Communications
in Computer and Information Science

Series Editors

Gang Li , *School of Information Technology, Deakin University, Burwood, VIC, Australia*

Joaquim Filipe , *Polytechnic Institute of Setúbal, Setúbal, Portugal*

Ashish Ghosh , *Indian Statistical Institute, Kolkata, West Bengal, India*

Zhiwei Xu, *Chinese Academy of Sciences, Beijing, China*

Rationale

The CCIS series is devoted to the publication of proceedings of computer science conferences. Its aim is to efficiently disseminate original research results in informatics in printed and electronic form. While the focus is on publication of peer-reviewed full papers presenting mature work, inclusion of reviewed short papers reporting on work in progress is welcome, too. Besides globally relevant meetings with internationally representative program committees guaranteeing a strict peer-reviewing and paper selection process, conferences run by societies or of high regional or national relevance are also considered for publication.

Topics

The topical scope of CCIS spans the entire spectrum of informatics ranging from foundational topics in the theory of computing to information and communications science and technology and a broad variety of interdisciplinary application fields.

Information for Volume Editors and Authors

Publication in CCIS is free of charge. No royalties are paid, however, we offer registered conference participants temporary free access to the online version of the conference proceedings on SpringerLink (http://link.springer.com) by means of an http referrer from the conference website and/or a number of complimentary printed copies, as specified in the official acceptance email of the event.

CCIS proceedings can be published in time for distribution at conferences or as postproceedings, and delivered in the form of printed books and/or electronically as USBs and/or e-content licenses for accessing proceedings at SpringerLink. Furthermore, CCIS proceedings are included in the CCIS electronic book series hosted in the SpringerLink digital library at http://link.springer.com/bookseries/7899. Conferences publishing in CCIS are allowed to use Online Conference Service (OCS) for managing the whole proceedings lifecycle (from submission and reviewing to preparing for publication) free of charge.

Publication process

The language of publication is exclusively English. Authors publishing in CCIS have to sign the Springer CCIS copyright transfer form, however, they are free to use their material published in CCIS for substantially changed, more elaborate subsequent publications elsewhere. For the preparation of the camera-ready papers/files, authors have to strictly adhere to the Springer CCIS Authors' Instructions and are strongly encouraged to use the CCIS LaTeX style files or templates.

Abstracting/Indexing

CCIS is abstracted/indexed in DBLP, Google Scholar, EI-Compendex, Mathematical Reviews, SCImago, Scopus. CCIS volumes are also submitted for the inclusion in ISI Proceedings.

How to start

To start the evaluation of your proposal for inclusion in the CCIS series, please send an e-mail to ccis@springer.com.

Victor Taratukhin · Artem Levchenko ·
Sohyeong Kim
Editors

Cultural Perspectives of Human-Centered and Technological Innovations

First International Workshop, CPHCATI 2024
Tokyo, Japan, January 27–28, 2024
Proceedings

Editors
Victor Taratukhin ⓘ
University of Münster
Münster, Germany

Artem Levchenko ⓘ
SAP Japan
Tokyo, Japan

Sohyeong Kim ⓘ
Stanford University
Stanford, CA, USA

ISSN 1865-0929　　　　　　　ISSN 1865-0937 (electronic)
Communications in Computer and Information Science
ISBN 978-3-031-77011-1　　　ISBN 978-3-031-77012-8 (eBook)
https://doi.org/10.1007/978-3-031-77012-8

© The Editor(s) (if applicable) and The Author(s), under exclusive license to Springer Nature Switzerland AG 2025

This work is subject to copyright. All rights are solely and exclusively licensed by the Publisher, whether the whole or part of the material is concerned, specifically the rights of translation, reprinting, reuse of illustrations, recitation, broadcasting, reproduction on microfilms or in any other physical way, and transmission or information storage and retrieval, electronic adaptation, computer software, or by similar or dissimilar methodology now known or hereafter developed.
The use of general descriptive names, registered names, trademarks, service marks, etc. in this publication does not imply, even in the absence of a specific statement, that such names are exempt from the relevant protective laws and regulations and therefore free for general use.
The publisher, the authors and the editors are safe to assume that the advice and information in this book are believed to be true and accurate at the date of publication. Neither the publisher nor the authors or the editors give a warranty, expressed or implied, with respect to the material contained herein or for any errors or omissions that may have been made. The publisher remains neutral with regard to jurisdictional claims in published maps and institutional affiliations.

This Springer imprint is published by the registered company Springer Nature Switzerland AG
The registered company address is: Gewerbestrasse 11, 6330 Cham, Switzerland

If disposing of this product, please recycle the paper.

Preface

We are pleased to present the proceedings of the International ICID 2024 Workshop on "Cultural Perspectives of Human-Centered Approaches and Technological Innovations" (CPHCATI 2024), which took place on January 27th–28th, 2024. This workshop, held in conjunction with the esteemed ICID (International Conference for Information Systems and Design) series, served as a precursor to the ICID 2024 conference, offering an insightful exploration of themes aligned with the broader scope of ICID.

CPHCATI 2024 aimed to unravel the intricate interplay between cultural perspectives, human-centered approaches, and technological innovations. With intellectual vigor evident in every session, the event welcomed researchers from Asia and beyond, fostering connections that transcended geographical boundaries. Against the vibrant backdrop of Tokyo, Japan, and utilizing a hybrid format accommodating both physical and virtual participation, the workshop provided a compelling platform for academic exchange. The event venue, GLOBIS University, Graduate School of Management, Tokyo Campus Annex, provided an ideal setting for intellectual discourse and collaboration.

ICID remains committed to its mission of serving as a nexus for open industry innovations within the academic realm, with a particular emphasis on the practical applications of Information Systems. The organizing committee meticulously reviewed 53 submissions, selecting 21 papers that demonstrated clear focus, depth, and practical applicability.

The proceedings from CPHCATI 2024 are organized into three sections:

- Cultural Perspectives on Technology
- Technological Innovations and Their Impact
- Sustainability and Environmental Impact of Innovations

The workshop initially adopted a preliminary offline/on-site format, with 20 in-person attendees and 83 participants joining online via video conferencing. Following the CPHCATI 2024 program, the conference spanned two days, featuring a plenary session on day 1 followed by 15 presentations on the first day and 19 presentations on the second.

These proceedings reflect our commitment to inclusivity and accessibility, ensuring that ICID remains a global platform for meaningful exchange and collaboration.

May 2024

Victor Taratukhin
Artem Levchenko
Sohyeong Kim

Organization

International Chair

Jörg BeckerUniversity of Münster, European Research Center for Information Systems, Germany

General Chairs

Victor TaratukhinUniversity of Münster, Germany
Artem LevchenkoSAP, Japan
Sohyeong KimStanford University, USA

International Program Committee

Vishal ShahCentral Michigan University, USA
Daigo MisakiKogakuin University, Japan
Mahendra SinghChuo University, Japan
Sergey BalandinTampere University of Technology, Finland
Lev VilkovProfessor Becker GmbH, Germany
Natalia PulyavinaStanford Center at the Incheon Global Campus, South Korea
Muzaffar DjalalovInha University Tashkent, Uzbekistan
Minhyoung KimHankuk University of Foreign Studies, South Korea

Organization Committee

Victor TaratukhinUniversity of Münster, Germany
Vishal ShahCentral Michigan University, USA
Artem LevchenkoSAP, Japan

Contents

Cultural Perspectives on Technology

Business Archaeology: From Foundational Discipline Definition
to Practical Implementation 3
  Victor Taratukhin and Natalia Pulyavina

Service Quality and Customer Satisfaction of Service Robots
in the Restaurants in India and Japan 15
  Mahendra Singh

Design Thinking Case Study: Developing a Training Program
for an International IT Company 29
  Artem Levchenko

The Role of Universities in Shaping an Innovative Ecosystem
and Sustainable Regional Development: The Experience of Inha
University in Tashkent and Prospects for the Future 43
  Muzaffar Djalalov and Dilshoda Mirzokhidova

Hybrid Design Thinking and Next-Gen Design Thinking Game: The Janus
2DT Ideathon Challenge 51
  Victor Taratukhin and Natalia Pulyavina

Towards Data-Driven Stress Management in Organizations: Innovative
Approaches and Application Development 63
  Kristina Dudkovskaia, Victor Taratukhin, and Jörg Becker

Advancing Mass Customization in Capital Goods Manufacturing Through
Standard Man Hours (SMH) Modelling and ESG Considerations 87
  Yagnesh Purohit and Shilpa Parkhi

Quality of Life as a Factor in Integrating Research into the Resilience
of Energy and Socio-Ecological Systems 107
  Liudmila V. Massel, Aleksei G. Massel, and Dmitrii V. Pesterev

Using Design Thinking Methodology for Advancing Employee
Knowledge and Skill Sets 120
  Aleksei Starostin and Natalia Pulyavina

Technological Innovations and Their Impact

Towards an Integrative Framework for AI Readiness and Market Disruption: The AI-Readiness and Market Dynamics Disruption Index (AIM-DDI) for Competitive AI Leadership 135
   Jorge Calvo

Designing Agents for Digital Twin of an Isolated Energy System 155
   Daria Gaskova, Aleksei Massel, Aleksey Tsybikov, and Nikita Shchukin

Design of Augmented Diffusion Model for Text-to-Image Representation Using Hybrid GAN 166
   Subuhi Kashif Ansari and Rakesh Kumar

A Hybrid Algorithm for Detection of Cloud-Based Email Phishing Attack 177
   Saahira Banu Ahamed, Anne Anoop, Rejna Azeez Nazeema, and Mujtaba Ali Khan

Using a Language Model to Analyze the Mental State of an Individual 188
   Arsenij Taratukhin and Mais Farkhadov Pasha Ogly

Digital Transformation as a Driver of the Fashion Industry 198
   Melnikova Anastasiya

Sustainability and Environmental Impact of Innovations

Key Drivers and Barriers to Digital Transformation of the Electric Power Industry in CIS Countries 213
   Tatsiana Zoryna, Olga Yurkevich, and Pavel Kabanov

Sustainability as Collective Action: Co-design Model Leveraging University Stakeholders to Design Sustainable Seaweed-Based Menu 225
   Hazel H. Kim, Summer D. Jung, Katherine Yoon, Evelyn Hur, and Soh Kim

Pioneering Renewable Energy Transition in US: A Comparative Case Study of Google, Apple, and Microsoft's Utilization of Power Purchase Agreements 237
   TaeHyung Kwon and Soh Kim

Towards a Renewable City: A Case Study of CleanPowerSF's Impact on Reducing GHG from Residential Buildings in San Francisco 250
   Jeung Lee and Soh Kim

Evaluation Model for the Quality of Electronic Services to Clients
of a Non-profit Institution 262
   Svetlana Begicheva and Antonina Begicheva

ESG 2.0: Revolutionizing Sustainability Through the Power
of Digitalization 273
   A. Zimin, N. Sedova, and N. Pulyavina

Author Index 283

Cultural Perspectives on Technology

Business Archaeology: From Foundational Discipline Definition to Practical Implementation

Victor Taratukhin[1](✉) and Natalia Pulyavina[2]

[1] University of Muenster, Muenster, Germany
victor.taratukhin@ercis.uni-muenster.de
[2] The Stanford Center at the Incheon Global Campus (SCIGC), Seoul, South Korea

Abstract. This paper extended the concept of Business Archaeology, defining its process, framework, and research ecosystem. The paper also emphasizes the practical application of Business Archaeology discipline, outlines the core components of the Janus Initiative, an academic research network focusing the future of innovation process. The Janus Initiative aims to connect various fields, including design thinking, strategic foresight, archaeology, and ethnography, among others. Furthermore, the paper examines the practical aspects of implementing the Next-Gen Design Thinking Game. This game has proven effective in fostering creative processes among students in Engineering, IT, and Management disciplines. It also serves as an effective tool for teaching the methods and approaches of Business Archaeology.

Keywords: Business Archaeology · Innovation · Janus Initiative · Next-Gen Design thinking · Next-Gen Design thinking Innovation Game

1 Introduction to Business Archaeology

Business Archaeology is a new cross-disciplinary discipline that tries to understand how people and organizations relate to the historical past and to apply the results to the modern world of business and management.

Defined in [1, 2] Business Archaeology is strongly connected to US Silicon Valley design culture and innovation environment. We propose that Business Archaeology is fundamental to developing new levels of knowledge of Corporate Past, Present, and Future scenarios of company innovation strategies and services.

In fact, Business Archaeology is not only a practical field of study but also provides the general principles and methods of the Future of Corporate Innovation [1, 2].

Business Archaeology, as a field, primarily focuses on research, preservation, and notably, the active utilization of knowledge to deepen our understanding of the corporate landscape, its history, present state, and prospects.

This integration of knowledge sets Business Archaeology apart from traditional archaeology. Despite this distinction, the discipline is rooted in archaeological theories and methodologies, showcasing the effectiveness of applying archaeological techniques to analyze business practices.

2 Business Archaeology Framework

Central to the Business Archaeology framework [2] is the concept of Cultural Diagnostics. Cultural Diagnostics enables a comprehensive journey from historical insights to contemporary company conditions, paving the way to conceptualize future advancements. At the heart of the Business Archaeology framework, Cultural Diagnostics serves as the key component. The process unfolds through phases below:

Exploring the Past. This phase emphasizes deep engagement with the company's historical context, aiming to form a representation of its past. This phase involves creating detailed profiles for past personas (employees or managers) and simulating historical events or scenarios. Such immersive exploration helps participants in viewing the company from the perspective of its former members, fostering a deep connection with its heritage. Following this immersion, an analysis of the company's current state is conducted.

Exploring the Present. In this phase the focus is constructing a contemporary persona, facilitating dialogues between historical and present personas, and developing an AS-IS model of the company's current situation. This stage assesses the preservation of the company's cultural identity over time.

Orchestrating Futures. This phase involves the conceptualization and understanding of potential future realities through the development of future scenarios and personas, alongside the innovation of new artifacts and environments.

Subsequently, these scenarios fall under a process of harmonization and orchestration. Harmonization involves the integration of new scenarios, while orchestration focuses on the strategic management and realization of these future visions. The Cultural Diagnostics component of the Business Archaeology Process is detailed above and visually represented in Fig. 1.

Business Archaeology as a discipline is certainly broader than the built-in method of cultural diagnostics. Business Archaeology employs a multidisciplinary approach, incorporating history, anthropology, sociology, psychology, and multiple management

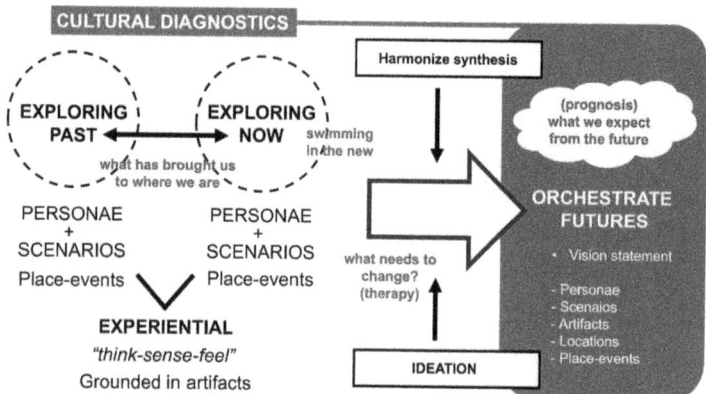

Fig. 1. Business Archaeology Framework (Cultural diagnostics part) Taratukhin, Shanks and Pulyavina [2].

disciplines. It is also a set of tools and approaches, both archaeological and related to methods of creating innovations, such as the Stanford Design Method (Design Thinking) [3, 4], and interdisciplinary tools from such fields as psychology, sociology, design, business games, etc. It uses a variety of sources, from company records to interviews of long-standing employees. The analysis includes not only success stories, but also failures and missed opportunities, offering a holistic view of business dynamics.

Considering the methods of Business Archaeology in more detail, we can define Business Archaeology Implementation Process (Exploring the Past stage and Orchestrate futures) below.

Bird's view is a stage of conceptual analysis of the problem. At this stage, it is possible to use **Janus cones** [5]. The Janus cones method helps to investigate the Past and foresee the Future. The method allows one to "plunge" into the history of the problem quickly and see the intersections in the study question development with other events of the Past. Context maps also can be an effective tool for this stage.

The Past (what is left, where, when)—Excavation, Seriation, Calendars, Historical Chronology, Geography analysis, and other methods.

The Past (company social organization)—Settlement Analysis and Site Hierarchy, Monuments, and Written Records Analysis. **The Past (what did they think)**—The method of constructing a person of the Past and the method of Archaeological Reconstruction.

The Future (what the Future looks like)—at this stage, the use of Janus cones oriented to the Future, Prototyping of the Future, and Heritage management can be useful Business Archaeology tools.

Below, we will present some examples of the use of archaeology methods as part of business archaeology.

3 Business Archaeology Tools and Methods

Business Archaeology tools and methods created the mechanism to study the past and to adapt the organizational culture of the present, to prepare for innovations within a constant change in corporate business environment.

Written records. Written records would seem to eliminate the need for doing archaeological research of material artifacts. However, written records only tell part of the story about the past, and that story is often idealized from one perspective (that of the recorder). In business archaeology, there is also an analysis of written sources which include both physical records and messages on corporate social networks and emails (Fig. 2).

Stratigraphy. Stratigraphy is the study of layered materials (strata) that were deposited over time. The basic law of stratigraphy, the law of superposition, states that lower layers are older than upper layers, unless the sequence has been overturned. Stratified deposits may include soils, rocks, as well as man-made items such as pits and postholes.

The adoption of stratigraphic principles by archaeologists greatly improved excavation and archaeological dating methods. By comparing natural strata and man-made strata, archaeologists are often able to determine a depositional history, or stratigraphic sequence—a chronological order of various layers, interfaces, and stratigraphic disturbances.

Fig. 2. Written records are subject to archaeological analysis (a) and Business Archaeology (b)

By analogy with archaeology, the identification of cultural layers and the search for necessary information are also possible in a business environment. Analysis of archives of materials, working places, determination of chronology, selection and construction of chronological sequences help to carry out cultural diagnostics of the company and to form the correct understanding of the past (Fig. 3).

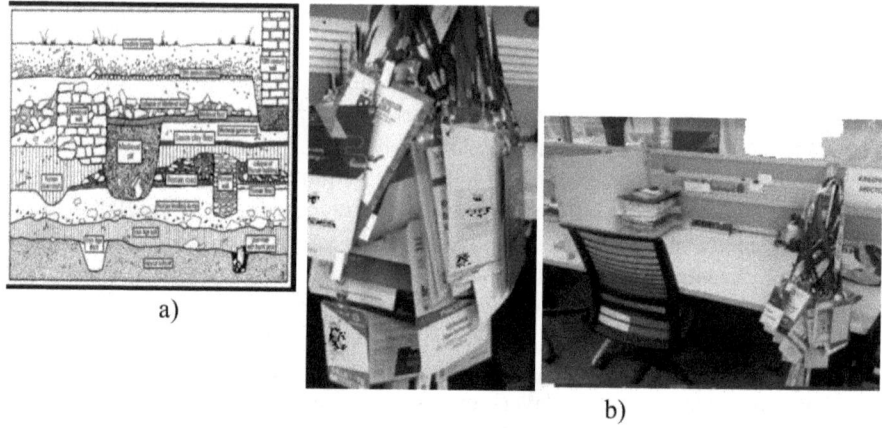

Fig. 3. Stratigraphy in archaeology (a) and business archaeology (b).

Seriation. In archaeology, seriation (or sequence dating) is a relative dating method in which assemblages or artifacts from numerous sites in the same culture are placed in chronological order. In cases where absolute dating methods, such as radiocarbon, cannot be applied, archaeologists should use relative dating methods to date archaeological finds. Seriation can be used to date stone tools, pottery fragments, and other artifacts. Generally, seriation is represented graphically. Plotting several curves can allow the archaeologist to develop a relative chronology for an entire site or group of sites.

In Business Archaeology a similar method can be used for better understanding of corporate branding, to build a unified approach to building a corporate logo, which opens up the possibility for building corporate chronologies.

Excavation method. In archaeology, excavation is the exposure, processing, and recording of archaeological remains, i.e. excavation sites or "digs". These locations range from one to several areas at a time during a project which can last from a few weeks to several years. Several excavation methods are used for deep foundation construction, such as full open cut method, bracing excavation, anchored excavation, island excavation methods, zoned excavation, top-down construction methods, etc.

Before excavating, the presence or absence of archaeological remains can often be suggested by non-intrusive remote sensing, such as ground-penetrating radar. During excavation, archaeologists often use stratigraphic excavation to remove phases of the site one layer at a time. This keeps the timeline of the material consistent with one another. It is usually done via mechanical means where artifacts can be spot-dated and processed through such methods as sieving or flotation. Afterward, digital methods are used to record the excavation process and its results.

By analogy with archaeology, business archaeology uses excavations along with serialization to reconstruct the company's past. The examples of archaeological excavations in Gobekli Tepe, and the results of the search for corporate artifacts in the Bucyrus Museum [6] are presented in Figs. 4 and 5.

Fig. 4. Excavation sites in archaeology (Gobekli Tepe site in 2018) and Business archaeology (Bucyrus Museum in 2022).

Chronology. Chronology has a central role in archaeology allowing scientists to understand the relative timing, rates, and nature of changing human societies. It provides the backbone for any historic narrative and allows us to relate individual events to the larger political context.

Archaeological timescale, also called archaeological chronology, is chronology that describes a period of human or protohuman prehistory. Some archaeological timescales are based on relative dating techniques, such as stratigraphy, which illuminate a sequence of change.

When applied to business archaeology, chronology is also the most important method of understanding the temporal relationships between the stages of a company's development and building dependencies between various milestones and business success. An example of a chronology from the Harley Davidson Motorcycle Museum is given in Fig. 5.

Fig. 5. Chronology at Harley Davidson Motorcycle Museum, Milwaukee, US.

Ethnoarchaeology. Ethnoarchaeology is the ethnographic study of peoples usually through the study of the material remains of a society. Ethnoarchaeology helps archaeologists in reconstructing ancient lifestyles by studying the material and non-material traditions of modern societies.

Ethnography can provide insights into how people in the past may have lived, especially in terms of their social structures, religious beliefs and other aspects of their culture. The application of ethnoarchaeology is also an essential element of the reconstruction of the company's past. It includes work on its artifacts and interviewing former employees of the company.

Cultural heritage, Cultural memory. Cultural memory includes tangible culture (such as buildings, monuments, landscapes, books, works of art, and artifacts), intangible culture (such as folklore, traditions, language, and knowledge), and natural heritage (including culturally significant landscapes, and biodiversity).

The new trend in scientific research related to the study of cultural heritage is to focus on noninvasive techniques as well as digital technologies. Many analytical methodologies and tools such as spectroscopy, chemometrics, and modeling, as well as the use of virtual reality systems in museums and archaeological sites are useful for heritage analysis.

In addition, in application to business archaeology, there is a great need to analyze external corporate objects, language, and knowledge, as well as corporate narrative. The method can be widely applied at various stages of cultural diagnostics, expanding the understanding of the corporate past, present and in the formation of future scenarios.

Next part shows the ecosystem of business archaeology as a science discipline and contains a description of possible applicable methods and tools. This ecosystem was developed based on a series of scientific seminars and brainstorming sessions at Stanford Archaeology Loft and collaborations with academic and industry partners.

4 Business Archaeology Research Ecosystem

Business archaeology research ecosystem development project was defined on strategic sessions at Stanford and named the Aristotle Project. The importance of Aristotle as a thinker is not only in his development of the theory of thinking, but in the practical significance of his works on logic and the unity of matter and form. That is why this project was named after him (Fig. 6).

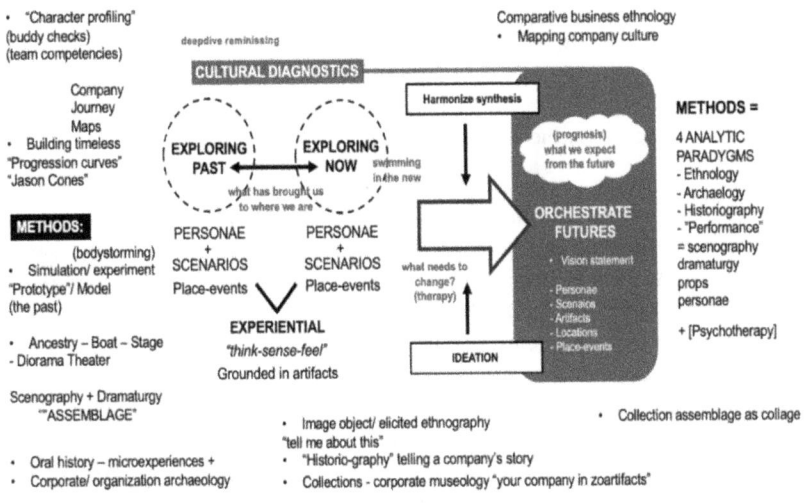

Fig. 6. Business Archaeology Research Ecosystem. Aristotle Project.

Analyzing the Business Archaeology Research Ecosystem, it is worth noting that, as was discussed in the Aristotle Project, in addition to the archaeological methods described above, tools and methods related to psychology, psychotherapy, sociology, simulation, museology, historiography, and even dramaturgy are actively used.

Further research is needed for a better understanding of the effectiveness of applying various approaches, methods, and tools within business archaeology.

Next, we should look at business archaeology as a scientific discipline and its structure. The Business Archaeology as a Scientific discipline is anchored in three pivotal dimensions: Research, Education, and Practice (Fig. 7). This framework envisions Business Archaeology as a discipline dedicated to innovating methods and tools, not merely by adapting archaeological techniques but through their integration with contemporary managerial practices.

Achieving this synthesis requires robust integration and the creation of joint academic programs and courses in Business Archaeology at both undergraduate and graduate levels, merging the fields of archaeology and management, and developing research topics for doctoral studies.

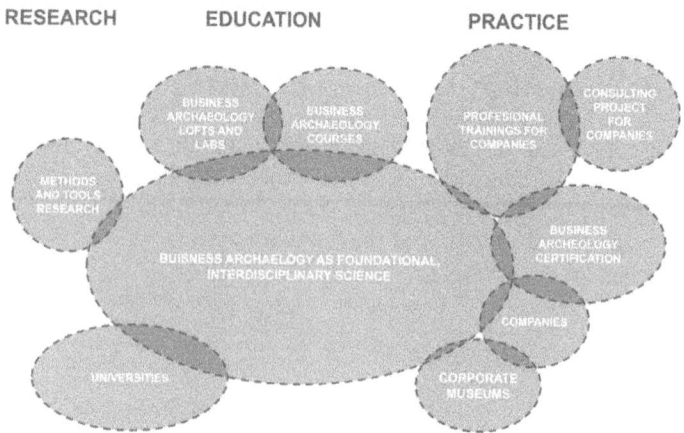

Fig. 7. Business Archaeology as a Scientific Discipline.

This interdisciplinary approach aims to lay a solid foundation for project-based learning, enabling students to engage in fieldwork and collaborate directly with businesses. The establishment of specialized Business Archaeology Lofts/Studios and Labs, inspired by models like the Stanford ME310 Loft, will enhance the practical aspects of the discipline, offering students unique opportunities to undertake industry-related projects within these innovative spaces.

Furthermore, the educational facet of Business Archaeology should extend to direct engagement with the industry, defining models of collaboration between academic institutions and businesses. It is critical to address the prevalent gap in corporate awareness regarding the importance of preserving corporate memory and understanding the methodologies and tools of Business Archaeology. Bridging this divide necessitates the development of a comprehensive cooperation model that encompasses industry-focused executive courses, certification in Business Archaeology, and consultancy projects aimed at businesses, thereby facilitating a more profound integration of academic insights with practical applications in the corporate world.

5 The Janus Initiative

The JANUS Initiative [1, 2] rooted in the name of Janus—the Roman god of transitions—provides a unique point of multidisciplinary discussions among scientists from the US, Germany, Denmark, South Korea, and other countries regarding the future of Corporate Innovation and Business Archaeology as the discipline. Janus Initiative is dedicated to exploring human innovation and design across time—past, present, and future—it bridges diverse domains from design thinking and strategic foresight to archaeology, ethnography, and anthropology; the initiative offers a holistic approach to understanding design innovation.

Another significant area of Janus Initiative discussions is the future of the Stanford Design Method (Design thinking) [3, 4]. Historically rooted in the traditional design thinking approach, Next-Gen Design thinking highlighted team members' cultural, organizational, and historical narratives [7]. The Next-Gen Design Thinking Game developed by the authors is an effective tool for supporting the Next-Gen Design Thinking process [8]. The website of the Janus initiative is presented below (Fig. 8).

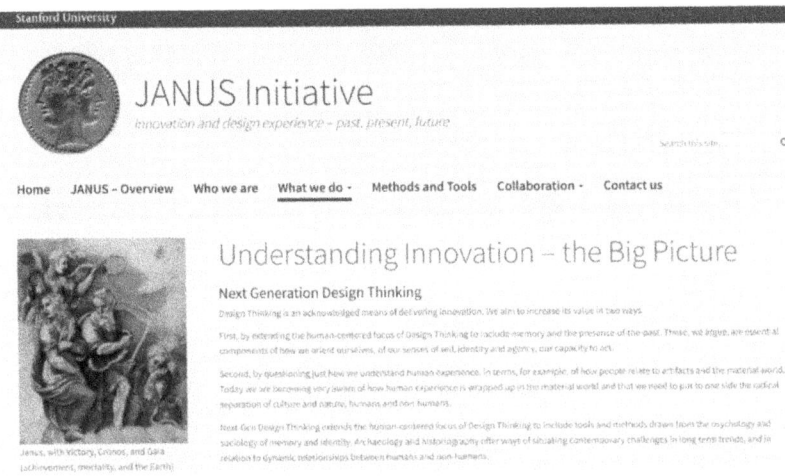

Fig. 8. Janus Initiative Web Page.

Next part will review Next-Gen Design Thinking Game in more detail.

6 Next-Gen Design Thinking Game

Business Archaeology Game (ArcheoSim) was an initial version of a Next-Gen Design Thinking Game that was designed by the authors as a tool of introduction to Business Archaeology then was extended for supporting creativity processes among Engineering, IT, and Management students. The game is both an online platform and physical set game—was first tested on international teams of 3–5 students working for 3–9 months on design thinking challenges.

As part of the experiment, participants with experience in the fields of industrial engineering, chemical engineering, sustainable finance, mobility, and human-computer interaction were divided into teams for preliminary evaluation of the game set.

The participants receive some artifacts from the past and have to recreate the ideas and principles of doing business of the people who invented it, to feel the spirit of Business Archaeology. The next step was to reconstruct current business of the company and to propose new ideas of corporate strategy based on artifacts analyzed. In addition to business artifacts, the team actively utilize design thinking tools and methods to create innovative solutions.

The key idea of the game is to make the past, the present and the future meet. We can see the direct analogy with archaeological practice: archaeologists study the past and to draw the necessary conclusions and to create a better future, considering the achievements and mistakes of their ancestors.

We can use different scenarios of the Game. During the testing stage, the players are divided into teams and each of the teams formulates and puts down the challenge containing possible innovation potential.

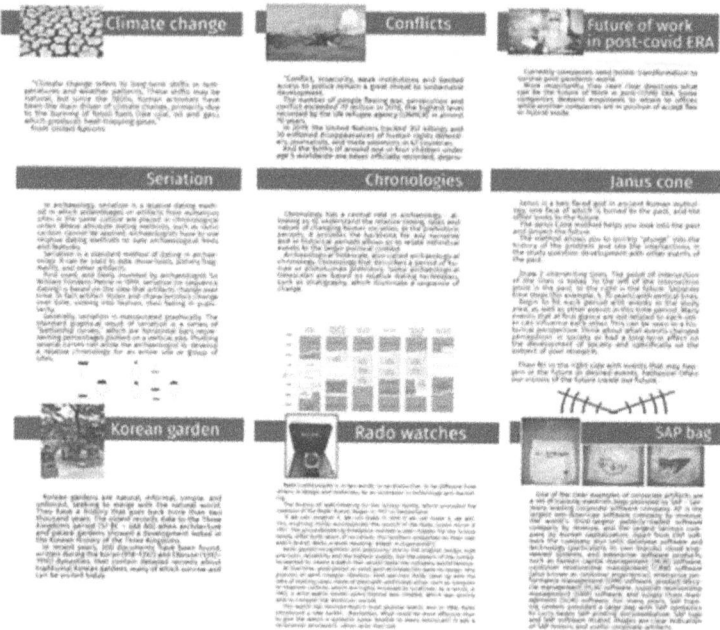

Fig. 9. Next-Gen Design Thinking Game.

The game set includes three types of cards with different backs: Artifacts, Tools, and Trends. The cards can be distributed between teams and the participants can take three types of cards during the session. The cards broaden the players' horizons, inspiring them to create new ideas by getting acquainted with other experiences. The Artifact cards provide information about brilliant business ideas from the past. The Trend cards contain possible business trends. The Tool cards offer specific methods from the Design Thinking to Archaeology with the help of which the players optimize the concept they have developed.

When working on a concept, the participants can use the Internet and other sources to analyze additional information about the different aspects related to the cards. The Artifacts, Tools, and Trends card examples are presented below (Fig. 9). Each team of participants draws three cards (one of each type) and has 15–30 min for team's discussion. After discussions, team's participants are presenting their ideas and prototypes.

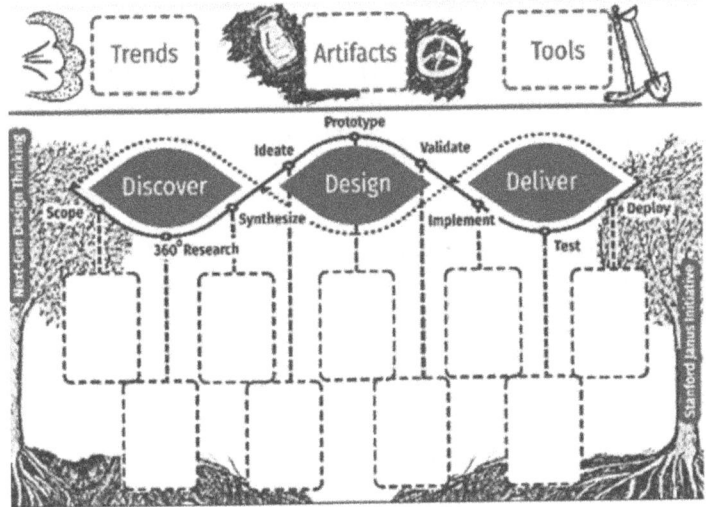

Fig. 10. Next - Gen Design Thinking Game. The Gameboard.

Team interaction is the key for the game because each participant contributes the discussion with their background, experience, and professional vision of the problem.

The results of the initial evaluation of ArcheoSim Game provided important feedback to authors and as the result of this evaluation the Gameboard with Design thinking process was introduced for tangible/physical version of the game (Fig. 10) and the new version of the Game was renamed to Next-Gen Design Thinking Game.

7 Conclusion

This paper provided an extended view to the concept of Business Archaeology, defining its process, framework, and research ecosystem. We analyze the practical application of this foundational discipline, outlines the core components of academic research network focusing the future of innovation process and Business Archaeology: the Janus Initiative. Furthermore, the paper examines the practical aspects of implementing the Next-Gen Design Thinking Game.

There is a need to broaden academic research within Business Archaeology, aiming to refine the categorization, application, and advancement of archaeological knowledge across various business scenarios.

To summarize, Business Archaeology is an important discipline to prepare the future leaders for success in challenging economic climate by arming them with unique competencies ordinating from a comprehensive understanding of the past. This skill set is critical for navigating the complexities and unpredictability's of the global business environment.

References

1. Shanks, M., Taratukhin, V., Pulyavina, N., Our Manifesto: Next-Gen Design Thinking, Business Archaeology, and Future of Corporate Innovation. Available at SSRN: https://ssrn.com/abstract=4618019 or https://doi.org/10.2139/ssrn.4618019 (2023)
2. Taratukhin, V., Shanks, M., Pulyavina, N.: Business Archaeology: Defining a New Foundational Discipline. Available at SSRN: https://ssrn.com/abstract=4617932 or https://doi.org/10.2139/ssrn.4617932 (2023)
3. Leifer, L.: Center for Design Research at Stanford University, In: Clarkson, P. (ed.) (2005)
4. Dym, C., Agogino, A., Eris, O., Frey, D., Leifer, L.: Engineering design thinking, teaching, and learning. IEEE Eng. Manage. Rev. **1**(34), 65–92 (2006)
5. Playbook for Strategic Foresight and Innovation, Stanford University: https://foresight.stanford.edu/methods, Last accessed 2024/03/29
6. Bucyrus Museum: https://bucyrusmuseum.org, Last accessed 2024/03/29
7. Taratukhin, V., Pulyavina, N.: The future of project-based learning for engineering and management students: Towards an advanced design thinking approach. In: Proceedings of the 125th ASEE Annual Conference and Exposition, Salt Palace Convention Center, Salt Lake City (2018)
8. Pulyavina, N., Taratukhin, V., Kim, S., Kim, S.: Accumulated practical experience of the past for building the future of design innovations: janus project and next-gen design thinking game. In: Taratukhin, V., Levchenko A., Kupriyanov, Y., (eds.) Communications in Computer and Information Science, vol 1767. Springer, Heidelberg (2023)

Service Quality and Customer Satisfaction of Service Robots in the Restaurants in India and Japan

Mahendra Singh[✉] [iD]

Chuo University, 742-1 Higashi-Nakano, Hachioji-shi, Tokyo 192-0393, Japan
mahenrsingh@gmail.com

Abstract. Robots have been in use for back-end business processes for a few decades. With the use of evolving digital technologies, these robots have become sophisticated enough to be used in customer-facing business operations, collaborating with the human beings. The use of service robots in restaurants is still in its early stages of adoption. This study aims at understanding the customer satisfaction and the level of service quality provided by the service robots in restaurants in India and Japan. For this study, SERVQUAL framework is used, which is a common framework for measuring and analyzing the service quality. This framework has five dimensions: tangibility, reliability, responsiveness, assurance, and empathy. In this research, an additional dimension of price is included. It was found that the service quality gap is not big between the expected quality and the actual service provided by the service robots on the tangibility and reliability aspects of service. However, big gaps between the expected quality of service and the actual service were found in the responsiveness, assurance, and empathy aspects of service. There is a need to further enhance the capabilities of the service robots to bridge the gap between the expected and current levels of responsiveness, assurance, and empathy aspects of service quality. By leveraging various evolving technologies such as AI, IoT, NLP, CRM, face recognition, digital payments, and integrating the kitchen work-flow information with the service robots could enhance the service quality of robots in the restaurants to a very large extent.

Keywords: Service Robots · SERVQUAL · Customer Satisfaction · Service Quality · Digital Transformation

1 Introduction

Human beings have been creating machines to make their lives easier and more comfortable. Earlier generations of machines have been mainly mechanical devices, but with the advent of the information systems, these machines got equipped with the capabilities to take the information inputs, process the information, store the information, and leverage the experience to make intelligent decisions. These machines powered with the information systems, sensors, and actuators are often called Robots, which have been in use for the industrial use. With the use of smart sensors, Internet of Things (IoT), computer vision, speech-recognition, advanced materials, cloud computing, natural language processing, wireless communication, artificial intelligence, and Industry 4.0, these robots got the ability to sense the environment and are being used in the collaborative environment with the human beings.

In recent years, further technological advancements and the Covid-19 pandemic triggered the use of contactless transactions, digital payments, and digital technologies. During the Covid-19 pandemic, customers preferred less human contact, which forced the organizations to consider digital transformation and use robots for customer service.

In Japan, some of the robots such as Pepper, developed by Softbank, have been in use in retail stores, even before the Covid-19 pandemic for some basic front-end customer interactions such as customer greetings, taking customer orders, providing information etc. However, in recent years, the use of robots for serving food is becoming popular in many restaurant chains in Japan, such as Skylark group and is also being used by some restaurants in other countries, such as The Yellow House robot restaurant in India. This study is aimed at understanding the service quality and customer satisfaction of the service provided by the service robots in the restaurants in India and Japan.

When the robots are used for front-end customer interactions and service, they are called service robots. These are the system-based autonomous and adaptable interfaces that interact, communicate, and deliver service to an organization's customers [19]. The service robots can conduct a wide range of customer services in a dynamic environment, collaborate with human beings, and have the capabilities to navigate in a populated environment with the human beings. Service robots have many potential benefits, such as improving the productivity, ensuring the consistent service quality, and reducing the staffing costs. Service robots enable enterprises to rapidly collect data from the environment, analyze the data on runtime, and serve the changing needs of the customers promptly [6]. The service robot market is expected to grow at a fast pace and is projected to reach US$84.8 billion by 2028 from the current market size of US$41.5 billion in 2023. Asia is expected to be the biggest market for service robots due to the large share by Japan, China, South Korea, supplemented with the increased demand in countries such as India and the Philippines due to the rise in disposable income and industrialization [8].

Using service robots for customer greetings, short communication, reserving seats, taking customer orders are some of the light front-end customer interactions. However, this research is aimed at understanding the gaps between the quality of service offered by the service robots and the customer expectation when the end-to-end service is provided by a human being in a restaurant. If those quality gaps could be reduced by leveraging the evolving technologies and new operational processes, then it would open a large avenue for the businesses to improve their productivity, ensure consistent service quality, and reduce the staffing costs. It is expected that the triggers for the use of service robots will differ according to the social, technological, and competitive landscape in a country. To reduce the effects of single country bias, this research is conducted in India and Japan, and a comparative analysis is conducted.

2 Research Motivation

The use of service robots for the front-end customer service in restaurants is a very recent development. It is very likely that the service provided by the robots in the current early years of evolution will have various shortcomings, and there will be a need for multiple rounds of research and development until the robots become perfect for customer-facing work responsibilities.

Currently, in certain cases, service robots are being used as a strategic differentiator for the business operations, while in some other situations, they are being used as a mechanism to deal with the labor shortage due to the aging and shrinking population in various developed countries. Japan and many European countries such as Italy, Finland, Portugal, Greece, Germany, Bulgaria, Croatia, and France are facing the problem of an aging population [11, 18]. The use of robots and automation could help the businesses in these countries to deal with the problem of labor shortages and lower their costs of business operations.

This research is aimed at understanding the service quality and customer satisfaction of the service provided by the service robots in the restaurants in India and Japan and providing recommendations for bridging the gaps between the expected and actual quality of the service.

For this research, India and Japan are selected for the comparative study as both are Asian countries but have significant differences in population demographics and the different possible motivations behind the adoption of service robots in the restaurants. India has the highest population in the world, with a large pool of young population, however Japan has shrinking birth rates and population. In India, service robots are possibly being adopted as a strategic differentiator in business, while in Japan service robots are being adopted to deal with the problems of aging population, labor shortages, and the increased costs of business operations. For this study, below are the research questions,

Q1. What is the current level of service provided by the service robots in the restaurants in comparison to the expected service by the customers in India and Japan?
Q2. What is the customer satisfaction level of the service provided by the service robots in the restaurants in comparison to the expected service by the customers in India and Japan?
Q3. What are the gaps between the quality of the service provided by the service robots in the restaurants and the expected service by the customers in India and Japan?
Q4. What are the possible reasons for the gaps between the quality of the service provided by the service robots in the restaurants and the expected service by the customers in India and Japan?
Q5. What could be the solutions to bridge the gaps between the quality of the service provided by the service robots in the restaurants and the expected service by the customers?

3 Theoretical Background

This research is focused on understanding the customer satisfaction of the service provided by service robots in the restaurants. For this study SERVQUAL framework is used, which is a common framework for measuring and analyzing the service quality. Service quality is the difference between the customer expectations of service and perceived service [10]. Originally, the SERVQUAL model had 10 conceptualized dimensions, but the refined SERVQUAL model has below 5 dimensions,

Tangibility: Appearance of physical facilities, appearance, and communication of the personnel in the service process and type of equipment provided in the service process.

Reliability: The ability of an organization to do a task or service as promised is called as reliability.

Responsiveness: The willingness of service provider to help the customers. Making a sincere effort to provide prompt service to customers.

Assurance: Ability of service provider to give a sense of trust and security to the customers.

Empathy: Ability of service providers to communicate with customers and provide individualized attention to them.

The last two dimensions (assurance and empathy) contain items representing seven original dimensions- communication, credibility, security, competence, courtesy, understanding/knowing customers, and access. The refined SERVQUAL model has only 5 dimensions, but they capture facets of all 10 originally conceptualized dimensions [9].

SERVQUAL is the most popular model in use for measuring service quality and customer satisfaction in service industries [3, 14]. For example, Shafiq et al. [15] used SERVQUAL to measure Generation Y's perceived service quality and its effects on their satisfaction towards the Malaysian hotel industry. It was found that all the elements of SERVQUAL, except tangibility, had a significant and positive relationship with customer satisfaction. Rezaei et al. [13] used SERVQUAL to assess the quality of the airline baggage handling system, which was conducted on 140 respondents from the EU, United States, India, Indonesia, and China. Reliability was found to be the most important dimension, followed by the responsiveness.

The SERVQUAL model could be used in any kind of service, and the dimensions and questions of the SERVQUAL model should be customized based on service and industry [10]. Since service robots is relatively a new topic of research and the use of service robots in restaurants is a very recent development, no published research on the service robots in restaurants was found.

There are various prior studies that have concluded the effect of price on customer satisfaction. Price and sales promotions have a positive effect on customer satisfaction. Customer satisfaction is the feeling of pleasure or disappointment, that arises after comparing the performance of the product or service against the expected performance. Service quality indirectly or partially mediates the effect of price on customer satisfaction [12]. Some researchers have found a direct positive relationship between price and customer satisfaction, while some others have found an inverse relationship between price and customer satisfaction in certain situations. An inverse relationship between price and customer satisfaction was found in the cases of high product/service specificity and product/service complexity [17]. While conducting research, sometimes it is appropriate to go beyond the fixed dimensions of a research model and test some additional dimensions [16]. Considering that price might have relationship with the customer satisfaction, Price is added as an additional construct in this research. Since, the use of service robots in the restaurants is a new development, no research papers were found on the use of service robots in restaurants. Using the SERVQUAL framework with the additional constructs of price and customer satisfaction might lay a foundation for the further research on this evolving business initiative of using robots in the service industry. Below is the research model for this study (Fig. 1).

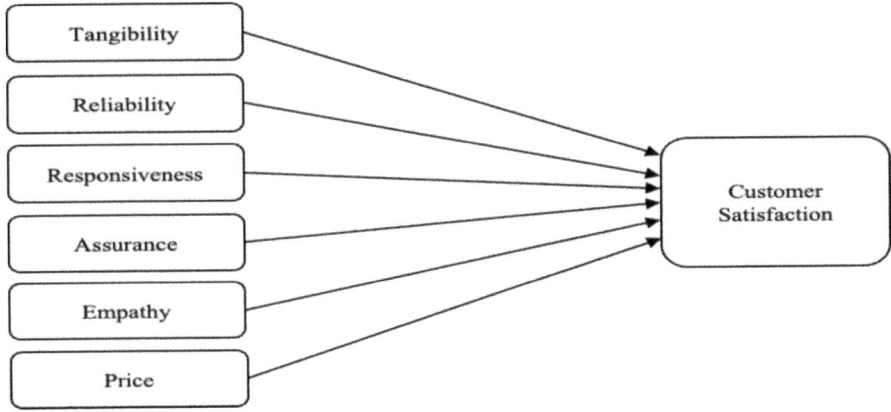

Fig. 1. Research Model.

4 Research Methodology

The SERVQUAL is a framework used for measuring the service quality and customer satisfaction for any kind of service. There are various prior studies on the use of SERVQUAL framework for understanding the customer satisfaction in the hotel and hospitality industry. However, no prior published research was found on the service quality and customer satisfaction of service robots in the restaurants. For deciding the research methodology, first an exploratory study was conducted through interviews with 5 academic professionals each in India and Japan, who had experienced the service robots in restaurants. Based on this exploratory study, some important elements of expected service by the customers in the restaurants were confirmed, such as greeting the customers, guiding the customers to the tables, taking the orders, confirming the order by verbally repeating it, taking the appropriate amount of time to serve the food, mentioning the name of the food brought to the table, taking any additional requests, billing, taking feedback, giving an appropriate response to the feedback, appropriate greetings when the customer leaves, etc. Based on these findings, in addition to the SERVQUAL questions, some new questions were added in the questionnaire. This research is conducted based on the data collected from 226 respondents in India and Japan. After collecting the data and conducting the analyses, the same 5 academic professionals each in India and Japan were interviewed to discuss the results and find the possible reasons for the research findings. To have credible data from interviews, ideally 4–10 participants are required with sound knowledge regarding the topic of discussion so that a significant contribution can be made in the preliminary research [1]. Total 10 respondents for preliminary research were chosen while considering the balance in the gender of the respondents selected for the interview.

This research is conducted based on the assumption that a service robot is expected to provide the same level of service as the human beings could provide. These expected elements of service are greeting the customers, guiding the customers to their tables, taking the orders, keeping a safe distance while moving and serving the food, bringing the food in hygienic condition, taking, and fulfilling additional orders, providing billing support, taking customer feedback, giving the appropriate response, and greeting the customers when they leave. These customer expectations are included in the questionnaire as a research instrument.

Various evolving technologies, such as smart sensors, IoT, computer vision, speech-recognition, advanced materials, cloud computing, wireless communication, artificial intelligence, and Industry 4.0 related technological developments, are enabling increased capability of the robots to work in a collaborative environment with human beings, but since the use of robots in restaurants is a new business initiative and is still at its early stage of adoption, the service provided by the robots in the hospitality industry is expected not to be of the same level as the service provided by the human beings.

5 Data Collection

A questionnaire was created with a total of 35 questions, 4 questions related to respondent demographics, 1 question to confirm that the respondent has experienced the restaurant using service robots, 4 questions related to the tangibility construct, 5 questions related to the reliability construct, 5 questions related to the responsiveness construct, 5 questions related to the assurance construct, 5 questions related to the empathy construct, 3 questions related to the price construct, and 3 questions related to the customer satisfaction.

All the measurement items were first compiled in a questionnaire in English, and then, the Japanese version of the questionnaire was created. The Japanese version of the questionnaire was reviewed by 3 native Japanese academic professionals, and it was independently translated back into English to ensure consistency between the English and Japanese versions of the questionnaires. Except for a few questions related to demographics and the question to confirm that the respondent has experienced the restaurant using service robots, all the questions in the questionnaire were based on a 5-point Likert scale that ranged from 1 (Strongly Disagree) to 5 (Strongly Agree).

Data was collected through the online questionnaire and face-to-face paper-based questionnaire in Japan and India from 226 respondents during a 4-month period, from July 2023 to September 2023. There were 8 invalid responses, so the total number of responses included in this research is 218. There were 108 valid respondents from India and 110 valid respondents from Japan (Table 1).

6 Analysis and Results

First, a factor analysis was conducted on the 5 constructs of the SERVQUAL model, and the additional constructs related to Price and Customer Satisfaction to examine the convergent validity, discriminant validity, and reliability of the constructs. A factor

Table 1. Respondent Demographics.

		India		Japan	
Gender	Male	55	51%	53	48%
	Female	53	49%	57	52%
	Total	108	100%	110	100%
Age	10–19	22	20%	20	18%
	20–29	29	27%	38	35%
	30–39	26	24%	30	27%
	40–49	17	16%	15	14%
	> 50	14	13%	7	6%
	Total	108	100%	110	100%
Annual Income	Level 1	38	35%	21	19%
	Level 2	26	24%	30	27%
	Level 3	14	13%	25	23%
	Level 3	13	12%	15	14%
	Level 5	11	10%	10	9%
	Level 6	6	6%	9	8%
	Total	108	100%	110	100%

Age is in number of years.
Annual Income Mapping Japan (Japanese Yen):
Level 1 is < 2M, Level 2 is > 2M & = < 4M, Level 3 is > 4M & = < 6M, Level 4 is > 6M & = < 8M, Level 5 is > 8M & = < 10M, Level 6 is > 10M.
Annual Income Mapping India (Indian Rupee):
Level 1 is < 450K, Level 2 is > 450K & = < 900K, Level 3 is > 900K & = < 1.35M, Level 4 is > 1.35M & = < 1.8M, Level 5 is > 1.8M & = < 22.5M, Level 6 is > 22.5M.
For income mapping https://salaryconverter.nigelb.me is used for the reference.

analysis is an interdependence technique whose primary purpose is to determine the underlying structure among the variables in the analysis [4]. Factor loadings in the range of ± 0.30 to ± 0.40 are considered to meet the minimal level for interpretation of structure and loadings, and ± 0.50 or greater are considered practically significant [4].

For convergent validity, a pattern matrix was examined to check the factor loadings of the measurement items on the respective constructs and the cross-factor loadings. A factor analysis was conducted using the principal component extraction method and promax rotation. Two measurement items were excluded from the analysis for both India and Japan data because of their low factor loading and high cross-loadings. One of these measurement items was related to the reliability construct and the other was related to the assurance construct.

Besides the two excluded measurement items for both India and Japan data, factor loadings of all other measurement items were either exceeding or were close to 0.7. None of the items had a factor loading of less than 0.6 and a cross loading higher than 0.25. Exclusion of the two measurement items resulted in passing the convergent validity test.

Discriminant validity shows to what extent factors are distinct and uncorrelated. For discriminant validity, correlations between the factors were observed and none of the correlations between the factors exceeded 0.7, which is an indicator of passing the discriminant validity test.

Validity is how well the concept is defined by the measures, whereas reliability relates to the consistency of the measures [4]. Reliability was tested through the computation of Cronbach's alpha for each factor. The generally agreed upon lower limit for Cronbach's alpha is 0.70 although it may decrease to 0.60 in exploratory research [7]. Cronbach's alpha for each construct was found to be higher than 0.7, as shown in the results below, hence passing the reliability criteria. Below are the results for the reliability test and convergent validity test for both India and Japan data (Table 2).

Multicollinearity means that the variance independent variables explain in dependent variables are overlapping each other and thus are not explaining unique variance in the dependent variable. The simplest and most obvious means of identifying collinearity is an examination of the correlation matrix for the independent variables. The presence of high correlations (generally 0.9 and higher) is an indication of collinearity. As shown in the factor correlation matrix below, none of the correlations between the independent variables were found to be more than 0.7. Therefore, no significant multicollinearity problem exists in the data (Tables 3 and 4).

The paired sample t-test is one of the most widely used statistical procedures for comparing the equality of the means of two paired populations. Customer satisfaction is the customer's feelings of pleasure or disappointment, which are generated after comparison of perceived expected quality of service with the actual service delivered [2, 5]. In this study, the perceived expected quality of service is supposed to be at 5, which is based on the traditional restaurants where human beings provide the service, and it is compared with the actual response of the respondents who have experienced the actual service at the restaurants with service robots. The paired t-test analysis is conducted for the India and Japan data, and the results are shown in the tables below. The paired t-test of India data suggests that there is not much difference between the expected quality of service and the actual service on the tangibility and reliability constructs. However, there are big gaps between the expected quality of service and the actual service on the responsiveness, assurance, and empathy constructs. For the overall satisfaction, there is not much difference between the expected quality of service and the actual quality of service. The paired t-test of Japan data also suggests that there is not much difference between the expected quality of service and the actual service on the tangibility and reliability constructs. However, there are big gaps between the expected quality of service and the actual service on the responsiveness, assurance, and empathy constructs. Also, for the overall satisfaction there is not much difference between the expected quality of service and the actual service (Tables 5 and 6).

A comparison of the factor correlation matrix for India and Japan suggests that there is a positive correlation of tangibility and reliability with the customer satisfaction. However, there is a negative correction of responsiveness, assurance, and empathy with

Table 2. Measurement Model.

		India			Japan	
Construct	Scale Item	Cronbach's Alpha	Factor Loading	Scale Item	Cronbach's Alpha	Factor Loading
Tangibility	TG1-I	0.895	0.811	TG1-J	0.885	0.740
	TG2-I		0.901	TG2-J		0.852
	TG3-I		0.857	TG3-J		0.888
	TG4-I		0.810	TG4-J		0.908
Reliability	RL1-I	0.934	Dropped	RL1-J	0.964	Dropped
	RL2-I		0.899	RL2-J		0.934
	RL3-I		0.895	RL3-J		0.953
	RL4-I		0.927	RL4-J		0.926
	RL5-I		0.890	RL5-J		0.888
Responsiveness	RS1-I	0.930	0.894	RS1-J	0.934	0.946
	RS2-I		0.814	RS2-J		0.896
	RS3-I		0.947	RS3-J		0.847
	RS4-I		0.806	RS4-J		0.890
	RS5-I		0.938	RS5-J		0.811
Assurance	AS1-I	0.884	0.875	AS1-J	0.892	0.874
	AS2-I		0.862	AS2-J		0.832
	AS3-I		Dropped	AS3-J		Dropped
	AS4-I		0.895	AS4-J		0.871
	AS5-I		0.807	AS5-J		0.899
Empathy	EM1-I	0.876	0.893	EM1-J	0.958	0.935
	EM2-I		0.850	EM2-J		0.934
	EM3-I		0.754	EM3-J		0.951
	EM4-I		0.696	EM4-J		0.841
	EM5-I		0.870	EM5-J		0.958
Price	PR1-I	0.954	0.955	PR1-J	0.878	0.900
	PR2-I		0.895	PR2-J		0.850
	PR3-I		0.972	PR3-J		0.926
Customer Satisfaction	CS1-I	0.918	0.716	CS1-J	0.988	0.915
	CS2-I		0.675	CS2-J		0.900
	CS3-I		0.841	CS3-J		0.885

the customer satisfaction for both India and Japan. Price has a positive correlation with customer satisfaction for India but has negative correlation for Japan data (Table 7).

Table 3. Factor Correlation Matrix (India).

	TG-I	RL-I	RS-I	AS-I	EM-I	PR-I	CS-I
TG-I	1.000						
RL-I	0.152	1.000					
RS-I	0.050	−0.186	1.000				
AS-I	−0.170	−0.168	0.216	1.000			
EM-I	−0.351	−0.013	−0.036	0.245	1.000		
PR-I	0.315	0.272	−0.065	−0.243	−0.176	1.000	
CS-I	0.318	0.422	−0.271	−0.142	−0.180	0.361	1.000

Table 4. Factor Correlation Matrix (Japan).

	TG-J	RL-J	RS-J	AS-J	EM-J	PR-J	CS-J
TG-J	1.000						
RL-J	0.336	1.000					
RS-J	−0.048	−0.002	1.000				
AS-J	−0.074	0.039	0.250	1.000			
EM-J	−0.132	−0.069	0.226	0.076	1.000		
PR-J	−0.208	−0.107	0.232	0.156	0.061	1.000	
CS-J	0.429	0.391	−0.258	−0.205	−0.279	−0.321	1.000

Table 5. Paired T-test (India).

	Mean	Ideal Scenario Gap	Standard Deviation	Standard Error Mean	t-value	Degree of Freedom	Significance
TG-I	4.62	−0.377	0.577	0.028	−13.591	431	<0.001
RL-I	4.30	−0.699	0.689	0.033	−21.074	431	<0.001
RS-I	2.46	−2.535	0.671	0.029	−87.861	539	<0.001
AS-I	2.29	−2.706	0.653	0.031	−86.159	431	<0.001
EM-I	1.81	−3.194	0.657	0.028	−113.005	539	<0.001
PR-I	3.75	−1.247	0.841	0.047	−26.700	323	<0.001
CS-I	4.55	−0.454	0.673	0.037	−12.134	323	<0.001

Customer demographics were analyzed to observe the customer satisfaction, and it was found that there is a negative correction between the age and income with the

Table 6. Paired T-test (Japan).

	Mean	Ideal Scenario Gap	Standard Deviation	Standard Error Mean	t-value	Degree of Freedom	Significance
TG-J	4.65	−0.355	0.516	0.025	−14.425	439	<0.001
RL-J	4.53	−0.475	0.596	0.028	−16.729	439	<0.001
RS-J	2.65	−2.351	0.868	0.037	−63.545	549	<0.001
AS-J	2.26	−2.741	0.638	0.030	−90.173	439	<0.001
EM-J	1.70	−3.298	0.728	0.031	−106.224	549	<0.001
PR-J	1.86	−3.142	0.615	0.034	−92.870	329	<0.001
CS-J	4.02	−0.976	0.970	0.053	−18.266	329	<0.001

Table 7. Correlation Analysis: Age and Income on Customer Satisfaction.

	India	Japan
Age	−0.062	−0.599
Income	−0.231	−0.571

customer satisfaction. This indicates that customer satisfaction with the service provided by the service robots in restaurants decreases with the increase in the age and income of the customers. In the case of Japan, the level of negative correlation between the customer satisfaction and age, as well as the customer satisfaction and income, is higher compared to the negative correction for India.

7 Conclusion and Recommendations

In this research, service quality and customer satisfaction of the service provided by the service robots in the restaurants is analyzed, and a few gaps between the expected service by the customers and the actual service provided by service robots are found. For conducting this research, the SERVQUAL model is used; however, the price as an additional construct is used as the price also plays an important role in the customer satisfaction.

Based on the analysis conducted, it is found that the gaps between the expected service and the service provided by the service robots on the tangibility and reliability aspects of service are not big for both India and Japan. The tangibility aspects of the service are about the size, appearance, cleanliness, audibility of robots. The reliability aspects of the service are about whether the service robots bring the right food to the right table in the appropriate condition without any errors.

The responsiveness aspects of the service are about greeting the customers, guiding the customers to an empty table, informing the customers about the estimated time required to serve food, taking additional requests, and being available when needed. It was found that the service robots are not currently providing such services. Considering the capabilities of the robots in some other use cases, such as the robot created by Softbank company in Japan named Pepper, greeting customers, and taking requests for tables is not difficult to implement in the service robots. Guiding the customers to the empty table requires the addition of some new workflow, such as whether the table is clean, seating capacity data of the table, Internet of Things (IoT) sensors, motion detectors, etc. If the robots are connected to data related to kitchen capacity, number of chefs, existing orders, and the average time required to prepare each food item, robots will be able to provide the estimated time to serve the food. Also, the number of robots to be deployed in a restaurant could be based on demand forecasting so as to have the right number of robots and the restaurant layout to ensure an appropriate level of availability of service robots.

The assurance aspects of the service are about robots confirming the order taken and then mentioning the name of the food brought to the table, providing the billing and payment service, answering customer queries, and instilling confidence and trust with customers. This aspect of service has a big gap between expectation and the actual service provided by the service robots. There is a need to add some more functionalities in the service robots to take the order and confirm it through screen or audio, mention the name of the food brought to the table, provide the billing and payment service through the input screen on the robot, use digital payment systems, and enhance communication ability through artificial intelligence systems such as generative AI and NLP, connect the robot to the restaurant database containing various information and frequently asked questions, etc. Integration of tablet computers on the tables with the robots can also help in providing the seamless customer service.

The empathy aspects of the service are about robots recommending the food as per customer preference, taking customer feedback, providing responses as and when appropriate, such as apologizing when the customer is dissatisfied, trying to understand the customer needs, and giving an individualized attention to the customers. This aspect of service also has a big gap between expectations and the actual service provided by the service robots. This gap could be reduced by understanding the customers and providing the intelligent customized communication and service through customer relationship management systems, artificial intelligence, natural language processing, and face recognition systems.

In this research, the customer's perception of price appropriateness is checked. It is found that the prices are perceived to be higher in the restaurants with service robots in India compared to the restaurants served by the human beings, while in Japan the restaurants with service robots are perceived to offer lower prices. This is mainly due to the differences in the objectives of deploying the service robots in the restaurants. Since Japan is facing the problems of labor shortage and aging population, robots are used to reduce the operational costs, and handle these problems, while in India service robots are being used as a strategic differentiator against other restaurants. Demographic analysis of customer satisfaction indicates that customer satisfaction reduces with an increase in age and income for both India and Japan. This is due to the reason that the younger people enjoy the interaction with the robots when visiting a restaurant, while senior and affluent customers expect a high level of personalized human service, and interacting with the robot might be a little inconvenient.

Responsiveness, assurance, and empathy aspects of service require further development and enhancements in the service robots to bridge the gap between the service provided by the service robots and that of human beings. By leveraging various existing digital technologies such as artificial intelligence, IoT, natural language processing, customer relationship management systems, face recognition systems, digital payment systems, and integrating the tablet computers, restaurant database, kitchen work-flow information with the service robots, could enhance the service quality of robots in the restaurants to a very large extent. Human errors are a natural occurrence when the service is provided by human beings however, by gaining the experience, knowledge, and capabilities through the evolution of digital technologies and process improvements, service robots have the potential to provide the service as good as human beings or even better.

8 Limitations

In this research, service provided by the robots in restaurants is compared with the service provided by the human beings. The questionnaire used for data collection is based on a 5-point Likert scale. It is assumed that humans can provide the ideal customer service, and the service provided by the robots is compared with the ideal service level of highest 5 points on Likert scale. However, the service provided by human beings is not always ideal or at the highest level of 5 points.

Data for this research is mainly collected from a very few cities in India and Japan, as the use of service robots in restaurants is still at its early stages of adoption and evolution. With further developments in digital technologies, it is expected that the service robots might become more sophisticated, intelligent, and capable. Also, it is expected that the customers and their expectations from service robots will also evolve in the future, opening a scope for a longitudinal study on the same topic.

References

1. Blumberg, B., Cooper, D.R., Schindler, P.S.: Business research methods. 9th edn. McGraw-Hill Education UK (2005)
2. Forozia, A., Zadeh, M.S., Gilani, M.H.: Customer satisfaction in hospitality industry: middle East tourists at 3-star hotels in Malaysia. Res. J. Appl. Sci. Eng. Technol. **5**(17), 4329–4335 (2013)
3. Gencer, Y.G., Akkucuk, U.: Measuring quality in automobile aftersales: AutoSERVQUAL scale. Amfiteatru Econ. **19**(44), 110–123 (2017)
4. Hair, J.F., Black, W.C., Babin, B.J., Anderson, R.E.: Multivariate Data Analysis. 7th edn. Pearson (2009)
5. Kim-Soon, N., Rahman, A., Visvalingam, L.: SERVQUAL: can it be used to differentiate guest's perception of service quality of 3 Star from a 4-star hotel. Int. Bus. Res. **7**(7), 38–47 (2014)
6. Lee, I.: Service robots: a systematic literature review. Electronics **10**(21), 2658 (2021)

7. MacCallum, R.C., Roznowski, M., Corinne, M.M., Reith, J.V.: Alternative strategies for cross-validation of covariance structure models. Multivar. Behav. Res. **29**(1), 1–32 (1994)
8. Markets and markets (n.d.). Service Robotics Market by Environment, Type (Professional and Personal and Domestic), Component, Application (Logistics, Inspection and Maintenance, Public Relations, Marine, Entertainment, Education, and Personal), and Geography—Global Forecast to 2028. https://www.marketsandmarkets.com/Market-Reports/service-robotics-market-681.html. Last accessed 2023/01/10
9. Parasuraman, A., Zeithaml, V.A., Berry, L.L.: Servqual: a multiple-item scale for measuring consumer perc. J. Retail. **64**(1), 12–40 (1988)
10. Parasuraman, A., Berry, L.L., Zeithaml, V.A.: Refinement and reassessment of the SERVQUAL scale. J. Retail. **67**(4), 420–450 (1991)
11. Population reference bureau: (2019). https://www.prb.org/resources/countries-with-the-oldest-populations-in-the-world/, last accessed 2023/01/09
12. Prasilowati, S.L., Suyanto, S., Safitri, J., Wardani, M.K.: The impact of service quality on customer satisfaction: the role of price. J. Asian Finance, Econ. Bus. **8**(1), 451–455 (2021)
13. Rezaei, J., Kothadiya, O., Tavasszy, L., Kroesen, M.: Quality assessment of airline baggage handling systems using SERVQUAL and BWM. Tour. Manage. **66**, 85–93 (2018)
14. Roslan, N.A.A., Wahab, E., Abdullah, N.H.: Service quality: a case study of logistics sector in iskandar malaysia using SERVQUAL model. Procedia Soc. Behav. Sci. **172**, 457–462 (2015)
15. Shafiq, A., Mostafiz, M.I., Taniguchi, M.: Using SERVQUAL to determine Generation Y's satisfaction towards hoteling industry in Malaysia. J. Tourism Futures **5**(1), 62–74 (2019)
16. Singh, M., Matsui, Y.: How long tail and trust affect online shopping behavior: an extension to UTAUT2 framework. Pacific Asia J. Assoc. Info. Syst. **9**(4), 1–24 (2017)
17. Stock, R.M.: Can customer satisfaction decrease price sensitivity in business-to-business markets? J. Bus. Bus. Mark. **12**(3), 59–87 (2005)
18. United Nations Population Division: World Population Prospects (2019). https://population.un.org/wpp/Download/Standard/Population/. Last accessed 2023/06/28
19. Wirtz, J., et al.: Brave new world: service robots in the frontline. J. Serv. Manag. **29**(5), 907–931 (2018)

Design Thinking Case Study: Developing a Training Program for an International IT Company

Artem Levchenko[✉] [iD]

SAP Japan Co., Ltd., Tokyo, Japan
`artem.levchenko@sap.com`

Abstract. The growth of the cloud technology market is driving a change in the strategies of IT companies. Previously, the priority for companies was on-Premises corporate information systems, i.e. systems delivered according to the SaaS model (Software as a Service). In positioning the benefits from the solution, the primary thing becomes dialogue with customers regarding economic benefits, rather than the functionality of the system. The implementation of new strategies forms the training requirements for employees. The article aims to develop a training program for IT employees of an international supplier of corporate systems. The analysis of scientific sources on the research topic is carried out, the problems are described, and the lack of scientific knowledge is highlighted in the use of Design Thinking methods for IT training. The use of system analysis made it possible to formalize the research tasks. The set theory was used to formalize the problem model—sets of subject areas and their characteristics are highlighted. To achieve the research goal, the methods of Design Thinking were applied. The article describes the study structure in terms of surveys and interaction with respondents using the methods of Design Thinking and the subsequent analysis of the data.

The proposed methods, based on the assessment of the company's management, made it possible to increase the effectiveness of the survey in terms of employee engagement. During the Design Thinking seminars, hundreds of subject topics were formalized, and dozens of topics were selected that corresponded to the set goal. The selected topics formed the basis of a training program for the IT staff of an international provider of corporate systems. Based on the feedback gathered from the staff, the seminar was highly appreciated. Positive reviews and results confirm that the goal of the study was achieved, and the methods used are more effective than those used previously.

Keywords: IT training · Systems Analysis · Design Thinking · SaaS

1 Introduction

The stable growth of cloud technologies in the global information technology market amounts to 16.9% in 2021. It will reach 1.3 trillion US dollars according to the forecasts of the IDC agency (International Data Corporation) [1, 2]. This growth, which is a consequence of the new strategies of large international IT solutions providers, is reflected in an increase in investment in the development of SaaS, PaaS, IaaS, and other XaaS models, and a decrease in investment in the promotion and development of the classic on-Premises model. Organizational changes are required to implement the new strategy in the departments of sales, implementation (customization) of an information product, and customer support when adapting an IT solution. Personnel training, which is a difficult task and often requires a creative approach, is one of the critical functions of the company's adaptation to implement a new strategy that prioritizes the development of the cloud technology business.

The SaaS business model is conceptually different from the classic on-Premises business. Under the classical scheme, the company's profit was based on the sale of solutions and services for their support, while in the case of the SaaS model, the basis is the adaptation of the solution and the renewal of the subscription to the solution. The specificity of cloud solutions lies in their unification for many users. Corporate IT solutions based on conventional technologies, by definition, cannot fulfill all the functional requirements of the customer and require a change in the customer's business in case of inconsistency with the typical models of business processes embedded in the SaaS system. The key to implementing a cloud system is the consistency of the work of the IT and business departments of the company.

The implementation scheme of classical systems was built as follows: the business department provides a list of functional requirements, and the IT department implements them. This scheme is incorporated, for example, into the ASAP methodology from SAP; at the conceptual design phase, a solution configuration design and a list of developments for the implementation of non-standard functional requirements are formed on the basis of all functional requirements. The approach is different when implementing SaaS solutions: the standard processes included in the solution are demonstrated, and a fit-gap analysis is formed. This analysis makes it possible to determine areas that cannot be implemented using the standard functionality of the solution and formulate requirements for changing business processes, organizational structure, regulations, and other elements of the enterprise's business. These works can be completed only in the case of a high level of involvement of business departments in the system implementation project. One fundamental element for making decisions about implementing a new corporate IT system in an enterprise is a business case describing the costs and projected benefits after the system deployment. In the case of an enterprise resource planning system, which is the central element of an enterprise's IT architecture, implementation takes several years. The initial project scope and SoW (the Statement of Work) often change, new client developments appear, the persons responsible for the project change, and not every company is engaged in tracking the execution of the initially confirmed business case.

In the case of the SaaS model, the key to renewing a subscription is the regular confirmation by department directors of the benefits of using the system. Therefore, returning to the position of a cloud technology provider, when implementing a new strategy and training employees, it is necessary to consider the requirements for employees' competencies in terms of negotiating with the top management of the enterprise about realizing the benefits of using SaaS systems. Historically, IT employees have a technical, not an economic, background. Therefore, training in calculating and tracking benefits and other knowledge required to negotiate with senior management of companies is still difficult for many technicians.

This study aims to formulate a training program for IT employees of an international supplier of corporate systems. Following the stages of system analysis, the following steps can be identified:

1. Statement of the problem—analysis of the subject area, the degree of its complexity, and the formation of tasks.
2. Analyzing available research on the relevant topic before and after choosing an approach to the solution.
3. Modeling and selecting alternative approaches to solving the problem—the rationale for using Design Thinking to solve the problem, not using classical methods based on expert assessments or surveys.
4. Developing a method for solving the problem—development of the format and framework of the Design Thinking workshop.
5. Developing a methodology for the practical Design Thinking application to solve the problem.
6. Conducting experiments by organized workshops.
7. Analysis of the results of experiments, assessment of possible strategies, and the formation of a solution—building a training program.

The article has a structure corresponding to the tasks. The introduction presents the problems, goals, and objectives of the study. The section with the analysis of scientific sources provides an overview of works on the research topic. In the theoretical part, the task is formalized, and the applied approaches and research methods are described. The implementation part describes the methodology and preparation for the experiment. In the experimental part, the investigation results are presented, and a solution is formed to achieve the goal of the study. In conclusion, a summary of the results obtained in the work, the findings, and directions for further research is described.

2 Literature Review

The study analyzed works in the following areas: problems and solutions for the adaptation of cloud technologies, the use of Design Thinking in education, the evolution of corporate systems considering the cultural characteristics of Japan (since the training program was formed for a branch of an IT company in Japan).

The existing literature on Design Thinking mainly describes the application of the method for innovation, including from the standpoint of organizational culture [3]. It has been argued that the advantage of Design Thinking lies in the connection between seemingly opposite ways of thinking, such as analytical and intuitive thinking. For Design Thinking to develop in a company, it must be embedded in a corporate culture that can maintain a dynamic balance between different types of thinking in innovation processes. Design Thinking is used in software companies. Research in Design Thinking shows that Design Thinking changes the way employees think [4]. Previously, an assessment was made of how the Design Thinking approach integrates with agile software development methodologies. The results show that most methods can be applied throughout the entire software development life cycle [5]. The integrated models have resulted in better interactions with the product end-users and development team, improving the quality and usability of the software. Design Thinking is used to collect customer requirements during product development. The industry case study [6] outlines the need for a better understanding of the needs of health stakeholders and the need to prepare new software requirements. Design Thinking was applied to solve this problem.

In addition to the use of methods in corporations, Design Thinking is used as a methodological approach in teaching engineering bachelors [7]. The approach focuses on creating innovative software products from scratch and goes beyond the typical analysis-design-implement-test process to reimagine the practice in terms of empathy-understanding-invention-prototyping-testing. An example of how universities plan to implement Design Thinking strategies to support project-based teaching of graduate students is presented in [8]. Design Thinking helps in software development and adapting an organization as it moves from a product orientation to an organization focus. For clarification, the article [9] presents an example from the field of care for the elderly in developing strategies for environmental sustainability using Design Thinking. From the educational point of view, using Design Thinking methods promotes the exchange of experience between the participants, enhances teamwork, and adds attractiveness to the communication between the trainer and the participants [10]. As previously stated, existing scientific articles mainly concern the application of methods to create new ideas [5, 11–13]. However, recently, the role of Design Thinking has been expanding from developing new solutions to improving team collaboration in applying new knowledge in practice [3, 14, 15]. In the case of the author of the article, it is used for educational purposes. For different scenarios of using Design Thinking, existing methods of Design Thinking and their combinations are changing. An industry example of Design Thinking is designing a sustainable, intelligent energy system [16]. In this example, an extension and modification of the classical methods were required. There are few articles on the connection between Design Thinking and cloud computing. The study [17] proposed a method for assessing the usability of a cloud platform service by implementing Design Thinking to analyze integration. Existing research broadly covers the application of Design Thinking to software development, but not to adapt cloud-based enterprise systems and educate employees. The relationship of the problems of adaptation to the cloud with the cultural specifics of individual countries has been discussed in several articles, but no definite solution has been found. This knowledge gap highlights the scientific value of the current research.

In terms of analyzing the specifics of cloud computing in the Japanese market, based on a questionnaire survey, a study was conducted on Japanese companies' awareness of cloud computing and main problems hindering the acceptance of cloud computing technologies in the market [18]. This study notes that cloud computing services have yet to be created and improved to make them look attractive and increase the speed of adoption in the Japanese market. In this regard, security concerns are the main hurdles to be overcome to strengthen the underlying IT infrastructure at the provider's disposal and deal with service disruptions and ensure uninterrupted service and continuous service availability. Interestingly, 13.2% of respondents still do not know the term "cloud computing." It is worth noting that none of the other respondents consider this a trend that will soon disappear.

Several works are worth noting from the point of view of technical aspects and specifics of cloud technologies. Aspects of a service-oriented IT architecture, micro-service model, and the challenges posed by multi-tier, distributed, and heterogeneous cloud architectures are described in [19]. Key concepts, architectural principles, modern implementation, and research challenges of cloud computing, such as automated service delivery and software frameworks, are highlighted in [20] and are still relevant. An area of emerging research challenges is also related to the self-adaptation of cloud applications. These exploratory problems, caused by the environment in which software applications are implemented, are described in [21]. Another area of cloud computing concerns is the architecture of cloud software systems caused by the increasing complexity of IT systems. There are unique challenges in this area, as the systems to be developed range from widespread social systems and enterprise applications to smart devices using IoT technologies [22]. It is argued that there is a need for model-driven techniques and methods to facilitate the specification of provisioning, deployment, monitoring, and adaptation of cloud systems at design time and their application at runtime [23]. The e-health industry has raised the challenges of using cloud services. These issues include regulation, security, access adaptation, connectivity, and resource allocation [24]. From a regional perspective, local issues, and the adoption of cloud services by local governments in Australia are highlighted in [25].

The analysis of the above works made it possible to study the subject area. It should be noted that there is a lack of scientific research in terms of the formation of a training program for IT employees of an international supplier of corporate systems using Design Thinking methods. This feature determines the scientific novelty of this research.

3 Theoretical Part: Approach Choice and Method Development

The problem is modeled from the position of a supplier of corporate information systems based on cloud technologies. Employees in the article are those employees who communicate directly with managers and top management of the client's enterprise. In the case of a shift in priority from discussing technical topics of system functionality to discussing economic topics of business benefits from using a SaaS system, the task of forming a training program comes down to identifying areas of knowledge (subject matters) that an employee should discuss but does not have sufficient competence. After identifying knowledge gaps, a training program is formed.

Through set theory, set C can be defined as a set of areas of knowledge (subject topics) in which an employee of a company has competencies:

$$C = \{c_i | g(c_i) > 0, i = 1, \ldots, m\} \subset U, \tag{1}$$

where c_i is a subject topic, $g(c)$ is a function of restrictions on permissible topics, which takes a positive value if the topic is valid for the research topic, m is the number of topics in the set, U is a universal set. The function of restrictions does not have an explicit form and takes values based on expert assessments.

Through the set R, areas of knowledge (subject topics) that are interesting for discussion by the top management of the client's enterprise are set:

$$R = \{r_i | g(r_i) > 0, i = 1, \ldots, l\} \subset U, \qquad (2)$$

where r_i is a subject topic, $g(r_i)$ is a function of restrictions on permissible topics, which takes a positive value if the topic is valid for the research topic, l is the number of topics in the set, U is a universal set. The function of restrictions does not have an explicit form and takes values based on expert assessments.

The set X with n elements x_i is the intersection of the sets $X = C \cap R$ and represents those topics that an employee of an IT company may have and that are of interest to the top management of the company. From the point of view of assessing the belonging of the competence to employees and its importance for the company's management, for each element x_i, three characteristics can be entered:

$$x_i = \langle I_i, F_i, V_i \rangle, \qquad (3)$$

$$I_i = \{Low, Medium, High\}, \qquad (4)$$

$$F_i = \{Low, Medium, High\}, \qquad (5)$$

$$V_i \subset N_0, \qquad (6)$$

$$i = 1, \ldots, n, \qquad (7)$$

where I_i—importance, the degree of importance for the management of the enterprise (client) of discussing this topic in terms of achieving economic benefits from using a SaaS-based system, this characteristic can take on the values Low (low significance), Medium (medium significance), High (high relevance); F_i—Feasibility, the level of competence of the IT company's employees in the x_i subject area, this characteristic can take on the values Low (low significance), Medium (medium significance), High (high significance); V_i—votes, characterizes the assessment of the importance of this topic for discussion with customers from the perspective of the IT company's employees in accordance with the new strategy of transition to cloud technologies.

To solve the problem, it is necessary to formalize the elements and their characteristics and then find x_i elements with the following property:

$$\begin{cases} I_i \subset \{Medium, High\}; \\ F_i \subset \{Low, Medium\}; \\ V_i = \max_{i=1,\ldots,n} V_i. \end{cases} \qquad (8)$$

To solve such multi-criteria tasks, it is necessary to turn to the company's experience, knowledge, and intuition of a wide range of qualified specialists. Conducting an expert survey is a successful method for solving such problems. Such a survey makes it possible to combine the opinions of specialists in various fields to obtain generalized results that consider unique ideas. There are many methods for conducting peer reviews. Some of the most popular are employee surveys and interviews with experts. These methods require employees to be motivated to spend time on interviews or filling out questionnaires. Interviewing is time-consuming if it is required to interview about a hundred employees, and polling is a method with low conversion rates due to poor employee engagement. Therefore, to solve this problem, methods of Design Thinking were proposed. This approach was chosen due to the following advantages: high employee involvement in the process; the opportunity not only to share knowledge but also to get new knowledge; polling several participants (respondents) with one facilitator (presenter, interviewer) saves time; the method involves the communication of the participants, which is an advantage during the period of isolation during a pandemic; the seminar can be held in a remote format; the presence of visual elements as a result of the workshop, which is a positive aspect for the presentation of the results of the session to the management [26].

The Hasso-Plattner Institute (HPI) identified six phases of Design Thinking as the basis for planning a workshop: understanding, observing, point of view, idea, prototype, verification (see Fig. 1). Phase selection is like a designer's intuitive workflow [27]. All stages are qualitatively important and, according to the methodology, cannot be skipped.

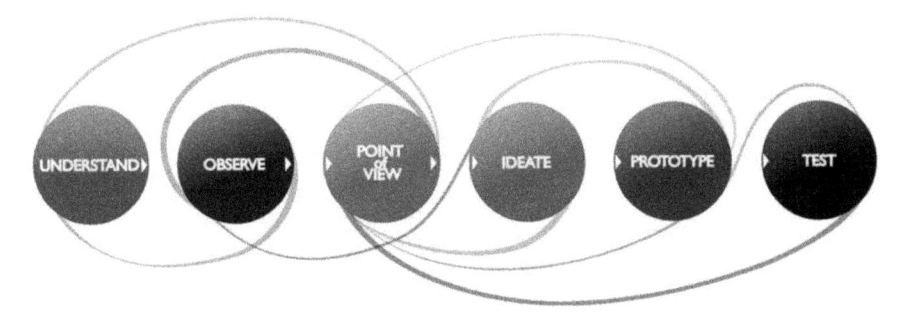

Fig. 1. HPI Design Thinking Process Model.

4 Implementation Part: Methodology Formation and Preparation for the Experiment

Since in 2021 in most countries, IT companies' employees work remotely and internal events from the point of view of the company are limited by corporate policies, the Design Thinking seminar was planned to be held remotely. There are many specialized programs for conducting Design Thinking workshops online. For example, the most popular tools are Mural, Miro, InVision, and Sprintbase. Each tool has a wide range of functionality for conducting virtual seminars in a Design Thinking format and would be suitable for conducting the necessary workshop. Mural was chosen due to its corporate subscription to the solution, extensive template base, and intuitive interface, resulting in less than ten minutes of training session facilitators.

A framework (structure, basis) of the seminar was prepared, making it possible to formalize the elements c_i, r_i, x_i, and determine the characteristics I_i, F_i, V_i corresponding to the elements. Since the seminar was held at the SAP company in the Japanese branch, the framework was prepared in English and Japanese. Figure 2 shows the framework in English.

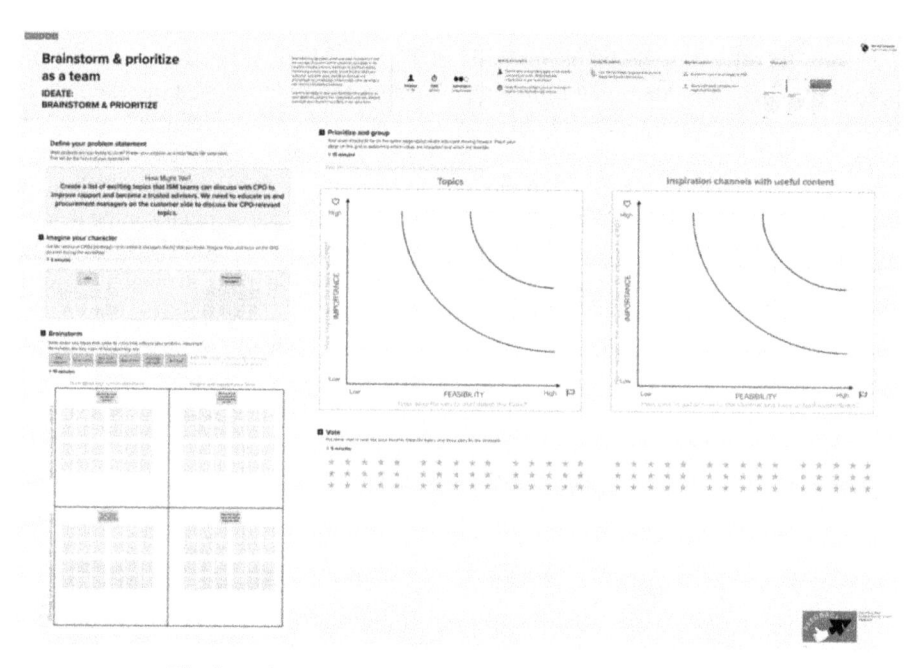

Fig. 2. A framework in a Mural app for holding a workshop.

Since it is impossible to present the framework completely in full size, and make the text readable from a picture, instead of printing several enlarged pictures, below is a description of the main characteristics of the framework and the sequence of tasks for the workshop.

The first task is called "Imagine your character." The task is to recall, in three minutes, authentic representatives of the top management of enterprises with whom the participants in the workshop worked or whom they know well. The assignment makes it possible to start the workshop with a simple activity and focus on the key role for the next stage of idea generation.

The second brainstorm assignment is to formalize and discuss ideas in four main areas in fifteen minutes: topics for discussion with the client's top management—what has been discussed in recent meetings and what has not been discussed before, but can be exciting and valuable for inclusion in the agenda of the meeting; channels and sources for obtaining relevant information on the listed topics—what employees already use (listen, watch, read) and what they do not use, but could do potentially. The exercise allows formalizing the elements of the sets c_i and r_i.

The third task, "Prioritize and Group," aims to define the I_i and F_i characteristics for the elements defined in the second task. In fifteen minutes, participants should determine the position of their idea in the Projections of Importance and Feasibility—how important it is to discuss this topic for the person from the first assignment and the role in general, and how competent the employee and the department are to discuss this topic. During the time given for exercise, there is a group discussion of the ideas, their location, and the integration of similar ideas into groups. At this stage, the elements x_i are determined based on the elements c_i and r_i. Those elements that were not intersections of the sets $C \cap R$ were cut off based on group discussions.

The fourth task, "Vote" (voting) allows determining the final characteristics of the elements of the sets V_i. In five minutes, each participant must choose the three most promising topics from his/her point of view and three sources for obtaining subject data for discussion of the selected topics.

For each workshop, 60 min were planned: 5 min of introduction, 50 min of working time, of which 38 min of working directly on tasks and 12 min for explaining tasks and reserve time, 5 min for completing the session—acknowledgments and a description of further steps. All company employees from one department who interact with the middle or top management of client enterprises were invited to participate in the workshop. Distribution of invitations came from the head of the department as an optional but desirable session for employees to participate. Invitations were sent with an offer of three different days and time frames for participation to increase the number of participants.

Before the workshop, a questionnaire was pre-formed to collect feedback after the workshop. The SAP Qualtrics solution was used to form the questionnaires. The questions of the questionnaire translated into Russian are presented in Table 1.

Table 1. Questions for providing feedback on the results of the workshop.

No.	Question	Format and answer options
1	Please choose your team	Drop-Down-List with the teams and "I don't remember" option
2	How did you like the Design Thinking workshop on a scale from 1 to 5? (5 stars is excellent)	From 1 to 5
3	Please let us know how much you agree or disagree with the following statements	Strongly disagree Somewhat disagree Neither agree nor disagree Somewhat agree Strongly agree
3.1	This event was well prepared	
3.2	The facilitation of the event was well done	
3.3	The selected topic was relevant to me	
3.4	The content was interesting to me	
3.5	I learned something new	
3.6	I plan to use the workshop results in my work once it will be published	

(continued)

Table 1. (*continued*)

No.	Question	Format and answer options
3.7	The virtual event platform was well selected	
3.8	There was enough opportunity to interact	
3.9	The timing of the event was appropriate	
4	Do you have any more ideas on how can we improve the Design Thinking workshop next time? Please insert as many ideas as you would like	Text field (many rows)
5	Is there anything else you would like to tell us?	Text field (many rows)

5 Experimental Part: Results Analysis and Solution Formation

As a result of mailing to 123 employees, 49 participants participated in the workshops, which is about 39.8% of the participants. According to the head of the department, the target audience is approximately 40–50% of employees who interact with managers and top management of customers' enterprises. Thus, the number of participants turned out to be at a high level. Ten parallel workshops were held over three-time intervals—three parallel workshops on the first two days and four parallel workshops on the third day. Nine workshops were conducted in Japanese, one in English. The workshops involved four facilitators. The number of participants in each workshop was from three to six people. A visual example of the results of the work of one of the groups in Japanese is shown in Fig. 3.

In the experiment, a set X was formed with the characteristics of the elements $x_i = I_i, F_i, V_i$. The number of ideas formulated was $i = 505$. The number of elements with $V_i > 0$ was 158. The ideas were transferred from Mural to Excel and translated from Japanese into English, and from English into Japanese.

For elements with $V_i > 0$, an expert correction of the wording was performed so that they were formalized in a single format. So, for example, the wording "Return on investment", "Need to discuss ROI" were reduced to "ROI". Next, elements x_i were selected, for which $I_i \subset \{Medium, High\}$, $F_i \subset \{Low, Medium\}$ and $V_i > 0$. The number of such elements was 44. From these 44 elements, the elements were first selected, for which $I_i = High$ and $F_i = Low$. There were 5 items in total. Out of the remaining 39 elements, seven elements x_i with the highest V_i were selected. As a result of the experiment, the selected 12 x_i elements became the basis for the employee training program in 2022, with a schedule of one subject area workshop per month. The topics fore training included topics related to the following areas of expertise: the organization of strategic partnerships, successful and unsuccessful examples of SaaS solutions by other companies, industry trends, calculating the return on investment after the implementation of a cloud-based solution, and others.

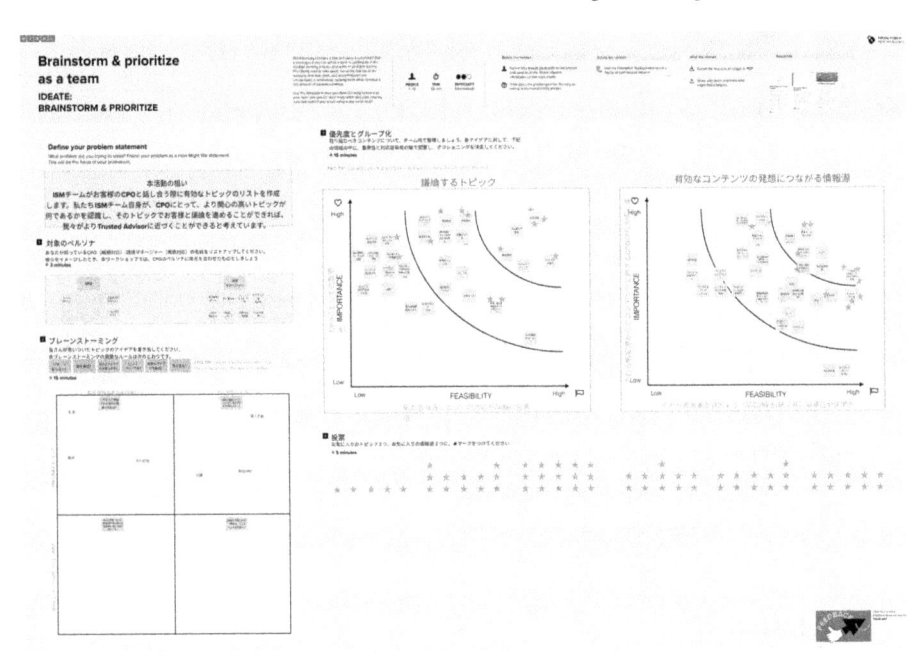

Fig. 3. Visual example of the results of the work of one of the groups in Japanese.

The results of the work were positively assessed by the company's leaders, which confirms the adequacy of the applied methodology. Compared to past expert knowledge and one-to-one survey approaches, the number of participants was less than 20%, compared to 39.8%, due to the author's approach. In addition to the assessment of the company's management, feedback from participants was analyzed. The feedback results are shown in Table 2.

In addition to the quantitative assessment, the seminar participants provided a qualitative assessment in comments (questions 4 and 5 in Table 1). Among the comments, there were many thanks, as well as recommendations for improvement—a proposal to hold a seminar for other departments; publish the framework before the workshop so that participants can get ready; more time for assignments and discussions between participants; more accurate distribution of invitations to the seminar (the mailing list was received by the customer support departments, which do not interact directly with the management).

The results obtained made it possible to identify areas for improvement in the following experiments. As a result of this experiment, the goal was achieved—forming a training program for IT employees of an international supplier of corporate systems. In addition to achieving the goal, the effectiveness of the use of Design Thinking methods for solving this class of problems of working with the collection and analysis of data for training has been confirmed. The following aspects limited the experiment: more than 80% of the participants were Japanese employees, the study was conducted within the same IT company. Further research is planned in terms of reducing the identified restrictions.

Table 2. The results of the survey with feedback on the seminar on a five-point scale.

No.	Question	Result
2	How did you like the Design Thinking workshop on a scale from 1 to 5? (5 stars is excellent)	4,5
3.1	This event was well prepared	4,25
3.2	The facilitation of the event was well done	4,625
3.3	The selected topic was relevant to me	4
3.4	The content was interesting to me	3,625
3.5	I learned something new	4
3.6	I plan to use the workshop results in my work once it will be published	3,75
3.7	The virtual event platform was well selected	4,125
3.8	There was enough opportunity to interact	3,75
3.9	The timing of the event was appropriate	4,5

6 Conclusion

The study achieved the goal of developing a training program for IT employees of an international supplier of corporate systems. The analysis of scientific sources on the subject topic was carried out, the problems were described, and the scientific deficit of knowledge was highlighted in the use of Design Thinking methods for IT training. As a result of the literature analysis, the goals were formalized. The use of system analysis made it possible to standardize the research tasks. The set theory was used to create a problem model and achieve the research goal—Design Thinking methods. The article describes in detail the structure of the study in terms of surveys and interaction of respondents using Design Thinking methods and the subsequent analysis of the data.

The proposed methods, based on the assessment of the company's management, made it possible to increase the effectiveness of the survey from 20% to 39.8% in terms of employee engagement. During ten Design Thinking workshops, 505 subject topics were formalized, and 44 topics corresponding to the set goal were selected. These 44 topics formed the basis of the training program for IT staff of an international supplier of corporate systems. Based on the collected feedback from employees, the seminar was rated 4.5 out of 5 points available. Positive reviews and results confirm that the goal of the study was achieved, and the methods used are more effective than those used previously.

Further research is planned to reduce the limitations of the experiment in terms of the influence of the cultural characteristics of the participants, increasing the number of attributes of the elements of sets, and surveying not only employees of one company but also companies in other countries and manufacturing industries.

References

1. IDC Forecasts Worldwide "Whole Cloud" Spending to Reach $1.3 Trillion by 2025, https://www.idc.com/getdoc.jsp?containerId=prUS48208321. Last accessed 2021/09/14
2. Gartner Forecasts Worldwide Public Cloud End-User Spending to Grow 23% in 2021, https://www.gartner.com/en/newsroom/press-releases/2021-04-21-gartner-forecasts-worldwide-public-cloud-end-user-spending-to-grow-23-percent-in-2021. Last assessed 2021/04/21
3. Prud'homme van Reine, P.: The culture of design thinking for innovation. J. Innov. Manage., **5–2**, 56–80 (2017)
4. Dobrigkeit, F.: Design thinking in practice: understanding manifestations of design thinking in software engineering. In: Proceedings of the 2019 27th ACM Joint Meeting on European Software Engineering Conference and Symposium on the Foundations of Software Engineering (ESEC/FSE 2019), pp. 1059–1069. Asso)iation for Computing Machinery, New York, NY, USA (2019)
5. Cesar Pereira, J.: Design thinking integrated in agile software development: a systematic literature review. Proc. Comput. Sci. **138**, 775–782 (2018)
6. Carroll, N.: Aligning Healthcare Innovation and Software Requirements through Design Thinking. In: 2016 IEEE/ACM International Workshop on Software Engineering in Healthcare Systems (SEHS). Association for Computing Machinery, Austin, TX, USA, pp. 1–7 (2016)
7. Corral, L.: Design thinking and agile practices for software engineering: an opportunity for innovation. In: Proceedings of the 19th Annual SIG Conference on Information Technology Education (SIGITE '18). Association for Computing Machinery, New York, NY, USA, pp. 26–31 (2018)
8. Taratukhin, V.: Next-gen design thinking for management education. Project-based and Game-oriented methods are critical ingredients of success. Develop. Bus. Simul. Experien. Learn., **47**, 261–265 (2020)
9. J. Clune, S.: Developing environmental sustainability strategies, the Double Diamond method of LCA and design thinking: a case study from aged care. J. Clean. Prod., **85**, 67–82 (2014)
10. Taratukhin, V.: Next-gen design thinking for management education. Project-based and game-oriented methods are critical ingredients of success. Develop. Bus. Simul. Experiential Learn. **47**, 261–265 (2020)
11. Carroll, N.: Aligning healthcare innovation and software requirements through design thinking. In 2016 IEEE/ACM International Workshop on Software Engineering in Healthcare Systems (SEHS). Austin, TX, USA: Association for Computing Machinery, pp. 1–7 (2016)
12. Taratukhin, V.: The future of project-based learning for engineering and management students: Towards an advanced design thinking approach. In: The American Society for Engineering Education Annual Conference and Exposition Proceedings, Salt Lake City, Utah, pp. 1–15. ASEE, USA (2018)
13. Corral, L.: Design thinking and agile practices for software engineering: an opportunity for innovation. In Proceedings of the 19th Annual SIG Conference on Information Technology Education (SIGITE '18), New York, NY, USA: Association for Computing Machinery, pp. 26–31 (2018)
14. Dilts, R.: Strategies of Genius: Sigmund Freud, p. 3. Meta Publications, Vol, Leonardo da Vinci, Nikola Tesla, Aptos, CA, USA (1994)
15. Dobrigkeit, F.: Design thinking in practice: understanding manifestations of design thinking in software engineering. In: Proceedings of the 2019 27th ACM Joint Meeting on European Software Engineering Conference and Symposium on the Foundations of Software Engineering (ESEC/FSE 2019), New York, NY, USA: Association for Computing Machinery, pp. 1059–1069 (2019)

16. Tushar, W.: Exploiting design thinking to improve energy efficiency of buildings. Energy **197**, 1–19 (2020)
17. Ng, K.H.: Design thinking for usability evaluation of cloud platform service-case study on 591 house rental web service. In: 2018 IEEE International Conference on Applied System Invention (ICASI). IEEE, Chiba, Japan, pp. 247–250 (2018)
18. Khare, A., Khare, K., Baber, W.: Why Japan's digital transformation is inevitable. In: Khare, A., Ishikura, H., Baber, W. (eds.) Transforming Japanese Business. Future of Business and Finance. Springer, Singapore, pp. 3–14 (2020)
19. Pahl, C.: Architectural principles for cloud software. ACM Trans. Internet Technol. **18–2**, 1–23 (2018)
20. Zhang, Q.: Cloud computing: state-of-the-art and research challenges. J. Internet Serv. Appl. **1**, 7–18 (2010)
21. Farokhi, S., Jamshidi, P., Brandic, I., Elmroth, E.: Self-adaptation challenges for cloud-based applications: a control theoretic perspective. In: 10th International Workshop on Feedback Computing 2015 (2015)
22. Chauhan, M.A.: Architecting cloud-enabled systems: a systematic survey of challenges and solutions. Softw.: Practice and Expertise **47**, 599–644 (2017)
23. Ferry, N.: Towards model-driven provisioning, deployment, monitoring, and adaptation of multi-cloud systems. In: 2013 IEEE Sixth International Conference on Cloud Computing. IEEE, Santa Clara, CA, USA, pp. 887–894 (2013)
24. Liu, W.: e-Healthcare cloud computing application solutions: Cloud-enabling characteristices, challenges and adaptations. In: 2013 International Conference on Computing, Networking and Communications (ICNC). IEEE Computer Society, San Diego, CA, USA, pp. 437-443 (2013).
25. Ali, O.: Cloud computing technology adoption: an evaluation of key factors in local governments. Inf. Technol. People **34–2**, 666–703 (2020)
26. Levchenko A.A.: A Design Thinking case study: Net Promoter Score improvement for SAP-based education courses/Levchenko A.A, V.V. Taratukhin. Proceedings of Twenty-first SAP Academic Conference Americas. USA: Online, pp. 40–43 (2021)
27. Plattner, H., Meinel, C., Weinberg, U.: Design Thinking. Mi-wirtschaftsbuch, Munich, Germany (2009)

The Role of Universities in Shaping an Innovative Ecosystem and Sustainable Regional Development: The Experience of Inha University in Tashkent and Prospects for the Future

Muzaffar Djalalov and Dilshoda Mirzokhidova(✉)

Inha University in Tashkent, Ziyolilar.Str. 9, Tashkent, Uzbekistan
dilshoda.mirzakhidova@gmail.com

Abstract. As the world continues to face numerous challenges, including economic uncertainty, environmental degradation, and technological disruption, universities are increasingly being called upon to play a pivotal role in shaping innovative ecosystems and fostering sustainable regional development. This conference abstract explores the case study of Inha University in Tashkent, Uzbekistan, to shed light on how universities can effectively contribute to these critical objectives, drawing from their experience and offering insights into the prospects for the future. Inha University in Tashkent, a branch of South Korea's renowned Inha University, has established itself as a leading educational institution in the Central Asian region. This abstract delves into the university's journey, highlighting its strategies, initiatives, and collaborations aimed at fostering innovation, entrepreneurship, and sustainable development in the local and regional context. Key aspects to be discussed include academic programs tailored to industry needs, research initiatives driving technological advancement, and the development of partnerships with government agencies, businesses, and non-profit organizations. Furthermore, this abstract examines the broader implications of Inha University in Tashkent's experience for the future of universities in shaping innovative ecosystems and sustainable regional development. It explores the transferability of lessons learned, the potential for replication in diverse global contexts, and the role of higher education institutions in promoting economic growth, environmental stewardship, and social progress. By analyzing the case of Inha University in Tashkent, this conference abstract contributes to a deeper understanding of the evolving role of universities in shaping innovative ecosystems and driving sustainable regional development. It provides valuable insights for policymakers, educators, and stakeholders interested in harnessing the potential of higher education institutions as catalysts for positive change in the modern world.

Keywords: Role of universities · Sustainable development · Innovative ecosystem

1 Introduction

In the era of globalization and rapid technological advancements, universities are increasingly recognized as key drivers of innovation and catalysts for regional development. They have metamorphosed into dynamic hubs that wield significant influence, not only in shaping the intellectual discourse but also in fostering innovation, entrepreneurship, and sustainable regional development. This conference paper delves into a compelling case study that exemplifies the transformative power of universities in the context of innovative ecosystem development and sustainable regional growth.

The experience of Inha University in Tashkent, Uzbekistan, offers an illuminating lens through which we can explore the multifaceted contributions that universities make to their local and regional landscapes. In a world marked by the rapid pace of globalization and technological advancement, the nexus between academia, industry, and government has never been more crucial. Inha University, as a unique entity born out of South Korea-Uzbekistan cooperation, epitomizes the profound potential universities possess in shaping the destiny of regions, fostering innovation ecosystems, and advancing sustainable development.

This paper endeavors to provide an in-depth analysis of University's role in shaping an innovative ecosystem and promoting sustainable regional development. We will delve into the institution's enduring commitment to education, research, and collaboration, emphasizing its impact on the local ecosystem. Moreover, we will explore the university's prospects and strategies for the future, underscoring its continued potential to drive innovation and contribute to the region's sustainable growth.

The journey of Inha University in Tashkent stands as a testament to the transformative influence universities can wield, transcending their academic boundaries to become engines of positive change. As we embark on this exploration of its experience, we delve into the profound implications it holds for the evolving landscape of higher education and its pivotal role in shaping innovative, sustainable, and prosperous regions.

In the past, universities primarily focused on disseminating and generating knowledge through their core academic activities of teaching and research. However, they are now increasingly adopting a more active role within their regions by embracing a "third mission" of external engagement with society (Etzkowitz and Leydesdorff, 2000; Gunasekara, 2006). As a result of this shift, there has been an increase in two-way and network connections with local stakeholders. Studies that have emphasized university-industry collaboration have been a prominent focus when examining universities' engagement with their regions, leading to a biased view of their regional roles [7]. Certainly, in light of governance models and policy frameworks that underscore greater involvement of stakeholders and the adoption of knowledge-driven decision-making, it is evident that collaboration between universities and regional governments has assumed a pivotal role. Universities are progressively assuming greater significance in shaping the processes involved in the formulation of regional strategies [1].

2 Materials and Methods

2.1 Higher Education System of Uzbekistan: The Government's Regulatory Role

The regulatory framework plays a crucial role in determining the innovation capability of individual entities, including universities and businesses, and consequently, the overall innovation system.

The Republic of Uzbekistan is resolutely and dynamically pursuing its primary objective—integration into the league of developed democratic nations. The fundamental mechanism driving this aspiration lies within the higher education system, which is constructed upon the processes of systematic organization, creative adaptation, and the utilization of accumulated wisdom from previous generations. In this new phase of development, it is imperative that the quality of personnel training aligns with the current requirements of a burgeoning civil society. Higher education has emerged as a focal point of governmental priorities within the context of elevating all facets of socio-economic life and fostering the establishment of civil society institutions. The continued advancement of higher education institutions is instrumental in facilitating innovative breakthroughs across all spheres of activity through the cultivation of skilled professionals. A crucial precondition for this progress has been the integration of key provisions from the "Strategy for Innovative Development of the Country for 2022–2026" into the operations of higher education institutions. This strategy has outlined the goal of achieving a 50% enrollment rate in higher education and enhancing the overall quality of education.

President Shavkat Mirziyoyev, through a decree issued on September 11, 2023 endorsed the Uzbekistan-2030 Strategy. This strategic plan aims to achieve several objectives, including providing equal opportunities for all citizens to unleash their potential, nurturing a well-educated and healthy generation, fostering a robust economy, and ensuring justice, the rule of law, and security within the nation.

Expanding Coverage of Higher Education: Under the Digital Uzbekistan 2030 initiative, the government is committed to increasing access to higher education for its citizens. This involves the establishment of more universities, colleges, and educational institutions to accommodate a growing number of students. The goal is to provide educational opportunities to a broader segment of the population, ensuring that talented individuals from all backgrounds have access to higher learning.

Improving the Quality of Training: To meet the demands of the modern digital era, the decree places a strong emphasis on enhancing the quality of education provided at higher education institutions. This involves updating curricula to align with the latest industry trends and technological advancements. Additionally, efforts are being made to attract highly qualified professors and researchers to these institutions, ensuring that students receive a world-class education.

The Digital Uzbekistan 2030 initiative recognizes that a well-educated workforce is essential for the country's economic development in the digital age. By expanding access to higher education and improving its quality, Uzbekistan aims to produce a skilled and competitive workforce capable of contributing to the country's technological advancement and global competitiveness. This comprehensive approach to higher education aligns with the broader vision of a digitally transformed and prosperous Uzbekistan by the year 2030.

3 Results and Discussions

3.1 Empowering Regional Development: The Impact of Inha University in Tashkent

Founded in 2014 by the decree of the President of Uzbekistan, Inha University in Tashkent has rapidly emerged as a prominent contributor to the local innovation ecosystem and sustainable regional growth. One of the key factors behind its success lies in the stringent quality education standards upheld through its partnership with the esteemed Korean institution, Inha University.

The university's core mission is to foster regional development and technological progress through education, research, and collaboration.

Inha University in Tashkent, renowned for its commitment to academic excellence and innovation, hosts two prominent schools at its campus, each contributing significantly to the educational landscape in Uzbekistan.

The School of Computer and Information Engineering at Inha University in Tashkent is at the forefront of technological advancement and computer science education. With a dedicated faculty and state-of-the-art facilities, this school provides students with a rigorous and comprehensive curriculum in computer engineering, software development, and information technology. Students here are immersed in a dynamic learning environment, fostering critical thinking, problem-solving, and hands-on experience in cutting-edge technologies. The school's programs not only equip students with essential skills but also prepare them to become leaders in the ever-evolving field of computer and information engineering.

The School of Business and Logistics at Inha University in Tashkent offers a distinctive and globally-oriented program known as "3 + 1." Under this program, students undergo three years of rigorous academic training in Uzbekistan, followed by an exciting and transformative one-year experience in South Korea. This unique approach to education not only provides students with a solid academic foundation but also exposes them to international perspectives and experiences.

During their three years in Uzbekistan, students receive comprehensive instruction in business and logistics, equipping them with essential knowledge and skills relevant to the modern business landscape. They benefit from the guidance of experienced faculty members and engage in a dynamic learning environment. The success of the "3 + 1" program is evident in the fact that over 300 students have completed their studies through this pathway.

In addition to its undergraduate programs, Inha University in Tashkent offers an innovative MBA program in Digital Transformation. This program is designed for professionals seeking to navigate the complexities of the digital age. As the digital landscape continues to evolve rapidly, this MBA program equips students with the knowledge and strategic insights needed to lead organizations through the challenges and opportunities presented by digital technologies. It provides a holistic understanding of digital transformation, encompassing areas such as data analytics, e-commerce, digital marketing, and emerging technologies. Graduates of this program emerge as digital leaders, ready to drive change and innovation in their respective industries.

In the current academic year, Inha University in Tashkent proudly boasts a vibrant and diverse student body, with a total enrollment of 1,672 students. These students come from various backgrounds and are driven by a shared commitment to academic excellence and innovation. This diverse community of learners represents the future leaders and professionals of Uzbekistan and beyond.

To ensure that these students receive a well-rounded and high-quality education, the university is supported by a dedicated team of 62 professors and educators. These accomplished individuals bring their expertise, passion for teaching, and commitment to research to the institution.

A pivotal aspect of Inha University in Tashkent's success lies in its unwavering commitment to upholding rigorous quality education standards, a legacy inherited from its Korean counterpart, Inha University. The Korean influence has played a pivotal role in shaping the curriculum, pedagogical methods, and research ethos, ensuring that students receive education of the highest caliber.

The graduates of Inha University in Tashkent have consistently demonstrated their exceptional capabilities and have gone on to become industry tech leaders both nationally and internationally. Their remarkable achievements showcase the university's commitment to producing top-notch talent in the technology sector.

For instance, Darkhonbek Mamataliev, a proud alumnus of Inha University in Tashkent, has risen to prominence as an iOS engineer at UBER in the United States. His contributions to one of the world's leading technology and transportation companies underscore the caliber of talent nurtured by the university.

Another illustrious graduate, Dilmurod Yangiboev, has forged a successful career as a Software Engineer at Tesla, a pioneering company renowned for its groundbreaking advancements in electric vehicles and sustainable energy solutions. Dilmurod's journey from the halls of Inha University in Tashkent to the forefront of the tech industry is a testament to the university's commitment to producing global tech leaders.

Furthermore, Fazliddin Anvarov has emerged as a distinguished figure in the technology sector within Uzbekistan. As a Youth Advisor at the Ministry of Digital Technologies of Uzbekistan, he plays a crucial role in shaping the nation's digital landscape. Fazliddin's contributions exemplify how Inha University in Tashkent graduates not only excel on the international stage but also make a significant impact in their home country's tech ecosystem.

These outstanding alumni are just a few examples of the many accomplished professionals who have emerged from Inha University in Tashkent. Their successes highlight the university's commitment to providing students with the knowledge, skills, and opportunities needed to become industry tech leaders, driving innovation and progress in the ever-evolving world of technology.

The essence of digital transformation in public educational structures is the effective use of the latest information technologies to transition to a personalized and result-oriented approach through the active use of all methods of communication and cognitive capabilities. The implementation of Uzbekistan's strategy at the stage of digitalization of the education system is gaining the necessary pace, this is facilitated by ongoing reforms, improvement of the regulatory framework and management using the experience of developed countries in digital transformation, including the Republic of Korea.

Research shows that the digital transformation of higher education in our conditions can be systematically considered in three directions:

1. The need for the full implementation of broadband networks and equipping educational institutions with modern equipment. The justification is that since February 2021, targeted work has been carried out by the Ministry for the Development of Information Technologies and Communications to connect all universities to the special "Education" tariff. More than 100 billion UZS have been allocated from the state budget for this activity and 200 billion UZS for equipment. The connection speed to Tas-IX networks has reached 100 Mbit/s on all Education tariffs;
2. High-quality digitization of new educational materials available online, conducting online courses—MOOC (Massive Open Online Courses). Electronic resources will facilitate self-training for students, since one device will have a huge amount of data in the form of textbooks, scientific articles, lectures and other educational materials. These measures in Uzbekistan are related to the implementation of the tasks defined in the Presidential Decree of April 29, 2019 "On approval of the concept of development of the public education system of the Republic of Uzbekistan until 2030";
3. Extensive training of young people in digital skills. This direction, as is known, is considered in the Decree of the President of the Republic of Uzbekistan dated October 5, 2020 "On approval of the strategy "Digital Uzbekistan-2030" and measures for its effective implementation", where by the end of 2023 in all districts and cities of the Republic of Karakalpakstan and regions of the regions Over 200 specialized schools with in-depth study of information technology will begin to function. The best teachers and specialists were recruited from Inha University in Tashkent (IUT) for professional training in computer programming skills.

IUT, remaining one of the drivers of the development of digital education in the region, involves not only the introduction of digital technologies, but also the expansion of continuous training of highly qualified specialists:

1. Online learning and constant monitoring of the quality of the educational process by partners from Inha University (Incheon).
2. Phased modernization of the Data Center (data center). This center is the largest data center in the country according to the TIER-2 standard after the national operator Uzbektelecom and provides services such as hosting, co-location and server rental.
3. Opening an IT school at the IUT Center for Continuing Education by 2024, as well as e-sports laboratories for students and students in specialized schools.
4. Corporate courses in the field of modern communication technologies (ORACLE, CISCO, Microsoft, SAP) and Strategic IT Leadership executive courses.
5. Implementation of international training programs (King Sejong Institute of the Korean Language).
6. Together with the IT Park, stimulating gifted students with opportunities for start-up projects and venture financing at the Incubation Center at the University.
7. Attracting foreign investment in Coworking, BPO Center and Cyber Security Laboratories at IUT.

This process implies not only the attraction of foreign teachers, the use of modern technical potential, joint software products with the help of partners from Korea, but also a fundamental change in the management of university education, the opening of new directions and specialties, scientific work of undergraduates using artificial intelligence.

A digital approach to the implementation of such areas as virtual management of student activities, remote admission of applicants, a new electronic resource center with the support of the Union youth of Uzbekistan, initiatives on popular international programs with famous universities from Korea and invitation of professors from other countries—opens up opportunities to give new impetus to the implementation of completely new smart solutions.

4 Conclusion

The analysis showed that further digital transformation of the university, which is fighting for the attention of new consumers of IT personnel in the labor market, is impossible without a modern environment for research and world experience in creating student campuses. This is our hope for the prospects for close cooperation between our partners from the Republic of Korea. Inha University (Incheon) was the first to propose opening a bachelor's program in Data Science and Information Security. With the support of the Medical Academy and Inha Hospital, work is underway on a joint master's program in the field of IT medicine. Active cooperation is also being established with leading outsourcing companies of the Republic of Korea in the field of Business Process Outsourcing (BPO), in particular with Geotwo Co. Ltd., SRPOST Inc., Joys Global and Global Optical Communications with the aim of involving students in the project at the BPO center at the university.

Inha University in Tashkent's achievements exemplify the transformative potential of universities in regional ecosystem development. By upholding stringent quality education standards, inherited from its Korean counterpart, the university has emerged as a beacon of innovation and sustainable growth in Uzbekistan. University stands as a shining example of how higher education institutions can serve as catalysts for regional development and ecosystem growth. Through its steadfast commitment to quality education standards, innovative programs, and strategic partnerships, this institution has made a significant and lasting impact on the region.

The university's dedication to fostering innovation, entrepreneurship, and the nurturing of an informed, proactive, and idealistic student body has not only produced highly skilled professionals but has also contributed to a culture of continuous learning and creativity. By providing an environment that encourages self-organized student activities and supports the aspirations of 'millennial' students, Inha University in Tashkent has amplified the region's potential for innovation and progress. As it continues on its trajectory of success, it not only shapes the region's future but also provides a valuable model for other institutions seeking to make a lasting impact on their communities.

References

1. Ansell, C., Gash, A.: Collaborative governance in theory and practice. J. Public Admin. Res. Theory **18**(4), 543–571 (2008). https://doi.org/10.1093/jopart/mum032

2. Ambasz, D., Nikolaev, D., Malinovskiy, S., Olszewski, O., Julien, A.S., Zavalina, P., Botero Alvarez, J.: Towards Higher Education Excellence in Central Asia: A Roadmap for Improving the Quality of Education and Research through Regional Integration. Washington, D.C.: World Bank Group. http://documents.worldbank.org/curated/en/099101023140578441/P17 90811f2f765ea101eb142301abf0100a90db82451
3. Cytlak, I., Mamadaminova, N.: Higher education during the pandemic. An Overview of the Higher Education System in Uzbekistan. Kultura-Społeczeństwo-Edukacja, **19**, 19–36 (2021). https://doi.org/10.14746/kse.2021.19.2
4. Fonseca, L., Nieth, L.: The role of universities in regional development strategies: a comparison across actors and policy stages. Euro. Urban Regional Stud. **28**(3), 298–315 (2021). https://doi.org/10.1177/0969776421999743
5. Kayumova, K.N., Tolipov, F.S., Siyaeva, G.A.: Higher Education in New Uzbekistan at Important Stages of Reform: Achievements, Challenges, and Solutions. КиберЛенинка (1970). Available at: https://cyberleninka.ru/article/n/higher-education-in-new-uzbekistan-at-important-stages-of-reform-achievements-challenges-and-solutions
6. PD-6079–10/05/2020. Available at: https://lex.uz/ru/docs/5031048
7. Pugh, R., Hamilton, E., Jack, S., Gibbons, A.: A step into the unknown: universities and the governance of regional economic development. Eur. Plan. Stud. **24**(7), 1357–1373 (2016). https://doi.org/10.1080/09654313.2016.1173201
8. Ulugbek: Statistics of the Number of Universities in Uzbekistan and How Many Students Study in Them. FLEDU.UZ (2023). Available at: https://fledu.uz/ru/statistika-chisla-vuzov-v-uzbekistane-i-skolko-studentov-v-nih-obuchayutsya/

Hybrid Design Thinking and Next-Gen Design Thinking Game: The Janus 2DT Ideathon Challenge

Victor Taratukhin[1](✉) and Natalia Pulyavina[2]

[1] University of Muenster, Muenster, Germany
`victor.taratukhin@ercis.uni-muenster.de`
[2] The Stanford Center at the Incheon Global Campus (SCIGC), Seoul, South Korea

Abstract. This article explores the key ideas behind the organization of the Janus 2DT Ideathon. The Janus 2DT Ideathon is an experimental event for integration of Digital Twin concept and Hybrid Design Thinking approach into a Next-Generation Design Thinking (NG DT) Framework. NG DT Framework expands traditional design thinking model, emphasizing the importance of additional elements such as sociocultural approach, hybridization, etc. Furthermore, the paper proposes a method for adapting the Next-Gen Design Thinking Game from a physical to a digital format. This recommendation further highlights the importance of employing a hybrid approach as the foundational strategy for future design thinking events.

Keywords: Innovation Methods · Design Thinking · Next-Gen Design Thinking · Next-Gen Design Thinking Framework Hybrid Design Thinking · Digital Twin · Ideathon Challenge

1 Introduction. Next-Gen Design Thinking Network

Next-Gen Design thinking is an extension of traditional design thinking approach and supports many challenges that innovators are already facing, and which will arise in the future as part of changing society in the time of instability. The important component of the new approach is the analysis of corporate memory and the expansion of the traditional process of design thinking using the method of cultural diagnostics, as well additional elements such as hybridization, gamification etc. Considering socio-cultural factors allows significantly expand the field of search for innovative solutions, considering the historical experience of the company and the organization. Such ideas initially developed by as part of Janus Initiative at Stanford discussions [1, 2] (and created the basis of new discipline—Business Archaeology [1, 3].

This approach, of course, provided certain features on the design thinking process itself, adapting design thinking to the needs of a particular organization and department.

The key philosophy of Next-Gen Design thinking is the use of an interdisciplinary approach, corporate experience of the past, business history and corporate narrative

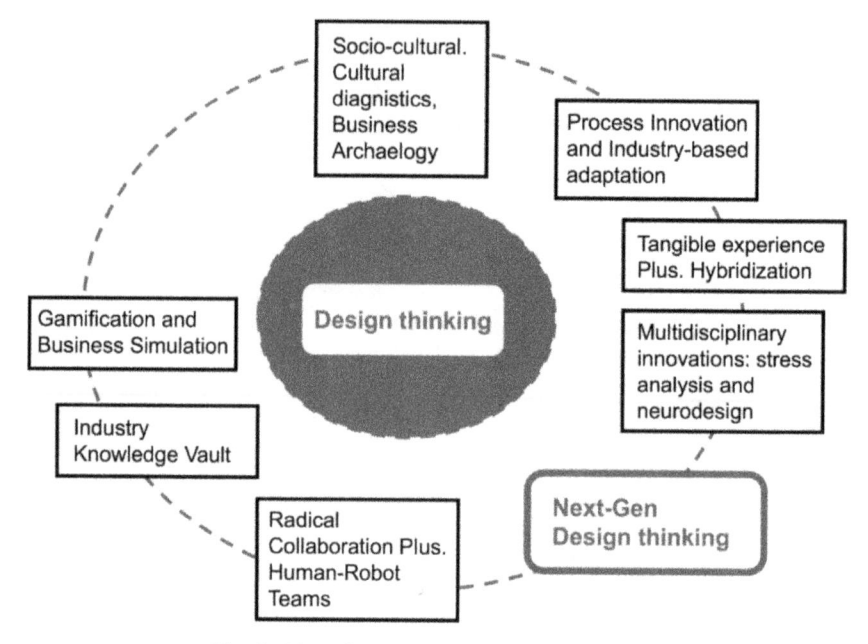

Fig. 1. Next-Gen Design Thinking Framework.

in dealing with corporate culture complexity. Next-Gen Design thinking framework is presented in Fig. 1.

This approach largely integrates the understanding of innovation as a process distributed over time and largely affecting not only the company in a specific period, but also being a constantly updated process. The developed method of design thinking (Next-Gen Design Thinking) is a significant expansion of the existing approach that regards the process of creating innovations primarily under the aspect of cultural values and the history of companies.

Analyzing the presented scheme, it is obvious that Next-Gen Design thinking (NG DT) constitutes an extension of traditional design thinking and at the same time answers many questions that innovators are already facing, and which will still arise in the future. The key elements of NG DT are described below.

Radical collaboration plus and Human-Robots teams. We are confident that future teams will be formed not only of people, but also of AI-based systems like ChatGPT, voice assistants like Alexa, etc. Thus, Next-Gen Design Thinking should have all the necessary tools to support hybrid teams of a new type. The first attempts to integrate ChatGPT into the work process of Industry-Academic teams were carried out in 2023 experiment conducted by author in real business environment and included question-answer communication, assistance in obtaining information on academic partnership and instructions generated by ChatGPT.

Additional research is required to study the basic principles of building a Human—Robot team, as well as building trust within such teams. Also, it is not only the availability of the necessary built-in AI assistants and information recording systems which will lead not only to the use of standard creative processes and approaches, but also allow adapting the standard approach to Design Thinking to new creative environment, automatically form a database of successful and unsuccessful projects, i.e. the space itself will remember both projects and their participants.

Industry knowledge Vault is an important metaphor describing the need to enrich design thinking with new, industrial artifacts and knowledge. And this concerns not only the introduction of people with industrial experience into the team, but also the creation of a set of industrial concepts, processes, and material objects for training creative teams. A good example of it is the introduction of new sets of cards into The Company Scenes that reflect a particular subject area.

Sociocultural. Cultural Diagnostics and Business Archaeology. The key philosophy of Next-Gen Design thinking is the use of an interdisciplinary approach, corporate experience of the past, business history and corporate narrative in dealing with corporate culture complexity. NG DT is a key approach to creating innovations specifically in corporate environments with strong corporate internal memory and cultural diversity. Business Archaeology as new discipline was introduced in detail in [1, 3]. Business archaeology is a new cross-disciplinary science that focuses on the past that may help in the present, on human experience and artifacts and examines itself through them. It aims to explore how individuals, communities, and organizations relate to history and memory, and to apply the results of this approach to business and management. Business archaeology offers a window into the future based on retrospective, tangible experience. In addition, business archaeology expands the human-centered approach of design thinking by putting a greater emphasis on historical roots of people's cultural values and their evolution, accentuating the memories and history that the business or community is based upon and describing how the past successes and failures of a corporation, community or organization can determine its ability to adapt to opportunities and challenges. In the center of the model, we see the process of cultural diagnostics (CD), which on the one hand is focused on finding new solutions for the future, on the other hand actively uses knowledge from the past through the analysis of people (through reconstruction of people, things, and events of the past). This includes analysis and reconstruction of business scenarios of the past through possible experimental approaches. The analysis of the past stages of business development allows one to start a journey to the present, considering the current state of the company and its future prototypes.

Process Innovation and Industry-based adaptation. There is a tendency to adapt the design thinking process to the needs of a particular company or Industry. In fact, Next-Gen Design thinking is a process of constant adaptation of the design thinking process, changing both the duration of the stages, the selection of various tools, and the number and type of prototype development. It can be accounted to changes in the company's business processes and adaptation to new conditions in an economic recession.

It seems that there will also be a process of enriching Design thinking with other creative technologies such as TRIZ, CRAFT (Creative algorithms, Frames and Tools), lateral thinking (there will be sources here), and so on. The enrichment of methods will take place not only at the level of mechanical fusion, but at the level of harmonization of various stages of the creative, innovation process.

Tangible experience Plus and Hybridization. Design thinking is characterized by a high level of tangible experience, but new conditions require the introduction of the concept of Tangible experience Plus and Hybridization. In the future, tangible experience will be possible with on-line Design thinking using the technical opportunities of AR and VR. On the other hand, the development of new approaches to the construction of physical prototypes, in particular the use of theater (there will be sources) and painting, will enrich the current mechanistic approach to prototyping. I would also like to highlight the methodology of rapid ideation, scenario construction and prototyping—Scenes Methods [4]. This method significantly speeds up the prototyping process and is the basis for expanding the industrial practices. There is also an attempt to reverse the transfer of digital doubles (in particular business processes) into the material world. The Tangible Business Processes Modeling (TBPM) experiment is an example of such a method [5].

This approach allows designers to significantly expand the horizons of their creativity. The implementation of these events showed the importance of further studying the main elements of Next-Gen Design thinking, the importance of forming a Design thinking mindset, evaluating the functioning of both specific participants in innovative seminars, and the principles of team formation.

Multidisciplinary innovations: Stress analysis and neurodesign. Better understanding of human abilities to adapt to new environments is not new. A lot of researchers tried to find the best way to improve human abilities and creativity. Interesting psychological experiment (Stanford Prison Experiment) was conducted at Stanford University in 1971, by the American social psychologist Philip Zimbardo. The experiment [6, 7] is a psychological study of a person's reaction to freedom violation, to the conditions of prison life and to the influence of an imposed social behavioral model. The role of stress factors as the most important mechanism for the formation of innovations is also noted, analyzed in presented in papers [8–10].

Recent research in the field of brain studies has led to the formation of a new research group—Stanford Neurodesign [11]—supervised by Larry Leifer. This center practices design activities and thinking from various perspectives, including neuroscience, embodied cognition, phenomenological, Gestalt, and other perspectives. The NeuroDesign Research Lab within the Center investigates embodied cognition and cognitive processes including human creativity, visual thinking, and tactile thinking in design activities. A particular research interest developed over the last thirty years relates to design team collaboration and related thinking patterns.

Gamification and Business Sumulation. In addition, management, project-oriented education, and game-based practices being embedded into the Next-Gen Design thinking process [12, 13] will enable engineering, IT, and management teams to develop design projects and entrepreneurial skills while working in real-life innovation challenges formulated by an industry partner. Next chapter is presented Next-Gen Design Thinking Game in detail.

2 Next-Gen Design Thinking Game

Next-Gen Design Thinking Game (NG DT Game) was initially designed by the authors as an effective tool of for introduction of Business Archaeology discipline and supporting creativity processes among Engineering, IT, and Management students.

Initially, the Game—both an online platform and physical set game—was tested on international teams of 3–5 students working for 3–9 months on design thinking challenges. The participants receive some artifacts from the past and must recreate the ideas and principles of doing business of the people who invented it, to understand Business Archaeology. The next step is to reconstruct current business trends of the company and try to create new ones based on studied artifacts. In addition to artifacts, the team used Design thinking tools to bring in an element of relevance to the current situation.

Some ideas on the ways of implementing a game-oriented approach to Design thinking methodology have already been discussed in [12, 13]. The idea of the game is to make the past, the present and the future meet. This is exactly what archaeologists do: they study the past so that people can draw the necessary conclusions and create a better future, considering the achievements and mistakes of their ancestors. One of the possible game scenarios presented below.

The players are divided into teams. Each of the teams formulates and propose a task (challenge) containing an innovation to work at. NG DT Game set includes three types of cards with different backs: Artifacts, Tools, and Trends (Fig. 2). The cards broaden the players' horizons, inspiring them to create new ideas. The Artifact cards provide information about business ideas from the past. The Trend cards contain some existing business trends. The Tool cards offer specific methods from the Design Thinking to traditional archaeological disciplines. With the help of which the players optimize the concept they have developed.

When working on a concept, participants can use the Internet and other sources to learn additional information about the aspects touched upon in the cards. Each team draws three cards (one of each type) and has 15–30 min for a discussion (Fig. 3). After that the teams take turns presenting their ideas and prototypes and testing them with the help of other teams. Team interaction is critically important for the game because each participant brining to the discussion their unique experience and professional vision of the challenge.

In addition to the basic set of artifacts, the game includes several additional subsets of cards reflecting the cultural features of the three countries—Korea, the North of Finland (Lapland) and Uzbekistan. These additional artifacts will participants to digging—in the culture of those countries.

As part of the experiment, participants with experience in the fields of industrial engineering, chemical engineering, sustainable finance, mobility, and human-computer interaction were divided into teams for preliminary evaluation of the game set.

The results of the initial evaluation of ArcheoSim Game provided important feedback to authors and as the result of this evaluation the Gameboard with Design thinking process was introduced for tangible/physical version of the game (Fig. 4) and the new version of the Game was renamed to Next-Gen Design Thinking Game.

Fig. 2. Next-Gen Design Thinking Game. Artifacts, Tools, and Trends.

Fig. 3. Next-Gen Design Thinking Game. Working with Cards.

Most of game participants also suggested the importance to create and to test different scenarios for on-line version of Next-Gen Design Thinking Game. On of the possible solutions is presented below.

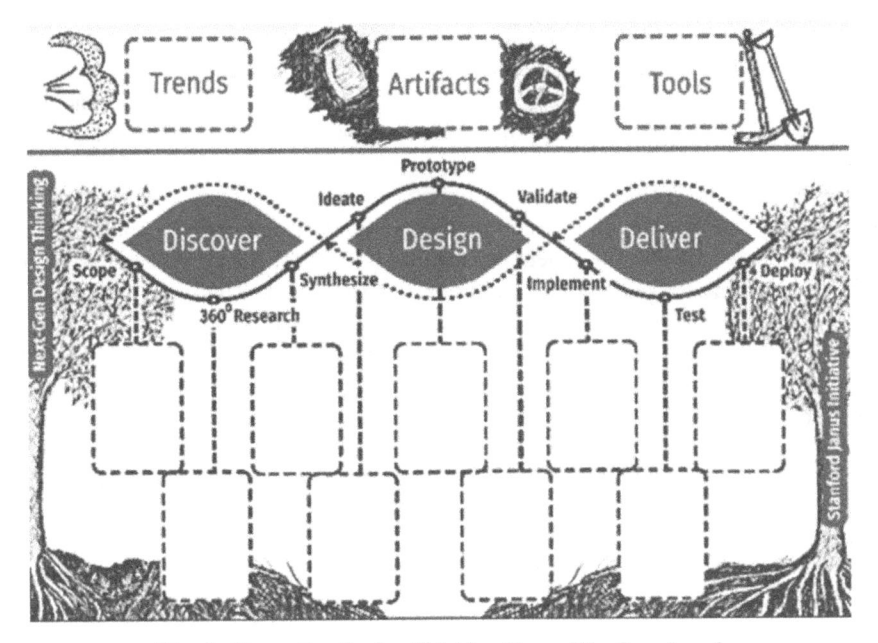

Fig. 4. Next - Gen Design Thinking Game. The Gameboard.

3 The Janus 2DT Ideathon

The Janus 2DT Ideathon (stands for Janus Project for Digital Twin—Design Thinking Ideathon) was proposed to conduct Design Thinking Project-oriented sessions researched in detail in [14, 15] in this case in hybrid format. The logo of the experiment reflects its significance as a role for a human, human-centered approach to creativity, and the creation and analysis of its digital twin as a concept (Fig. 5).

Fig. 5. Janus 2DT Ideathon Logo.

Digital twins are virtual copies of physical objects, processes, or systems that can be used to simulate interactions in the real world and test various scenarios without physical prototypes. The idea to use digital twin is not new one, digital twin approach was very well known in computer simulation, computer design, CAD/CAM [16], and manufacturing systems [17], etc.

Ideathon is a short continuous event, mainly for students and young professionals, at which the organizers, most often in collaboration with certain companies, address current and global issues for the subsequent generation of ideas for their solution. Participants work in small groups and offer, in addition to hypotheses, working prototypes of a possible solution and the results of brief testing of this prototype.

To test the prototype of the on-line platform, an experimental Ideathon Janus 2DT was conducted in April 2023 in which students and IT company employees, who acted as mentors and juries, took part.

Janus 2DT Ideathon uses Miro software solution [18], and the teams used Zoom for video communication and Google Forms for surveys (Fig. 6).

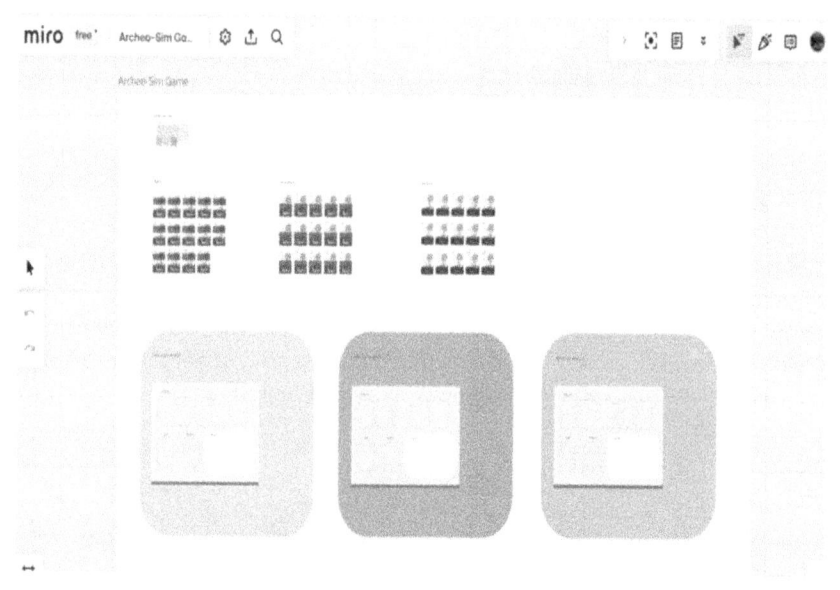

Fig. 6. On-line version of Next Gen Design Thinking Game (Janus 2DT experiment).

Firstly, all the participants gathered in Zoom and did an introductory survey, the results of which are analyzed in the next part. Then the participants briefly got acquainted with the methodology of design thinking and then to learn each others.

Then the task was generated with the help of physical ball with the UN Sustainable Development Goals on in [19] (Fig. 7). The sixth Sustainable Development Goal fell on the ball, i.e. clean water, and sanitation.

The task of the participants was set as follows: to help the BRICS countries get access to clean water if it is a problem in this area, participants were tasked with addressing the challenge of providing access to clean water in developing countries, where this remains a pressing issue.

Fig. 7. UN Sustainable Development Goals and UN SDGs Soccer Ball (UN SDGs; UN SDGs Soccer Ball).

The teams communicated using the Miro environment [18] and Zoom software (Fig. 8). Throughout the session, teams constructed Persona and Empathy maps to understand better the people affected by the lack of clean water in BRICS regions. These tools enabled our participants to empathize with and design solutions tailored to the needs and circumstances of those facing water and sanitation challenges in developing countries.

After all the stages were over, the teams used the Miro environment to select one idea and presented it as part of an on-line presentation. The final presentation is also shown in Fig. 8.

In addition, during Janus 2DT experiment additional tests were conducted by experts and researchers to access the stress indicators and stress level of participants, the stress index was calculated. In general, three responses of participants prevailed: sleep, communication, and physical activity. Also, the survey identified "triggers" that may increase the amount of energy or improve performance. In the survey, they had to note several triggers from a possible list: sleep, healthy eating, self-care and mindfulness practices, work and training, social interaction, and physical activity [20].

Such research defining the basis of initial ideas how to define the digital twins of participants Also, during experiment, to reduce the stress level, number of physical activity events were conducted at time break (Fig. 9).

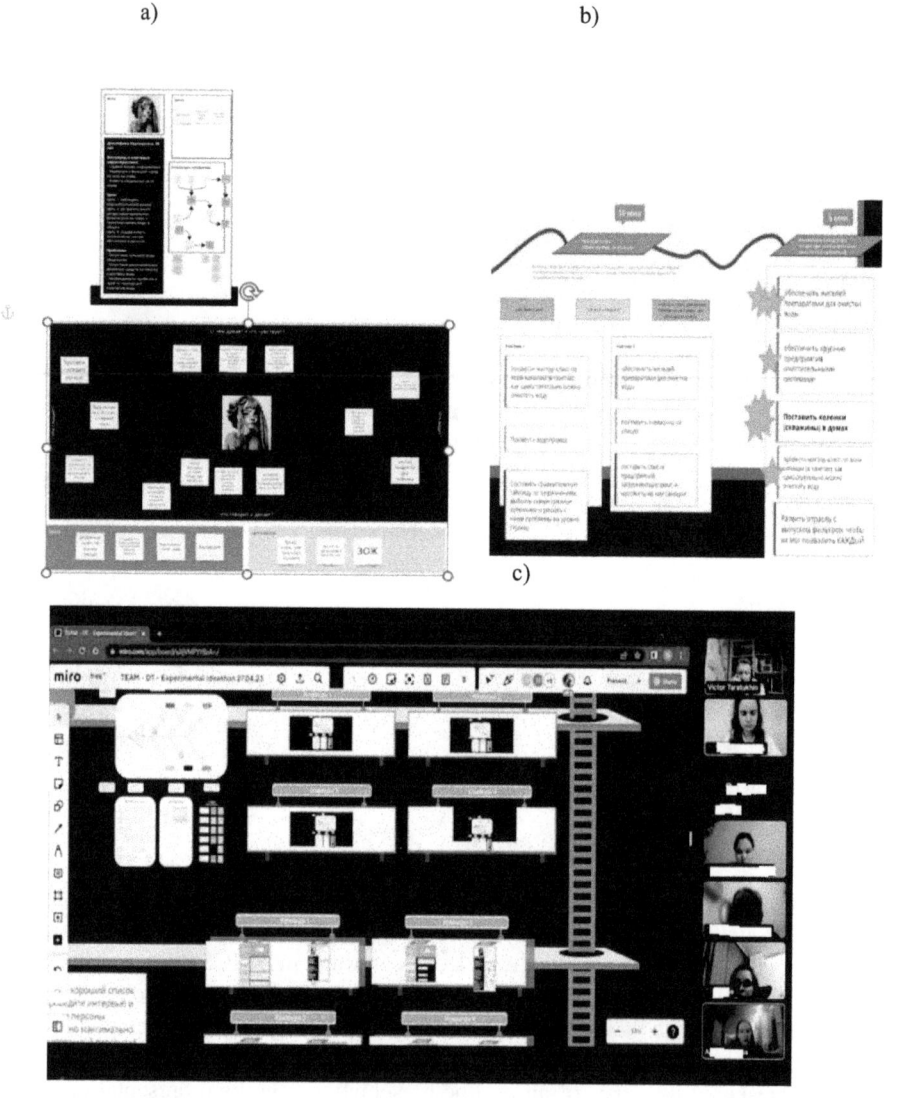

Fig. 8. a) Persona and Empathy map; b) Ideathon Process c} Janus 2DT on-line experiment Final Presentation.

The Janus 2DT Ideathon results summarized in two Master students' degree dissertations [20] and new hybrid Ideathon experiment planning is under way.

4 Conclusion

The Janus 2DT on-line experiment showed the effectiveness of using a hybrid approach to creating innovation, tested the possibility of using a game-oriented approach and business simulation.

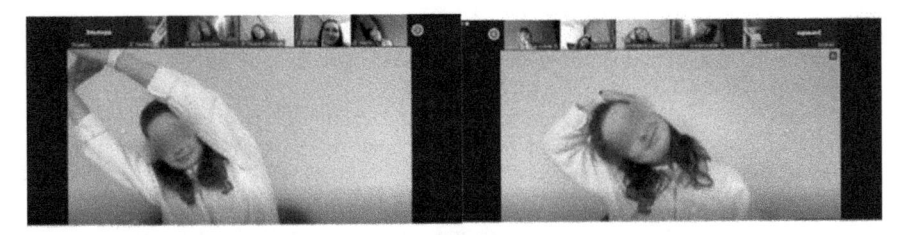

Fig. 9. Physical activity on-line event for Janus 2DT participants.

Hybrid Design Thinking is part of Next-Generation Design Thinking (NG DT) Framework introduced in this paper. NG DT Framework is a significant extension of traditional design thinking method, adding an important team's hybridization, process innovation, sociocultural approach, etc.

This research is also the basis of additional experiments to assess the stress level in teams work and the future of work environment [21].

References

1. Shanks, M., Taratukhin, V., Pulyavina, N., Our Manifesto: Next-Gen Design Thinking, Business Archaeology, and Future of Corporate Innovation: Available at SSRN: https://ssrn.com/abstract=4618019 or https://doi.org/10.2139/ssrn.4618019 (2023)
2. Shanks, M., Taratukhin, V., Pulyavina, N.: Janus Initiative Web Page, https://web.stanford.edu/group/archaeolog/cgi-bin/archaeolog/janus-initiative/, last accessed 2024/04/16
3. Taratukhin, V., Shanks, M., Pulyavina, N., Business Archaeology: Defining a New Foundational Discipline: Available at SSRN: https://ssrn.com/abstract=4617932 or https://doi.org/10.2139/ssrn.4617932 (2023)
4. SAP Scenes Web Page, https://experience.sap.com/designservices/approach/scenes, last accessed 2024/04/16
5. Edelman, J., Grosskopf, A., Weske, M., Leifer, L.: Tangible business process modeling: a new approach. In: Proceedings of International Conference on Engineering Design, Palo Alto, US (2009)
6. Zimbardo, P., Haney, C., Banks, W.C., Jaffe, D. The Stanford Prison Experiment: A Simulation Study of the Psychology of Imprisonment conducted, https://studylib.net/doc/18407847/the-stanford-prison-experiment, last accessed 2024/04/16
7. Bosch, X.: The lucifer effect: understanding how good people turn evil. Jama-Journal of The American Medical Association—JAMA-J AM MED ASSN. 298, 1338–1339 (2007). https://doi.org/10.1001/jama.298.11.1338-b
8. Anikushina, V., Fedyay, S., Kuznetsova, P., Vinokhodova, A., Shved, D., Taratukhin, V., Stutterheim, C., Savinkina, A., Becker, J., Gushin, V.: Effects of fatigue and long-term isolation on human behavior. Transp. Res. Proc. **66**, 57–69, ISSN 2352–1465 (2022)
9. Anikushina, V., Taratukhin, V., Stutterheim, C.: Natural language oral communication in humans under stress. Linguistic cognitive coping strategies for enrichment of artificial intelligence. Proc. Comput. Sci., **123**, 24–28 (2018)
10. Anikushina, V., Taratukhin, V., Vinokhodova, A., Gushin, V., Stutterheim, C.: Creativity and Cognitive Performance of Space Crews: An isolation mixed-gender study, Conference poster presentation. The UN World Space Forum, Vienna, Austria (2019)
11. Stanford NeuroDesign Group, https://neurodesign.stanford.edu/, last accessed 2024/04/16

12. Taratukhin, V., Pulyavina, N., Becker, J.: Next-gen design thinking for management education. project-based and game-oriented methods are critical ingredients of success. In: Proceedings of the 47th Annual ABSEL Conference (2020)
13. Pulyavina, N., Taratukhin, V., Kim, S., Kim, S.: Accumulated practical experience of the past for building the future of design innovations: janus project and next-gen design thinking game. In: Taratukhin, V., Levchenko A., Kupriyanov, Y., (eds.) Communications in Computer and Information Science, vol 1767. Springer, Heidelberg (2023)
14. Taratukhin, V., Baryshnikova, A., Kupriyanov, Y., Becker, J.:Digital business framework: shaping engineering education for next-gen in the era of digital economy. Proceedings of the ASEE Annual Conference & Exposition, Louisiana (2016)
15. Taratukhin, V., Pulyavina, N.: The future of project-based learning for engineering and management students: Towards an advanced design thinking approach. In: Proceedings of the 125th ASEE Annual Conference and Exposition, Salt Palace Convention Center, Salt Lake City (2018)
16. Taratoukhine, V., Bechkoum, K.: Towards a Consistent Distributed Design: A Multi-Agent Approach. In Proceedings of the IEEE International Conference on Information Visualization, London, UK, 384–389. (1999)
17. Taratukhin, V., Yadgarova, Y.: Towards a socio-inspired multiagent approach for new generation of product life cycle management. Procedia Computer Science **123**(123), 479–487 (2018)
18. Miro Website https://miro.com/, last accessed 2024/04/16
19. UN Sustainable Development Goals. https://sdgs.un.org/goals, last accessed 2024/04/16
20. UN SDGs Soccer Ball. https://shop.undp.org/products/sdg-soccer-ball, last accessed 2024/04/16
21. Kozlova, E.: The Role of Breakthrough Information Technologies in Developing Main Approaches to Stress Management in Future Business Environments. (Scientific Advisor: Victor Taratukhin), MSc thesis (2023)

Towards Data-Driven Stress Management in Organizations: Innovative Approaches and Application Development

Kristina Dudkovskaia[✉], Victor Taratukhin[✉], and Jörg Becker[✉]

University of Münster, Münster, Germany
kdudkovs@uni-muenster.de,
{victor.taratukhin,joerg.becker}@ercis.uni-muenster.de

Abstract. The main asset and a central engine of any organization are its employees, its team. Business success depends to a large extent on their well-being and effective collaborative work. But very often such a factor as high stress at work leads to burnout of valuable employees, worsens the performance and quality of work results, badly affects the health of employees and even colleagues. However, not all managers especially in companies with a distributed territorial structure have objective information about subordinates - deterioration in working atmosphere, severe work-load imbalance among teams and team members, sharp negative changes in relationships with colleagues, customers and supervisors, etc. The study proofs that stress-related issues can be detected using passive corporate data. In order to do so, first of all, an extensive list of stress factors, possible stress predictors and compensation mechanisms from literature is compiled. Then, based on findings a framework is proposed to categorize parameters that can be calculated using data from corporate systems. The framework is illustrated and tested via an application prototype using selected parameters from theoretical framework, open-source datasets such as DReddit and Enron, advanced NLP techniques such as Recurrent neural network, Bidirectional Encoder Representations from Transformers model, and Linguistic Inquiry and Word Count. Upon detecting elevated stress levels, the developed application prototype generates a personalized list of identified stress factors and stress compensators. By leveraging existing corporate systems and requiring minimal user input, the proposed approach offers a non-intrusive and efficient tool for identifying and tracing workplace stress and promoting employee well-being.

Keywords: Work-related stress · Stress management · Employee data analytics

1 Motivation

1.1 Stress-Related Unhealthy Tendencies

Stress and burnout have become increasingly problematic issues in modern society in general and also among employees across various organizational scales, industries, and nations. The constant high mental demands or repetitive routine work, permanent technological progress or stagnation, a giant corporate or a small startup, office onsite work, or remote workplace - often contradictory factors contribute to the same results - growing problem of stress and burnout among employees in different industries and countries. Employee burnouts are challenging to predict as often employees report that they feel perfectly well. The COVID pandemic has further shown the importance of engaging with employees based on digital data with the rise of remote work settings.

So, a data-driven approach is needed to identify stress-related issues and enable stress management in organizations. For organizations, it is essential to have qualitative data to understand their employees better and, in general, move beyond anonymized surveys to eliminate biases in management. The issue of uncontrollable work-related stress and unpredictable burnout has tangible consequences for individual well-being, individual and organizational efficiency, and, as a result, for the organization's success. The multifaceted nature of stress and the studies conducted in this field indicate that the eventual method will rely on multiple modalities.

This paper aims to propose a novel approach for the detection and mitigation of elevated stress levels among employees using corporate data sources, with the ultimate goal of fostering a better and more productive work environment.

The Federal Institute for Occupational Safety and Health (BAuA) in Germany conducted a study in 2018 on stress levels among the working population. The study revealed that 61% encountered work-related stress, 11.3% classifying their stress levels as severe. Stress and burnout are linked to many health issues, ranging from minor disorders to severe chronic illnesses. A study conducted by Cohen et al. (2015) found a correlation between work-related stress and cardiovascular illness, gastrointestinal issues, as well as mental health disorders such as melancholy and anxiety (Cohen et al., 2015). Numerous studies explicitly affirm that workplace stress has a detrimental effect on productivity and the attainment of company objectives. Multiple reasons can be discerned, encompassing but not limited to promoted absenteeism and turnover, diminished employee engagement, reduced job satisfaction, impaired decision-making capacity, and heightened risk of accidents and injuries. Thus, it is imperative to develop **a multifaceted approach that utilizes various modalities to detect and mitigate elevated stress levels among employees**, ultimately fostering a healthier work environment.

1.2 Difficulties in Implementing and Supporting Existing Solutions

Setting up and maintaining stress management systems in organizations can take much work. In recent years, there has been a rise in the use of novel strategies for stress management, to monitor the well-being of employees and deliver interventions: wearable devices and mobile applications, which can monitor the stress levels of employees and provide customized tactics for stress reduction, mindfulness exercises or relaxation techniques.

In-person programs can be perceived as time-consuming, while IT technologies typically necessitate customization, employee training, and encouragement to ensure successful acceptance and sustained usage. Furthermore, organizations need help in terms of their willingness to adopt and integrate new technologies and tools. Besides, new tools may cause additional technostress.

Hence, it is imperative to adopt inconspicuous methodologies for monitoring employee conduct and gathering analytical data from preexisting organizational systems (Biggs, A., Brough, 2022). Thus, novel approaches and frameworks should be **easy of implementation, easy to support and adaptable for remote work settings**.

1.3 People and Work-Settings Are Different

In addition, it should be noted that centralized stress management plans may lack the necessary adaptability to address the specific needs of individual employees effectively. Numerous strategies have been devised to alleviate stress among employees. Organizations have widely embraced conventional stress management strategies, including counseling, stress reduction courses, and employee assistance programs (EAPs).

Nevertheless, it is essential to acknowledge that these approaches may not adequately tackle the wide range of stressors encountered by employees across various nations. This is primarily due to their tendency to prioritize broad interventions rather than tailored, personalized solutions. Conventional methodologies for stress management typically encompass centralized techniques that employ top-down strategies, including employee assistance programs, workload modifications, and stress management training. Although the strategies above might yield advantages, their implementation and sustainability can pose challenges inside scaling organizations, given the diverse range of employee demands and pressures (Cooper, 2018).

One more problem with centralized stress management is that it can be hard to tell which employees are under much stress. Conventional techniques, such as surveys and self-report instruments, are not accurate to response biases and may not comprehensively assess an individual's stress levels (Heinen et al., 2017). Furthermore, it may not be practical to depend on employees for the assessment of their stress levels in specific organizational contexts, as employees may exhibit reluctance to disclose their difficulties due to concerns regarding social stigma or potential adverse impacts on their professional advancement. So, people tend to not to talk about their problems at work.

Thus, novel approaches and frameworks should possess qualities such as **user-friendliness, personalized approaches, accuracy, non-biased assessments**. These qualities will contribute to the successful management of stress and the promotion of employee well-being.

2 Factors and Predictors to Measure Work-Related Stress

In order to follow the initial approach to analyse various work-related stress factors and predictors, it is imperative to conduct a comprehensive literature review of stressors of different types within the organizational context. Where appropriate, for each stressor, objective indicators should be identified by which the presence of the stressor can be determined. The primary objective of the literature review is to compile an extensive list of stress factors, possible stress predictors and compensation mechanisms from literature. In addition, where possible, a compensatory mechanism or approach should be selected to help reduce the stressor.

Work-related stress is a distinct form of stress that arises within the framework of an individual's occupation and work setting (Podsakoff et al., 2007; Leiter and Maslach, 2017). Employees are exposed to a range of complex elements such as workplace design, work culture and management practices. Another critical difference between regular stress and work-related stress is how much the stressors are affected by the workplace and the person's role in the company (Golden et al., 2008; Dhawan, 2022). Other variables can contribute to its occurrence, including inflated job expectations, reduced supervision, inadequate organizational support, and interpersonal relations (Cooper and Marshall, 1976; Robert A. Karasek, 1979). In turns, interpersonal relations are a complex factor even in daily life and in the context of a collaborative work environment, which may also include remote work settings, the dynamics of interpersonal relationships can be intricate and multifaceted. These dynamics encompass various aspects, such as conflicts that may arise between colleagues or supervisors, disparities in expectations, and struggles for power (Golden et al., 2008). These dynamics have the potential to intensify stress levels and makes its management much more difficult in comparison to general stress, which typically revolves around personal matters or relationships unrelated to the workplace.

Thus, let us delve into the intricacies of different models, approaches and researches to find out work-related stress factors. For example, the job demand-control-support model has been widely studied and has identified job demand and job control as significant workplace risk factors. The model is being looked at in great detail because it shows the complicated relationship between the demands of work and the freedom individuals are given to do their jobs. Haque and Oino's 2019 study highlights the challenges of stress reduction and human capital management in work environments. They examined stressors like excessive control, pressure, long working hours, and distractions that can lead to adverse effects like depression, reduced concentration, health problems, and frustration. B. Bakker et el. (2004) in their Job Demands-Resources (JD-R) highlighted such stress factors as work pressure, role overload, and situations when job's emotional and physical demands are higher than person's resources in general or in a specific period of time. According to the research, role overload can imply both a role mismatch with the individual and cases when the individual is given tasks outside of their primary role and beyond their official job description (Bakker et al., 2004).

Another view on work-related stress is Challenge-Hindrance Stress Framework (CHS) proposed by Podsakoff, & LePine (2005) (LePine et al., 2005). This approach implies that there are two main types of stressors: hindrance stressors that do not potentially promote growth, learning, and development, challenge stressors that potentially promote growth, learning, and development. When employees cope with hindrance stressors more often they experience strain, lower job satisfaction (challenges for nothing), demonstrate lower productivity, lower engagement. Among other famous frameworks about work-related stress are Effort-reward imbalance (Peter et al., 1998), Person-Environment Fit (Sell, M.V., French, J.R., Caplan, R.D., & Harrison, 1984), job demand-control model (Robert A. Karasek, 1979), Oldenburg burnout inventory - (Demerouti, 1999) and (Maslach et al., 1981). These papers are summarized in a Table 1. These different researches are analyzed and decomposed in the same way: stressors, predictors and compensators mentioned by the authors.

Through an in-depth exploration of the essential elements comprising the work environment, scholars try to model complex mechanisms that have a significant impact on occupational stress, individual well-being, and the overall level of job satisfaction (Fishta and Maria, 2020). But several others have been studied, such as job insecurity, procedural (in)justice, workplace conflict or bullying (Harvey et al., 2017), and workplace violence (Magnavita et al., 2019). It is hard to figure out what environmental factors cause daily stressors that are different from chronic stress. That proofs the need to use passive organizational data to obtain every day stressors. In other words, it is imperative to bridge this knowledge gap in order to formulate precise solutions that effectively trace the obstacles encountered by individuals in their day-to-day professional endeavours. A recent study by Charzyńska et al. (2023) on work-related stress among healthcare professionals in Iran during the COVID-19 pandemic reveals a complex terrain with five discrete profiles. Variables like age, marital status, service area, workplace, and overtime strongly predict profile membership. That mean that these factors are also important for analysis. In Germany, according to a study conducted by the European Agency for Safety and Health at Work (EU-OSHA, 2007), it was observed that there are variations in work-related stress variables among different countries. According to (Huang et al., 2002), the United States experiences significant levels of stress due to extended working hours, demanding job requirements, and low job stability (Huang et al., 2002). Conversely research has demonstrated that employees, in Europe often experience heightened stress levels due to a lack of control over their work environment and an insufficient balance, between work and personal life (Cox et al., 2005). Nixon et al. (2011) conducted a study that revealed that employees experience considerable levels of stress due to factors such as high job demands, inadequate job control, role ambiguity, and role conflict (Nixona et al., 2011). Furthermore, a study conducted by LePine et al. (2005) highlights the significant influence of work-family conflict on the levels of stress experienced by employees. Specifically, people who face challenges in effectively managing the demands of their work and personal lives tend to experience heightened levels of stress.

The workplace has been recognized as tremendous stress factor itself due to the presence of technological improvements (LePine et al., 2005). In addition, Tarafdar et al. (2011) emphasized the significance of technostress. This phenomenon arises from the ongoing requirement to adjust to emerging technologies and the perceived obligation to stay abreast of technological advancements (Tarafdar et al., 2011). Day et al. (2012) conducted a study wherein they observed that the state of being constantly connected and the anticipation of being accessible beyond regular working hours can result in heightened levels of stress among workers (Day et al., 2012).

The start of the COVID-19 epidemic has aggravated the circumstances since a substantial percentage of the labor force has shifted to telecommuting. The current trend towards telecommuting has presented novel difficulties and sources of tension for individuals engaged in remote work. It is imperative to comprehend these variables and ascertain efficacious approaches to mitigate stress among individuals working remotely, as this is crucial for upholding the well-being and productivity of employees. Based on Eurofound's findings, it was seen that in the year 2020, a significant proportion of workers in the European Union, roughly 37%, transitioned to remote work as a consequence of the pandemic (Daphne Ahrendt, Jorge Cabrita, Eleonora Clerici, John Hurley, Tadas Leončikas, Massimiliano Mascherini, 2020). In parallel, the United States experienced a higher percentage of individuals engaged in remote work, reaching 42%. The rise of remote work has presented companies with new difficulties in monitoring and managing employee well-being, as conventional methods of supervision and support are no longer suitable. Recent studies have elucidated various aspects that contribute to the experience of stress among those engaged in remote work. According to a study conducted by Park et al. (2020), the absence of work-life balance, feelings of social isolation, and challenges in communication emerge as notable stressors for individuals engaged in remote work (Park et al., 2018). In a study conducted by Xiao et al. (2020), it was found that individuals engaged in remote work encounter stress as a result of the indistinct demarcation between their professional and personal lives. This lack of separation can result in excessive work demands and challenges in disengaging from work-related activities. Technological issues have been recognized as significant sources of stress for individuals engaged in remote work (Xiao et al., 2020). Suh and Lee's (2020) study found that remote workers who experienced technical difficulties and insufficient technological assistance were more likely to experience "Zoom fatigue" which refers to the fatigue and strain that come from spending much time participating in video conferences (Suh and Lee, 2017; Fauville et al., 2021). According to a study conducted by Nieuwenhuijsen et al. (2010), it is suggested that the most effective approach to preventing stress-related disorders (SRDs) involves treating a combination of many psychosocial risk factors. Even though the study only used a few questions, it clearly shows that high job expectations, less job control, not getting enough help from coworkers and supervisors, and less procedural and relational fairness are all linked to a higher risk of stress-related disorders (SRDs). The consequences of these findings have substantial relevance for assessing the extent to which individual cases of SRD are related to work. In addition, this study shows the possible benefits of looking at the psychosocial work environment as a way to reduce the number of SRDs that happen (Nieuwenhuijsen et al., 2010).

In order to understand and effectively deal with stress at work in this chapter different factors and predictors that can be used to track, identify and measure work-related stress were observed with a help of literature. In the Table 1 the list of stressors is partly described, encompassing job stressors, predictors and possible compensation and coping mechanisms that can be applied in the organizational context.

Table 1. Examples of stressors from literature (short list for illustration)

Author	Model	Stressor	Early sign/Predictor	Compensator
Bakker et al., 2004	The job demands-resources (JD-R)	Work pressure, role overload, Job's emotional and physical demands are higher than person's resources	Disengagement, Changes in performance (lower or higher), Reducing employees' self-confidence in solving work-related problems, Turnover, Absenteeism	Autonomy and participation in decision-making, Manager and colleagues' support, Clear career opportunities, Good team's climate, Role clarity, Feedback loop
LePine et al., 2005	Challenge-Hindrance Stress Framework	All kinds of hindrance stressors that do not potentially promote growth, learning, and development	Lower job satisfaction (challenges for nothing), Lower productivity, Lower engagement, Strain	Challenge stressors that potentially promote growth, learning, and development
Ragu-Nathan et al., 2011, Day et al., 2012	-	Technostress (technology adoption)	State of being constantly connected and the anticipation of being accessible beyond regular working hours, Increased time on repetitive processes	Additional trainings and consultations
Maslach et al., 1981	Maslach Burnout Inventory (MBI and MBI-GS), Questioner	Strain, individual's expectations are not met, achievement in the past didn't satisfy an employee, seem not significant	Exhaustion, cynicism (lack of interest in the job and job meaningfulness), depersonalization (becoming impersonal, callous, hardening), reduced personal accomplishment	Relaxed atmosphere, work on worthwhile things
T. Theorell, 2012	Likert scaled Effort-reward imbalance	High job demands, no clear reward motivation or low reward (subjectively or objectively)	Negative feeling about work, impatience and irritability, inability to limit work obligations	Clear motivation system, Workload monitoring
Park et al., 2018, Xiao et al., 2020	-	Remote work setting, demarcation between their professional and personal lives, challenges in communication	Disengagement, Procrastination, Fewer social interactions	-

3 Stress-Related Data Categorization and Processing

Based on the findings described in the Sect. 2, a framework is proposed to categorize parameters that can be obtained or calculated using data from corporate systems. Possible corporate data sources are included in the framework. The columns are:

– Category: categorization of the employee-associated features such as User profile, Personal, Social, Engagement, Behavioral, Productivity:
– Parameter: name of the parameter to obtain or calculate
– Calculation methods: possible methods to obtain the parameters

- Reference to a predictor stress predictors list: reference to the factor or predictor from the list from Sect. 2
- Data source: possible corporate systems and informational infrastructure part that can serve as a data source to obtain or calculate the parameter.

The short list of the parameters is provided in Table 2.

Table 2. Examples of parameters (short list for illustration)

Category	Parameter	Calculation Methods	Reference to a predictor stress predictors list	Data source
User profile	Age, Position, Education, Location, Department, Work Schedule (prefers to work early or late)	Fact	-	Employee card in the HR system
Personal	Openness/Readiness to engage, Agreeableness, Emotional Stability	LIWC	Opposite to disengagement, Neuroticism	Microsoft Teams, Microsoft Exchange, Slack
Personal	Problem-Solving Style	BERT-based classification mode	Reducing employees' self-confidence in solving work-related problems	Microsoft Teams, Microsoft Exchange, Slack
Social	Emotional symbols used (positive/negative/often/rarefor a person)	Sentiment analysis using VADER (Valence Aware Dictionary and sentiment Reasoner)	Engagement	Microsoft Teams, Microsoft Exchange, Slack
Social	Using forcing words in dialogue's internal/external ('you must', 'I don't care you must' vs 'please')	LIWC, IBM Watson Tone Analyzer	Often feel sickened by work tasks	Microsoft Teams, Microsoft Exchange, Slack
Behavioral	Response time	Time analysis of communication timestamps, Time for completion of tasks, accepted code commits	Procrastination, Lower productivity, Cynicism (lack of interest in the job and job meaningfulness)	Jira, Github, Microsoft Teams, Microsoft Exchange, Slack, Zoom, Google Meet, Trello
Behavioral	Procrastination Tendency	Time for completion of tasks, accepted code commits	Procrastination, Lower productivity	Jira, Github, Microsoft Teams, Microsoft Exchange, Slack, Trello

4 Organizational Data Processing

In this section a framework approach for organizational data processing is presented (Fig. 1). In essence, the presented framework is a concept of a system core that represents the main data flows of the analytical system when processing the organizational data. **It is important to note that the listed parameters from Employee data categorization calculated only once cannot provide information about the stress level of a person.** First, based on historical data, it is needed to calculate the usual metrics for each user. Ensure the identified patterns are consistent over a significant period (e.g., several weeks to months) to confirm that they are usual for a specific user. **Then, calculating parameters and identifying considerable deviations provides data for identifying the fact of stress and the possible stressors.**

1. First of all, a list of source systems needs to be defined. The examples of possible data sources are
   - Communication platforms: Microsoft Teams, Microsoft Exchange (mail, calendar), Zoom, Slack
   - Task managers and digital archives: Jira, GitHub, Confluence, Trello,

- Other corporate systems: Human Resource management systems, Helpdesk systems, Customer Relationship Management tools, Active Directory, etc.
2. Data frames are then generated each embodying the data pertinent to individual employees as extracted from each respective system.
3. Then the data is processed using simple algorithms and sophisticated models. The resulting features are calculated (Table 3).
4. Based on historical data average values for each employee is calculated establishing a benchmark for typical state for a specific person against which metrics can be measured.
5. The data processing is a repetitive process. When the sharp deviations are detected in comparison to the average values based on historical data the system should notify managers.
6. If stress is identified, a correlation matrix is prepared for an individual employee, where the last row is stress, the rows are the parameters, and the values in the cells are the correlation coefficient of stress from the specified parameters. Thus, positive correlation reveals stressors, and negative correlation reveals factors-compensators of stress.

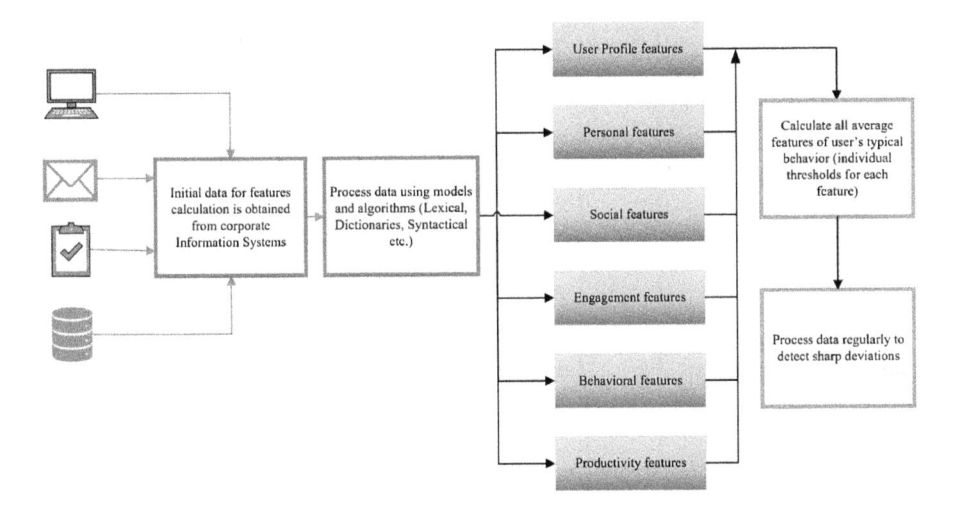

Fig. 1. Work-related stress identification process-oriented framework

5 Stress-Related Data Analysis Strategy

5.1 Tool Selection for Data Analysis

In order to select a suitable tool for analyzing employees' passive data from corporate systems, a brief analysis of popular methods used for similar tasks

Table 3. Algorithms examples for employee parameters categorization)

Parameter	Algorithm example	Data source example
Work Schedule (full-time, part-time, prefers to work early or late), Working hours	1. Normalizing all timestamps to a standard time zone to ensure consistency. Filter out non-working days and public holidays based on the regional calendar to focus on typical workdays. 2. Calculating the total active hours for each user by summing the time spent on activities each day 3. Determining the regularity and frequency of early starts and late finishes to infer preferred working hours 4. Ensuring the identified patterns are consistent over a significant period (e.g., several weeks to months) to confirm the work schedule categorization 5. Presenting the inferred Work Schedule for each user, indicating whether they are full-time or part-time and if they have a preference for starting early or working late	Microsoft Exchange, Microsoft Teams, Slack
Procrastination Tendency	1. Gathering information on task assignments, deadlines, and completion dates from Jira. This data should include the time when a task was assigned, when work began, and when it was finally marked as complete. 2. Extracting changes in deadline extensions 3. Calculating the time interval between when a task is assigned and when the first active work on the task is logged in Jira. A significant delay might indicate a tendency to procrastinate. 4. Comparing the planned completion dates with the actual completion dates of tasks. 5. Counting the flagged cases	Jira, Teams, Git, Trello, Slack, Microsoft Exchange, Microsoft Teams
Attention to Detail	1. Gathering relevant data from Jira and Git. This includes data on code reviews, commit histories, and task scheduling. 2. For Git: looking for commits that have not been merged into the main branch due to issues initiated by the user 3. For Jira: identifying tasks that have been moved back in the workflow to earlier stages for additional work by the user	Jira, Teams, Git, Trello, Slack

was performed. Although it has its peculiarities, work stress is a particular case of ordinary stress. "People reveal themselves by the words they use." Since the early 90th, researchers have analyzed paper-based diary texts to study family processes, happiness, well-being, and social and personal aspects of everyday life. And surprisingly, the methods used in this research are helpful for analyzing employees' digital footprints. Since the early 2000s, researchers have been trying to mine insight from what people write using statistical methods and improved modern tools like Natural Language Processing (NLP) and Machine Learning (ML) techniques to analyze textual data. One of the popular aims was identifying stress, depression, anxiety markers, suicidal markers, and also determining stress levels (Al-smadi, 2019). There is a multitude of petabytes of data generated manually by users on social media, which is why social media posts are the primary source of initial data for such research (Lin and Albert, 2014). They are a kind of descendant of diaries.

In addition, the immediate relevance of such a science as psycholinguistics and its value for this study cannot be overlooked. An experimental study conducted by Anikushina, Taratukhin and Stutterheim showed that stress negatively affects speech activity, creativity and problem-solving skills. Among the psycholinguistic parameters that deteriorate, the authors identified responsiveness, task relatedness, and speech coherence (Anikushina et al., 2018).

Several research studies have been dedicated to identifying characteristics that can act as indicators of stress in written content (Mello et al., 2011). The features can be categorized into three types: lexical, syntactic, and semantic features. Several algorithms can be employed to process further obtained linguistic features, such as Support Vector Machines (SVM), Naïve Bayes, and Decision Trees (Al-smadi, 2019), with levels of accuracy ranging from 65% to 85% (Lin and Albert, 2014). However, several challenges need to be addressed to train models and obtain a sufficient level of accuracy. The first challenge is the need for open-source, significant, labeled datasets to train and test the algorithms.

Additionally, the linguistic features used to identify stress markers may vary across different types of textual data, requiring the development of context-specific models. For example, on women's forums, people write much more emotionally and openly. In contrast, in work chats, it is tough to notice barely visible deviations through conversations about business.

Many researchers have worked on the task of stress detection using NLP and machine learning in social interactions. A study published in the "Journal of Big Data" explored stress detection using natural language processing (NLP) and machine learning (ML) over social media interactions. The research leveraged large-scale datasets with tweets for sentiment analysis, utilizing machine learning algorithms and the BERT model for sentiment classification. They also employed Latent Dirichlet Allocation for topic identification related to textual data, which helped in detecting emotions online that could be linked to stress or depression. This study's use of BERT for sentiment classification and emotion detection aligns closely with this work (Nijhawan et al., 2022).

What is more, machine learning (ML) is widely used in the health sector for stress and depression analysis. (Arya and Kumar, 2021), the review highlighted the application of machine learning in health, particularly in mental stress detection using various data sources such as social networking sites and clinical datasets. They underscored the potential of ML algorithms in mental health, citing the use of SVM and Naïve Bayesian algorithms for predicting stress from user-generated content on social media. Their findings demonstrate the versatility and effectiveness of machine learning in analyzing mental health-related data.

(Cho et al., 2020) analyzed ML algorithms for diagnosing mental illness, considering various techniques and their limitations. They achieved a significant accuracy rate with SVM classifiers. Additionally, Deshpande and Rao introduced an emotion AI technique to detect depression, employing SVM and Naïve Bayes algorithms with Twitter data. These studies highlight the effectiveness of machine learning in analyzing mental health, especially in the context of social media content.

In a recent paper (Garg, 2023), the author analysed the F1 metrics of 29 researchers where various algorithms and methods were used for mental health analysis of social media posts, including Stress, Depression, and Suicide risk assessment. RNN, BERT, and Multi-task demonstrated the highest F1 metric - 80.34%.

This research incorporates advanced NLP techniques like BERT and RNN for stress analysis in organizational contexts. The selected tools are well-aligned with the current research trends in using machine learning for mental health analysis. The emphasis on leveraging diverse data sources, including text from emails and social media, and the application of sophisticated algorithms is consistent with the approaches discussed in the above studies. This demonstrates the relevance and potential impact of the research in contributing to the development of nuanced and compelling stress detection and management strategies. The cross-dataset application is a highlight of this approach to testing, showcasing an innovative approach to machine learning. The choice to use both BERT and RNN models allows for a comparative analysis of different approaches to NLP tasks, though this aspect could be further explored. The prototyping approach including stress-related data analysis strategy is presented below (Fig. 2).

5.2 Data Sets Selection

Testing the approach requires open datasets containing information about the work interactions of a group of people over as long a period as possible. The group of people should be relatively stable, meaning the data set should include interactions between the same people. The open data sources for analyzing employee interactions about work-related topics may not be easily accessible due to privacy and data protection concerns. Enron data set fit for the stress level assessment, including analysis of interaction between different employees. For the testing purposes several data sets were considered (Table 4):

Table 4. Datasets with corporate correspondence

Name	Number of emails
Enron	619,446 between 158 users
Atari mail archive	4,128 from Jed Margolin
Hillary Clinton Email Archive (wikileaks)	30,000 sent to and from Hillary Clinton's private email server

Dreddit Dataset

The creators of the labelled dataset (Turcan and McKeown, 2019) discuss the importance of stress identification due to its association with numerous negative health outcomes and its prevalence in online communications. They highlight the dataset's potential applications, which include diagnosing physical and mental illnesses, gauging public mood in politics and economics, and tracking the effects of disasters. For labelling they used Amazon Mechanical Turk. They were asked to assign category from 3 options: "Stress", "Not Stress", or "Uncertain". A post is designated as indicative of stress solely when a minimum of five annotators have consistently marked it as such. From 187,444 posts only around 1,900 were marked as stressed. The DReddit dataset is particularly valuable because it contains longer posts from Reddit, which provide more context and complexity compared to other platforms like Twitter. This allows for the exploration of more nuanced expressions of stress and a deeper understanding of its indicators. The authors' contributions to the field are threefold:

- Providing the DReddit dataset, which includes both stressful and non-stressful text.
- Establishing supervised models for predicting stress.
- Offering an analysis of the dataset that provides insight into the stress detection problem.

5.3 Prototyping and Testing Process Specification

Phase 1. Training labeled data. Reddit Self-reported Depression Diagnosis (RSDD)

1. Data sets with stress-related mark-up selection. Data sets should include a history of employee correspondence with the sender and addressee name, date, and text of the message. Data sets can also be labelled social media posts. Posts or correspondence should be labelled with a specific stress level. These data sets should be used for training and testing of models.
2. Preliminary analysis of labelled data. Analyse corresponding scientific papers, columns, data structure, data volume, number of users, and data set shortcomings. Pre-process data with Python for further analysis.
   (a) Initial data Ingestion: The notebook effectively begins by loading the Dreaddit dataset using Pandas, showcasing fundamental data handling capabilities.
   (b) Initial Data Exploration: Displaying the first few rows of the dataset provides an excellent initial insight into the structure and content of the data.
   (c) Creating a New Feature: The addition of a binary 'stress' column based on specific keywords is an intelligent approach to feature engineering. This step shows an understanding of how-to tailor data to fit the needs of a specific analysis. Included keywords: "anxiety," "stress," "survivorofabuse," and "domesticviolence" is labelled as 1 (stress), the rest as 0.
3. Process data using popular semantic/lexical/punctuation models to add analytical features (from the list of predictors).
4. Perform correlation analysis between binary stress feature and other features added using Python.

5. Split labelled data into training and testing data (80/20
6. Neural network architecture selection which will be used for training models. In this case, several network types will be tested to identify different stress predictors.
7. Data Loading for training: Loading of the dataset using pandas.
8. Data pre-processing:
   (a) Choose features to predict the target variable and extract features from the dataset, such as date, text bode, target label, and additional features, for text body, delete links, hashtags, and unnecessary symbols.
   (b) Tokenize the text using:
      i. BERT Tokenizer Implementation: The utilization of the BERT tokenizer from the 'transformers' library is a strong choice for text data preparation, ensuring that the data is appropriately formatted for the BERT model.
      ii. RNN Tokenizer and Data Preparation: The implementation of a separate tokenizer for the RNN model and subsequent data padding demonstrates a good understanding of the different requirements of these two model types.
9. Perform model training:
   (a) BERT Model Training: The training process for the BERT model, including compiling and fitting the model, is methodologically sound. However, the model's performance, as indicated by the accuracy metrics, suggests potential issues, possibly due to overfitting or an imbalance in the dataset.
   (b) RNN Model Training: The RNN model's training shows a gradual improvement in accuracy over epochs. This progression indicates a learning pattern but also highlights the potential for overfitting, as seen in the increasing divergence between training and validation accuracy.
10. Calculate Precision on the test data frame.
11. Implementation and use of the model: Once the models are trained and validated, it can be used to predict the stress level of employees based on their current and changing parameters taking into account temporal dynamics.

Phase 2. Experiment data processing and analysis of results. Enron data set

1. Data sets without mark-up selection. Data sets should include a history of employee correspondence with the sender and addressee name, date, and text of the message.
2. Preliminary analysis of labelled data. Analyse corresponding scientific papers, columns, data structure, data volume, number of users, and data set shortcomings. Pre-process data with Python for further analysis.
   (a) Data Adaptation for BERT: The pre-processing of the Enron dataset for compatibility with the BERT model is well-executed. However, it would be beneficial to see an analysis of how the different nature of the Enron dataset might affect the model trained on Dreaddit data.
   (b) Data Adaptation for RNN: Similarly, adapting the Enron data for the RNN model is a crucial step, and the notebook handles this well by ensuring consistency in data processing.

3. Process data using popular semantic/lexical/punctuation models to add analytical features (from the list of predictors).
4. Model Predictions: Process data by all models including trained model. The final output with predicted stress levels from both BERT and RNN models is a critical part of the analysis, though it would benefit from a deeper discussion on the comparison of these predictions and their implications.
5. Perform a correlation analysis between stress label (0/1) and other obtained features
6. Describe results and select informative feature

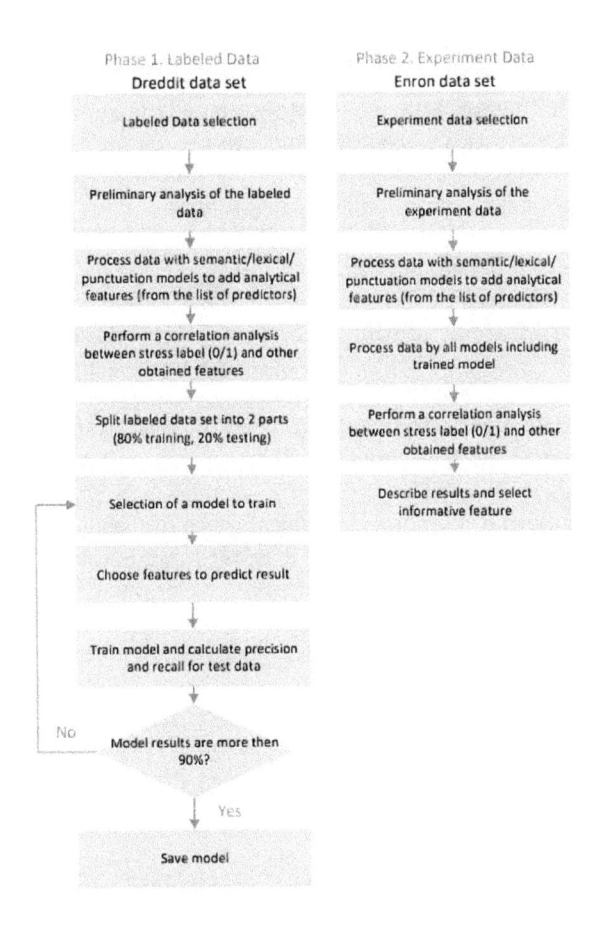

Fig. 2. Prototyping and testing approach

6 Results Testing

This part of the paper describes an attempt at applying advanced NLP techniques to challenging datasets. While there are areas for improvement, particularly in model tuning and in-depth analysis of results, the work effectively demonstrates the potential and challenges of applying machine learning models to real-world text data. The notebook is well-documented, with clear explanations of each step. The code quality is generally high, though some additional comments in complex sections could enhance readability. Data Handling and Preparation assessment:

1. Efficiency in Data Downloading and Extraction: The notebook begins with an efficient approach to downloading and extracting the Enron email dataset. This demonstrates a good understanding of handling external data sources.
2. Email Parsing and DataFrame Creation: The custom functions 'parse email' and 'read emails' are well-constructed for parsing and structuring the email data into a pandas DataFrame. This showcases a thoughtful approach to data transformation and pre-processing.
3. Handling of LIWC Analysis Results: The importation and processing of LIWC (Linguistic Inquiry and Word Count) analysis results are executed skilfully. The manipulation of CSV files into DataFrames and subsequent data cleaning processes are indicative of proficient data wrangling skills.
4. Correlation Analysis and Visualization: The notebook's use of correlation matrices and seaborn heatmaps for visualizing relationships in the data is commendable. It provides a clear and intuitive understanding of the underlying patterns in the dataset.
5. Time Series Analysis: The exploration of time-series data, especially visualizations involving well-being, social connect, and motivation scores, is executed effectively. This part of the notebook is particularly strong in demonstrating the temporal dynamics of the datasets.
6. Grouping and Aggregating Data: The techniques used for grouping and aggregating data show a deep understanding of pandas functionality. This section is crucial for summarizing and interpreting large datasets.

BERT testing:

- Epoch 1/3 accuracy: 0.4700 - val loss: 0.6931 - val accuracy: 0.3222
- Epoch 2/3 accuracy: 0.4687 - val loss: 0.6931 - val accuracy: 0.3222
- Epoch 3/3 accuracy: 0.4762 - val loss: 0.6931 - val accuracy: 0.3222

RNN testing:

- Epoch 1/10 accuracy: 0.6780 - val loss: 0.6218 - val accuracy: 0.6884
- Epoch 2/10 accuracy: 0.6885 - val loss: 0.6230 - val accuracy: 0.6884
- Epoch 3/10 accuracy: 0.6868 - val loss: 0.6249 - val accuracy: 0.6884
- Epoch 4/10 accuracy: 0.7648 - val loss: 0.6370 - val accuracy: 0.6585
- ...
- Epoch 10/10 accuracy: 0.9965 - val loss: 0.8600 - val accuracy: 0.6162

Results analysis

Two models Bert and RNN were trained on a training dataset containing labeled textual data from social media posts. Then validation was performed on the testing part of the labeled dataset. The obtained accuracy for a validation part of the dataset for RNN were 69% and for Bert 32%. The Enron dataset was then processed by trained models and the identified stress indicators were analyzed using the following metrics and actions:

1. For each user several stress-marked emails were read and analyzed if they contained stress related content. If this system were actually applied to a real organization, we wouldn't be reading posts. But in this study, we can read these emails and assess to what extent they contain stress-related content in terms of human comprehension. What is interesting that, the models identified negative stress as well as positive stress, which is still stress.
   "*I was DYING by the last game. I told you I had a rough day!!! I've never felt that out of shape. So what are you still doing here?*"
   "*Well, it wasn't that bad. I was delayed a half an hour from Newark and then was only about a half an hour late getting into Houston. I made it to bed by 12:15 am and managed to drag myself out of bed at 5 am. I have a bunch of work to do this week which SU*KS,*"
   "*So tired I am.*"
2. For each user were calculated the following parameters (Fig. 3 and Fig. 4):
   (a) Total number of sent messages grouped by weeks
   (b) Total number of stressed messages marked by RNN grouped by weeks
   (c) Total number of stressed messages marked by Bert grouped by weeks
   (d) Total number of stressed messages marked by RNN grouped by weeks divided by Total number of sent messages grouped by weeks *100%

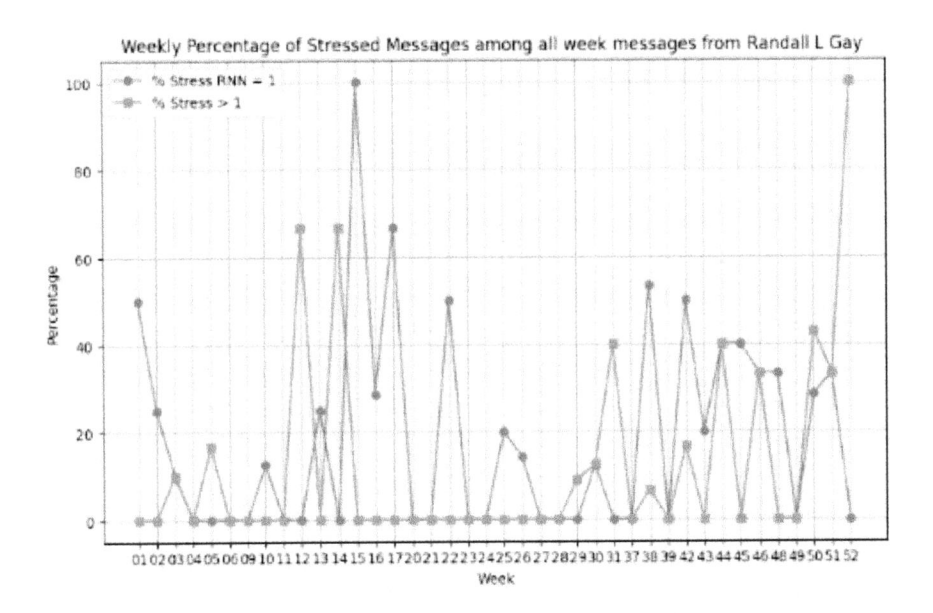

Fig. 3. Weekly percentage of Stressed Messages among all week messages from Randall L Gay

(e) Total number of stressed messages marked by Bert grouped by weeks divided by Total number of sent messages grouped by weeks *100%
3. The percentages of stressed messages for each week for each user were plotted to observe the dynamics of stressed messages proportions.
4. A data frame was compiled containing in strings data for each user with the following columns (Fig. 5):
   (a) Unique user name
   (b) Total number of sent messages for the whole period
   (c) Total number of stressed messages for the whole period marked by RNN
   (d) Total number of stressed messages for the whole period marked by Bert
   (e) Percentage of stressed massages for the whole period marked by RNN
   (f) Percentage of stressed massages for the whole period marked by Bert
5. Top stressed people according to RNN
6. Correlation matrix showing the correlations values of stress labels to linguistic features (Fig. 6).
7. For each user were automatically calculated the features that had high (>0.1) positive correlations to stress marks. In other works what were the identified stress factors for them (Fig. 3 and Fig. 4).
8. For each user were automatically calculated the features that had high (<-0.1) negative correlations to stress marks. In other works what were the identified stress compensators (Fig. 6).
9. A pivot table can be made that illustrated how many people within the organization were negatively affected by which factors. In other words, what were the top stressors within the organization.

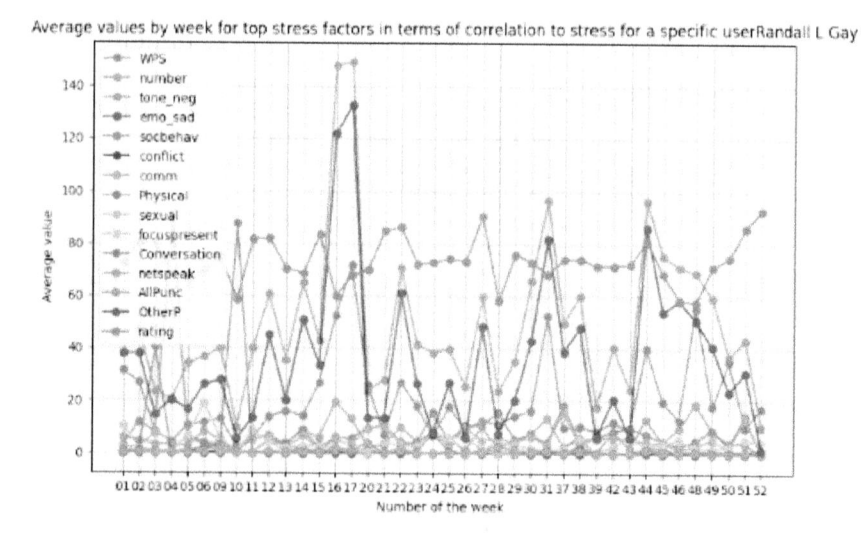

Fig. 4. Average values by week for the top stress factors in termn of correlation with stress metric predicted by the models for a specific user

X-From	Count	Stress RNN > 0.3 Count	Stress > 1 Count	RNNpercent
Amelia Alder	1	1	0	100,00%
Darin Talley	1	1	1	100,00%
Clint Dean	6	3	0	50,00%
Martha Benner	2	1	0	50,00%
Sherri Reinartz	15	6	1	40,00%
Geoff Storey	13	5	1	38,46%
Martin Cuilla	16	6	2	37,50%
Lysa Akin	62	21	3	33,87%
Karen K Heathman	3	1	0	33,33%
Dana Davis	126	38	13	30,16%
Tom Donohoe	10	3	0	30,00%
Judy Hernandez	221	66	52	29,86%
Susan Scott	409	110	34	26,89%
Cathy Phillips	50	13	1	26,00%
Andrea Ring	127	33	26	25,98%
Vince J Kaminski	3470	898	479	25,88%
Sherri Sera	190	49	16	25,79%
Kate Symes	1329	342	389	25,73%
Sally Beck	1017	260	137	25,57%
James Derrick	51	13	3	25,49%

Fig. 5. Enter Caption

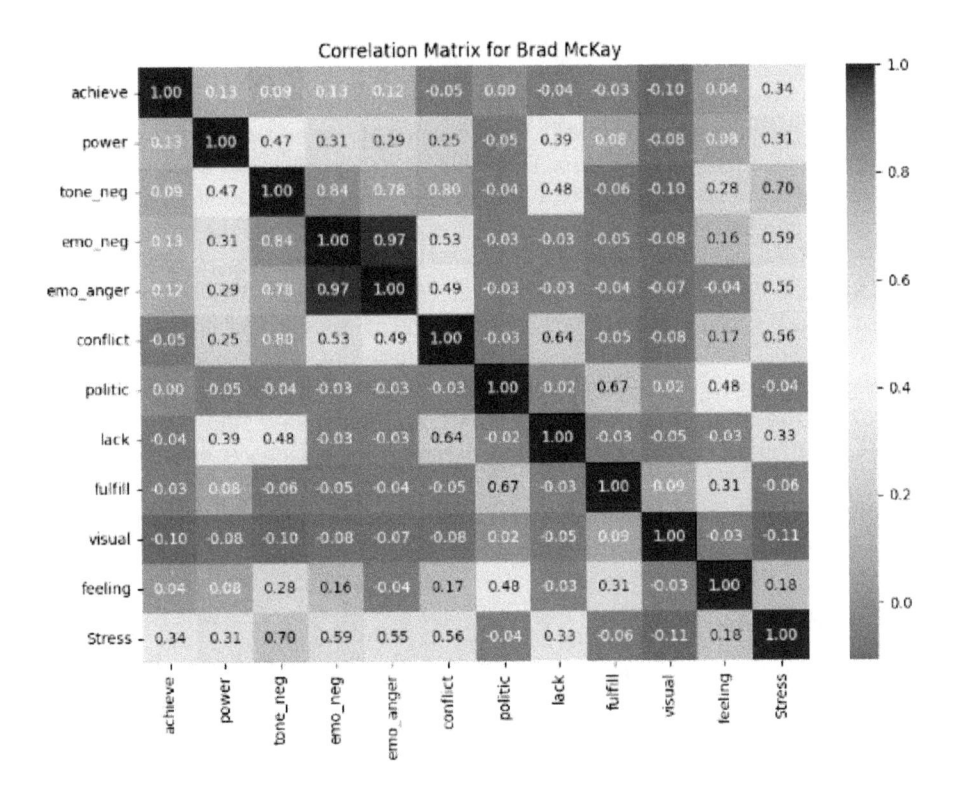

Fig. 6. Enter Caption

10. A pivot table can be made that illustrated how many people within the organization were positively affected by which factors. In other words, what were the top compensators within the organization.
11. For each user the social dynamics can was shown on the chart.
12. For each user if the stressed messages were detected a rating of opponents can be compiled. In other words, with whom the user communicated the most often when experienced stressed according to the models.

7 Conclusion

7.1 Findings and Results

The current paper represents a sophisticated and innovative attempt at applying passive corporate data, analytical algorithms and advanced NLP techniques to identify work-related stress in an organizational context. The research included a compilation of a list of work-related stress factors, early stress predictors, and possible compensators obtained from a literature review. Based on the findings, a framework is proposed to categorize parameters that can be obtained or calculated using data from corporate systems. Possible corporate data sources are included in the framework. Algorithms examples were specified for parameters. In order to select a suitable tool for analyzing employees' passive data from corporate systems, an additional literature review was synthesized with the current research and recent advancements in natural language processing (NLP) and machine learning (ML) for detecting stress and mental health issues through social media interactions. For this work, two models, Bert and RNN, were selected and trained on a training dataset containing labelled textual data from social media posts. Then, validation was performed on the testing part of the labelled dataset. The obtained accuracy for a validation part of the dataset for RNN was 69% and for Bert 32%. The Enron dataset was then processed using the LIWC tool and trained models, and the identified stress indicators were analyzed. The results of the analysis include not only the identified stress markers but also the individually identified factors of stress and possible compensators. The results were verified manually and using data analysis techniques. The experiment results have shown that passive information systems data can be used for the development of a non-intrusive and invisible tool that can provide valuable insights about employee stress levels and provide solutions for personalized stress management interventions.

7.2 Limitations

- In this study, data from a social network in which people expressed emotions more openly than they normally would in a work context was used for training. The use of social media data for model training may not accurately reflect the nuances of workplace communication. Unfortunately, the existence of stress labelled data sets with a real corporate correspondence is not identified by the author of these research.

- In general, people can always skirt topics that are emotional for them. The fact of stress can be identified by other passive signs. However, this behavior can make it more difficult to identify the core reason of stress.
- Good accuracy in identifying stress and possible stressors and compensators requires a long period of historical data collection and statistics for each employee.

7.3 Implications and Future Directions

This study has significant and far-reaching implications for the employee's well-being and organizational stress management. Firstly, it demonstrated the potential of utilizing passive corporate data, combined with cutting-edge analytical algorithms and advanced NLP techniques, as a non-invasive mechanism for monitoring work-related stress. The ability to identify stress factors, predictors, and compensators through analysis of routine corporate system interactions offers a discreet method for organizations to support employee well-being proactively. The proposed framework, which systematically organizes parameters that can be derived from corporate data, serves as a blueprint for businesses seeking to integrate stress detection into their employee wellness programs. By incorporating sources of corporate data and algorithmic examples, the framework provides a practical guide for implementing stress analysis tools. Furthermore, the research experimental findings prove the relevance of these technologies in addressing mental health concerns in the workplace. The application of algorithms, LIWC, Bert and RNN models to corporate correspondence texts illustrates the feasibility of adapting such models for the corporate environment, despite the variance in accuracy levels. The exploration of the Enron dataset using LIWC and the trained models sheds light on the types of stress indicators that can be captured within professional communication. These findings open avenues for future research to improve the approach for stress detection.

- The further development of a prototype is one of the possible directions of this study
- There is a need to develop a classification that selects a personalized stress management plan depending on the combination of identified stressors and compensators.
- According to literature review it was observed that there are variations in work-related stress variables among different countries. The approach specified in this study can be used for analysis of the differences.
- Is essential to establish information security policies and procedures that ensure confidentiality throughout the whole process on data analytics. Data leaks containing personal data is a widely-spread problem over last decades.
- The work-related stress management system reporting function should evolve towards higher abstraction level from the context from which the conclusions are drawn.
- More domain-specific dictionaries with features should be tested to identify stressors and compensators more accurately

- The psycholinguistic component of this study could be of interest to the developers of CRM (e.g. Helpdesk systems) in order to control the politeness of staff when communicating with customers.
- It is necessary to build processes that should be triggered once stress has been detected. It is imperative to approach stress management as a perpetual and evolving procedure.
- It must be determined who the users of the system are. It should be a team manager, HR manager, or the employee himself for self-reflection.
- Regarding the model tuning and validation - given the challenges in model performance, particularly with the BERT model, further tuning and validation, possibly with a different learning rate or additional layers, might be beneficial. In addition, deep analysis of Misclassifications: Investigating specific cases where the models' predictions diverge or fail could provide deeper insights into their performance and potential areas for improvement. A more in-depth analysis of the results, especially concerning the differences in predictions between the two models, would add significant value to the work.

References

Al-smadi, M.: Using long short - term memory deep neural networks for aspect - based sentiment analysis of Arabic reviews. Int. J. Mach. Learn. Cybern. (2019). https://doi.org/10.1007/s13042-018-0799-4

Anikushina, V., Taratukhin, V., Von Stutterheim, C.: Natural language oral communication in humans under stress. Linguistic cognitive coping strategies for enrichment of artificial intelligence. Procedia Comput. Sci. **123**, 24–28 (2018). https://doi.org/10.1016/j.procs.2018.01.005

Arya, V., Kumar, A.: Machine learning approaches to mental stress detection: a review. Ann. Optim. Theory Pract. **4**, 55–67 (2021). https://doi.org/10.22121/AOTP.2021.292083.1074

Bakker, A.B., Demerouti, E., Verbeke, W.: Using the job demands-resources model to predict burnout and performance. Hum. Resour. Manage. **43**, 83–104 (2004). https://doi.org/10.1002/hrm.20004

Biggs, A., Brough, P.: Explaining Intervention Success and Failure: What Works, When, and Why? Springer, Dordrecht (2015)

Charzyńska, E., Soola, A.H., Mozaffari, N.: Patterns of work-related stress and their predictors among emergency department nurses and emergency medical services staff in a time of crisis: a latent profile analysis. BMC Nurs. 1–10 (2023)

Cho, G., Yim, J., Choi, Y., Ko, J., Lee, S.: Review of machine learning algorithms for diagnosing mental illness. Psychiatry Invest. 262–269 (2020)

Cohen, B.E., Edmondson, D., Kronish, I.M.: State of the art review: depression, stress, anxiety, and cardiovascular disease. Am. J. Hypertens. **28**, 1295–1302 (2015). https://doi.org/10.1093/ajh/hpv047

Cooper, C.: Well-being - absenteeism, presenteeism, costs and challenges (2018). https://doi.org/10.1093/occmed/kqn124

Cooper, C.L., Marshall, J.: Occupational sources of stress: a review of the literature relating to coronary heart disease and mental ill health. J. Occup. Psychol. 11–28 (1976)

Cox, T.O.M., Leka, S., Ivanov, I., Kortum, E.: Work, employment and mental health in Europe (2005). https://doi.org/10.1080/02678370412331272651

Ahrendt, D., et al.: Living, working and COVID-19. Publications Office of the European Union (2020)

Day, A., Paquet, S., Scott, N., Hambley, L.: Perceived information and communication technology (ICT) demands on employee outcomes: the moderating effect of organizational ICT support. J. Occup. Health Psychol. **17**, 473–491 (2012). https://doi.org/10.1037/a0029837

Demerouti, E.: Oldenburg burnout inventory. Eur. J. Psychol. Assess. (1999)

Dhawan, S.: Group dynamics and team effectiveness in organisations. J. Asiatic Soc. Mumbai **96**(9(I)), 110–125 96, 110–125 (2022)

Enron wikipedia.org (2023). https://en.wikipedia.org/wiki/Enron

EU-OSHA, 2007. EU-OSHA Annual report 2007: bringing safety and health closer to European workers, European Agency for Safety and Health at Work

Fauville, G., Luo, M., Queiroz, A.C.M., Bailenson, J.N., Hancock, J.: Nonverbal Mechanisms Predict Zoom Fatigue and Explain Why Women Experience Higher Levels than Men. SSRN Electron. J. 1–18 (2021). https://doi.org/10.2139/ssrn.3820035

Fishta, A., Maria, E.: Psychosocial stress at work and cardiovascular diseases: an overview of systematic reviews. Int. Arch. Occup. Environ. Health 997–1014 (2020). https://doi.org/10.1007/s00420-015-1019-0

Garg, M.: Mental health analysis in social media posts: a survey. Arch. Comput. Methods Eng. **30**, 1819–1842 (2023). https://doi.org/10.1007/s11831-022-09863-z

Golden, T.D., Veiga, J.F., Dino, R.N.: The impact of professional isolation on teleworker job performance and turnover intentions: does time spent teleworking, interacting face-to- face, or having access to communication-enhancing technology matter? J. Appl. Psychol. **93**, 1412–1421 (2008). https://doi.org/10.1037/a0012722

Haque, A.U., Oino, I.: Managerial challenges for software houses related to work, worker and workplace: stress reduction and sustenance of human capital. Polish J. Manag. Stud. **19**, 170–189 (2019). https://doi.org/10.17512/pjms.2019.19.1.13

Harvey, S.B.: Can work make you mentally ill? A systematic meta-review of work-related risk factors for common mental health problems. Occup. Environ. Med. 1–10 (2017). https://doi.org/10.1136/oemed-2016-104015

Heinen, I., Bullinger, M., Kocalevent, R.D.: Perceived stress in first year medical students - associations with personal resources and emotional distress. BMC Med. Educ. **17**, 1–14 (2017). https://doi.org/10.1186/s12909-016-0841-8

Huang, G.D., Feuerstein, M., Sauter, S.L.: Occupational stress and work-related upper extremity disorders: concepts and models. Am. J. Ind. Med. **41**, 298–314 (2002). https://doi.org/10.1002/ajim.10045

Johnson, K.R., Park, S., Chaudhuri, S.: Mindfulness training in the workplace: exploring its scope and outcomes. Eur. J. Train. Dev. **44**, 341–354 (2020). https://doi.org/10.1108/EJTD-09-2019-0156

Leiter, M.P., Maslach, C.: Burnout and engagement: contributions to a new vision. Burn. Res. **5**, 55–57 (2017). https://doi.org/10.1016/j.burn.2017.04.003

LePine, J.A., Podsakoff, N.P., LePine, M.A.: A meta-analytic test of the challenge Stressor-hindrance stressor framework: an explanation for inconsistent relationships among Stressors and performance. Acad. Manag. J. **48**, 764–775 (2005). https://doi.org/10.5465/AMJ.2005.18803921

Lin, F.R., Albert, M.: Hearing loss and dementia - who is listening? 7863 (2014). https://doi.org/10.1080/13607863.2014.915924

Magnavita, N., Di Stasio, E., Capitanelli, I., Lops, E.A., Chirico, F., Garbarino, S.: Sleep problems and workplace violence: a systematic review and meta-analysis. Front. Neurosci. **13** (2019). https://doi.org/10.3389/fnins.2019.00997

Maslach, C., Jackson, S.E., Leiter, M.P.: The maslach burnout inventory manual. Eval. Stress a B. Resour. 191–218 (1981)

Mello, S.D., Dale, R., Graesser, A.: Disequilibrium in the mind, disharmony in the body, pp. 1–13 (2011). https://doi.org/10.1080/02699931.2011.575767

Nijhawan, T., Attigeri, G., Ananthakrishna, T.: Stress detection using natural language processing and machine learning over social interactions. J. Big Data (2022). https://doi.org/10.1186/s40537-022-00575-6

Nixona, A.E., Mazzolab, J.J., Bauera, J., Kruegerc, J.R., Spectora, P.E.: Can work make you sick? A meta-analysis of the relationships between job stressors and physical symptoms. Work Stress **25**, 1–22 (2011). https://doi.org/10.1080/02678373.2011.569175

Park, Y.A., Fritz, C., Jex, S.M.: Daily cyber incivility and distress: the moderating roles of resources at work and home. J. Manage. **44**, 2535–2557 (2018). https://doi.org/10.1177/0149206315576796

Peter, R., Alfredsson, L., Hammar, N., Siegrist, J., Theorell, T.: High effort, low reward, and cardiovascular risk factors in employed Swedish men and women: baseline results from the WOLF Study, pp. 540–547 (1998)

Podsakoff, N.P., Lepine, J.A., Lepine, M.A.: Differential challenge stressor-hindrance stressor relationships with job attitudes, turnover intentions, turnover, and withdrawal behavior: a meta-analysis. J. Appl. Psychol. **92**, 438–454 (2007). https://doi.org/10.1037/0021-9010.92.2.438

Karasek Jr, R.A.: Job demands, job decision latitude, and mental strain: implication for job redesign. Adm. Sci. Q. **24**, 285–308 (1979)

Sell, M.V., French, J.R., Caplan, R.D., Harrison, R.V.: The mechanisms of job stress and strain. Conf. Proc. (1984)

Suh, A., Lee, J.: Understanding teleworkers' technostress and its influence on job satisfaction. Internet Res. **27**, 140–159 (2017). https://doi.org/10.1108/IntR-06-2015-0181

Theorell, T.: Stress reduction programmes for the workplace. Handb. Occup. Heal. Wellness 1–576 (2012). https://doi.org/10.1007/978-1-4614-4839-6

Tarafdar, M., Tu, Q., Ragu-Nathan, T.S., Ragu-Nathan, B.S.: Crossing to the dark side: examining creators, outcomes, and inhibitors of technostress. Commun. ACM **54**, 113–120 (2011). https://doi.org/10.1145/1995376.1995403

Turcan, E., McKeown, K.: Dreaddit: a reddit dataset for stress analysis in social media. LOUHI@EMNLP 2019 - 10th International Workshop on Health Text Mining and Information Analysis Proceedings, pp. 97–107 (2019). https://doi.org/10.18653/v1/d19-6213

Xiao, H., Zhang, Y., Kong, D., Li, S., Yang, N.: The effects of social support on sleep quality of medical staff treating patients with coronavirus disease 2019(COVID-19) in January and February 2020 in China. Med. Sci. Monit. **26**, 1–8 (2020). https://doi.org/10.12659/MSM.923549

Advancing Mass Customization in Capital Goods Manufacturing Through Standard Man Hours (SMH) Modelling and ESG Considerations

Yagnesh Purohit[1(✉)] and Shilpa Parkhi[2]

[1] Symbiosis International Deemed University (SIU), Pune, India
yagnesh.purohit17@gmail.com
[2] Symbiosis Institute of Business Management, (SIBM), Pune, India

Abstract. In the contemporary industrial landscape, mass customization emerges as a beacon for manufacturers seeking to broaden their product offerings, blending bespoke craftsmanship with off-the-shelf efficiency. This scholarly inquiry focuses on the domain of mass customization within the welding and fabrication sectors, shedding light on its multifaceted implications for supply chains, labour dynamics, and environmental sustainability.

Our research delves into the intricacies of mass customization strategies within capital goods fabrication, drawing insights from welding, fabrication, and allied industries. Employing a multidisciplinary approach that melds data analytics and business acumen, we delve into the pivotal role of skills and job parameters, which wield significant influence over standard man-hours (SMH) and the feasibility of mass customization endeavours.

Beyond theoretical discourse, our study offers practical insights into multi-criteria decision-making techniques, furnishing tangible evidence of our proficiency in delineating job roles and skill requisites for achieving mass customization excellence.

This scholarly endeavour contributes substantially to industrial innovation, data-informed decision-making, and manufacturing efficiency, enriching the discourse on mass customization within capital goods fabrication. By unravelling the intricate interplay of skill parameters, job specifications, and SMH, our findings and recommendations serve to benefit both industry practitioners and academic scholars, thereby advancing the realm of mass customization.

Furthermore, our research illuminates mass customization as a strategic management tool, harmonizing productivity amplification with heightened customer satisfaction. Through a comprehensive examination of fundamental principles and methodological approaches, we unveil untapped opportunities and future trajectories, fostering ongoing dialogue and exploration across diverse industrial domain's efficiency.

Keywords: Mass customization · Standard Man Hour (SMH) · Manufacturing efficiencies · Design for Mass customization

1 Introduction

Mass customization involves the production of personalized goods or services with the efficiency of mass production techniques. In 1993, Pine coined this notion as the capacity to deliver tailored goods or services in varying quantities, on demand, to a diverse range of individuals, at various locations, and for diverse purposes [1]. The concept of mass customization emerged approximately half a century ago. It was first introduced by Toffler in his book 'Future Shock' published in 1970 [2]. Davis further elaborated on this idea in 'Future Perfect' in 1990 [3].

The creation of a product is intricately shaped and constrained by a myriad of factors, encompassing supply chain logistics, manufacturing procedures, and customer inclinations. The product's design wields influence over manufacturing expenses, the smooth functioning of the supply chain, and, in the end, the contentment of consumers. The complexity emerges in crafting a perfect product design that amplifies customer contentment while keeping manufacturing and linked expenses at their lowest, all the while balancing the often-conflicting goals of elevating product quality and variety while trimming costs. In making design decisions, these three interlinked facets of design must be meticulously weighed and contemplated.

An essential aspect of managing product variety involves determining the appropriate range of options that align with consumer expectations. Customers typically favor a broader array of product options at their disposal, which encourages manufacturers to expand their product offerings. Nevertheless, this expansion also ushers in complexities in the manufacturing process and the potential for conflicts among different product configurations. To prevent customers from selecting components that don't work together, product configurators often provide suggestions for creating valid configurations. Yet, the presence of impractical configurations can harm customer perceptions and undermine the sustainability of mass customization. One approach to tackle this challenge is to minimize or remove components that are inherently incompatible. It's vital to strike a balance, though, as completely eliminating all incompatible components could significantly reduce the diversity of available products. Hence, reducing the number of incompatible components can effectively address the product configuration issue while preserving a desirable level of product variety [4].

2 The Examination of Existing Scholarly Works—The Literature Review

In the comprehensive examination undertaken, reliance was predominantly placed on Scopus, Web of Science and Google Scholar to scour the extensive landscape of relevant research articles. Approximately 600 publications were scrutinized, employing subject searches with keywords such as "Mass customization, Standard work Hour (SWH), Standard Mam Hour (SMH) model, Modularization, DFMC, DFM, economization, agile manufacturing, order to make, rapid production, design to order, capital goods, and mass manufacturing." This meticulous process yielded the identification of around 300 publications aligned with the specific focus of the research.

Table 1 serves as a valuable resource for researchers, practitioners, and enthusiasts interested in Mass Customization, offering a quantitative snapshot of the diverse scholarly landscape surrounding this topic.

Table 1. Summary of scholarly written publications.

Publication type	Statistics
Article Published	5,030
Data Sets	49
Grants	552
Patents	676

(*Source* app.dimesion.ai)

Article Published (5,030): This category encompasses a substantial number of scholarly articles that delve into the subject of Mass Customization. These articles are likely to provide in-depth analyses, theoretical frameworks, empirical studies, and critical discussions contributing to the existing body of knowledge on Mass Customization.

Data Sets (49): The presence of data sets indicates a significant emphasis on empirical research within the realm of Mass Customization. These publications may offer valuable datasets for researchers, enabling them to conduct further analyses, validate hypotheses, or draw evidence-based conclusions.

Grants (552): The inclusion of grants signifies financial support for research endeavors related to Mass Customization. These publications may detail the funding sources, facilitating transparency and providing insights into the level of investment in this field.

Patents (676): The mention of patents suggests a focus on innovation within Mass Customization. These publications may involve discussions on novel technologies, processes, or systems that have been patented, reflecting an interest in intellectual property and advancements in the field.

The trend depicted in Fig. 1 illustrates the evolution of research output on Mass Customization over different time periods. Several noteworthy observations can be made:

Early Stages (1989–1999): The initial years show a gradual increase in the number of publications, with a notable spike in the late 1990s. This period signifies the emergence of Mass Customization as a subject of scholarly interest.

Significant Growth (2000–2010): The early 2000s witnessed a substantial surge in research output, indicating a growing recognition of Mass Customization as a critical area of study. The number of publications more than doubled during this decade, reflecting heightened academic and industrial attention.

Steady Expansion (2011–2020): From 2011 to 2020, the trend continues with a steady expansion of research output. Although there are fluctuations, the overall trajectory maintains an upward momentum, suggesting sustained interest and investment in Mass Customization research.

Recent Acceleration (2021–2023): The most recent years showcase a notable acceleration in research output, with a sharp increase from 2021 onwards. This surge could be attributed to various factors, such as advancements in technology, increasing industrial applications, or heightened awareness of the importance of Mass Customization in contemporary business strategies.

Overall, the trend reveals a dynamic and evolving landscape, with Mass Customization gaining prominence over the years. The consistent growth in research output signifies the enduring relevance and significance of this field, indicating its continued impact on academia and industry alike. Researchers and stakeholders can use this trend analysis to understand the historical context and anticipate future developments in Mass Customization research.

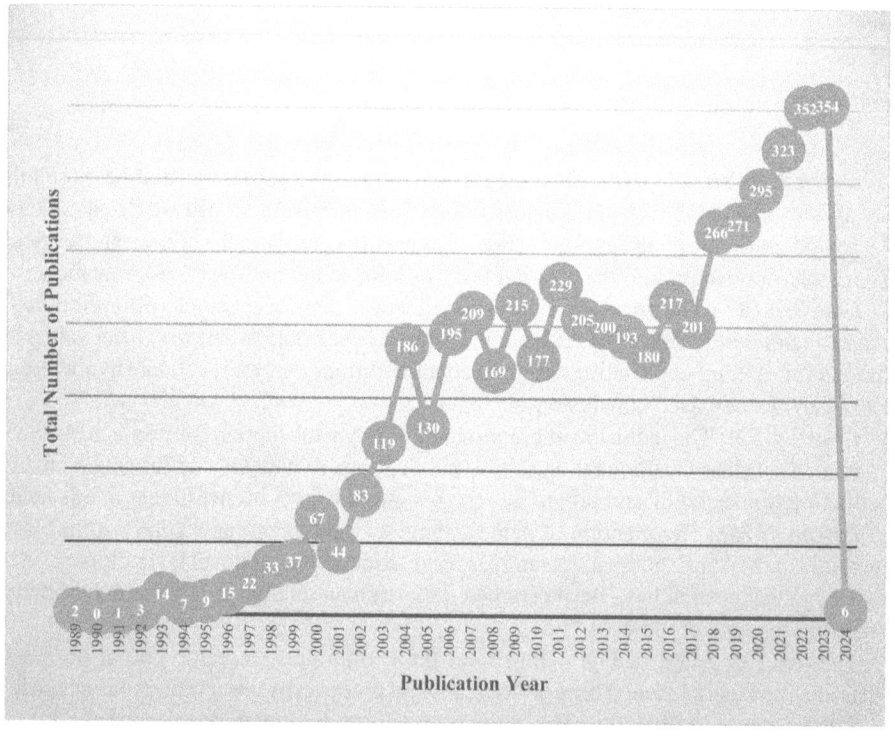

Fig. 1. Distribution of articles across time intervals. (*Source* app.dimesion.ai)

Figure 2, employing a Pareto chart, meticulously delineates the distribution of Mass Customization-related articles across diverse research fields, providing an intricate portrayal of the scholarly landscape. This visual representation not only accentuates the concentration of research endeavours but also quantifies these contributions in precise percentage terms, adhering to the fundamental tenets of the Pareto principle.

A meticulous examination reveals the paramount role played by Engineering and Management in this scholarly discourse, collectively constituting a formidable 67% of the entire corpus of publications. Engineering, with its substantial 34% contribution, emerges as a focal point, attesting to its pivotal role in shaping the narrative surrounding

Mass Customization. Concurrently, the Management domain, encapsulated within Commerce, Management, Tourism, and Services, echoes its prominence with a substantial 33% contribution, further emphasizing its indispensable standing in this interdisciplinary field.

This refined analysis underscores the dual prominence of Engineering and Management within Mass Customization scholarship, acknowledging their considerable share of the scholarly output. The inclusion of percentage-based information not only adds precision to the assessment but also serves as a strategic compass for nuanced planning, resource allocation, and collaborative initiatives within these influential domains, propelling the scholarly understanding and impact of Mass Customization to new heights.

Articles published across diverse research fields

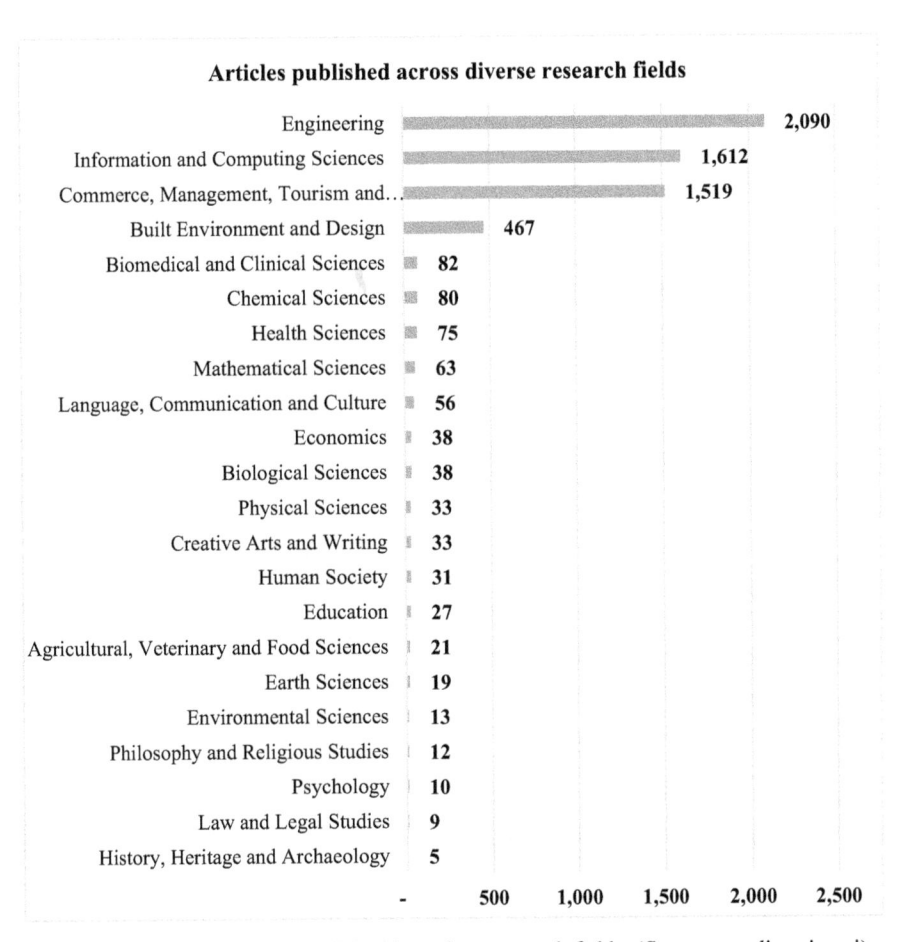

Research Field	Number of Articles
Engineering	2,090
Information and Computing Sciences	1,612
Commerce, Management, Tourism and...	1,519
Built Environment and Design	467
Biomedical and Clinical Sciences	82
Chemical Sciences	80
Health Sciences	75
Mathematical Sciences	63
Language, Communication and Culture	56
Economics	38
Biological Sciences	38
Physical Sciences	33
Creative Arts and Writing	33
Human Society	31
Education	27
Agricultural, Veterinary and Food Sciences	21
Earth Sciences	19
Environmental Sciences	13
Philosophy and Religious Studies	12
Psychology	10
Law and Legal Studies	9
History, Heritage and Archaeology	5

Fig. 2. Number of articles published in various research fields. (*Source* app.dimesion.ai)

3 Mass Customization in Industrial Application

In the contemporary world, navigating through volatility, uncertainty, complexity, and ambiguity demands businesses to establish a new normal. When faced with these challenges, it becomes imperative to adopt fresh approaches to management. Aligning these novel directions with customer needs guarantees positive outcomes in the modern landscape. Mass customization emerges as a potent strategy capable of driving rapid growth and building a trustworthy brand among customers. It offers the unique opportunity to balance economies of scale while reaping the benefits of competitive pricing [5].

Table 2 provides a concise overview of the SWOT analysis, unveiling the strengths, weaknesses, opportunities, and threats associated with mass customization. These insights offer valuable guidance to firms seeking rapid growth and aiming to establish a global presence.

Table 2. Concise overview of the SWOT analysis

Strength	Weakness
Rapidity in supply	Higher in complexity
Gives modularity to processes	Rapid re-design and re-structuring
Boost just in time concept	Difficult to achieve mass market efficiency
A set configured management tools already available in firms for mass customization	Calls for changes in all function of management
Enables state of art production	
Gives time and cost benefits	
Opportunity	*Threat*
It provides the option to engage in multistage management	Demands deep customer understanding, including behaviour
Balances unique needs with economies of scale	Delayed Product Differentiation (DPD)
SMEs can also implement this concept	Shortens lead time for management support functions
Fulfils personalized requirements	
ERP has revolutionized the way products are tailored to meet individual customer needs	
Facilitates cyber-physical production	
Effectively caters to in-process design changes	
Enhances decision support matrix	
Provides adaptability for manufacturing and management	

In summary, the literature review provides a comprehensive examination of the evolution of mass customization, tracing its trajectory from conceptual origins to practical applications in the era of Industry 4.0 and smart manufacturing. It underscores the significance of technology, data-driven insights, and customer-centric approaches in the contemporary landscape of manufacturing and retail, where personalized products are increasingly accessible and efficient. Additionally, it highlights a notable research gap in SMH modelling within the capital goods fabrication industry, suggesting a promising avenue for exploration and innovation. In conclusion, today's business environment requires adaptability and innovation, with mass customization emerging as a powerful solution. It enables firms to achieve sustainable growth while meeting customer needs effectively. By seizing the opportunities of mass customization, companies can excel in today's dynamic and competitive landscape.

To comprehensively understand the various factors influencing the SMH model, a series of hypotheses have been formulated. These hypotheses aim to explore the relationships between specific skill parameters and job parameters and their impact on the required Standard Man Hour (SMH) for a given job.

3.1 Parameters for Standard Man Hour (SMH)

(A) **Fit-up Proficiency**:

Null Hypothesis (H0): The proficiency level of workmen in fitting does not influence the necessary SMH for a specific task.

Alternative Hypothesis (Ha): The fitting skill of workmen significantly affects the required SMH for a given job.

(B) **Welding Proficiency**:

Null Hypothesis (H0): The welding proficiency of workmen has no effect on the necessary SMH for a given task.

Alternative Hypothesis (Ha): The welding skill of workmen influences the required SMH for a given job.

(C) **Material Classification**:

Null Hypothesis (H0): The classification of job material does not affect the necessary SMH for a given task.

Alternative Hypothesis (Ha): The category of job material significantly influences the required SMH for a given job.

(D) **Weight of Job**:

Null Hypothesis (H0): The weight of the job does not affect the necessary SMH for a given task.

Alternative Hypothesis (Ha): The job weight significantly influences the required SMH for a given job.

(E) **Volume of Weldmetal**:

Null Hypothesis (H0): The volume of welds in the job does not affect the necessary SMH for a given task.

Alternative Hypothesis (Ha): The weld volume of the job significantly influences the required SMH for a given job.

These hypotheses lay the groundwork for investigating the interplay between skill-related parameters and job-related parameters in determining Standard Man Hours within fabrication processes. The objective is to evaluate whether these parameters exert a statistically significant impact on the time needed to complete a job, thus aiding in the optimization of fabrication processes and the attainment of timely, high-quality results.

The following sections of this study will delve into empirical research and analyses aimed at rigorously testing these hypotheses. Through this exploration, valuable insights will be gained into the factors influencing SMH and, consequently, the efficiency of mass customization in the fabrication of capital goods.

3.2 Multi-Criteria Decision Making (MCDM) Strategies

MCDM strategies entail evaluating multiple criteria, each representing a unique facet of the decision-making process. These criteria may encompass factors such as cost-effectiveness, quality standards, scalability potential, and environmental considerations. By assigning suitable weights to each criterion, decision-makers can objectively assess and rank available manufacturing methods.

This systematic evaluation with MCDM strategies not only improves decision-making accuracy but also ensures that the selected manufacturing method aligns with the specific requirements and objectives of the project or product. Such an approach mitigates the risk of relying solely on intuition or incomplete information when making decisions.

3.2.1 Analytic Hierarchy Process (AHP)

1. **Objective Definition and Attribute Assessment:** The process commences by clearly defining the objectives driving the decision-making process. Concurrently, relevant attributes or criteria are scrutinized to form the foundational decision hierarchy.
2. **Relative Importance Determination:** Each attribute's relative importance or value is discerned concerning the overarching goals and objectives. This evaluation often employs a scale to reflect the significance of each attribute accurately.
3. **Construction of Pairwise Comparison Matrix:** Through pairwise comparisons, the relative importance of attributes is systematically captured, culminating in the creation of a matrix (H1) that delineates the interrelationships among attributes.
4. **Geometric Mean Calculation and Weight Normalization:** Geometric means for each row in the pairwise comparison matrix are computed and subsequently normalized to derive attribute weights, yielding the matrix denoted as H2.
5. **Matrix Multiplication and Division:** By performing matrix operations between H1 and H2, H3 is generated, followed by obtaining H4 through division. These matrices serve as pivotal tools in assessing attribute importance.
6. **Maximum Eigenvalue (max) and Consistency Index (CI) Computation:** The average value of matrix H4 facilitates the determination of the maximum Eigenvalue (max), while Eq. (1) is utilized to compute the Consistency Index (CI), gauging the decision matrix's coherence. A CI below 0.1 signifies acceptable consistency.

7. **Random Index (RI) Establishment and Consistency Ratio (CR) Evaluation:** RI is established based on the decision-making issue's attribute count, aiding in the calculation of CR. A CR not exceeding 0.1 indicates satisfactory consistency.
8. **Holistic Performance Evaluation:** Performance scores are meticulously computed for each option or alternative based on the established criteria and their corresponding weights.
9. **Ranking and Selection:** Subsequently, the options undergo ranking based on their performance scores. The option garnering the highest score is deemed the optimal approach and is accorded the top rank.

3.2.2 Technique for Order of Preference by Similarity to Ideal Solutions (TOPSIS)

1. **Objective Definition and Key Characteristic Assessment:** In this initial phase, the objectives are precisely delineated, and key characteristics or criteria pertinent to both the null hypothesis (H0) and the alternative hypothesis (Ha) are thoroughly evaluated.
2. **Construction of Data Matrix:** All pertinent data pertaining to the identified characteristics are systematically organized and presented within a matrix structure.
3. **Determination of Relative Weights:** Relative weights for each characteristic are computed, reflecting their respective significance in relation to the overarching objective. The cumulative sum of these weights amounts to one, ensuring comprehensive coverage of the decision domain.
4. **Normalization of Weighted Values:** The weighted values are normalized by multiplying each element within the matrix columns by the corresponding weights attributed to each characteristic concerning the null hypothesis (H0).
5. **Identification of Optimal and Suboptimal Options:** Through meticulous calculations, the optimal and suboptimal options are discerned, shedding light on their performance against the established criteria.
6. **Assessment of Distance Metrics:** Subsequent to identifying the best and worst options, distance metrics are employed to gauge the relative proximity of each option to these extremes. This assessment aids in comprehending the effectiveness of each option concerning the defined criteria, facilitating informed decision-making.

4 Implication on Management Practices

Mass customization is a business strategy that aims to merge the advantages of mass production and individualized customization, and its impact on management practices across diverse industries is significant. It triggers a transformation in how companies conduct their operations and engage with their clientele, challenging conventional management norms. Below, we delve into distinctive consequences:

Transition from Push to Pull Models: Mass customization necessitates a shift away from the conventional push production model and the adoption of a pull model. In contrast to forecasting demand and proactively manufacturing goods, companies now respond to specific customer orders. This shift demands a supply chain that is more agile and responsive to customer demand, prompting a reassessment of inventory management and production scheduling practices [6].

Reliance on Data-Driven Decision-Making: Mass customization places a significant emphasis on data analysis. Managers must effectively utilize extensive customer data to gain insights into preferences, purchasing patterns, and market trends. This shift towards data-driven decision-making necessitates investments in analytics tools and expertise to make informed choices [7].

Flexible Manufacturing: Traditional manufacturing setups typically prioritize economies of scale, resulting in inflexible production processes. Mass customization, however, demands the presence of flexible manufacturing systems capable of swift adaptation to evolving product configurations. The process of designing new products is significantly influenced by considerations for production. To maintain competitiveness in the market, the concept of Design for Manufacturability (DFM) emphasizes the importance of cost and time reduction throughout the product design process.

A set of process design principles can be outlined as following three points [8].

1st: Streamlining the number of stages, components, and connections can enhance reliability while reducing expenses on purchases and inventories.

2nd: The utilization of standardized components and the development of modular designs can lead to cost savings, quicker procurement lead times, and increased reliability.

3rd: Contemplating designs that are compatible with automated or robotic production processes can help reduce labor costs.

These principles underscore the significance of integrating manufacturing considerations into the product design phase to optimize efficiency and competitiveness.

Incorporating DFM into the product design phase can result in cost savings and reduced lead times in the manufacturing process [9].

Diversity of Talent and Skills: Effectively managing a mass customization operation requires a broad spectrum of skills. Engineers, designers, data scientists, and marketing experts must collaborate seamlessly. Managers play a crucial role in establishing cross-functional teams and cultivating a workplace culture that promotes interdisciplinary cooperation among these diverse skill sets.

Customization of Operations: Conventional management practices typically adopt a uniform, one-size-fits-all approach. However, in the context of mass customization, operations themselves may require customization. Companies need to create flexible processes and systems that can be adjusted to accommodate individual customer requirements, all while upholding operational efficiency [10].

Customer-Centric: Mass customization revolves around prioritizing customer needs. Managers must emphasize understanding customer preferences and feedback, fostering a customer-centric culture. Involving consumers as design partners enhances satisfaction. DFM techniques reduce costs by consolidating components [11].

Complexity in Supply chain: Effectively navigating a mass customization supply chain presents a markedly greater challenge compared to conventional supply chains. Companies are tasked with procuring a diverse spectrum of materials and components to meet customization demands. This intricate landscape demands the implementation of pioneering supply chain management approaches.

Digital Transformation: To effectively implement mass customization, companies need to embark on a digital transformation journey. This entails the comprehensive integration of digital technologies across the entire organization, spanning from production processes to customer interfaces. Managers play a crucial role in leading and skilfully navigating this transformation process [12, 13].

Communication Challenges: Navigating mass customization entails distinct marketing and communication hurdles. Companies must craft precise marketing strategies for each customer segment, leveraging sophisticated personalization techniques. Managers spearhead these efforts, ensuring uniformity across all customer interactions and touchpoints.

The communication of the following four points to buyer, which invoke willingness of customer to buy the product is having paramount importance [14].

1st: Rapid production of the product design is feasible.

2nd: The product is going to be cost-effective to manufacture.

3rd: Minimized changes to the manufacturing process for diverse product requirements.

4th: Ensured that manufactured item meets predefined quality standards.

Quality and Environmental Considerations: The customization of products adds complexity to the realm of quality control and assurance. To address this challenge, managers must establish stringent quality standards and put in place real-time monitoring and feedback systems. These measures are essential to ensure that each customized product consistently meets the desired quality standards. Additionally, environmental considerations should also be factored into the customization process to align with sustainability goals and practices.

5 Environmental, Social, and Governance (ESG) Considerations

ESG Practices refers to a set of principles and criteria that companies and organizations follow to align their operations and activities with Environmental, Social, and Governance (ESG) considerations. These practices aim to promote sustainability, ethical behavior, and responsible corporate citizenship. Here's a breakdown of each component:

Firms that embrace robust ESG principles aim to harmonize their financial outcomes with their influence on society and the environment. These principles are not just regarded as a moral obligation but also as means to reduce risks, bolster their standing, draw investors, and foster enduring sustainability. The incorporation of mass customization and the utilization of Standard Man Hours (SMH) or Standard Work Hours (SWH) offer a method for finely aligning all three ESG objectives during the planning and implementation phases. ESG practices have gained significant importance in the business world as investors, customers, and regulators increasingly consider a company's ESG performance when making decisions and assessments. Many organizations now publish ESG reports to transparently communicate their efforts and progress in these areas.

Alfaify et al. [15] have delved into the realm of rapid manufacturing, and their research suggests that leveraging quick production technology can lead to a reduction in the number of components required in an assembly. Theoretically, this reduction in the number of components to just one, through the use of rapid manufacturing techniques, can result in a substantial decrease in overall production costs.

Shahbazi et al. [16] emphasize the pivotal role of mass customization for cost and time reduction in production. Drawing practical insights from a review of related literature, the authors offer strategies to curtail overall processing costs and lead times for production. Two key strategies identified by them. 1st: Reducing Component Count: This involves integrating existing systems or adopting innovative processes such as additive manufacturing to minimize the number of components required in the assembly. 2nd: Standardization and Modular Design: Employing standardized and modular design principles to streamline production processes and enhance efficiency. These strategies, based on the synthesis of prior research, contribute to more efficient and cost-effective production methods.

To enhance the efficiency of reconfiguring the production line, three methodologies have been proposed by Fazio et al. [17]. 1st: Abstract Combination: This methodology focuses on abstracting and combining elements to simplify the production process. 2nd: Component Combination Analysis: It involves a thorough analysis of components to identify opportunities for combining or optimizing them. 3rd: Component Elimination Procedure: This methodology targets the elimination of unnecessary components from the production process.

In an industrial design context, the incorporation of these three methodologies has been put into practice. The outcomes reveal that the reduction in the number of components proves to be an exceptionally effective approach. This not only enhances production efficiency but also streamlines the process of reconfiguring the production line. Consequently, it contributes to the achievement of progressively higher ESG targets, aligning with sustainability and efficiency objectives.

Asadi et al. [18] have examined the consequences of product integration and modularity in production and assembly systems. Through a case study centered on the automotive "Body-in-White," their investigation demonstrates that modular products provide significant adaptability but face constraints in promptly adapting to swift market shifts. In contrast, integral products perform better during market fluctuations but tend to be less cost-effective. The authors suggest that the path forward involves finding a harmonious equilibrium between product integration and product flexibility. This balanced approach is seen as the key to optimizing both cost-effectiveness and adaptability to dynamic market conditions.

Asif et al. [19], highlights that in the conceptualization and planning stage, continuous improvement efforts are often individually optimized for specific aspects of production, such as assembly, manufacturing, cost, or raw material selection. This fragmented approach is deemed ineffective and prone to inconsistencies. To enhance the efficiency of both manufacturing and assembly processes, the study introduces a multi-objective decision-making strategy that incorporates mass customization principles and systematically integrates product requirements with industry expertise. This research utilizes a case study involving a CNC machine tool equipped with a rotating tool holder carousel to evaluate the expenses and socio-environmental advantages of different design options. The findings illustrate that the suggested approach can significantly slash overall production expenses and lower the frequency of replacements. However, the study also acknowledges the challenge of determining whether a process developed for one specific product can be successfully applied to other goods during design and development.

As per Kunic et al. [20], Crafting modular products can proficiently meet the call for a wide array of product variations and simplify the automation process in production or assembly lines. This paper introduces a framework that concurrently addresses the design of automated production systems and modular products. To optimize the efficiency of designing products for automation, the framework incorporates the use of the design structure matrix and modular function deployment. The study's results illustrate that the proposed framework excels in managing multiple product variations that consist of numerous components. The framework's application is demonstrated in the context of the furniture assembly sector, showcasing its effectiveness in handling the complexities of diverse product lines and automation requirements.

In alignment with ESG considerations, Brunoe et al. [21] employ modular product design as a strategy to reduce production costs. Their research addresses concerns related to "quality degradation resulting from modularization" and "reconfiguration expenses" by introducing a non-linear coding approach using an integer paradigm. This model is designed to optimize the selection of components or subsets within modular items, with a focus on minimizing the overall environmental impact and resource utilization of the production system. The approach is applied to a specific case involving the modular construction of a ball screw and a DC motor, with outcomes demonstrating its effectiveness in achieving cost reduction while adhering to ESG principles.

Vaz-Serra et al. [22], delve into the application of mass customization principles in the production of sheet metal components, taking into account environmental and sustainability considerations within the ESG framework. Their study proposes two strategies for reducing costs and environmental impact: standardizing geometric forms and designing integrated parts. Additionally, the authors introduce a methodology for the integration of components and subassemblies within the parts, not only improving production efficiency but also aligning with ESG goals related to resource efficiency and waste reduction.

Incorporated ESG principles by adhering to industry standards, optimizing product integration, and making thoughtful supplier choices [23].

Designing product families and optimizing supply chains is vital not only for business efficiency but also for aligning with ESG principles. This process involves creating groups of related products and strategically planning the supply chain to maximize sustainability, minimize environmental impact, and enhance social responsibility. By doing so, companies can effectively meet consumer demands, reduce waste, and contribute to a more sustainable and ethical business ecosystem [24].

Incorporate Product Lifetime principles into product development while considering the structure of the supply chain. This approach not only extends product durability but also considers the sustainability and efficiency of the entire supply chain. By doing so, businesses can minimize resource consumption, reduce waste, and promote responsible sourcing and distribution practices, all in alignment with ESG objectives [25].

Take into account both environmental sustainability and social responsibility. This approach ensures that business practices and decisions prioritize ecological preservation, such as reducing carbon emissions and conserving resources, while also addressing social issues like fair labor practices, diversity, and community engagement. By embracing these principles, organizations can contribute to a more sustainable and ethical business landscape in line with ESG criteria [26].

Optimize modularity while considering the level of product integration. Striking the right balance between modularity and integration is essential for both business efficiency and ESG compliance. This approach ensures that products can be efficiently assembled, maintained, and upgraded while minimizing waste and resource consumption, aligning with sustainability and social responsibility goals [27].

Carefully consider component selection for mass-customized products, taking into account ESG considerations. This approach involves choosing components that not only meet customization requirements but also adhere to sustainability principles, ethical sourcing, and social responsibility standards. By making responsible component choices, companies can deliver personalized products while aligning with ESG values and promoting a more sustainable and ethical business model et al. [28].

Consider the limitations imposed by guaranteed service time and carbon emissions. This perspective ensures that business operations and product designs adhere to commitments related to service quality and environmental sustainability. By addressing these constraints, companies can better meet customer expectations, reduce their carbon footprint, and align with ESG principles, promoting responsible and sustainable practices [29].

Factor in the limitations imposed by carbon emission regulations. This approach ensures that business operations and product development align with environmental sustainability standards and legal requirements. By proactively addressing these constraints, companies can comply with carbon emission regulations, reduce their environmental impact, and contribute to a more sustainable and ESG compliant business ecosystem [30].

Select product and supply chain iterations with a focus on improving sustainability, efficiency, and social responsibility. This approach involves refining and optimizing both the product design and supply chain processes to align with ESG objectives. By continuously reviewing and enhancing these iterations, companies can reduce their environmental impact, promote ethical practices, and contribute to a more sustainable business ecosystem [31].

Reconfigure product and supply chain design strategies while considering both ESG and Mass Customization (MC) elements. This approach entails adapting the design of products and supply chains to not only fulfill customized demands but also uphold sustainability, social responsibility, and ethical standards. By continually refining these strategies, companies can reduce their environmental impact, promote ethical practices, and provide tailored solutions that align seamlessly with both ESG and MC goals [32].

Thoroughly analyze demand, capacity, bill of materials, lead time, and transportation flow constraints. This comprehensive examination ensures that business operations and supply chain processes consider these factors, contributing to efficient resource allocation, reduced waste, and adherence to ESG principles with implementations of MC techniques. By addressing these restrictions, companies can better manage customer demand, optimize production capacity, and minimize environmental and social impacts, in line with ESG objectives [33].

Determine the ideal degree of re-manufacturability. This involves identifying the most efficient and sustainable level at which products can be remanufactured, considering both ESG criteria and business objectives. Striking the right balance in re-manufacturability ensures that products can be effectively refurbished, reducing waste and resource consumption while meeting environmental and social responsibility goals [34].

Strategize for demand and supply alignment, supplier choice, and inventory level optimization using mass customization with a strong focus on ESG considerations. This approach involves planning to ensure that supply meets demand efficiently, selecting suppliers who adhere to sustainability and ethical standards, and optimizing inventory levels to minimize waste and resource consumption. By incorporating ESG principles into these planning processes, businesses can achieve sustainable and responsible operations [35].

Consider a product's configuration, the degree of product integration, and supplier selection carefully, factoring in ESG principles. This approach ensures that product designs, integration levels, and supplier choices align with sustainability and ethical standards. By making responsible decisions in these areas, companies can deliver products that meet customization needs while adhering to ESG values and promoting a more sustainable and ethical business model [36].

Efficiently optimize the level of product integration and supplier selection while incorporating ESG principles. Plan demand and supply strategies with sustainability in mind, and design modular products that align with both customization requirements and environmental responsibility. Additionally, prioritize supply chain transparency to ensure ethical practices and adherence to ESG standards throughout the entire process. By integrating these considerations, businesses can deliver tailored solutions while upholding responsible and sustainable practices [37, 38].

Conduct a comprehensive examination of the societal and environmental implications, with a primary focus on environmental preservation. This involves carefully assessing how actions and decisions affect both society and the natural world. Prioritize the safeguarding of the environment by considering sustainability practices and measures. By doing so, businesses can contribute to a healthier planet while also being mindful of their social responsibilities [39, 40].

Consider both financial gains and carbon emissions, taking into account the economic and environmental benefits. This approach involves evaluating the potential profits alongside the carbon footprint of various actions and decisions. By doing so, businesses can make informed choices that not only enhance their financial well-being but also contribute to environmental preservation, thus achieving a balance between economic and environmental advantages [41, 42]. A mixed-integer linear programming approach is possible to optimize the allocation of production tasks for individual products. The objective is to simultaneously cut down on supply chain costs and carbon emissions, resulting in advantages for individuals, the environment, and profitability [41]. Additionally, a stochastic mixed-integer programming model is suggested, incorporating economic variables, environmental impacts, and demand uncertainties, emphasizing the potential benefits for people, the planet, and financial returns [42].

6 Promising and Trending Future Research Trajectories

Certainly, implementing strategies like Mass Customization, SMH model, Modularization, DFMC, DFM, and Human Resource Development (HRD) can have significant positive impacts on organizations. Here's a breakdown of how each of these strategies can benefit organizations:

Mass Customization: Mass customization allows organizations to provide tailored products to individual customers at a competitive cost. This can lead to increased customer satisfaction, stronger brand loyalty, and a competitive edge in the market.

Standard Man Hour (SMH) Model: The SMH model helps organizations estimate and optimize the time required for various tasks in manufacturing and other processes. This can lead to improved resource allocation, better project planning, and increased productivity.

Modularization: Modular design simplifies product development and manufacturing by breaking products into standardized modules or components. This enhances flexibility, reduces lead times, and facilitates easier adaptation to changing customer requirements.

DFMC (Design for Mass Customization): DFMC focuses on designing products with an emphasis on efficient manufacturing and cost-effectiveness. By optimizing product designs for easy manufacturing, organizations can reduce production costs and improve product quality.

DFM (Design for Manufacturing): DFM ensures that product designs are manufacturable with minimal complexity. This reduces the risk of production errors, enhances product quality, and streamlines the manufacturing process.

DFSC (Design for Supply Chain): DFSC involves considering supply chain factors during product design. This leads to better supply chain integration, reduced logistics costs, shorter lead times, and improved overall supply chain efficiency.

Human Resource Development (HRD): Mass customization is centered around catering to the unique and personalized preferences of customers, making their satisfaction a paramount objective. Achieving this goal necessitates alterations in design and processes, where the role of human resources becomes pivotal. Investigating the influence of diverse human resource management practices, such as training, collaboration initiatives, job rotation, and group or individual incentives and rewards, on the capacity for mass customization within the field of management offers promising avenues for future research.

7 Conclusion

We have meticulously distilled manufacturing, supply chain management, and bespoke design synthesis strategies for mass customization. What distinguishes our analysis is its holistic view of these design imperatives, exploring their intricate interplay. We delve deep into design attributes, frameworks, and decision-making protocols, charting pathways for advancing DFMC, DFM, and DFSC domains amidst dynamic environmental factors and customer behaviours. Our review serves as a navigational guide for manufacturers, addressing challenges in management while leveraging mass customization and

SMH modelling tools in a fiercely competitive arena, considering people, the planet, and profitability. In the evolving landscape of the manufacturing industries, the convergence of Mass Customization, the SMH model, and Modularization stands as a catalyst for transformation in the era of Industry 4.0. These interlinked concepts, when harnessed effectively, not only promise enhanced operational efficiency but also align the industry with Environmental, Social, and Governance (ESG) principles, thereby fostering sustainability.

Figure 3 presents a definitive perspective of the research conducted on mass customization, characterized by scholarly and distinctive attributes.

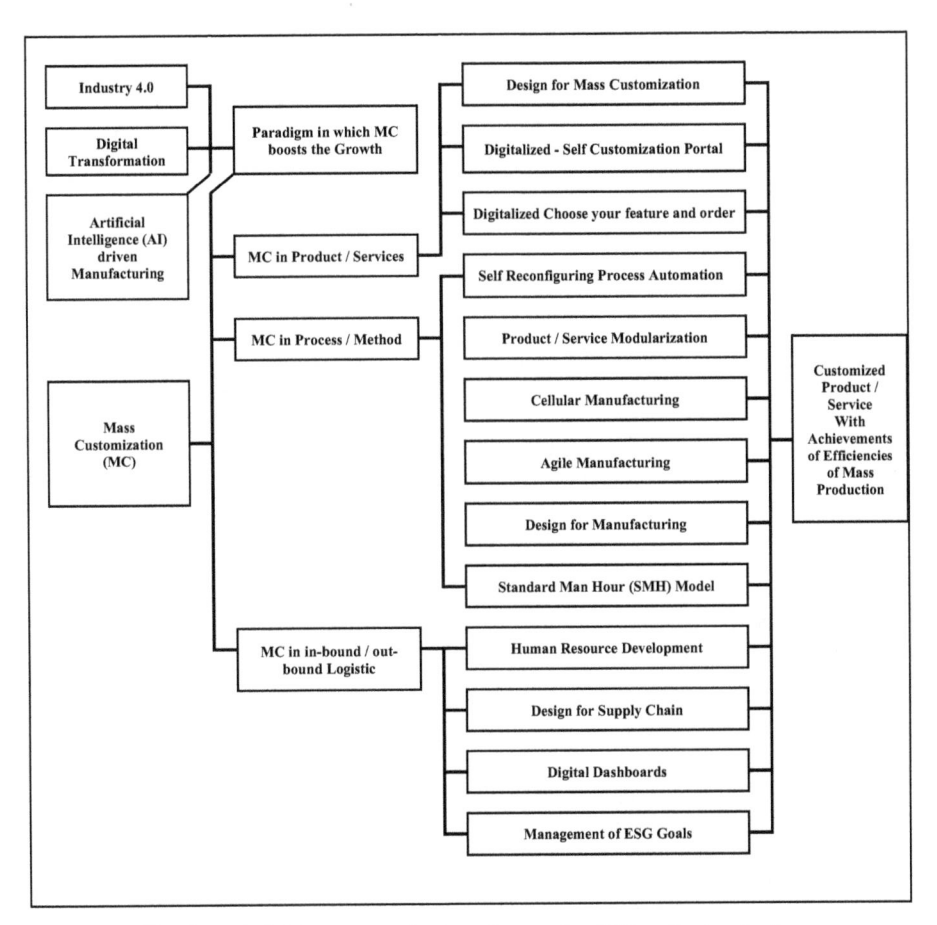

Fig. 3. A definitive perspective based on study of Mass Customization

In conclusion, the manufacturing industries find themselves at a pivotal juncture, where Mass Customization, the SMH model, and Modularization intersect with ESG principles, Industry 4.0, DFMC, DFM, DFSC, and HRD. This convergence represents an opportunity not only to optimize operations but also to uphold sustainability and ethical values. To thrive in this new industrial era, organizations must embrace these principles holistically, recognizing that the heart of this transformation lies in nurturing a workforce equipped for innovation and guided by the values of responsibility and adaptability. As they embark on this transformative journey, these industries can not only meet the demands of the present but also shape a more sustainable and agile future.

As we continue our journey of exploration, we anticipate that the fusion of SMH and MCDM methodologies will become an invaluable asset for industries seeking to excel in both efficiency and quality. It represents a convergence of precision, sustainability, and innovation, propelling manufacturing into a future where mass customization and environmental responsibility are harmoniously intertwined, shaping a more prosperous and responsible world of production.

References

1. Pine, B.J.: Mass customizing products and services. Plan. Rev. **21**(4), 6–55 (1993)
2. Toffler, A.: Future shock, 1970. Pan, Sydney (1970)
3. Davis, S.M.: Future perfect. In Human Resource Management in International Firms: Change, Globalization, Innovation, in Evans, P., Doz, Y., Laurent, A. (eds.). London, Palgrave Macmillan UK, pp. 18–28 (1990). https://doi.org/10.1007/978-1-349-11255-5_2
4. Modrak, V., Soltysova, Z.: Management of product configuration conflicts to increase the sustainability of mass customization. Sustainability (Switzerland), **12**(9) (2020), https://doi.org/10.3390/su12093610
5. Purohit, Y., Parkhi, S.: Evolution study of mass customization and its SWOT analysis for business management practices. J. Namibian Stud.: History Polit. Cult. **35**, 3413–3428 (2023). https://doi.org/10.59670/jns.v35i.4236
6. Hou, S., Gao, J., Wang, C.: Design for mass customisation, design for manufacturing, and design for supply chain: A review of the literature. IET Collab. Intell. Manuf. **4**(1), 1–16 (2022)
7. Cinelli, M., Ferraro, G., Iovanella, A., Lucci, G., Schiraldi, M.M.: A network perspective for the analysis of bill of material. Procedia CIRP **88**, 19–24 (2020)
8. Formentini, G., Boix Rodríguez, N., Favi, C.: Design for manufacturing and assembly methods in the product development process of mechanical products: a systematic literature review. J. Adv. Manuf. Technol., **120**(7–8), 4307–4334 (2022)
9. M. I. Abd Razak, M. A. Khoiry, W. H. Wan Badaruzzaman, and A. H. Hussain, "DfMA for a Better Industrialised Building System. Buildings 2022, 12, 794." s Note: MDPI stays neutral with regard to jurisdictional claims in published …, 2022
10. Ferro, R., Cordeiro, G.A., Ordóñez, R.E.C., Beydoun, G., Shukla, N.: An optimization tool for production planning: a case study in a textile industry. Appl. Sci. **11**(18), 8312 (2021)
11. Tripathi, V., et al.: Development of a data-driven decision-making system using lean and smart manufacturing concept in industry 4.0: a case study. Math. Probl. Eng., **2022** (2022)
12. Bai, X., Huerta, O., Unver, E., Allen, J., Clayton, J.E.: A parametric product design framework for the development of mass customized head/face (eyewear) products. Appl. Sci. **11**(12), 5382 (2021)
13. Marconi, M., Papetti, A., Scafà, M., Rossi, M., Germani, M.: An innovative framework for managing the customization of tailor-made shoes. In Proceedings of the Design Society: International Conference on Engineering Design, Cambridge University Press, pp. 3821–3830 (2019)
14. Mandolini, M., Campi, F., Favi, C., Cicconi, P., Germani, M.: An analytical cost model for investment casting. In Proceedings of the Design Society: DESIGN Conference, Cambridge University Press, pp. 987–996 (2020)

15. Alfaify, A., Saleh, M., Abdullah, F.M., Al-Ahmari, A.M.: Design for additive manufacturing: a systematic review. Sustainability **12**(19), 7936 (2020)
16. Shahbazi, S., Jönbrink, A.K.: Design guidelines to develop circular products: action research on nordic industry. Sustainability **12**(9), 3679 (2020)
17. De Fazio, F., Bakker, C., Flipsen, B., Balkenende, R.: The disassembly map: a new method to enhance design for product repairability. J. Clean. Prod. **320**, 128552 (2021)
18. Asadi, N., Jackson, M., Fundin, A.: Implications of realizing mix flexibility in assembly systems for product modularity—a case study. J. Manuf. Syst., **52**, 13–22 (2019)
19. Asif, F.M.A., Roci, M., Lieder, M., Rashid, A., Mihelič, A., Kotnik, S.: A methodological approach to design products for multiple lifecycles in the context of circular manufacturing systems. J. Clean. Prod. **296**, 126534 (2021)
20. Kunic, A., Naboni, R., Kramberger, A., Schlette, C.: Design and assembly automation of the robotic reversible Timber Beam. Autom. Constr. **123**, 103531 (2021)
21. Brunoe, T.D., Soerensen, D.G.H., Nielsen, K.: Modular design method for reconfigurable manufacturing systems. Procedia CIRP **104**, 1275–1279 (2021)
22. Vaz-Serra, P., Wasim, M., Egglestone, S.: Design for manufacture and assembly: a case study for a prefabricated bathroom wet wall panel. J. Build. Eng. **44**, 102849 (2021)
23. Taherdoost, H., Brard, A.: Analyzing the process of supplier selection criteria and methods. Procedia Manuf. **32**, 1024–1034 (2019)
24. Wang, Q., Qi, P., Li, S.: A concurrence optimization model for low-carbon product family design and the procurement plan of components under uncertainty. Sustainability **13**(19), 10764 (2021)
25. Chen, J., Wang, H., Fu, Y.: A multi-stage supply chain disruption mitigation strategy considering product life cycle during COVID-19. Environ. Sci. Pollut. Res., pp. 1–15 (2022)
26. Honarvar, M., Alimohammadi Ardakani, M., Modarres, M.: A particle swarm optimization algorithm for solving pricing and lead time quotation in a dual-channel supply chain with multiple customer classes. Adv. Oper. Res., **2020** (2020)
27. Huang, D., Xu, X., Zhang, Y., Xia, X.: Improved interactive genetic algorithm for three-dimensional vase modeling design. Comput. Intell. Neurosci., **2022** (2022)
28. Briskorn, D., Wensing, T.: The replenishment problem with multiple articles and an order threshold. Comput. Oper. Res. **136**, 105485 (2021)
29. Luo, Y., Wei, Q., Ling, Q., Huo, B.: Optimal decision in a green supply chain: bank financing or supplier financing. J. Clean. Prod. **271**, 122090 (2020)
30. Yılmaz, Ö.F., Özçelik, G., Yeni, F.B.: Ensuring sustainability in the reverse supply chain in case of the ripple effect: a two-stage stochastic optimization model. J. Clean. Prod. **282**, 124548 (2021)
31. Taifouris, M., Martín, M., Martínez, A., Esquejo, N.: Simultaneous optimization of the design of the product, process, and supply chain for formulated product. Comput. Chem. Eng. **152**, 107384 (2021)
32. Varl, M., Duhovnik, J., Tavčar, J.: Changeability and agility enablers in one-of-a-kind product development and design processes. Res. Eng. Des., pp. 1–18 (2021)
33. Wang, J., Wang, X., Yu, M.: Multi-period multi-product supply chain network design in the competitive environment. Math. Probl. Eng. **2020**, 1–15 (2020)
34. Zhou, Y., Liu, X.-Q., Wong, K.-H.: Remanufacturing policies options for a closed-loop supply chain network. Sustainability **13**(12), 6640 (2021)
35. Abdallah, K.S., El-Beheiry, M.M.: The effect of planning horizon and information sharing on the optimisation of the distribution network of a fast-moving consumer goods supply chain. J. Transp. Supply Chain Manage. **16**, 788 (2022)
36. M. Azam, M. S. Ali Khan, and S. Yang, "A decision-making approach for the evaluation of information security management under complex intuitionistic fuzzy set environment," Journal of Mathematics, vol. 2022, pp. 1–30, 2022

37. Katsaliaki, K., Galetsi, P., Kumar, S.: Supply chain disruptions and resilience: a major review and future research agenda. Ann. Oper. Res., pp. 1–38 (2021)
38. Dadhich, M., Hiran, K.K.: Empirical investigation of extended TOE model on corporate environment sustainability and dimensions of operating performance of SMEs: A high order PLS-ANN approach. J. Clean. Prod. **363**, 132309 (2022). https://doi.org/10.1016/j.jclepro.2022.132309
39. Hajiaghaei-Keshteli, M., Fathollahi Fard, A.M.: Sustainable closed-loop supply chain network design with discount supposition. Neural Comput. Appl., **31**(9), 5343–5377 (2019), https://doi.org/10.1007/s00521-018-3369-5
40. Konyalıoğlu, A.K., Zafeirakopoulos, İ.B.: A literature review on closed loop supply chains. In Proceedings of the International Symposium for Production Research 2019, Springer, pp. 547–556 (2020)
41. Beheshtinia, M.A., Feizollahy, P., Fathi, M.: Supply chain optimization considering sustainability aspects. Sustainability **13**(21), 11873 (2021)
42. Wang, C.-N., Nhieu, N.-L., Chung, Y.-C., Pham, H.-T.: Multi-objective optimization models for sustainable perishable intermodal multi-product networks with delivery time window. Mathematics **9**(4), 379 (2021)

Quality of Life as a Factor in Integrating Research into the Resilience of Energy and Socio-Ecological Systems

Liudmila V. Massel(✉), Aleksei G. Massel, and Dmitrii V. Pesterev

Melentiev Energy Systems Institute SB RAS, 130, Lermontova Street, Irkutsk 664033, Russia
massel@isem.irk.ru

Abstract. It is proposed to use the quality of life as an integration factor of resilience research of energy and socio-ecological systems. Resilience is not considered in the classical sense, as sustainability, but as the ability of a system to return to equilibrium after disturbances. Resilience criteria of energy, ecological and social systems are introduced. Cognitive modeling is proposed as one of the main tools in resilience research. Examples of cognitive modeling are given. Architecture of Web-oriented Information-Computing System (WICS) and general architecture of the intelligent integrate instrumental environment for research into the Resilience of Energy, Ecological and Social Systems (REESS) are shown.

Keywords: Resilience · Quality of life · Energy and socio-ecological systems · Ontology and cognitive modeling · Resilience criteria · Tools for research

1 Introduction

Resilience is not considered in the classical sense, as sustainability, but as the ability of a system to return to equilibrium, or rather, the ability to return to equilibrium and develop, despite further shocks and disturbances [1]. Recently, a direction defined by the term "Resilience", has attracted great interest [1–6]. In Russia, these studies are conducted mainly in the field of technical sustainability, while in Western Europe they consider this area more broadly and also include environmental, psychological, social and economic resilience. On the other hand, the factors that determine social resilience in foreign studies echo the factors used to assess the quality of life in these studies carried out in Russia.

Socio-ecological systems are understood as natural systems that are very sensitive to anthropogenic impacts and social [7]. According to the ecological approach, resilience is a measure of the permanence of ecosystems and their ability to adapt to changes and disturbances and still maintain the same relationships between the population or the state [2]. The concepts of permanence, change and unpredictability in this definition differ from efficiency, constancy and predictability in technical stability. Eco-system resilience refers to the ability to absorb disturbances and reorganize while the system undergoes change.

Issues of energy and environmental security are of great importance in resilience research. An important aspect of ensuring the country's energy security (ES) [8, 9] is the study of the negative impact of natural disasters on energy systems in order to reduce the risks of major systemic accidents that have a significant impact on the quality of life of the population. Natural risks such as earthquakes, storms, floods, and extreme heat waves are cited as the main causes of cascading failures in power systems. Recent evidence suggests that climate change is leading to an increase in the number of extreme natural disasters that can lead to systemic accidents.

When considering social resilience, the following factors are identified: moral values, realistic optimism, stable role models, receiving social support, mental and emotional flexibility, meaning in life and goals, spiritual practices, physical activity, and the ability to confront fears. There is a strong focus on the link between disaster risk reduction and resilience. One of the factors of social resilience is quality of life.

Quality of life has not been taken into account in energy research in Russia until recently. In addition, the population traditionally belonged to the category of household consumers, whose needs were taken into account last. The development of such a scientific direction as research into quality of life requires reconsidering the current situation and considering quality of life as a category associated not only with health, but also with the influence of external factors: environmental, economic and energy, including population provision with energy resources, which is directly related to the problem of energy security. This problem was considered by the authors in [10].

2 The Quality of Life

This concept was first introduced into the scientific revolution in the 60's of the last century in connection with attempts by foreign researchers to model the trajectories of industrial development. There are many different definitions of the quality of life, but this concept is most fully disclosed in the context of health care.

The world scientific community understands quality of life as a set of objective and subjective parameters that characterize the maximum number of aspects of a person's life, his position in society and satisfaction with it. The integral indicator of quality of life summarizes indicators of health, social well-being, subjective social well-being and well-being. Quality of life ontology integrating energy, environment and social factors is shown in Fig. 1.

The quality of life is differentiated from the widely used concept of "standard of living," which refers exclusively to the material component. J. Forrester suggested that the level and quality of life are inversely related to one another: the higher the standard of living associated with the growth rate of industrial production, the faster mineral resources are depleted, the faster the natural environment is polluted, the higher the population density, People's health is worse, there are more stressful situations, that is, the quality of life is deteriorating.

The ontology was developed in a team represented by the authors (developer T.N. Vorozhtsova).

The ontology shown in Fig. 1 illustrates the integration role of the "quality of life" indicator and reflects the connection between the concepts "regional economy", "regional energy" and "regional ecology". Energy facilities create a negative anthropogenic

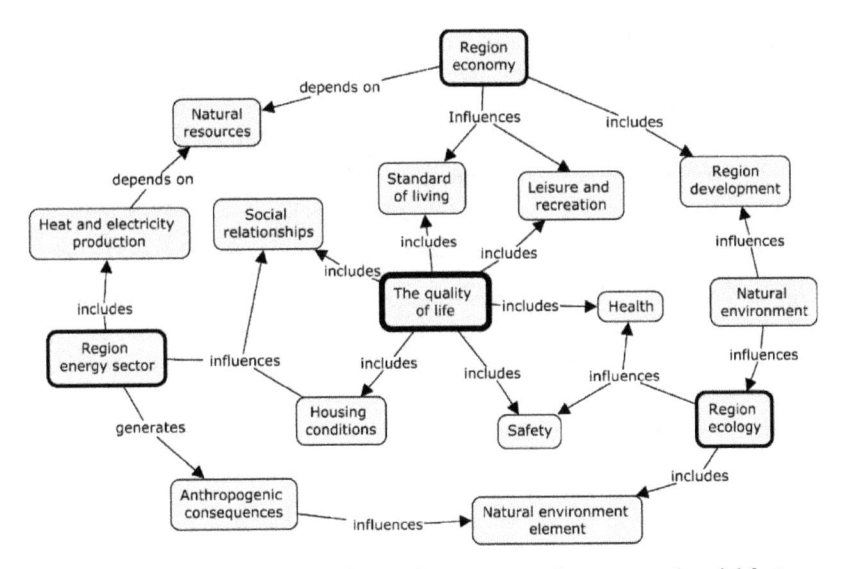

Quality of Life as a Factor in Integrating Research 109

Fig. 1. Quality of life ontology integrating energy, environment and social factors

impact on elements of the natural environment, and, accordingly, deteriorate the ecology of the region, what affects on the health and safety of people, reducing the level of quality of life.

On the other hand, energy resources are necessary to improve housing conditions and social infrastructure, which increases the quality of life. The economy of the region is connected with the development of the region, depends on the natural resources necessary for the production of heat and electricity and affects the standard of living, and, indirectly, the quality of life. In turn, natural conditions are related to the ecology of the region and also affect the development of the territory, and, accordingly, the economy of the region.

Thus, the quality of life depends on the state of the energy infrastructure (the provision of energy resources of the required quality and in the required volume), the environmental situation in the region, which affects health and safety – important factors in the quality of life, and the economic development of the region, which determines the standard of living, what also affects on the quality of life. It follows that to assess the quality of life it is necessary to integrate the results of studies on the resilience of energy, environmental and social systems.

3 Resilience Criteria

For energy systems, such criteria may be indicators of the availability of energy resources of the required quality and in the required volume (i.e. quantitative criteria - indicators of energy security). An example of energy security indicators for regional level is shown in Fig. 2 [9].

For ecological systems: MPC values (maximum permissible concentrations) can act as quantitative criteria for resilience of ecological systems. Qualitative criteria can be, for example, total and specific (per person and GDP (gross domestic product)),

CO_2 emissions; greenhouse gas emissions trend; efficiency of energy production and consumption; share of renewable energy sources and nuclear power plants, etc.

For social systems, resilience criteria can be the main indicators of quality of life: the state of the environment, health, social relationships, self-realization (work, education), safety, emotional and financial well-being; provision of energy resources.

Until recently, energy research has not taken into account the quality of life. In addition, the population has traditionally been classified as household consumers, whose needs were taken into account last. The development of such a scientific direction as research into the quality of life requires reconsidering the current situation and considering the quality of life as a category associated not only with health, but also with the influence of external factors, including such as the provision of energy resources to the population, which is directly related to the problem energy security.

Since objective-subjective indicators are used to assess the quality of life, to comprehensively solve the problem it is necessary to involve qualitative methods of system analysis, in particular, semantic modeling, which can be considered together with mathematical modeling in the presence of the quantitative information necessary for mathematical models.

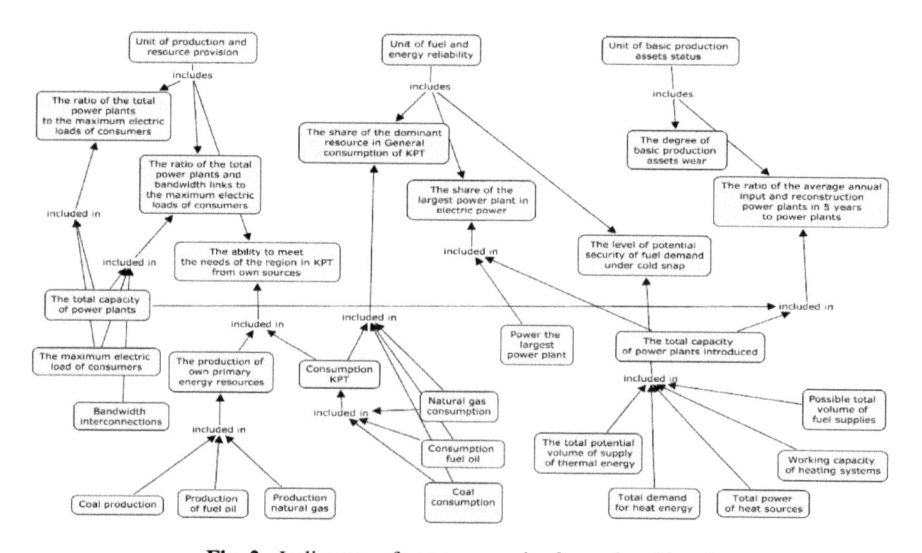

Fig. 2. Indicators of energy security for regional level

The ontology was developed in a team represented by the authors (developer T.N. Vorozhtsova).

Comments on Fig. 2. Energy security indicators are classified according to the range of numerical values on the scale: "norm – pre-crisis – crisis". If the indicator values are within the range defined as "norm", the system is in a stable state. It is possible to carry out preventive measures to maintain the system in this state. If the values of the indicators move into the "pre-crisis" range, there is a risk of the system transitioning to an unstable state, and prompt measures are necessary to prevent the transition to the "crisis" range. If the indicator values are in the "crisis" range – in an emergency situation (ES), it is necessary to take liquidation measures to transfer the system to a stable state and eliminate the consequences of the emergency.

In Figs. 2, 3 groups of indicators are identified (for the regional level): 1) "Unit of production and resource provision", 2) "Unit of reliability of fuel and energy supply" and 3) "Unit of basic production assets status". In the last unit, important indicators are "The degree of basic production assets wear" and "The ratio of the average annual input and reconstruction in 5 years to capacity of the region power plants"; the latter is associated with the indicator "Total capacity of power plants introduced in the region" from the first Unit of production and resource provision.

Second "Unit of reliability of fuel and energy supply" includes indicators: 1) "Share of the dominant resource in the general consumption of boiler and furnace fuel", 2) "Share of the largest power plant in electric power (it includes indicators: "Power of the largest power plant" and "Total capacity of power plants introduced") and 3) "The level of potential security of fuel demand under cold snap."

The first "Unit of production and resource provision" includes the following indicators: 1) "The ratio of the total power plants to the maximum electrical load of consumers" (it includes the indicators "Total capacity of power plants", "Maximum electrical load of consumers" and "Bandwidth of system interconnections"; 2) "The ratio of the total power plants and Bandwidth links to the maximum electrical load of consumers"; 3) "The ability to meet the region's needs in boiler and furnace fuel from its own sources." The latter is determined by the indicators "Production of own primary fuel and energy resources" (determined by the indicators "Coal production", "Production of fuel oil", "Natural gas production") and "Consumption of boiler and furnace fuel" (determined by the indicators "Natural gas consumption", "Consumption fuel oil" and "Coal consumption".

All these indicators are calculated using the multi-agent software package "INTEC-A" (see Fig. 8 and comments to this).

Ontology of the energy sector impact on the environment is shown in Fig. 3.

Comments on Fig. 3. Figure 3 shows that humans create and use energy enterprises including electric power stations, boiler plants, enterprises for resource extraction and transportation. These enterprises pollute the environment: water, air and soil. Pollution from energy facilities, both directly and through vegetation, affects fauna. In addition to the direct negative impact of pollution, humans are adversely affected by contaminated flora and fauna, the products of which a person consumes.

4   Tools for Resilience Research

Under the leadership of L.V. Massel proposed and developed the idea of using cognitive modeling for an integral assessment of quality of life [11, 12]. This is one of the types of semantic modeling, based on the construction of cognitive models that describe the main concepts of the simulated situations and the cause-and-effect relationships between the concepts. Their graphical display is called cognitive maps. Cognitive modeling is actively being developed and used both in Russia (for example, at the Institute of Management Problems of the Russian Academy of Sciences) [13] and in Greece [14, 15], etc. The author's tool CogMap is used for cognitive modeling (Fig. 4).

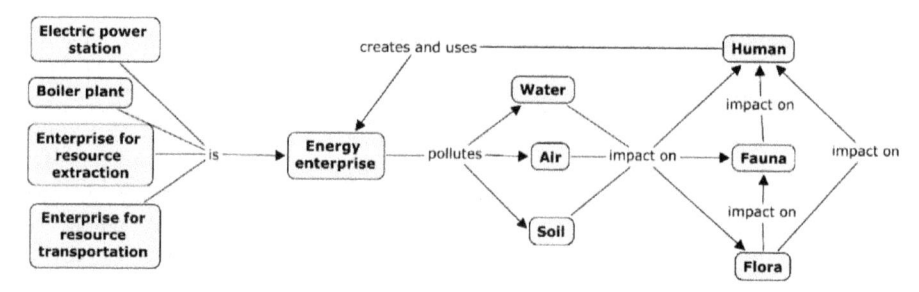

Fig. 3. Ontology of the energy sector impact on the environment

An example of a cognitive map illustrating the impact of lower air temperatures on energy production is shown in Fig. 4. As the temperature decreases, the need for heat and electricity increases (the relationship between the concepts is negative). In turn, an increase in the demand for heat and electricity requires an increase in the production of these resources (positive connections), and, accordingly, the introduction of additional capacities (positive connection). An increase in the production of energy resources requires an increase in fuel consumption (positive connection), and an increase in fuel consumption leads to a decrease in its reserves (negative connection). To replenish fuel reserves, either an increase in its production or an increase in the purchase (export) of fuel is required (positive connections).

Thus, if the changes in concepts are the same: an increase (or decrease) in the value of one concept leads to an increase (or decrease) in another - the connections are positive. If the changes are multidirectional: an increase (or decrease) in one concept, on the contrary, leads to a decrease (or increase) in another concept – the connections are negative. In more complex cases, it is possible to calculate the weighting coefficients of connections that determine the degree of influence of one concept on another.

With the help of the cognitive modeling tool CogMap, developed by the team represented by the authors, a cognitive map of the integral assessment of the quality of life was built, based on the SF-36 methodology used by sociologists in Russia, which included the external factor "Provision of energy resources"; to determine it, a questionnaire was created for a social survey of the population (Figs. 5, 6) [11, 12].

Adaptation of the situational management concept [16], previously used by the authors in research on energy security, to resilience research allows the use previously developed the entire range of semantic modeling tools (ontological, cognitive, event-based and probabilistic, based on Bayesian belief networks).

Tools will also be used to support knowledge management technology, ensuring the transformation of cause-and-effect relationships of cognitive maps into rules for the production of an expert system and their subsequent analysis using the inference mechanism of the expert system [17].

To assess the resilience of environmental systems, the information and computing system WICS (Fig. 7), developed by a team represented by the authors (developer V.R. Kuzmin), will be used to assess environmental pollution by objects [18].

Comments on Fig. 5, Fig. 6.
On these cognitive maps:

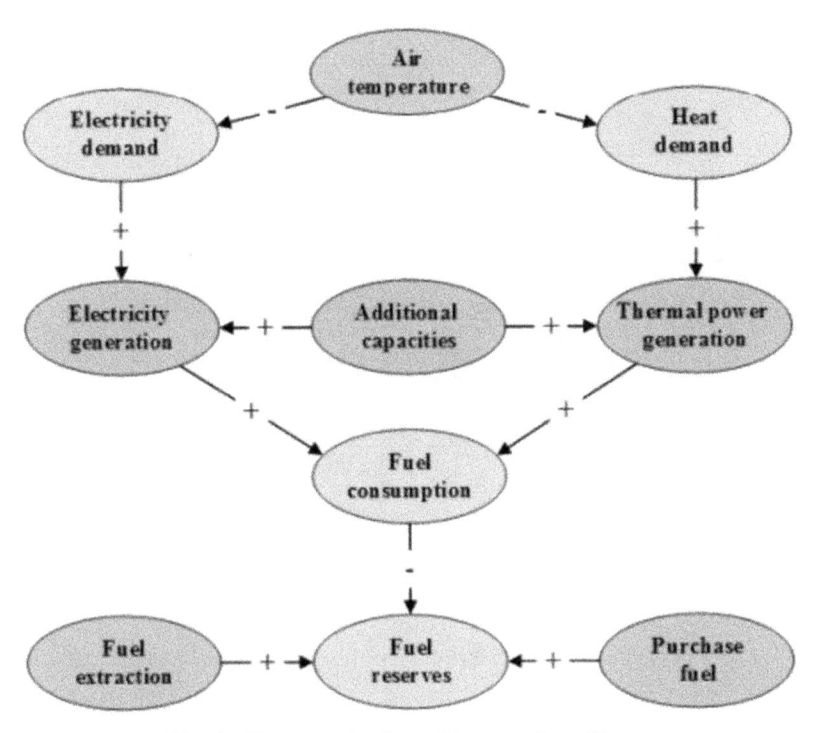

Quality of Life as a Factor in Integrating Research 113

Fig. 4. The example of cognitive map for cold treat

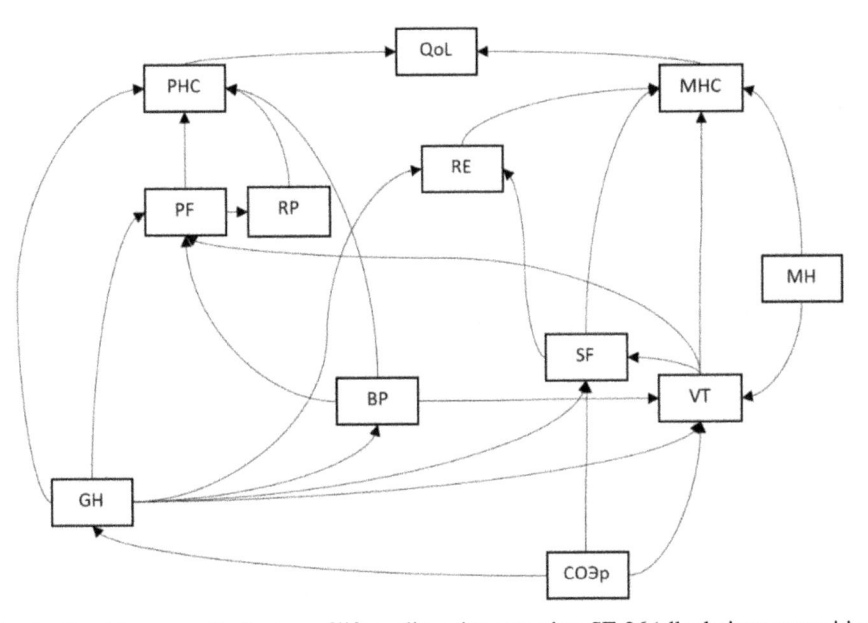

Fig. 5. Cognitive map of indicators of life quality using procedure SF-36 (all relations are positive)

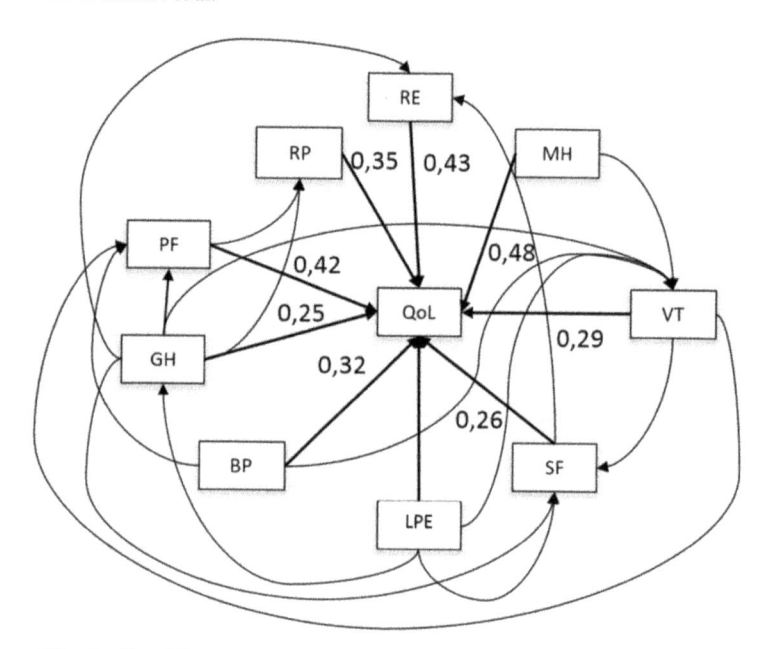

Fig. 6. Cognitive map of indicators of life quality using procedure SF-36

- PF – Physical Functioning;
- RP (Role-Physical Functioning) – role functioning conditioned by physical state;
- BP (Bodily pain) – pain intensity;
- GH – General Health;
- VT (Vitality) – life activity;
- SF – Social Functioning;
- RE (Role-Emotional) – role functioning preconditioned by emotional state;
- MH – Mental Health;
- PHC (Physical health) – general component of physical health;
- MHC (Mental health) – general component of mental health;
- QoL (QualityofLife) – integral indicator of quality of life;
- СОЭр (DSEr) – degree of supply with energy resources.

Cognitive map in Fig. 5 illustrates the relationships between the main health-related quality of life factors. The signs " +" and "-" are not indicated, since all connections are positive. It has been shown that Degree of Supply with Energy Resources (DSEr) influences on GH – General Health, SF – Social Functioning and VT (Vitality) – Life Activity. Figure 6 shows a cognitive map (corresponding to the map in Fig. 5) indicating the weighting coefficients that determine the degree of influence of factors on the integral indicator of quality of life. The weights of the influence factors of supply with energy resources (DSEr) on QoL have not yet been determined.

Comments on Fig. 7

- IS PEF – implements calculations of quantitative indicators of pollutant emissions (pollutants) from an energy facility based on regulatory methods;

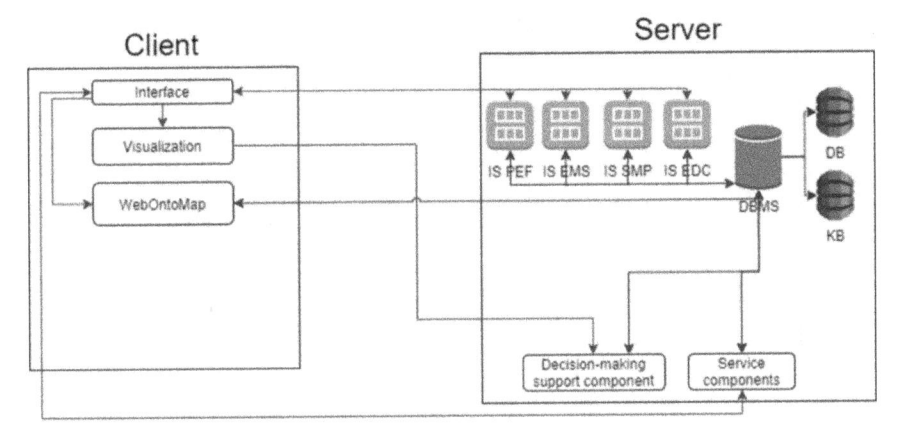

Quality of Life as a Factor in Integrating Research   115

Fig. 7. Architecture of Web-oriented Information-Computer System (WICS)

- IS EMS – implements calculations of pollutant dispersion based on standard methods using the results obtained from the IS PEF subsystem;
- IS SMP – provides the user with the results of analysis of snow samples;
- IS EDC – provides work with calculations of economic damages based on existing methods and uses the calculation results obtained from the IS PEF subsystem;
- DB – database;
- KB – knowledge base;
- DBMS – Data Base Management System.

The client part includes components that provide a user interface, visualization, and a Web-based tool, WebOntoMap. The server part includes the above-mentioned subsystems for calculating quantitative indicators of pollution (PEF, EMS, SMP, EDC), DB, KB and DBMS, as well as a decision support component for improving the environmental situation and service components.

Architecture of the intelligent integrate instrumental environment for research into the **R**esilience of **E**nergy, **E**cological and **S**ocial **S**ystems (REESS) is shown in Fig. 8.

Comments on Fig. 8

- OntoMap, CogMap, BayNet and EventMap – authors tools for supporting ontological, cognitive, probabilistic (based on Bayesian belief networks) and event modeling;
- TCogMap – subsystem for converting cognitive maps into production rules of an expert system;
- WICS is a web-based information and computing system for assessing environmental pollution by energy facilities, as well as damage resulting from pollution;
- INTEC is a multi-agent software package for quantitative assessment of the state (stability) of the fuel and energy complex (TCogMap, WICS and INTEC are also proprietary developments);
- Protégé is a publicly available ontological modeling tool;
- ProExSys – accessible shells for production expert systems.
- The dotted arrows indicate that the transfer of data from these blocks to INTEC is carried out with the involvement of researchers, solid arrows – data transfer is automated.

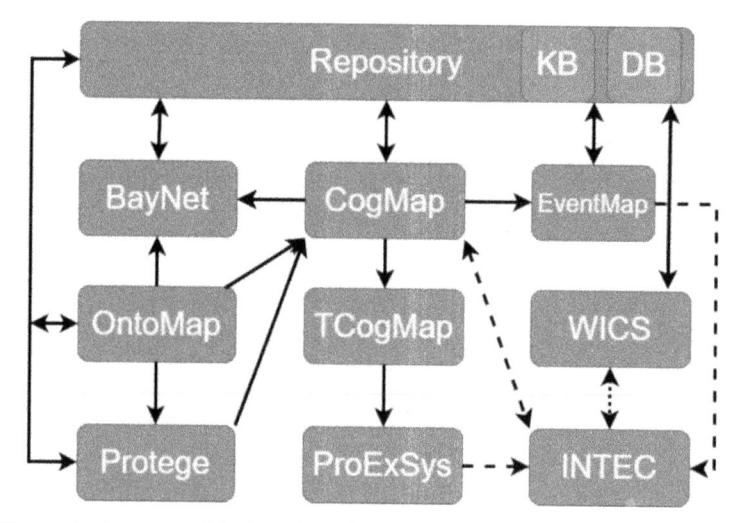

Fig. 8. Architecture of the intelligent integrate instrumental environment REESS

In Fig. 8 shows the main semantic modeling support tools (OntoMap, CogMap, BayNet and EventMap). At this stage, ontological and cognitive modeling tools are used (OntoMap, CogMap, TCogMap), but in the future it is also planned to use event and probabilistic modeling tools (BayNet and EventMap). Ontologies built using OntoMap or the open source CMapTools can be translated into the Protégé system, which has more capabilities, for example, allowing inference on ontologies. Ontologies are the basis for constructing cognitive maps (cause-and-effect relationships of concepts and weighting coefficients of connections between concepts are added). The Repository stores knowledge bases (with constructed ontologies, cognitive maps and rules of production expert systems) and WICS and INTEC databases.

The technology for converting cognitive maps into production rules of an expert system is debugged using the CLIPS shell, but it is possible to connect shells of other production expert systems (ProExSys).

Energy security indicators used as resilience indicators are calculated using the multi-agent software package "INTEC-A", and environmental resilience indicators associated with the calculation of environmental pollution by energy facilities are calculated using the WICS. Currently, the results of cognitive modeling are transferred to "INTEC-A" manually, but work is underway to integrate CogMap into "INTEC-A", after which the transfer of these results will be automated.

In addition, the composition of energy security indicators (resilience indicators) will be expanded: environmental and social blocks will be added. The environmental block may include such indicators as "Emissions of harmful substances into the atmosphere from electric power enterprises per unit area of territory", "Ratio of CO_2 emissions to the volume of gross consumption of fuel and energy resources", "CO_2 emissions per capita", etc. The social block, for example, for the energy sector, may include the following indicators: "The share of the average per capita income of the population spent on paying for energy resources", "The amount of wages in the energy sector in relation to the average in the economy", "The level of growth in the number of specialists working in the energy sector", "The effectiveness of scientific-research and development work in the field of traditional and non-traditional energy." After these blocks are included in the energy security indicators, the transfer of data from the WICS to the "INTEC-A" will be automated.

A generalized technology for researching energy and socio-ecological systems using tools integrated into REESS is given in Table 1.

The AQLI system (3 column) – a system for assessing quality of life indicators – was developed in a team represented by the authors (developer M.V. Kozlov) and is currently undergoing trial operation. It is proposed to use it to test the population and determine the main quality of life indicators.

Table 1. Generalized technology for researching energy and socio-ecological systems

Stage of technology	Resilience criteria	Tools	Results of stage	Where (to whom) results are transmitted
Energy Resilience Assessment	Energy Security Indicators	CogMap, ProExSYS, BayNet, INTEC-A	Cognitive maps, Knowledge base, ProExSYS, Probabilistic models, INTEC-A calculation results	Expert Researcher, Decision Maker, Knowledge base, CogMap, WICS
Ecology Resilience Assessment	MPC (maximum permissible concentration of contaminants)	WICS	Results of calculations of emissions and distribution of pollutants	INTEC-A, Expert Researcher, Decision Maker
Quality of Life Assessment (Resilience of Social Systems)	Quality of Life Indicators	CogMap, ProExSYS, AQLI – system for Assessing Quality of Life Indicators	Cognitive maps Knowledge base of ProExSYS (Expert System)	INTEC-A, Expert Researcher, Decision Maker

The novelty of the proposed approach is determined both by the multidisciplinary nature and integration of research into the resilience of energy and socio-ecological systems, and by the need to attract the attention of technical sciences to the concept of quality of life, which should play one of the determining roles in these studies.

The proposed tools were used in studies of the sustainability of energy and socio-ecological systems of the Baikal natural territory (Siberia, Russia).

Computational experiments were carried out to assess the resilience of the electric power system of the Siberian Federal District (Russia) on the example of the threat of low water using machine learning methods [19] and to assess the impact of energy facilities on the environment in the central ecological zone of the Baikal natural territory (Russia) using system WICS [20].

5 Conclusion

Integration of resilience research in energy and socio-ecological systems is relevant, given the increasing risks of natural and man-made disasters. It is necessary to attract the attention of technical sciences to the concept of "quality of life", which can be an integrating factor in these studies. Considering the need to take into account subjective factors in quality of life research, the role of semantic (ontological and cognitive) modeling in these studies is increasing. A collection of tools for studying the resilience of energy and socio-ecological systems is presented, which are combined within the framework of the intelligent integrated tool environment REESS. The novelty of the approach is formulated and the area of application is determined: research into the resilience of energy and socio-ecological systems in the Baikal natural territory (Siberia, Russia), which is represented by the authors.

Acknowledgements. The work was carried out within the framework of a project under the state order of MESI SB RAS, topic no.: FNEU-2021-0007, reg. no.: AAAA-A21-121012090007-7.

References

1. Davoudi, S.: Resilience: a bridging concept or a dead end. Plan. Theory Pract. **13**(2), 299–307 (2012)
2. Holling, C.: Engineering resilience versus ecological resilience. In: Schultz, P. (ed.) Engineering Within Ecological Constraints, pp. 31–43. National Academy Press, Washington, D.C. (1996)
3. Nan, C., Sansavini, G., Kröger, W.: Building an integrated metric for quantifying the resilience of interdependent infrastructure systems. In: Panayiotou, C., Ellinas, G., Kyriakides, E., Polycarpou, M. (eds.) CRITIS 2014. LNSC, vol. 8985, pp. 159–171. Springer, Cham (2016). https://doi.org/10.1007/978-3-319-31664-2_17
4. Cimellaro, G., Reinhyorn, A., Bruneau, M.: Seismic resilience of a hospital system. Struct. Infrastruct. Eng. **6**(1–2), 127–144 (2010)
5. Wang, Y., Chen, C., Wang, J., Baldick, R.: Research on resilience of power systems under natural disasters – a review. IEEE Trans. Power Syst. **31**(2), 1604–1612 (2016)
6. Wang, Z., Nistor, M.S., Pickl, S.W.: Analysis of the definitions of resilience. In: 20th IFAC World Congress, Toulouse, France, 9–14 July 2017, pp. 11136–11144 (2017)
7. Dictionary of Geography (2015). https://geography_ru.academic.ru/. Accessed Feb 2024
8. Pyatkova, N.I., Voropay, N.I., Cheltsov, M.B. (eds.): Energy Security of Russia: Problems and Solutions. Publishing House of the SB RAS (2011). 198 p. (in Russian)
9. Senderov, S.M. (ed.): Ensuring Russia's Energy Security: Choosing Priorities. MESI SB RAS. Science, Novosibirsk (2017). 116 p. (in Russian)

10. Massel, L.V., Pesterev, D.V.: Quality of life as a factor in the integration of research into the resilience of energy, socio-ecological and socio-economic systems. Inf. Math. Technol. Sci. Manag. **3**(23), 5–16 (2021). https://doi.org/10.38028/ESI.2021.23.3.001
11. Massel', L.V., Blohin, A.A.: Cognitive modeling of indicators of quality of life: the proposed approach and example of use. Bull. NSU. Ser.: Inf. Technol. **14**(2), 72–79 (2016). (in Russian)
12. Massel', L.V., Blohin, A.A.: The method of cognitive modeling of quality of life indicators taking into account external factors. Sci. Educ. Sci. Publ. MSTU Bauman **4**, 65–75 (2016). https://doi.org/10.7463/0416.0839061. (in Russian)
13. Trahtengerc, E.A.: Computer Support of Decision-Making. SINTEG, Moscow (1998). 376 p. (in Russian)
14. Groumpos, P.P.: Intelligence and fuzzy cognitive maps: scientific issues, challenges and opportunities. Stud. Inform. Control **27**(3), 247–264 (2018). https://doi.org/10.24846/v27 i3y201801
15. Stylios, C.D., Bourgani, E., Georgopoulos, V.C.: Impact and applications of fuzzy cognitive map methodologies. In: Kosheleva, O., Shary, S., Xiang, G., Zapatrin, R. (eds.) Beyond Traditional Probabilistic Data Processing Techniques: Interval, Fuzzy etc. Methods and Their Applications. SCI, vol. 835, pp. 229–246. Springer, Cham (2020). https://doi.org/10.1007/978-3-030-31041-7_13
16. Pospelov, D.A.: Situational Management. Theory and Practice. Science, Moscow (1986). 284 p. (in Russian)
17. Massel', L.V., Massel, A.G., Pesterev, D.V.: Usage management technology using ontologies, cognitive models and production expert systems. News SFedU. Eng. Sci. **4**, 140–152 (2019). (in Russian)
18. Kuzmin, V.R.: Development of an information subsystem for calculating and visualizing harmful emissions from energy facilities. Inf. Math. Technol. Sci. Manag. **1**(17), 142–154 (2020). https://doi.org/10.38028/ESI.2020.17.1.011. (in Russian)
19. Massel, L.V., Massel, A.G., Mamedov, T.G., Gaskova, D.A., Tsybikov, A.R., Shchukin, N.I.: Assessing the resilience of energy systems using machine learning methods. Inf. Math. Technol. Sci. Manag. **4**(28), 248–260 (2022). https://doi.org/10.38028/ESI.2022.28.4.020. (in Russian)
20. Kuzmin, V.R., Massel, L.V.: Information and computing system for assessing the impact of energy facilities on the environment. Softw. Prod. Syst. **1**, 60–70 (2023). https://doi.org/10.15827/0236-235X.141.060-070. (in Russian)

Using Design Thinking Methodology for Advancing Employee Knowledge and Skill Sets

Aleksei Starostin[✉] and Natalia Pulyavina

Plekhanov Russian University of Economics, Moscow, Russia
starostin.a.v@hse.ru, pulyavina.ns@rea.ru

Abstract. This article explores the transformative impact of applying design thinking approach to the development of employee training systems, with a particular emphasis on human-centered innovation. Focusing on the unique context of marketplaces' pickup-points staff within the Commonwealth of Independent States (CIS) countries, the research delves into the application of design thinking principles to the evolution of training programs.

The study highlights the pivotal role of human-centered design in reshaping training systems, ensuring that they not only meet the evolving needs of employees but also contribute to enhanced organizational effectiveness. By infusing design thinking methodologies, the article unveils a paradigm shift towards a more empathetic and user-centric approach to crafting training programs.

The examination of pickup-points staff within the CIS countries injects a distinctive layer into the analysis, recognizing and navigating the cultural nuances and specificities inherent in this context. The application of design thinking emerges as a potent catalyst for tailoring training systems to resonate authentically with the diverse workforce, fostering heightened engagement and optimizing learning outcomes.

The study includes forming a portrait of the target audience of employees, identifying the factors that most significantly influence an employee's completion of educational programs.

This article provides insights into the potential of human-centered innovation in reshaping organizational learning landscapes. The findings offer practical implications for businesses, shedding light on how design thinking can be harnessed to create adaptive and culturally responsive training systems.

Keywords: Design thinking · Reshaping training programs · Human-centered education innovations · Learning & Development · Marketplaces

1 Introduction

In today's dynamic and fast-paced work environment, the continuous development of employee knowledge and skill sets is essential for the success of any organization. As businesses strive to adapt to evolving market demands and technological advancements, the need to cultivate a workforce equipped with the latest competencies has become a strategic imperative.

Amid this backdrop, the application of design thinking methodology in educational programs can become a compelling approach to foster employee growth and proficiency. Design thinking, a human-centered problem-solving methodology, has emerged as a pivotal approach in addressing complex challenges across various domains. Its application in educational programs has garnered attention due to its potential to revolutionize the learning experience for employees within organizational settings.

Design thinking is centered around understanding the needs of the end-users, generating innovative ideas, and creating practical solutions through an iterative process of prototyping and testing. In the context of educational programs, this methodology offers a unique framework to foster a culture of continuous learning and skill development among employees.

By incorporating design thinking principles into educational initiatives, organizations can tailor learning experiences to address specific skill gaps and challenges faced by their workforce. This approach not only enhances employee engagement but also promotes a deeper understanding of the relevance of learning within the context of their roles and the overall organizational objectives.

In this article, we delve into the theoretical foundations of utilizing design thinking in educational programs, explore its practical applications, and examine survey results to understand its efficacy in advancing employee knowledge and skill sets. By doing so, we aim to shed light on the transformative potential of design thinking in shaping the future of employee education within organizations.

2 Theoretical Overview

2.1 Defining Design Thinking and Its Key Stages

Design thinking is a human-centered, iterative approach to problem-solving that has gained traction across diverse industries for its ability to foster innovation and user-centric solutions [1]. At its core, design thinking is characterized by a set of principles that guide the creation of effective solutions to complex problems.

In modern design thinking, the following key stages of this approach are distinguished [1, 4]:

1. Empathy. At this stage, we will need to create a current portrait of a company employee who is the target audience of training products. This is possible by conducting a large survey of the entire franchise network of order pick-up points.
2. Ideation. At this stage, it is necessary to notice some characteristic features in the portraits of employees from various CIS countries and draw conclusions about how this can be applied in training. The result of this phase should be an understanding and specific ideas on how training materials can be adapted for employees in different countries.
3. Prototyping. We need the prototyping stage to create a specific tangible test product, which we will later examine for consistency and effectiveness. The result of this phase should be an example of training material for employees of one of the CIS countries.
4. Testing. Testing a prototype is an opportunity to evaluate how well training materials, firstly, successfully cope with their function - how effectively they convey the

meaning of work processes. And, secondly, how much they improve the perception and accessibility of educational material.

In the realm of employee education, design thinking serves as a guiding framework to develop learning experiences that go beyond traditional, one-size-fits-all approaches [2]. Moreover, design thinking encourages a shift from a content-centric to a learner-centric approach, where the focus is on understanding the unique requirements of employees and crafting educational interventions that resonate with their everyday challenges and aspirations.

2.2 Application of Design Thinking to Training Programs for Employees

Design thinking offers a transformative framework for reimagining educational programs within organizations, with a specific focus on enhancing employee knowledge and skill sets. The application of design thinking principles to educational initiatives for employees can yield several notable benefits [3, 7]:

1. Tailored learning experiences. Design thinking allows organizations to tailor educational programs to address specific skill gaps and learning needs of employees. By understanding the unique challenges and aspirations of the workforce, educational content and methodologies can be customized to deliver relevant and impactful learning experiences.
2. User-centric approach. By placing employees at the center of the educational design process, organizations can create learning interventions that resonate with their day-to-day experiences and professional aspirations. This user-centric approach enhances engagement and promotes a sense of ownership over the learning journey.
3. Creativity and innovation. Design thinking encourages a culture of creativity and innovation within educational programs. By fostering an environment that values experimentation and out-of-the-box thinking, organizations can inspire employees to approach learning with a fresh perspective, leading to the discovery of novel solutions and approaches.
4. Alignment with organizational goals. By aligning educational programs with the broader strategic objectives of the organization, design thinking ensures that learning initiatives contribute directly to the enhancement of employee capabilities that are essential for achieving organizational success.

While design thinking offers numerous benefits for educational programs, its application may also present certain drawbacks that organizations should consider. Here are some potential drawbacks [2]:

Resistance to change. Introducing design thinking into existing educational frameworks may encounter resistance from employees and educators accustomed to traditional learning approaches. Overcoming this resistance and fostering a culture that embraces design thinking principles may require extensive change management efforts.

Lack of clear metrics for evaluation. Measuring the effectiveness of educational programs developed through design thinking can be challenging. Traditional metrics may not fully capture the impact of design thinking on skill development, making it essential to develop new evaluation frameworks tailored to the iterative and user-centric nature of design thinking.

In conclusion, while design thinking offers significant benefits for educational programs, such as fostering innovation and creativity, it is important to acknowledge and address potential drawbacks. Organizations should be prepared to navigate resistance to change by implementing robust change management strategies.

3 Using Design Thinking Methodology for Training Program Development

3.1 Empathy

The first step in design thinking is to empathize with the learner. This involves understanding their needs, motivations, and challenges. By conducting user research, including interviews, observations, and surveys, organizations can gain valuable insights into the learner's perspective [1, 5].

Our path to developing new human-centric training programs also began with studying our target audience – owners, employees and managers of Ozon marketplace order pick-up points in the CIS countries. Ozon works as a franchise network – there are many business owners, who hire managers and employees for working in their pick-up points under the company's brand.

Thus, a quantitative survey was conducted, within the framework of which we established the socio-demographic, behavioral and psychological characteristics of the target audience. In total, 15,613 people participated in the study out of a population of approximately 130,000 people, which means that the study covered approximately 12.01%. General sociological data on the survey are presented below (Table 1).

Table 1. General sociological data on the survey.

Country	Position in a pick-up point	Women	Men	Total
Russian Federation	Employee	7646	1395	9041
	Manager	560	180	740
	Owner	2755	2047	4802
Republic of Kazakhstan	Employee	164	59	223
	Manager	10	5	15
	Owner	140	126	266
Republic of Belarus	Employee	185	33	218
	Manager	7	9	16
	Owner	72	114	186
Republic of Armenia	Employee	22	11	33
	Manager	1	1	2

(*continued*)

Table 1. (*continued*)

Country	Position in a pick-up point	Women	Men	Total
	Owner	21	41	62
Republic of Kyrgyzstan	Employee	2	1	3
	Manager	2	2	4
	Owner	2	0	2
Total	Employee	8019	1499	9518
	Manager	580	197	777
	Owner	2990	2328	5318
	–	11589	4024	15613

The table shows the overall distribution of those who completed the survey by country, role at the point of delivery of orders, and by gender.

As part of the study, we drew attention to the differences in ideas about work in different countries (Fig. 1).

Fig. 1. Attitudes towards working in a pick-up point depending on the country

First of all, it turned out that in Armenia and Kazakhstan employees more often view work at a pickup point as a part-time job than as a full-time job. However, in other republics the situation is changing - for employees from Kyrgyzstan and Belarus, work at a pick-up point is perceived as a full-time job.

Of course, the sample in the CIS countries is not very large for a more detailed analysis, but based on the available data we can conclude that cross-cultural characteristics can influence a person's attitude towards his activities.

The next aspect that was important for us to pay attention to when studying the target audience was language. Despite the fact that the CIS countries are the heirs of the USSR and many citizens know Russian at the everyday level, we put forward a hypothesis that the national language of a particular republic is accessible to a larger number of employees (Fig. 2).

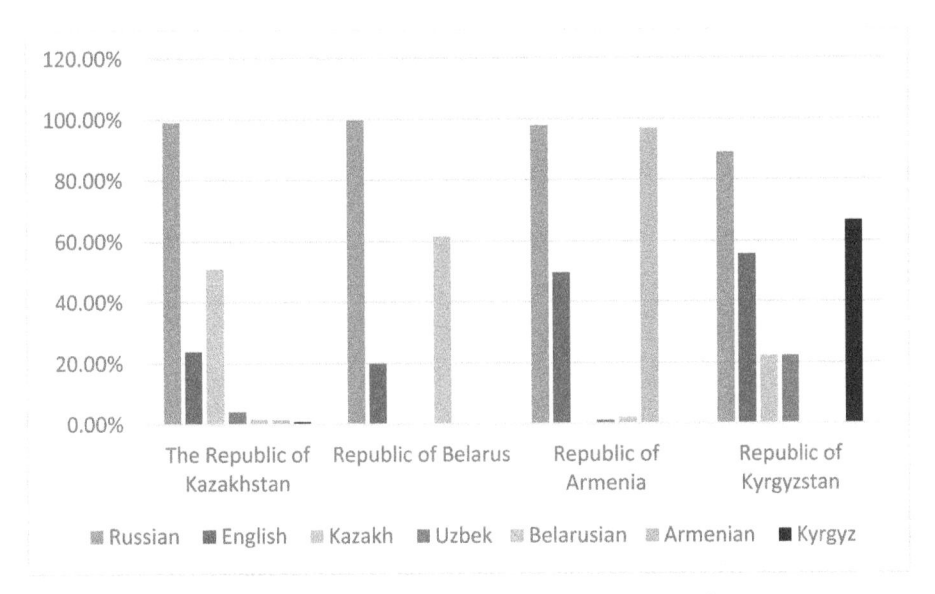

Fig. 2. Distribution of native speakers by CIS countries

It is noteworthy that in all countries the Russian language is predominantly spoken, and the percentage of national languages is not so high among employees of order pick-up points. However, in Armenia, unlike other countries, the proportion of people who know the local language is maximum in comparison with all other republics. From this we can conclude that for Belarus, Kazakhstan, and Kyrgyzstan, the issue of translating training programs into a local language is not as relevant as for Armenia.

And last but not least, the factor that we paid attention to during the study is employee values. The table below provides summary data on the TOP-3 values for each of the countries studied (Table 2).

For the most part, the percentage of the most important values among the CIS countries does not change, but in Armenia we see a slightly different picture: instead of health - a more personal value - family has come first. And instead of self-development, the third tier was taken by career.

What else can be noted is that in the CIS countries, in addition to Russia, large percentage shares fall on the TOP-3 values, while in Russia the values are more variable and distributed.

As a result of the research in the form of a survey, we compiled avatar portraits of the most typical personalities of employees of order pick-up points in various countries (Table 3).

Based on the previous steps described, we create a summary table with differences between countries for adapting training materials (Table 4).

Table 2. Distribution of valuables among employees of pickup points in the CIS countries

Country	Top-1 value	Top-2 value	Top-3 value
Russian Federation	Health (25.13%)	Family (13.77%)	Self-development (13.22%)
Republic of Kazakhstan	Health (24.81%)	Family (20.27%)	Self-development (11.93%)
Republic of Belarus	Health (27.60%)	Family (22.68%)	Self-development (12.30%)
Republic of Armenia	Family (27.01%)	Health (21.84%)	Career (10.92%)
Republic of Kyrgyzstan	Health (31.58%)	Family (31.58%)	Self-development (21.205%)

Table 3. Personas of pick-up point employees by country.

Kazakhstan	Armenia	Belarus
Age - 21 years old Level of education - higher (current final year student) Female gender No children, not married Works for 6 months The main values are health, family, self-development Treats work as a part-time job	Age - 27 years Level of education - higher Female gender No children, married Works for 10 months Core values: family, health, career Treats work as a part-time job	Age - 25 years Level of education - secondary specialized (graduated from college) Male gender No children, not married Works for 12 months The main values are health, family, self-development Treats work as the main place of work

Based on the summary data in the table above, we can conclude how learning models need to be adapted. Each CIS country needs its own approach based on many factors.

3.2 Ideation

Once the learner's needs and pain points are identified, the next step is to generate ideas for innovative training solutions [1, 6]. Design thinking encourages brainstorming and creative thinking to come up with a wide range of ideas. This ideation phase is all about pushing boundaries, challenging assumptions, and exploring new possibilities.

For the brainstorm, an expert survey was conducted among the top management of the Ozon company, as well as specialists in personnel training and development of electronic courses.

Based on the results of the brainstorm, we updated the table from the previous paragraph, moving from psycho-social features to ideas for adapting training materials (Table 5).

Table 4. Factors that should be taken into account when localizing employee training materials

Country	Attitude to work	Translation into local language	Values
Republic of Kazakhstan	Many people treat working at a pick-up point as a part-time job	Preferable, but least critical	Practically no different from Russian ones
Republic of Belarus	Mostly people treat it like their main job	Preferable, but not critical	Practically no different from Russian ones
Republic of Armenia	Some people treat working at a pickup point as a part-time job	Critically needed	Collective values prevail over individual ones
Republic of Kyrgyzstan	Mostly people treat it like their main job	Preferable, but not critical	Practically no different from Russian ones

Thus, based on this stage of the study, it becomes obvious that the number of training programs available to the company must increase exponentially in order to meet the cross-cultural characteristics of all CIS countries.

3.3 Prototyping

In the prototyping phase, organizations transform their ideas into tangible prototypes. These prototypes can take various forms, such as interactive modules, simulations, or gamified learning experiences. The key is to create a low-fidelity representation of the training program that allows for quick iteration and feedback [8].

As a pilot, we decided to develop microlearning cards for Kazakhstan. They required minimal use of additional human resources on the part of the company, so they could be quickly assembled and prepared for testing.

Since translation of materials into Kazakh for Kazakhstan is the least critical language aspect among all countries, this option was once again confirmed as optimal at this stage.

We took one of the operating processes, which at the time of the study was being prepared for scaling. The company had already created an electronic course that took about 40 min to complete. As part of the prototyping, cards were created that explain the same process without diving into small details, but much faster - in 5–7 min (Fig. 3).

3.4 Testing

Testing is a crucial step in design thinking, as it allows organizations to gather feedback and refine their training programs. By involving learners in the testing process, organizations can gain valuable insights into the effectiveness of their prototypes and make necessary adjustments. Testing promotes a culture of continuous improvement, where feedback from learners is used to iterate and refine the training program until it meets their needs and expectations.

Table 5. Ideas for adapting training programs to accommodate cross-cultural considerations

Country	Attitude to work	Translation into local language	Values
Republic of Kazakhstan	Do not condemn the attitude to work as a temporary place of work. Switch to the microlearning format - short cards, with the help of which an employee can absorb information faster than from long electronic courses	Translation of materials in the presence of free human resources	–
Republic of Belarus	Create expanded and more detailed instructions and courses	Translation of materials in the presence of free human resources	–
Republic of Armenia	Make it possible to choose the type of training materials - microlearning cards or detailed instructions	Translate materials into Armenian, but taking into account local peculiarities - not a literal translation, but a transliteration of some terms and others	Modify the approach to real-life workflow simulators. Add an element of mutual assistance within the team, taking into account the desire for collectivism
Republic of Kyrgyzstan	Create expanded and more detailed instructions and courses	Translation of materials in the presence of free human resources	–

Fig. 3. Example of microlearning cards applied after a design thinking iteration in Armenian

Considering the widespread attitude of employees to a pickup point as a place for part-time work, their satisfaction with training materials has increased - this is evidenced by the result of the company's NPS survey on training materials - during the testing of microlearning cards, NPS increased from 26% to 38%.

The second critical criterion for assessing the success of a design thinking implemetation project is contact in support. The company spends more than $500,000 a year on maintaining a pick-up point support staff, and labor reduction in this area is one of the company's priorities.

Based on the results of implementing the design thinking approach in training, the contact rate of support requests decreased by 3%. Thus, the organization's estimated savings are $15,000 2 months after implementation.

Thus, both the business task of operational training of employees and their loyalty to the company are solved.

3.5 Result of Iteration

So, the learning model formulated using the design thinking method actually achieves its goals.

However, something else worth considering when developing international training programs is also the transmission of the company's corporate values by employees of international enterprises. This is important for any franchise - without a holistic image of the organization it is impossible to build a strong brand, but when entering international markets, it is vital.

A consumer abroad must understand that a brand that comes to its market clearly knows how to convey not only the value of its services and goods, but also some background of its business - history, moral values, etc.

And here corporate training plays an important role - outside of it, an employee may have nowhere to learn what values the company carries and how to convey them.

However, it is quite obvious that direct disclosure of all values "head-on" is not enough for an employee to understand them in order to be able to transmit them in the future.

As part of the empirical study, we noted the following aspects that must be taken into account when developing corporate training programs for an enterprise to enter international markets:

1. The same values in different countries are understood differently by people. Despite the fact that the CIS countries in our study have a significant common historical and social past, at the current moment citizens understand the same aspects of life very differently. For example, within the framework of our research, it can be noted that residents of many countries put personal health in first place when it comes to personal values. However, this does not mean that they all perceive the name "Health" in the same way. In Kazakhstan, health is usually understood as a sufficiently developed level of medicine, which makes it possible to quickly cure emerging diseases, while in Belarus it is the absence of diseases as such. And this is just one example that illustrates possible polar views within the same phenomena.

   That is, the value must not only be conveyed to employees, but its content must be explained in detail. This will help move away from a diverse understanding to a homogeneous perception of the brand by both employees (primarily) and ultimately clients.

2. Simply listing values will not be perceived by employees as something worth paying attention to. Most likely, the presentation slides with corporate culture will be closed 2 s after opening (especially considering the factor of treating the job as a temporary or part-time job). It follows that the values must be implemented in other training programs. That is, each operational process must illustrate the achievement of certain organizational goals. For example, a course on issuing orders should direct the employee to be customer-oriented; a course on receiving deliveries from couriers should be built in favor of teamwork and partnerships between various departments of the organization. This will not only help convey to employees what the organization's vision is regarding rules and regulations, but also highlight how an employee should behave in typical corporate situations.

4 Conclusion

Design thinking stands as a powerful and transformative framework for revolutionizing training programs and fostering impactful learning experiences for employees. Through its human-centered approach, integration of gamification and collaboration, and commitment to iterative refinement, design thinking empowers organizations to unleash the full potential of their workforce and instill a culture of perpetual learning and advancement.

By embracing design thinking, organizations not only elevate the quality of their training initiatives but also nurture an environment where creativity, innovation, and adaptability thrive. The emphasis on empathy and user-centric design ensures that educational programs resonate with the unique needs and aspirations of employees, fostering a sense of ownership and engagement in their professional development journey.

As the business landscape continues to undergo rapid evolution, the role of design thinking in shaping the future of organizational learning cannot be overstated. Its influence will be pivotal in enabling organizations to remain agile, innovative, and competitive in the dynamic markets of tomorrow.

In harnessing the principles of design thinking, organizations can pave the way for a workforce that is not only adept at navigating change but also empowered to drive innovation and success in the ever-evolving business ecosystem.

References

1. Panke, S.: Design thinking in education: perspectives, opportunities and challenges. Open Educ. Stud. 1(1), 281–306. https://doi.org/10.1515/edu-2019-0022
2. Micheli, P., Wilner, S.J., Bhatti, S., Mura, M., Beverland, M.B.: Doing design thinking: conceptual review, synthesis and research agenda. J. Prod. Innov. Manag. (2018)
3. Melles, G., Anderson, N., Barrett, T., Thompson-Whiteside, S.: Problem finding through design thinking in education. In: Inquiry-Based Learning for Multidisciplinary Programs: A Conceptual and Practical Resource for Educators, pp. 191–209. Emerald Group Publishing Limited (2015)
4. Gergen, K., Gill, S.: Beyond the Tyranny of Testing: Relational Evaluation in Education. Oxford University Press (2020)
5. Gill, S., Thomson, G.: Human-Centred Education: A Practical Handbook and Guide. Routledge (2016)

6. Coculová, J., Tomčíková, L.: Analyzing the employment of expatriates as high-performance workers in terms of their impact on selected areas of the company. In: SHS Web of Conferences (2020)
7. Lauring, J., Selmer, J.: Person-environment fit and emotional control: assigned expatriates vs. self-initiated expatriates. Int. Bus. Rev. **27**(5) (2018)
8. Davidekova, S., Gregus, M.: Impacts of globalization on socio-economic domain of employees. In: International Scientific Conference Globalization and Its Socio-Economic Consequences, University of Zilina, The Faculty of Operation and Economics of Transport and Communications (2017)

Technological Innovations and Their Impact

Towards an Integrative Framework for AI Readiness and Market Disruption: The AI-Readiness and Market Dynamics Disruption Index (AIM-DDI) for Competitive AI Leadership

Jorge Calvo

GLOBIS University Graduate School of Management, 5-1 Niban-cho, Chiyoda-ku, Tokyo 102-0084, Japan
`jorge.calvo@globis.ac.jp`

Abstract. The rapid advancement of artificial intelligence (AI) has positioned it as a critical lever for business transformation and competitive advantage. However, the challenge for organizations lies in understanding their readiness for AI integration and the potential impact of AI-driven market disruptions. This paper introduces the AI-Readiness and Market Dynamics Disruption Index (AIM-DDI) Framework, an innovative approach designed to evaluate an organization's preparedness for AI and its ability to navigate and capitalize on market disruptions. By assessing both internal capabilities—spanning AI strategy, infrastructure, talent, implementation, and ethics—and external market dynamics—considering customer expectations, competitor AI maturity, industry disruption potential, regulatory environment, and the AI talent ecosystem—the AIM-DDI Framework provides a comprehensive perspective on an organization's position and potential strategic directions in the AI-driven landscape. Through a detailed examination of AI's role in business strategy, innovation, and competitive dynamics, this paper elucidates the pivotal influence of AI on strategic decision-making and market positioning. The AIM-DDI Framework offers a holistic toolkit for organizations to identify their strengths, pinpoint areas for improvement, and strategically leverage AI for sustainable competitive success.

Keywords: Strategy · Competitive Advantage · Market Disruption · Disruptive Innovation · AI Readiness · AI Maturity · AIM-DDI Framework · Strategic Planning

1 Introduction

In the dynamic realm of AI-driven transformation, it is imperative for businesses to ascertain their strategic positioning through a comprehensive framework that scrutinizes both their intrinsic capabilities and the external forces exerted by the market. This dual analysis is pivotal for informed strategic planning and decision-making in the contemporary era dominated by AI advancements. To this end, we introduce the AI-Readiness and Market Dynamics Disruption Index Framework (AIM-DDI Framework), a holistic methodology designed to assess the potential impact of AI-driven disruption on an organization according to its market context.

This framework delves into the internal dynamics of the organization, encompassing aspects such as AI strategy, infrastructure, talent, implementation, and ethical governance, while also considering the external AI ecosystem characterized by market demand, competitive landscape, and regulatory influences. The AIM-DDI Framework offers a nuanced perspective, ensuring a thorough understanding of an organization's standing amidst the rapidly evolving AI technological landscape and its broader implications.

2 A Comprehensive Review Towards an Integrative AIM-DDI Framework

A thorough exploration and dialogue concerning AI readiness and market disruption models emerge as essential pillars within the integrative AIM-DDI framework. The evaluation of the readiness for AI and the diverse array of market disruption models unveils a multifaceted and elaborate landscape emphasizing the significance of a comprehensive strategy analysis to fully comprehend the manifold implications of AI on both organizations and industries. Rooted deeply in the AIM-DDI framework is a recognition of the existing voids prevalent in the literature, explicitly focusing on addressing the dual dimensions of AI readiness within organizations and its potential to disrupt the market.

Most contemporary frameworks focus solely on the internal aspects of an organization's readiness for AI, neglecting the broader market impacts or external market implications without delving into organizational readiness itself. The existing literature on AI readiness in organizations presents valuable insights into the essential preparatory actions and capabilities needed for AI implementation. However, it must offer a comprehensive perspective on how this readiness contributes to market disruption and competitive advantages.

The scarcity of resources underscores the crucial requirement for a framework such as AIM-DDI to bridge these existing gaps effectively and offer a thorough understanding of the complex interplay among organizational readiness market dynamics and competitive positioning. The framework's primary objective is to enhance organizational readiness for AI adoption and shed light on leveraging this readiness to capture market opportunities and secure a sustainable competitive advantage. This holistic approach guarantees that organizations are not just capable of embracing AI technologies proficiently but also strategically positioning themselves to thrive in the everchanging and tumultuous market landscape, ultimately maximizing their growth potential.

Recent investigations into market disruptions emphasize the substantial influence of AI in disrupting and reshaping industry landscapes and altering competition dynamics (Yadav and Dwivedi 2023; Samadhiya et al. 2023). However, these studies often overlook the crucial organizational capabilities needed for such transformative changes (Shen and

Li 2017; Qin 2019). Additionally, the automation-augmentation paradox underlines the complexity of implementing AI technologies, stressing the importance of a balanced approach that fosters economic prosperity and social benefits (Kumar et al. 2023). In a more thorough investigation, these studies uncover the potential for AI to revolutionize corporate practices and strategies significantly, resulting in fundamental shifts in market frameworks and competitive dynamics.

The AIM-DDI framework emerges as a game changer setting out to bridge existing gaps by unveiling an integrated model. Delving into the depths of AI readiness, from technological infrastructure to organizational culture and skill enhancement, this framework also explores external forces like market disruption. The essence lies in empowering organizations with a sturdy compass to sail through the complexities of AI adoption and unlock its full potential for gaining sustainable competitive edges. The AIM-DDI framework focuses on overcoming the multifaceted challenges that organizations inevitably encounter amidst AI integration, facilitating adaptability within the dynamic technology and business realms. By skillfully blending internal and external perspectives, this model armors organizations with strategic insights and actionable advice essential for triumphing in the age of AI-driven innovation and transformation.

2.1 Exploring How AI Shapes Business Strategy

Integrating AI into corporate strategies has become a vital element for companies striving to enhance efficiency, competitiveness, and innovation. An abundance of literature focusing on businesses' preparedness for AI in strategic planning reveals the transformative capacity of AI technologies. This detailed analysis delves deeply into the core aspects of AI readiness in strategic business planning, shedding light on the methods, effects, and challenges that accompany AI integration. This thorough examination aims to enrich our understanding of the importance of infusing AI within business strategies and its profound implications on organizational operations and industry positioning.

AI Readiness and Strategic Planning entail an organization's readiness to embrace and incorporate AI technologies into its strategic framework effectively. Research by Mittal (2020), Najdawi (2020) and Utomo and Setiastuti (2019) emphasizes the importance of assessing AI readiness through methodologies like multicriterion decision analysis and the Singapore Smart Industry Readiness Index to classify the approach to Industry 4.0 of companies (Tzu-Chieh et al. 2020). These approaches assist in pinpointing the levels of technological procedural and organizational readiness, enabling the development of precise strategies for seamless AI integration. Exploring the depths of AI readiness isn't just about the technical aspects but also about intertwining AI initiatives with the organization's broader strategic objectives. Mittal's study underscores the significance of a thorough evaluation comprising elements such as data readiness, talent capabilities, and cultural preparedness for AI assimilation.

The influence of AI on business strategy is vast and varied, significantly impacting critical aspects such as supply chain resilience, workforce management, and enterprise competitiveness, as illuminated in studies by Zamani et al. (2022), Erick et al. (2021) and Nurhaida et al. (2023). A crucial point to note is the essential role of leadership and strategic vision in propelling AI readiness and integration across organizations.

This underscores the vital connection between leadership styles and successfully incorporating AI technologies into business strategies. This ongoing interplay suggests that effective leadership with a strategic outlook plays a pivotal role in shaping an environment that fosters adopting and utilizing AI advancements for a competitive edge in the business domain.

In the dynamic world of modern business, the introduction of AI brings a treasure trove of benefits; however, riding this wave presents significant hurdles for organizations. These challenges range from a resistance to change wrestling with ethical dilemmas safeguarding data, like a dragon guards its treasure, to the critical need for a skilled workforce. Renowned scholars like Sulthan et al. (2023) and Venkatesh and Jakka (2023) delve into these barriers highlighting the paramount importance of expertly navigating ethical challenges and making substantial investments in personnel training for the-seamless implementation of AI technologies.

Recent studies extensively examine how AI impacts decision-making and organizational competitiveness. The research by Makar (2023) and Zhao et al. (2023) sheds light on AIs' pivotal role in enhancing decision-making processes, emphasizing the use of advanced data analytics and machine learning algorithms to provide strategic insights for businesses. This not only fosters innovation but also cultivates sustainable competitive advantages.

The research findings underscore the importance of transcending technical barriers to achieve AI readiness extending into strategic organizational and human resource realms. The constant evolution of AI underscores the vital need for a comprehensive strategy incorporating technical know-how, leadership dynamics, ethical considerations, and employee competencies. Companies proficient in navigating these diverse elements can exploit AI capabilities to secure a competitive edge, drive innovation, and streamline operational efficiency. This analysis highlights the complex interplay between technology and organizational factors in adapting to the AI era, affirming that successful AI assimilation demands a multifaceted approach that aligns with broader business goals, nurtures a supportive leadership ethos, upholds ethical standards, and fosters continual skill enhancement among employees.

2.2 How AI Shapes Competitive Business Landscapes

The infusion of AI into enterprises' operation models has triggered a profound metamorphosis in the competitive landscape across manifold sectors. This in-depth scrutiny critically evaluates the pivotal importance of AI in augmenting businesses' competitive advantage, specifically emphasizing strategic management, fostering innovation, and navigating the intricate dynamics of challenges and opportunities it presents. The AI has catalyzed a paradigm shift across diverse business functions in how new business strategies must be formulated. The adoption of AI-driven technologies, as exemplified by breakthroughs like ChatGPT, has sparked a profound transformation in the landscape of corporate competitive intelligence systems (Nurhaida et al. 2023). This evolution heralds a new era of intelligence enhancement tailored to reinforce competitive advantages within enterprises (Linna 2023). Incorporating AI capabilities is pivotal in driving organizational metamorphosis, equipping businesses with a competitive edge characterized by enhanced agility and a penchant for innovation (Wetering et al. 2023). Noteworthy is the strategic amalgamation of AI with core business models particularly within the domain of the renowned Blue Ocean Strategy (Kim, W. C., and Mauborgne, R. 2015), highlighting the significant impact of AI in achieving competitive superiority and solidifying market leadership (Abbas Muhammad and Fayez Ghazi 2016).

AI integration in Strategic Management is crucial for driving business innovation and maintaining competitiveness in the market landscape. A recent study by Fischer et al. (2022) highlights the importance of AI in streamlining the B2B sales process, emphasizing how integrating AI-driven technologies can significantly enhance a company's overall performance. Kordons's (2020) research extensively explores utilizing AI-driven systems to give organizations a competitive edge. It highlights the crucial importance for businesses to embrace AI solutions to enhance operational efficiency and fortify their position in the global market. Integrating AI in strategic management not only streamlines current processes but also unlocks new avenues for decision-making resource allocation and customer engagement fostering innovation and growth.

The integration of AI into corporate operations presents significant hurdles, such as the imperative for improved semantic understanding, robust information security measures, and tackling potential biases within AI models (Linna 2023). These challenges underscore the complexity accompanying AI technology adoption in various business sectors. Conversely, AI ushers in numerous opportunities for companies, fostering an environment ripe for innovation and heightened competitiveness. Notably, a study by Benabed and Boeru (2022) delves into the pivotal role AI plays in the globalization of stock markets and how it aids businesses in securing competitive edges amidst the swift transformations occurring within the economic sphere.

The potential of AI to enhance organizational competitiveness stands out as a critical focus. Ongoing technological advancements are poised to transform strategic planning and reshape decision-making processes and market positioning strategies. A recent study conducted by Calderaro and Blumfelde (2022) sheds light on the challenges faced by the European Union's digital sovereignty due to the rapid progress of AI technologies. This study underlines the extensive impact that AI exerts on the development and implementation of business strategies on a global scale. This discussion explores the intricate relationship between AI progress and organizational evolution.

In the grand landscape of the digital era, AI emerges as a crucial force driving businesses towards increased competitiveness, ushering in unprecedented opportunities for strategic innovation and solidifying a leading position in the market domain. As companies navigate the intricate realm of incorporating AI into their processes, a meticulous and forward-thinking strategy that encompasses not just technological upgrades but also ethical considerations and a steadfast commitment to continuous innovation becomes imperative to harness the full spectrum of benefits that AI offers.

2.3 Delving into AI's Impact on Business Transformation

The landscape of business transformation has been reshaped to unprecedented levels by AI, leading to heightened efficiency, groundbreaking innovation, and enhanced competitive edge. Our literature review consolidates findings from recent research to delve deep into AI-driven metamorphosis within the business realm. By scrutinizing

AI's impact, exploring the opportunities it bestows, and addressing challenges it introduces, this review provides a detailed exploration of AI's profound effects on business transformation.

The integration of AI in the business realm is reshaping operations profoundly, enhancing efficiency, automating routine tasks, and deriving valuable strategic insights from vast data collections. According to Yadav and Dwivedi (2023), various industries are witnessing a substantial shift as companies strategically incorporate AI into their operational frameworks. Moreover, Shvetsova (2023) explores the multifaceted impact of AI on businesses, emphasizing its ability to streamline processes and raise awareness about ethical dilemmas, including potential privacy breaches and market competition. This technological progression has compelled firms to reassess their strategies, recognizing AIs' pivotal role in fostering innovation and optimizing performance strategies in today's business landscape.

AI has revolutionized business model innovation through its extensive influence. It not only enhances current business operations but also kickstarts innovative business approaches. Rubab (2023) underlines the pivotal role of AI-driven technologies like machine learning and natural language processing in reshaping multiple industries. These advanced technologies equip businesses with predictive analytics capabilities and the means to deliver customized customer experiences, thus transforming traditional business models.

Exploring further into the practical applications of AI in business, Goyal and Ashraf (2023) illuminate a captivating case study centered on Swiggy. This case study proves how AI integration can enhance efficiency and raise quality standards. In the realm of business progress, AI offers numerous opportunities for transformative shifts. However, amid this pursuit of advancement, many challenges and risks surface, requiring careful navigation. As highlighted by a study from Nigmatov and Pradeep (2023), AI holds the potential to automate various organizational processes and unlock fresh revenue generation avenues. Despite the bright outlook, hurdles such as algorithmic bias and cybersecurity vulnerabilities pose significant threats demanding proactive risk mitigation strategies.

Diving deeper into the ramifications of AI, Quaquebeke and Gerpott (2023) provocatively speculate on the potential for AI to supplant traditional leadership roles eventually. This bold assertion raises pertinent inquiries about the evolving dynamics of human involvement. AI is critical in driving transformative shifts and aligning strategic goals in organizational dynamics and strategic planning. A recent study by Bilan et al. (2022) extensively explored AI applications in organizational management through a thorough bibliometric review. The research illuminated the evolving research clusters and emerging trends in this field, highlighting the increasing importance of AI-driven advancements. Furthermore, the scholarly inquiry led by Kanitz et al. (2023) explored the transformative impact of generative AI on reshaping organizational change endeavors. The study underscored how integrating AI technologies could substantially amplify the efficacy and efficiency of change initiatives.

The pivotal role of ethical considerations and governance practices in AI within business operations is widely acknowledged. Leveraging the advantages of AI while effectively managing potential drawbacks requires a sophisticated approach. This involves critical aspects such as safeguarding data privacy, minimizing algorithmic bias, and addressing the impact on employment opportunities. Furthermore, discussions on digital leadership and integrating AI into strategic management frameworks underscore the indispensable need for ethical leadership and well-defined governance mechanisms to oversee the integration of AI technologies in corporate settings. A deep understanding of the ethical dimensions and governance protocols governing AI implementations is essential for promoting responsible and sustainable utilization of AI in the business landscape.

AI emerges as a compelling driver of substantial transformations within businesses, offering diverse paths for fostering innovation, streamlining processes, and gaining a competitive edge. However, harnessing the full potential of AI mandates a vigilant approach toward navigating complex ethical dilemmas, addressing a myriad of hurdles linked to technology integration, and reimagining the core strategies and frameworks underpinning organizational operations. As corporations progressively embed AI into their business landscapes, a meticulous examination of these critical facets assumes the indispensability of paving the way for sustained and enduring success. Embracing the ethical implications of overcoming technological obstacles and reshaping organizational paradigms are essential in this transformative journey.

The fusion of digital technology, AI, and disruptive trends offers a blend of benefits and challenges. Westerman et al. (2014) highlighted the critical role of digital competencies and strong leadership in navigating the digital environment. Expanding on this, Davenport and Ronanki (2018) examined AI's role in enhancing human abilities, emphasizing the augmentation of human capabilities. Birkinshaw and Lancefield (2023) presented a nuanced analysis of disruptions from demand and supply perspectives, offering a strategic framework for understanding innovation and competitive dynamics. This paper aims to synthesize these perspectives into a unified model for practical application in business evolution and leadership.

The proposed models include three key components:

1. Effective Leadership: Echoing Westerman et al. (2014), it underscores the importance of leadership in fostering innovation and adaptability, enabling swift adaptation to digital progress.
2. Human Augmentation through AI: Referencing Davenport and Ronanki (2018), and Daugherty and Wilson (2018), the model views AI as a partner to human intellect, enhancing decision-making and productivity. This highlights the strategic integration of AI into operations and decision-making processes.
3. Embracing Innovation: It stresses the necessity for organizations to engage in demand-side innovation (creating new customer needs) and supply-side innovation (transforming service/product delivery), drawing on Birkinshaw and Lancefield (2023).

The authors advocate for a comprehensive digital transformation strategy, smoothly integrating AI and leveraging disruptions. It advises organizations to:

1. Develop leadership skills adept at navigating and adapting to changes in digital and AI technologies.

2. View AI not just as a tool but as a key strategic asset for augmenting human capabilities and reshaping competitive landscapes.
3. Maintain competitiveness and leadership by actively engaging in demand disruption and supply chain innovation.

2.4 Conclusion

In sum, blending digital acumen, effective leadership, AI augmenting human capabilities, and a deep understanding of disruptive forces lays a solid foundation for organizations aiming for success in the digital era. This holistic approach enables businesses to skillfully navigate digital transformation challenges, maintaining their competitive edge in a dynamic environment. Future research should explore the application of this model across various sectors and contexts to better understand its implications for business strategies and management.

The comprehensive review of the Integrative AIM-DDI Framework underscores the critical importance of AI readiness and market disruption models as foundational elements for understanding and leveraging AI's transformative potential in business. This framework not only fills the existing gaps in literature by addressing both organizational readiness and market disruption capabilities but also offers a holistic approach to navigating the complex interplay between AI integration and competitive strategy. By emphasizing the need for a multifaceted strategy that encompasses technological infrastructure, organizational culture, skill enhancement, and market dynamics, the AIM-DDI framework equips organizations with the insights and tools necessary to thrive in the rapidly evolving business landscape.

The review highlights the significant impact of AI on strategic planning, business model innovation, and competitive advantage, illustrating the vast opportunities and challenges that come with AI adoption. It calls for a balanced approach that considers technical, ethical, and strategic dimensions, ensuring that AI integration supports not only operational efficiency and innovation but also ethical governance and sustainable competitive positioning.

As businesses continue to navigate the complexities of AI adoption, the AIM-DDI framework serves as a valuable guide for achieving readiness, embracing market disruptions, and securing a sustainable competitive edge. The journey towards AI integration is intricate and multifaceted, requiring ongoing adaptation, ethical consideration, and strategic foresight. Ultimately, the successful assimilation of AI technologies hinges on a comprehensive understanding of both internal organizational readiness and external market dynamics, ensuring that businesses are not only prepared for the present but also poised for future innovation and growth.

3 The AI-Readiness and Market Dynamics Disruption Index (AIM-DDI)

In an era defined by rapid technological advancements, the imperative for businesses to innovate is not just a strategic advantage but a survival necessity. This is particularly true with the rise of AI, a force so transformative that it compels companies to confront a critical juncture: become a disruptor or risk being disrupted. The AIM-DDI framework is rooted in a deep analysis of existing literature, industry best practices, and empirical research, aiming to synthesize a wide array of perspectives into a coherent and actionable model. It addresses the dual dimensions of AI readiness within organizations—technological and cultural—and its potential to disrupt markets, thereby providing a holistic view of the strategic implications of AI integration.

The AIM-DDI is a comprehensive framework designed to help businesses navigate the complex landscape of AI-driven disruption, assessing both their internal capabilities and the external market forces at play. It presents a new approach to understanding and navigating the multifaceted challenges and opportunities presented by AI in the business context. This methodology is designed to bridge the gap between theoretical research and practical application, offering a comprehensive toolset for organizations to assess their AI readiness, understand market disruption models, and strategically leverage AI for competitive advantage.

3.1 Internal AI Maturity: The Foundation of Disruption

At the heart of a company's potential to disrupt lies its internal AI maturity, a multifaceted measure of its readiness to leverage AI technologies. This readiness is not merely about adopting new tools but involves a holistic integration of AI into the strategic, operational, and ethical fabric of the organization.

1. AI Strategy and Vision: The cornerstone of AI maturity is a clear, actionable strategy that aligns AI initiatives with business objectives, ensuring that technological investments drive towards overarching goals.
2. Data Infrastructure: Robust data management systems form the backbone of effective AI deployment. Without a solid data infrastructure, even the most advanced AI algorithms cannot function optimally.
3. AI Talent and Expertise: The availability of skilled personnel, coupled with a culture that fosters innovation and continuous learning in AI, determines an organization's ability to develop and implement cutting-edge AI solutions.
4. AI Implementation and Use Cases: The extent of AI integration into products, services, and operations signifies the organization's practical application of AI, transcending beyond theoretical models to real-world impact.
5. AI Ethics and Governance: Responsible AI use underpinned by ethical guidelines and governance structures is paramount, ensuring that AI technologies enhance societal well-being while mitigating risks.

3.2 External AI Maturity: Understanding the Market Dynamics

Beyond the confines of individual organizations, the external AI maturity landscape shapes the context in which businesses operate, influenced by customer expectations, competitive pressures, and broader industry trends.

1. Customer Expectations and Adoption: The demand for AI-enhanced offerings and the market's readiness to adopt such innovations set the pace for companies to align their products and services with evolving consumer needs.

2. Competitor AI Maturity: The level of AI adoption among competitors serves as a benchmark and a driver for organizations to accelerate their AI initiatives, ensuring they remain competitive or gain a market edge.
3. Industry Disruption Potential: The likelihood and extent of AI reshaping industry practices highlight the transformative power of AI, urging companies to innovate lest they fall prey to emerging paradigms.
4. Regulatory Environment and AI Governance: The regulatory backdrop influences the pace and direction of AI innovation, with supportive policies fostering growth and stringent regulations posing potential hurdles.
5. AI Talent and Education Ecosystem: The availability of AI expertise, driven by educational institutions and industry collaborations, fuels the innovation engine, empowering companies to push the boundaries of what's possible with AI.

3.3 The AIM-DDI Score of AI Competitiveness: The Boundary Between AI as a Strength or as a Weakness

Incorporating a mathematical approach to calculating the AIM-DDI score and detailing its implications enhances the analytical depth of our understanding of an organization's position in terms of AI maturity. By calculating the ratio of an organization's AI maturity to the external AI maturity, we arrive at the AIM-DDI score. This method provides a clear, quantifiable metric that facilitates straightforward interpretation.

$$AIM - DDI\ score = \frac{Internal\ AI\ Maturity\ Score}{External\ AI\ Maturity\ Score}$$

- If the AIM-DDI Index is greater than 1 (AIM-DDI > 1), the organization's AI capabilities are strong, indicating a competitive advantage in AI maturity.
- Conversely, if the AIM-DDI Index is less than 1 (AIM-DDI < 1), the company needs to enhance its AI maturity capabilities to lead effectively in its market.

Drawing a graphical representation related to the AIM-DDI framework with two axes—Organization AI Maturity (Internal) on the X-Axis and Market AI Maturity (External) on the Y-Axis—allows us to visually assess a company's AI maturity relative to its market and context. The chart's diagonal line differentiates between AI maturity as a strength (below the diagonal) or a weakness (above the diagonal) for a given company. This distinction also suggests a demarcation between Blue Ocean and Red Ocean strategies (see Fig. 1).

The Blue Ocean strategy emphasizes creating uncontested market spaces, making the competition irrelevant by focusing on innovation, differentiation, and low costs, effectively generating new demand and opportunities. Conversely, the Red Ocean strategy involves competing in existing market spaces, striving for a larger share of the market through competitive advantages over rivals. The distinction between these strategies underlines the transformative potential of AI maturity, where leveraging AI effectively can lead a company into uncharted waters of opportunity (Blue Ocean) versus remaining in fiercely competitive, saturated markets (Red Ocean).

The Blue Ocean strategy represents a shift in strategic thinking from competition to creating new market space, which is vital for organizations looking to harness AI

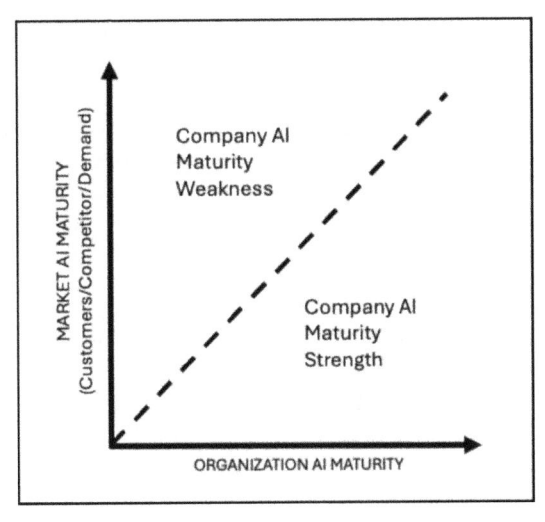

Fig. 1. The graphic boundary between AI as a strength or as a weakness. (Color figure online)

for transformative success. As companies navigate the AI landscape, understanding and applying these strategic concepts can be pivotal in defining their market position and competitive edge.

Positioning an organization within this framework involves assessing its standing on the two axes: Internal AI Maturity (X-Axis) and External AI Maturity (Y-Axis), giving rise to four distinct quadrants:

1. Vulnerable Observers (Lower Left): Companies here have yet to fully embrace AI, and while immediate market pressures may be low, they risk obsolescence as the pace of AI adoption accelerates. Proactive investments in AI capabilities are crucial to avoid being sidelined by the tidal wave of technological change.
2. Pressured Responders (Upper Left): Faced with a market rapidly embracing AI, these companies must quickly bridge their internal AI maturity gap to fend off disruption. Agility in adopting AI and forming strategic alliances can help turn pressure into opportunity.
3. AI-Driven Leaders (Upper Right): With advanced internal AI capabilities in a market ripe for innovation, these organizations are poised to lead and shape the future of their industries. Continuous innovation and leveraging AI to set new standards will ensure their sustained leadership. Leading AI-Driven companies are preparing to enter less mature markets and industries.
4. Latent Disruptors (Lower Right): Possessing advanced AI capabilities in a less mature market presents a unique opportunity to redefine the competitive landscape. These companies can harness their AI prowess to unveil groundbreaking products and services, setting the stage for disruption.

As we will elaborate further, pinpointing a company's position within these quadrants provides crucial insights into its strategic priorities and exposes potential vulnerabilities.

For those in the early stages of AI maturity, the focus should be on building a solid foundation, from talent acquisition to infrastructure development and ethical guidelines. For market leaders and hidden disruptors, the emphasis shifts to leveraging their advanced capabilities to drive innovation and redefine industry norms. The journey through the landscape of AI-driven disruption is not a solitary endeavor but a strategic chess game that requires foresight, agility, and a deep understanding of both internal capabilities and external market dynamics. By evaluating their position within the proposed framework, companies can chart a course that not only navigates the tumult.

4 Developing the Scale for the AIM-DDI Framework

This methodology section outlines the theoretical underpinnings, research design, and analytical approaches employed in developing the AIM-DDI framework. It details the systematic process of data collection, analysis, and model formulation, emphasizing the interdisciplinary nature of the research and the integration of insights from economics, business administration, and information technology.

To synthesize the insights derived from evaluating the internal and external factors outlined in the AIM-DDI Framework Metrics, a cumulative approach is employed. Each factor within the organizational AI maturity (X-axis) and the external AI maturity (Y-axis) is assessed on a scale from 0 to 5, with 0 indicating the lowest level of maturity and 5 representing the highest. The sum of these ratings across all factors provides a comprehensive metric that reflects the organization's overall position in terms of AI readiness frame and its potential to disrupt or be disrupted in the marketplace.

4.1 Cumulative Scoring Method

- Organizational AI Maturity Score: The sum of scores from the five internal factors (AI Strategy and Vision, Data Infrastructure, AI Talent and Expertise, AI Implementation and Use Cases, AI Ethics and Governance) provides a total score for the organization's AI maturity. This score ranges from 0 (indicating no AI maturity) to 25 (indicating full AI maturity across all dimensions).
- External AI Maturity Score: Similarly, the sum of scores from the five external factors (Customer Expectations and Adoption, Competitor AI Maturity, Industry Disruption Potential, Regulatory Environment and AI Governance, AI Talent, and Education Ecosystem) yields a total score for the external AI maturity. This score also ranges from 0 to 25, reflecting the AI maturity of the market and industry in which the organization operates.

X-Axis Scale: Organization AI Maturity (0–25)

The X-axis represents the internal AI maturity of the organization, measured through the following questions:

1. AI Strategy and Vision (0–5):
    0. No AI strategy or vision in place.
    1. Initial discussions about AI but no formal strategy.

2. AI strategy is defined but not integrated into the business strategy.
  3. AI strategy is aligned with business strategy, but implementation is in early stages.
  4. AI strategy is fully integrated into business strategy and is being implemented across some departments.
  5. AI is a core part of the business strategy with full implementation across all departments.
2. Data Infrastructure (0–5):
   0. No data infrastructure in place.
   1. Basic data collection processes in place, but data is siloed and not easily accessible.
   2. Good data collection processes and some level of data integration.
   3. Robust data infrastructure with integrated data from various sources.
   4. Advanced data management with real-time data analytics capabilities.
   5. Cutting-edge data infrastructure with predictive analytics and fully leveraged big data.
3. AI Talent and Expertise (0–5):
   0. No AI expertise or talent within the organization.
   1. Limited AI expertise, possibly through a few individuals or a small team.
   2. Growing AI team with a focus on specific use cases or departments.
   3. Established AI department with a range of skills, involved in multiple projects.
   4. Strong AI expertise across the organization with ongoing training programs.
   5. Leading-edge AI talent with a culture of continuous learning and innovation.
4. AI Implementation and Use Cases (0–5):
   0. No AI implementations or use cases.
   1. Experimental or pilot AI projects.
   2. A few successful AI projects with limited scope.
   3. Multiple AI projects across different departments with some showing significant benefits.
   4. AI is systematically used for decision-making and operations in many areas.
   4. AI is deeply integrated into products, services, and operations, driving major efficiencies and innovations.
5. AI Ethics and Governance (0–5):
   0. No consideration of AI ethics or governance.
   1. Initial awareness of AI ethics and governance issues but no formal policies.
   2. Development of AI ethics guidelines and some governance structures.
   3. Comprehensive AI ethics policies and governance frameworks in place.
   4. Active monitoring and enforcement of AI ethics and governance, with regular updates.
   5. Industry-leading practices in AI ethics and governance, with active contributions to setting standards.

Y-Axis: Customers/Competitor/Demand AI Maturity (0–25)

The Y-axis assesses the external environment, focusing on the AI maturity of customers, competitors, and overall market demand:

1. Customer Expectations and Adoption (0–5):
   0. Customers have no expectation or awareness of AI-enhanced products/services.

1. Growing customer awareness but low adoption of AI-enhanced offerings.
   2. Moderate level of customer expectations with some seeking AI-enhanced experiences.
   3. High customer expectations with good adoption of AI-enhanced products/services.
   4. Customers demand AI-enhanced offerings and see them as a differentiator.
   5. AI is central to customer expectations, driving significant influence on purchasing decisions.
2. Competitor AI Maturity (0–5):
   0. Competitors are not using AI in their operations or offerings.
   1. Some competitors are experimenting with AI.
   2. Many competitors have successful AI implementations in niche areas.
   3. Competitors widely adopt AI, integrating it into their products and operations.
   4. Majority of competitors leverage AI for competitive advantage.
   5. AI is a key battleground in the industry, with leading competitors pushing the boundaries.
3. Industry Disruption Potential (0–5):
   0. The industry shows little to no signs of potential disruption by AI.
   1. Early indicators of AI's potential to disrupt certain aspects of the industry.
   2. Clear examples of AI starting to change industry practices or business models.
   3. Significant shifts in industry dynamics due to AI, with new entrants challenging incumbents.
   4. AI is a major driver of industry transformation, reshaping value chains and customer experiences.
   5. AI has become the cornerstone of industry innovation, fundamentally redefining market leaders and creating entirely new business models and opportunities.
4. Regulatory Environment and AI Governance (0–5):
   0. Stringent regulations severely restrict AI development and deployment.
   1. Regulations are present but unclear or inconsistently applied, causing uncertainty.
   2. A regulatory framework is being developed, with some guidelines in place.
   3. Clear regulations and standards support ethical AI development and deployment.
   4. Regulations encourage AI innovation while ensuring ethical and responsible use.
   5. The regulatory environment is highly conducive to AI innovation, with strong support for ethical AI, data privacy, and security standards, fostering a trustworthy AI ecosystem.
5. AI Talent and Education Ecosystem (0–5):
   0. A significant shortage of AI talent, with very limited educational programs in AI.
   1. Some educational institutions are beginning to offer AI-related programs, but talent remains scarce.
   2. A growing number of AI professionals and educational programs, but demand outpaces supply.
   3. A healthy ecosystem of AI talent, with multiple educational pathways and ongoing professional development opportunities.
   4. A strong AI talent pool, supported by world-class educational institutions and industry-academia collaborations.
   5. A vibrant and globally recognized AI talent and education ecosystem, driving innovation and setting global standards in AI research and application.

The sum of all factor levels within the AIM-DDI Framework Metrics serves as a crucial result, offering organizations a strategic tool for navigating the AI landscape. This comprehensive score facilitates informed decision-making, strategic planning, and the identification of key areas for development and investment in the journey towards AI-driven transformation and market leadership.

4.2 Interpreting the Results

The cumulative scores offer a quantifiable measure of an organization's readiness to leverage AI for competitive advantage and its susceptibility to market disruptions caused by AI advancements. A higher score on the organizational AI maturity axis suggests a strong internal foundation for AI integration, while a higher score on the external AI maturity axis indicates a dynamic and potentially disruptive market environment.

By analyzing these scores, organizations can identify strategic areas of focus to enhance their AI capabilities, mitigate vulnerabilities, and capitalize on market opportunities. This cumulative approach not only simplifies the assessment of complex and multifaceted AI readiness factors but also provides a clear metric for benchmarking progress over time and against competitors.

The classification into four distinct quadrants—Vulnerable Observers, Pressured Responders, AI-Driven Leaders, and Latent Disruptors—provides a strategic framework for understanding an organization's current position and potential trajectory in the realm of AI adoption and market disruption. This segmentation is based on two critical dimensions: internal AI maturity and the external AI maturity of the market. Each quadrant represents a unique set of characteristics and strategic implications, guiding organizations on how to navigate the complexities of AI integration and competitive positioning.

By identifying which quadrant an organization falls into, leaders can gain insights into their company's strengths, weaknesses, and the external forces at play. This understanding is crucial for developing tailored strategies that align with their current status and future aspirations in the AI-driven business environment. From those just beginning to explore AI's potential to those leading the charge in AI innovation, the quadrant framework offers a roadmap for action. It highlights the need for building capabilities, responding to competitive pressures, leveraging AI strengths for market leadership, or seizing the opportunity to disrupt the industry.

5 Navigating the Quadrants of the AIM-DDI Framework

This section sets the stage for a deeper exploration of each quadrant's characteristics and strategic implications, offering organizations a clear perspective on how to approach AI adoption and utilization. Whether the goal is to build, respond, lead, or disrupt, understanding one's position within these quadrants is a critical step toward navigating the "Disrupt or Be Disrupted" landscape with confidence and strategic acumen. Positioning an organization within this framework involves assessing its standing on two axes: Internal AI Maturity (X-Axis) and External AI Maturity (Y-Axis), giving rise to four distinct quadrants (see Fig. 2).

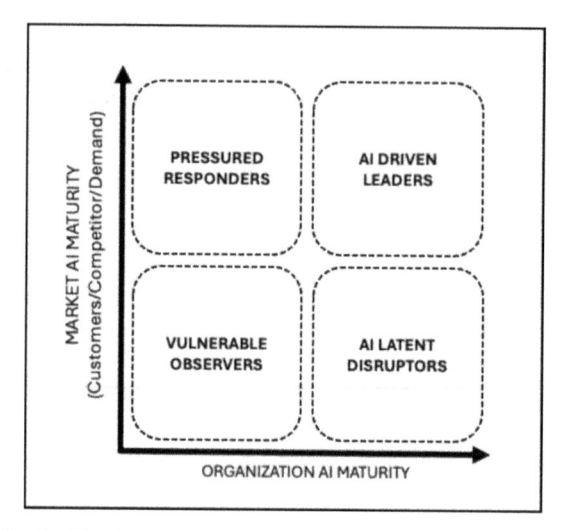

Fig. 2. The Integrative AIM-DDI Framework and Quadrants.

1. Vulnerable Observers (Lower Left): Companies here have yet to fully embrace AI, and while immediate market pressures may be low, they risk obsolescence as the pace of AI adoption accelerates. Proactive investments in AI capabilities are crucial to avoid being sidelined by the tidal wave of technological change.
   - Characteristics: Organizations here have low internal AI maturity and face a market with low external AI maturity. They are not yet leveraging AI significantly within their operations, nor are they pressured by a market that is rapidly adopting AI.
   - Strategic Implications: These organizations are in a relatively safe zone but risk falling behind as the market evolves. They need to begin building their AI capabilities and preparing for future market shifts to avoid becoming disrupted as AI adoption accelerates.
2. Pressured Responders (Upper Left): Faced with a market rapidly embracing AI, these companies must quickly bridge their internal AI maturity gap to fend off disruption. Agility in adopting AI and forming strategic alliances can help turn pressure into opportunity.
   - Characteristics: Companies in this quadrant are in markets where AI is becoming increasingly important, but they lack internal AI capabilities. They are facing pressure from competitors and market expectations to adopt AI.
   - Strategic Implications: These organizations are at risk of being disrupted if they do not act swiftly. They need to prioritize the development of AI capabilities and look for strategic partnerships or acquisitions to enhance their AI readiness and meet market demands.
3. AI Driven Leaders (Upper Right): With advanced internal AI capabilities in a market ripe for innovation, these organizations are poised to lead and shape the future of their industries. Continuous innovation and leveraging AI to set new standards will ensure

their sustained leadership. Leading AI-Driven companies are preparing to enter less mature markets and industries.

- Characteristics: These organizations are at the forefront of AI adoption both internally and within the market. They have strong AI capabilities and operate in a competitive environment where AI is a critical factor.
- Strategic Implications: As leaders, these companies should continue to innovate and push the boundaries of AI applications. They are in a position to disrupt the market further and should focus on expanding their influence and setting new industry standards.

4. AI Latent Disruptors (Lower Right): Possessing advanced AI capabilities in a less mature market presents a unique opportunity to redefine the competitive landscape. These companies can harness their AI prowess to unveil groundbreaking products and services, setting the stage for disruption.

- Characteristics: Companies here have high internal AI maturity but operate in markets that have not yet fully embraced AI. They possess significant AI capabilities that are not yet common in their industry.
- Strategic Implications: These organizations have a unique opportunity to become disruptors. They should leverage their advanced AI capabilities to introduce new products, services, or business models, thereby reshaping the market and setting new competitive standards.

5.1 The Path Forward

Identifying a company's position within these quadrants illuminates strategic priorities and reveals potential vulnerabilities. For entities at the nascent stages of AI maturity, the imperative is to establish a robust foundation. This encompasses everything from talent acquisition and infrastructure development to the formulation of ethical guidelines. Conversely, for those positioned as market leaders or latent disruptors, the focus pivots towards exploiting their sophisticated AI capabilities to spearhead innovation and set new benchmarks for the industry.

By understanding their position within these quadrants, organizations can better strategize their approach to AI adoption and utilization. Whether by building capabilities, responding to market pressures, leveraging strengths to lead the market, or capitalizing on unique opportunities to disrupt, companies can navigate the "Disrupt or Be Disrupted" dilemma more effectively.

In essence, navigating the terrain of AI-induced disruption transcends mere participation; it demands strategic acumen akin to playing a game of chess, where foresight, agility, and an intricate comprehension of both internal strengths and the external competitive landscape are paramount. By critically assessing their stance within this strategic framework, organizations can delineate a trajectory that adeptly steers through the whirlwind of AI advancements, effectively distinguishing substantive opportunities from fleeting trends.

6 Conclusion

The swift advancement of artificial intelligence (AI) technology offers exceptional prospects as well as significant obstacles for businesses spanning various sectors. Within this intricate scenario, the AIM-DDI Framework stands out as a crucial instrument for companies aiming to traverse the challenging terrain of AI implementation and market upheaval. This article thoroughly explains the elements of the AIM-DDI Framework, showcasing its ability to evaluate an organization's readiness for AI implementation internally and its propensity to cause and endure disruption within market dynamics.

Employing the AIM-DDI Framework enables organizations to enhance their comprehension of their AI maturity by identifying strengths, areas needing enhancement, and strategic avenues for utilizing AI to attain a competitive edge. This framework accentuates the necessity of a comprehensive strategy that embraces not only technology proficiency but also forward-thinking strategies, ethical concerns, and flexible leadership in the era of AI.

In the effort to leverage the powerful impact of AI, globally, the AIM-DDI Framework acts as a crucial tool in directing key strategic choices for sustainable progress and creativity. Yet, this path is ongoing. The ever-evolving realms of technology and markets demand constant updates to the framework, accommodating new trends, technologies, and approaches.

In order to determine the suitability of the AIM-DDI Framework in various industries and situations, future studies should be conducted. These studies should delve into the unique challenges and prospects related to AI implementation in each industry. Additionally, longitudinal research could offer valuable perspectives on the predictive capabilities of the framework and its influence on organizational effectiveness over an extended period. As artificial intelligence continues to reshape the business landscape, the AIM-DDI Framework demonstrates the importance of strategic preparedness and flexibility in harnessing the benefits of the digital era.

References

Abbas, M., Hussein, S., Ghazi, F., Al Bayat, A.L.: Alignment between the blue ocean strategy and the entry and exit from the market strategies and their impact in achieving competitive advantage: exploratory study of a sample of managers in Al-Rafidain Bank. J. Al-Ma'moon Coll. (27) (2016)

Benabed, A., Boeru, A: Globalization of the stock market and the impact of artificial intelligence on challenging businesses. In: LIMEN - International Scientific-Business Conference - Leadership, Innovation, Management and Economics: Integrated Politics of Research (2022). https://doi.org/10.31410/LIMEN.2022.1

Bilan, S., Šuleř, P., Skrynnyk, O., Krajňáková, E., Vasilyeva, T.: Systematic bibliometric review of artificial intelligence technology in organizational management, development, change and culture. Bus.: Theory Pract. **23**(1), 1–13 (2022). https://doi.org/10.3846/btp.2022.13204

Birkinshaw, J., Lancefield, D.: How professional services firms dodged disruption. MIT Sloan Manag. Rev. **64**(4) (2023). [Article Reprint #64405]. https://sloanreview.mit.edu

Calderaro, A., Blumfelde, S.: Artificial intelligence and EU security: the false promise of digital sovereignty. Eur. Secur. **31**(3), 415–434 (2022)

Daugherty, P.R., Wilson, H.J.: Human + Machine: Reimagining Work in the Age of AI. Harvard Business Review Press (2018)

Davenport, T.H., Ronanki, R.: Collaborative Intelligence: Humans and AI Are Joining Forces. Harvard Business Review (2018). https://hbr.org/2018/07/collaborative-intelligence-humans-and-ai-are-joining-forces

Erick, N.R.J., Mirbabaie, M., Stieglitz, S., Salomon, J.: Maneuvering through the stormy seas of digital transformation: the impact of empowering leadership on the AI readiness of enterprises. J. Decis. Syst. (2021). https://doi.org/10.1080/12460125.2020.1870065

Fischer, H., Seidenstricker, S., Berger, T., Holopainen, T.: Artificial intelligence in B2B sales: impact on the sales process. Artificial intelligence in B2B sales: impact on the sales process. Artif. Intell. Soc. Comput. **28**, 135–142 (2022)

Goyal, M., Ashraf, D.G.: To study the impact of AI on business and customer services - a case study on Swiggy. Int. J. Adv. Res. Sci. Commun. Technol. (2023)

Kanitz, R., Gonzalez, K., Briker, R., Straatmann, T.: Augmenting organizational change and strategy activities: leveraging generative artificial intelligence. J. Appl. Behav. Sci. **59**(3), 345–363 (2023)

Kim, W.C., Mauborgne, R.: Blue Ocean Strategy: How to Create Uncontested Market Space and Make the Competition Irrelevant. Harvard Business Review Press (2015)

Kordon, A.K.: Applied artificial intelligence-based systems as competitive advantage. In: 2020 IEEE 10th International Conference on Intelligent Systems (IS), pp. 6–18 (2020)

Kumar, A., Bhattacharyya, S., Krishnamoorthy, B.: Automation-augmentation paradox in organizational artificial intelligence technology deployment capabilities; an empirical investigation for achieving simultaneous economic and social benefits. J. Enterp. Inf. Manag. **36**(6), 1556–1582 (2023). https://doi.org/10.1108/JEIM-09-2022-0307

Linna, G.: The impact of ChatGPT on enterprise competitive intelligence systems. Inf. Syst. Econ. (2023). https://doi.org/10.23977/infse.2023.040909

Makar, K.Š.: Driven by Artificial Intelligence (AI) – improving operational efficiency and competitiveness in business. In: 2023 46th MIPRO ICT and Electronics Convention (MIPRO), pp. 1142–1147. IEEE (2023)

Mittal, P.: A multi-criterion decision analysis based on PCA for analyzing the digital technology skills in the effectiveness of government services. In: 2020 International Conference on Decision Aid Sciences and Application (DASA), pp. 490–494. IEEE (2020). https://doi.org/10.1109/DASA51403.2020.9317241

Najdawi, A.: Assessing AI readiness across organizations: the case of UAE. assessing AI readiness across organizations: the case of UAE. In: 2020 11th International Conference on Computing, Communication and Networking Technologies (ICCCNT). IEEE (2020). https://doi.org/10.1109/ICCCNT49239.2020.9225386

Nigmatov, A., Pradeep, A.: The impact of AI on business: opportunities, risks, and challenges. In: 2023 13th International Conference on Advanced Computer Information Technologies (ACIT), pp. 618–622. IEEE (2023)

Nurhaida, D., Amran, E., Nugraha, E.R., Osman, A.F., Shafira, A.N.: Utilizing Artificial Intelligence (AI) Technology to support MSMEs businesses: ChatGPT. Dinamisia: Jurnal Pengabdian Kepada Masyarakat **7**(4), 910–918 (2023)

Qin, Z.: Disruption and strategic outsourcing to the competitor in the common market. Int. J. Oper. Res. Inf. Syst. (IJORIS) **10**(1), 1–20 (2019)

Quaquebeke, N., Gerpott, F.H.: The now, new, and next of digital leadership: how artificial intelligence (AI) will take over and change leadership as we know it. J. Leadersh. Organiz. Stud. **30**(3), 265–275 (2023)

Rubab, S.A.: Impact of AI on business growth. Bus. Manag. Rev. **14**(2), 229–236 (2023)

Samadhiya, A., et al.: The influence of artificial intelligence techniques on disruption management: does supply chain dynamism matter? Technol. Soc. **75**, 102394 (2023)

Shen, B., Li, Q.: Market disruptions in supply chains: a review of operational models. Int. Trans. Oper. Res. **24**(4), 697–711 (2017)

Shvetsova, O.: The impact of AI on business ecosystem development: pro and contra. In: Emerging Technologies and Future of Work, vol. 117 (2023)

Sulthan, N., AlGahtani, F., Mahjoub, M., Al-Surf, M., Navas, S.: Physician entrepreneurs and AI technology: an in-depth study of knowledge, competence, adoption, and sustainability in the GCC region. Emirati J. Bus. Econ. Soc. Stud. **2**(2), 28–38 (2023)

Lin, T.-C., Margaret, K.J.W., Sheng, L.: To assess smart manufacturing readiness by maturity model: a case study on Taiwan enterprises. Int. J. Comput. Integr. Manuf. **33**(1), 102–115 (2020). https://doi.org/10.1080/0951192X.2019.1699255

Utomo, S., Setiastuti, N.: Industri 4.0: Pengukuran Tingkat Kesiapan Industri Tekstil dengan Metode Singapore Smart Industry Readiness Index. Journal Techno Nusa Mandiri **16**(1), 29–36 (2019)

Venkatesh, D., Jakka, S.R.: Digital recruitment technology implementation: a study of select companies in Yadadri Bhuvanagiri dist. of Telangana state, India. Asian J. Econ. Bus. Account. **23**(6), 32–42 (2023). https://doi.org/10.9734/AJEBA/2023/v23i6939

Westerman, G., Bonnet, D., McAfee, A.: Leading Digital: Turning Technology into Business Transformation. Harvard Business Review Press (2014)

Van de Wetering, R., de Weerd-Nederhof, P., Bagheri, S., Bons, R.: Architecting agility: unraveling the impact of AI capability on organizational change and competitive advantage. In: Shishkov, B. (eds.) BMSD 2023. LNBIP, vol. 483, pp. 203–213. Springer, Cham (2023). https://doi.org/10.1007/978-3-031-36757-1_12

Yadav, M.K., Dwivedi, N., Sondhi, H.: Systematic literature review on sustainable marketing and artificial intelligence. In: 2023 10th International Conference on Computing for Sustainable Global Development (INDIACom), pp. 583–588. IEEE, March 2023

Zamani, E., Smyth, C., Gupta, S., Dennehy, D.: Artificial intelligence and big data analytics for supply chain resilience: a systematic literature review. Ann. Oper. Res. **327**(2), 605–632 (2022)

Zhao, Y., Xu, L., Wang, T.: Design and implementation of enterprise AI business service system based on NHibernate architecture. In: 2023 IEEE 6th International Conference on Knowledge Innovation and Invention (ICKII), pp. 345–349. IEEE, August 2023

Designing Agents for Digital Twin of an Isolated Energy System

Daria Gaskova(✉)[ID], Aleksei Massel[ID], Aleksey Tsybikov[ID], and Nikita Shchukin[ID]

Melentiev Energy Systems Institute SB RAS, Lermontov st. 130, 664033 Irkutsk, Russia
gaskovada@gmail.com

Abstract. The use of renewable energy sources is an urgent task in the territories with decentralized energy supply. The introduction of new digital technologies allows one to analyze the possibility and expediency of implementing energy technologies in specific territorial conditions. Currently, one of the main trends of digital energy transformation is Digital Twins, which in some cases are considered synonymous with the digitalization of the energy sector. Whereas the technology of Digital Twins is actively developing, there is no single standard for the development of software tools. The article presents the previous stages of research on the design of architecture and components of the digital twin and the corresponding approach based on the application of ontological modeling. The presented study introduces aspects of designing software tools that are part of the Digital Twin architecture. The agent-service approach is used in the design of components of the Digital Twin architecture. The design of software tools is based on examples of tasks relevant to isolated power systems (solar power plant and wind farm) as an energy system with a relatively small set of parameters. The experience gained will be further extended to other energy systems.

Keywords: Knowledge Engineering Methods · Ontological Approach · Renewable Energy Sources

1 Introduction

The introduction of new digital technologies allows one to analyze the possibility and expediency of implementing energy technologies in specific territorial conditions. Reducing the cost of implementing and maintaining energy systems based on the use of renewable energy sources contributes to the deployment of such systems in isolated areas remote from centralized energy supply. The analysis of threats to energy security is carried out during the design and implementation of such energy technologies. Threats include the repair of specialized power equipment, physical and moral deterioration of equipment, uneven and unstable load schedules, etc. The increased reliability requirements with this respect should also be taken into account for such systems operating in decentralized areas. Figure 1 briefly presents some aspects of energy supply to consumers isolated from the power grid. Digital Twin technology allows one solving such tasks at the stages of exploration, design, management and forecasting of systems.

© The Author(s), under exclusive license to Springer Nature Switzerland AG 2025
V. Taratukhin et al. (Eds.): CPHCATI 2024, CCIS 2233, pp. 155–165, 2025.
https://doi.org/10.1007/978-3-031-77012-8_11

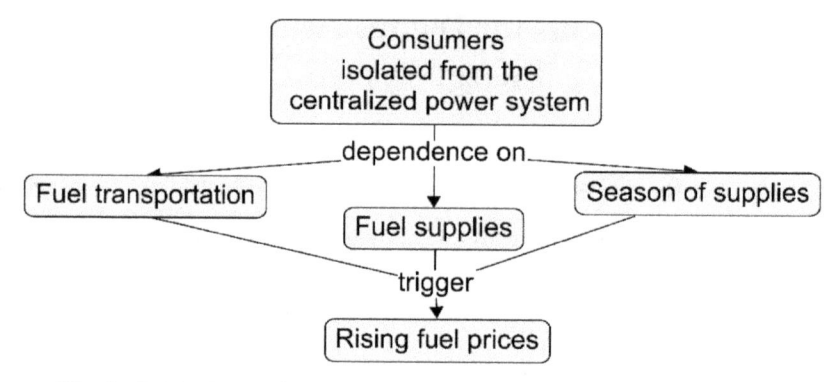

Fig. 1. Some aspects of energy supply to consumers from isolated territories.

The development of Digital Twins is not strictly regulated at the moment. The authors present a study in the field of designing Digital Twins for solving energy problems. The article contains a description and links to the previous stages of the study and the current stage devoted to the design of a Digital Twin component for performing mathematical modeling in the field of energy.

1.1 Some Aspects of Digital Twin Technologies

Technologies represented on the Gartner Inc. Hype Cycle for Emerging Technologies (2018) [1] includes Digital twins, which are at the peak of expectations. And although the trend of digital twins has been declared one of the breakthrough technologies in the energy sector for 10 years in the report of the Global Energy Association [2], there is no single definition of this term. The general meaning of this term is to create a constantly updated digital model used for conducting experiments and testing hypotheses, predicting the behavior of an object and solving problems of managing its life cycle based on real or experimental data [3]. The Digital Twin technology combines both the virtual environment of the enterprise (data coming from sensors, mathematical and simulation models, etc.) and the physical one (actuators, machines, circuits, etc.), and also describes the process of interaction between these environments and complements it with automation technologies.

Digital Twins include five types of components [4] in its architecture: i) a computational core that implements mathematical, simulation and information models; ii) data collection and analysis systems for observation, cognition, monitoring tasks, as well as control systems for a physical object (an element or part of a Digital Twin); iii) systems providing storage of the collected data, including databases, cloud storage, distributed file systems, etc.; iv) service components that provide services and an interface for users; v) Internet of Things platform that provides connections between components.

Weather forecasting is an important feature of designing Digital Twin counterparts of renewable energy sources, since the its behavior strongly depends on external factors, such as solar radiation or wind speed. Machine learning models for predicting such data are used to consideration the feature. Application of recurrent neural networks is suitable for solving the weather forecasting problem. Recurrent neural networks are a type of neural network that aims to process sequences [5]. That neural network allows one to predict information based on historical data, as well as analyze input data. Such popular networks as LSTM and GRU were taken as an example in the study. Machine learning methods have been widely used in solving various energy problems. However, most practical and research tasks are solved due to classical mathematical models that describe the behavior of energy objects.

The development of Digital Twins of energy facilities will expand the possibilities of solving problems of design, forecasting and management in energy systems by modeling the structure of facilities and production processes, simulating their activities using various models.

1.2 Mathematical Models in the Energy Sector

Energy sector is an infrastructure industry, the main task of which is to ensure energy supply to consumers with the required reliability and acceptable quality of energy. The infrastructural role is inherent in electric, gas and heat supply systems with a well-developed transport and distribution network infrastructure. These energy systems are usually divided into production, transport and energy supply systems [6]. Production and transport energy systems are integrated when using the energy carrier of one system into another (for example, gas as fuel in power plants and boiler houses, electricity in gas pumping units, and so on). This integration defines the leading role of energy systems in the energy complex.

Energy models, as well as energy infrastructure, differ in their territorial and sectoral coverage, level of detail (for example, their temporal and spatial aspects) and their initial conditions and assumptions [7]. There is no universal energy model that could completely solve the problems of energy planning for all isolated areas. Various energy models and their combinations serves to solve this issue as decision support tools. An overview of the methodologies and models used in isolated territories is presented in [8]. Such models are often based on Stochastic Mathematical Programming, Fuzzy Mathematical Programming and Interval Mathematical Programming, Probability-Constrained Programming, Two-stage Stochastic Programming, Multi-stage Stochastic Programming, Fuzzy Flexible Programming, Fuzzy Probabilistic programming, Interval Linear Programming. Five open-source frameworks for modeling renewable energy systems were compared in [9]: urbs, The Baltic Model of Regional Electricity Liberalization (Balmorel), Genetic Optimization of a European Energy Supply System (GENESYS-2), Global Energy System Model (GENeSYS-MOD), Open Energy Modeling Framework (oemof). One of the results of the study is the conclusion that the core equations are mathematically very similar.

The proposed study is offered to design program tool, which connect appropriate solvers to solve mathematical equations. It is proposed to design such software tools as agent services both for storing descriptions of mathematical models and for calling solvers. Ontological modeling methods are used to integrate disparate mathematical models within the framework of the ontological approach to the construction of digital twins (Sect. 1.4).

1.3 Knowledge Engineering Methods

The concept of ontological engineering refers to knowledge engineering, a branch of engineering activity aimed at using knowledge in computer systems to solve complex problems. Ontological engineering develops the basic principles of knowledge engineering and combines two main technologies for designing large systems: object-oriented and structural analysis [10]. The goal of ontological engineering is to structure and manage knowledge using ontologies. Ontological engineering is used to support strategic decision-making in the energy sector. It ensures the allocation of the connections between various factors (environmental, economic, social, energy, etc.) and the consistency of interdisciplinary energy research.

Another important aspect of ontological engineering is applying of ontologies and ontology systems in the design of software products, including for energy facilities, systems and the energy sector as a whole. Various studies demonstrate the advantages of ontologies. Some of them relate with support the development of industrial energy management systems [11], analysis of energy systems [7], development of web services for district energy management [12], research on the energy sector in general [13], for instance.

The authors are part of a team that performs scientific research [14] in which ontological engineering is considered as a stage in the design of Digital Twins. Ontological approach to the construction of Digital Twins in the energy sector is proposed for this purpose.

1.4 Ontological Approach Proposed for Digital Twin Designing

Digital Twins have shown good results at different stages of the life cycle of objects and systems. The main problem in building digital twins is the lack of a unified concept of interconnection and general interaction between different levels of management [6].

The ontological approach to the construction of Digital Twins suggests, first of all, the construction of a single ontological space of knowledge, filling it with content and, further, the formalization and use of ontologies in the design of information models and the selection of mathematical models for the implementation of tasks of energy object, system or sector [14]. The ontological approach allows one to integrate different models (i.e. mathematical or informational) at the stage of system design. The approach contributes to the formalization of the description of information flows necessary for the operation and integration of software components of the Digital Twin (agent-based design) for their operation in a single information space. Figure 2 shows the main idea of the approach.

The ontological approach makes it possible to integrate description of models of different kinds at different levels into a single modeling complex considering information relationships and data exchange [6]. The transition from scientific tools (mathematical models and software) to Digital Twin is accompanied by the development of digital programs, web applications and web services, including programs based on the reengineering of outdated software that implements mathematical models.

Ontologies are frequently employed in the design of Digital Twins, by way of illustration, Internet of Things ontology for building Digital Twin in cyber physical systems

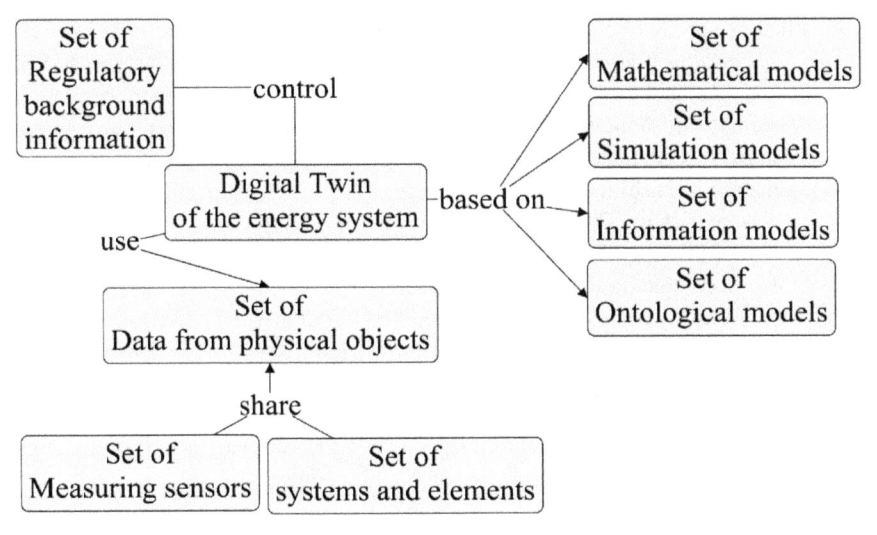

Fig. 2. The scheme of interaction of the parts of the Digital Twin.

[15]. Steindl et al. [16] present a service-oriented architecture of the digital twin of an energy system, including a common knowledge base of components and an ontological modeling module. Akroyd et al. [17] combined different ontologies and provided a geospatial description to create a digital twin in the field of land use.

Ontologies for designing Digital Twins of a wind farm [18] and a solar power plant [19] were proposed at the previous stages of the study in accordance with the ontological approach. Results of ontological engineering of the subject area of solar power plant and wind farm provided the basis for architectures of Digital Twins. The data model has been developed and implemented based on ontologies of equipment, weather conditions, energy tasks, and links between them. The corresponding database scheme is implemented in the PostgreSQL relational database.

2 Designing of Agents-Service Mathematical Modelling

Section 1.1 provides the types of Digital Twin components. The computational core implements mathematical, simulation and information models. Section 2 is devoted to the implementation of a part of the computational core that implements one set of models – mathematical models describing the behavior of energy objects.

The proposed research includes the development of Digital Twin components as agents-services. Agents are computing units that support local states and parallel computing, which are able to reach the state of other agents in communication processes and automatically perform actions in certain environmental conditions [20]. An agent acts as a service in the agent system that provides services to other agents or external users. Agents can perform work in parallel, together, and interacting with each other. Such systems containing agents interacting with each other are called multi-agent systems [21]. One of the advantages of this approach is modularity. Agents can be developed and modified independently of each other with minimal or no changes in the entire software package. This approach allows one to easily to make changes to the system, add new agents or modify existing ones without disrupting the operation of other components. Modularity simplifies the development and maintenance of the system, since updates and fixes can be implemented separately. Independent agents and services contribute to improving the maintainability (the ability to refine, improve), extensibility and scalability of the software system. This approach describes the creation of various combinations of agents to perform specific tasks. This is primarily relevant when connecting and switching various mathematical equation solvers.

Agent-based technologies are used in the energy sector to solve various tasks with developing systems such as Intelligent Decision-making Support Systems [21], Modelling of Renewable Energy Market [22], framework for Digital Twins for multi-robots of the smart warehouse [23], etc.

Figure 3 demonstrates the interaction scheme of agent-services as part of the Digital Twin of an isolated power system for mathematical modeling.

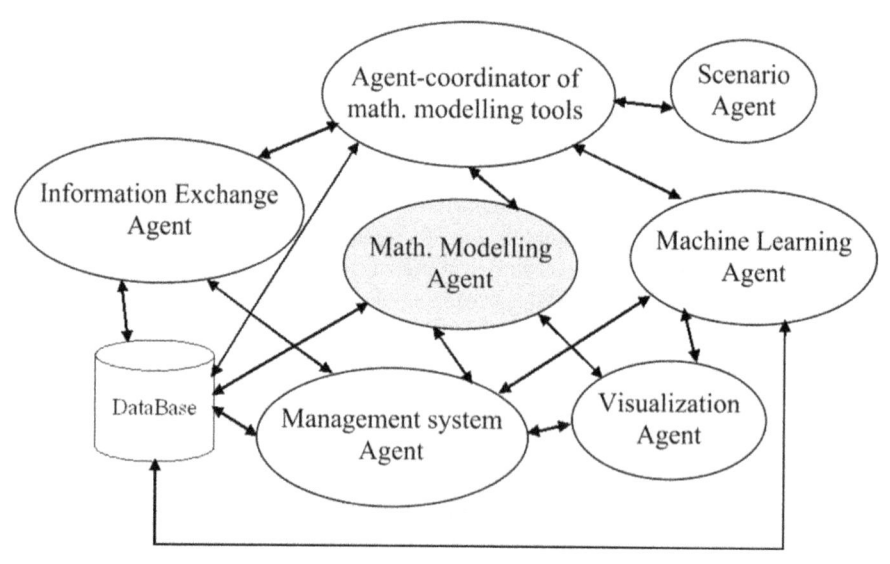

Fig. 3. Scheme of agent-services as part of the Digital Twin of an isolated power system for mathematical modeling.

Each agent in the agent-service approach performs its tasks aimed at achieving the set goal. The main goals of the service agents shown in Fig. 3 are shown below.

Agent-coordinator of mathematical modelling tools is controls agents, which responsible for work of mathematical modelling tools. Every tool is an agent too.

Information exchange agent serves to organize the exchange between agents in multi-agent system or between agents and data flow from sensors and systems of physical objects.

Machine learning agents solve the tasks of predicting various characteristics in the functioning of objects. The data obtained during forecasting is used for planning and decision-making. This type of agent can be used for a different set of tasks that digital counterparts must solve, including predictive analytics tasks. In addition, this agent solves the problems of data imputation and emulation.

Management system agent performs the functions of transferring the received calculations to the object management systems.

Visualization agents work to provide different types of visualization of data and objects depending on the required level of decision-making. Tabular interfaces and dashboards are designed at the current stage of work.

Mathematical modeling agent allows one to process mathematical models describing the behavior of energy objects and perform the function of calculating the necessary characteristics.

Consider the principle of the Mathematical modeling agent's work in more detail. Mathematical modeling agent-service operates as follows in the simplest version:

1. Entering a list of necessary formulas for a mathematical model into the user interface (GUI).
2. Conversion of formulas into a structured program format.
3. Formation of the calculation scenario and selection of datasets, if necessary.
4. Selecting a solver and performing calculations according to a given scenario and parameters.
5. Uploading calculation results as a dataset.

Figure 4 shows operation scheme of the components of the mathematical modeling agent-service. The dotted line shows the interaction with external services.

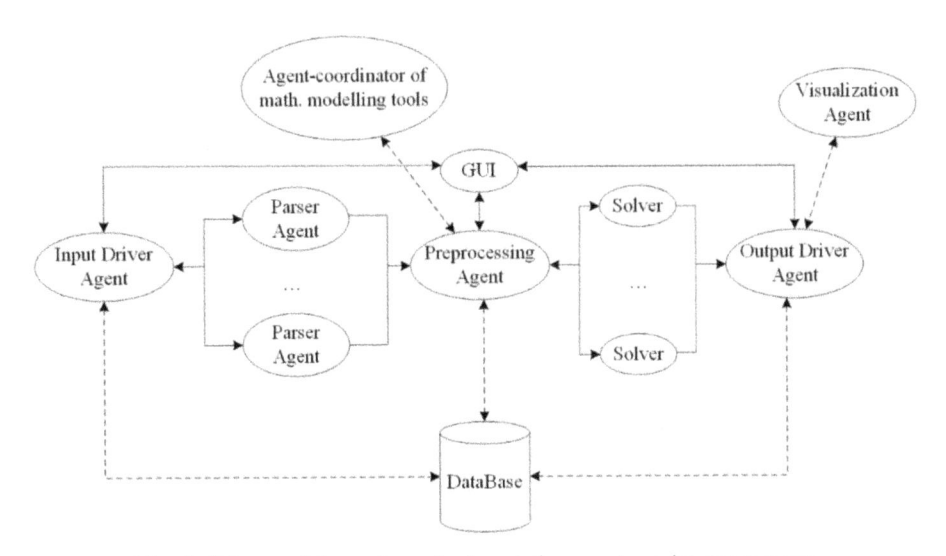

Fig. 4. Scheme of the mathematical modeling agent-service components.

Input Driver is used to work with a user who enters mathematical formulas for storage and further calculations. Formulas are written to datasets (JSON, csv, xlsx).

Parsers service to translate function from input language into a program format. The number of parsers is declared only by the number of ways to write formulas.

Preprocessing component provides an opportunity through the GUI to create scenarios for working with mathematical formulas and interacting with a dataset. Scenario agent there manages the scenarios and interactions of the solvers.

Solver is a software library for solving a mathematical tasks and obtaining output data. The number of solvers depends directly on the functionality of other solvers.

Output driver displays updated data sets and saves them after conversion.

Database stores mathematical models and datasets. Such data is diverse and requires a flexible data model. The existing version on PostgreSQL is implemented only for a solar power plant. This database is difficult to expand for a wind farm and therefore it was chosen to use a NoSQL database.

Table 1 resents agent-services and the stages of their basic work for mathematical modeling.

Table 1. Technology of using the mathematical modeling agent-service.

Stages	Agent-services (components)	Results
Formulas input	GUI, Input Driver, DataBase	Standardized formula
Converting formulas to a program format	Parser, DataBase	Structured program format formulas
Formation of the calculation scenario	GUI, Preprocessing, Scenario Agent, DataBase	The script of the formula execution order, selected solvers and additional parameters
Calculation	Solver	Updated data sets
Displaying results of calculation	GUI, Output Driver, DataBase, Visualization Agent	Tables, dashboards with updated data sets

The results of calculations in the current study are supposed to be used in two ways (Fig. 5): i) solving problems of functioning and forecasting for physical object systems; ii) simulation modeling near real conditions or training simulators. This study focuses on the second option. Part of the Digital Twin for visualizing the simulation of the behavior of a wind farm is being developed on the Unity cross-platform engine.

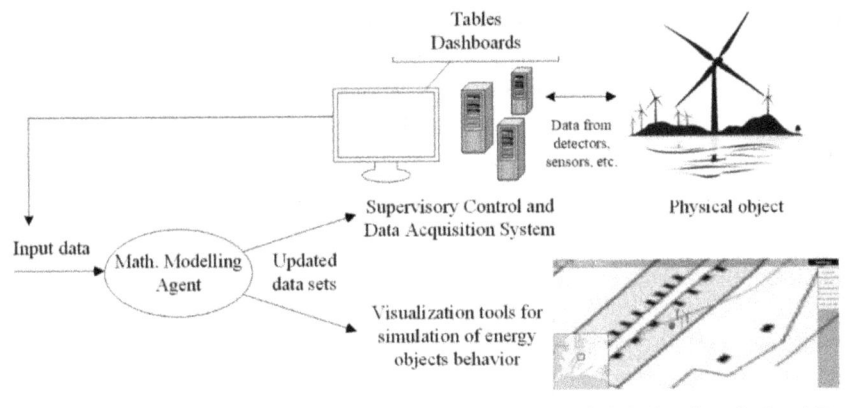

Fig. 5. Ways to use a mathematical modeling agent in the Digital Twin of an Isolated Power System.

3 Conclusion and Future Work

The article presents the design of Digital Twin components (computational core) implementing mathematical models for various tasks of modeling the operation of an isolated power system on the example of solar power plant and a wind farm. PostgreSQL relational database was used at the previous stages of work. However, relational databases are limited in flexibility and sensitive to changes in the database structure. Non-relational (NoSQL) database is proposed to use as an alternative to overcome the limitations in future work. NoSQL databases offer a more flexible data storage model that meets the requirements of changing data structures. Such databases allow one to add and remove data fields, change their types and relationships without having to change the database structure. This makes NoSQL databases more suitable for tasks where flexibility and adaptability are required. They also provide higher performance and scalability when processing large amounts of data. Such advantages of databases are relevant for the Digital Twins design.

In the future, NoSQL will be used to store mathematical models, which are planned to be used in Digital Twin. Such a database will also be used to store and use collections of data.

The organization of data storage is an important task for the integration of traditional mathematical models in the field of energy and machine learning models into a unified computer model. Research team implements making program prototypes to develop agent-services for simulation modeling near real conditions or training simulators. Mathematical models for determining the operating parameters of a wind farm and modeling a solar power plant taking into account changes in environmental parameters [18, 19] were used to develop data models and prototyping a mathematical modeling agent-service. LSTM for short-term forecasting of insolation, air temperature and wind speed for several isolated settlements of the Baikal Natural Territory were developed to simulate environmental parameters. At the same time, the problem of imputation of incomplete data obtained from open sources was solved. The further direction of work is related to the development of prototypes of agent-services for the implementation of a unified computer model, visualization and testing on a digital platform that is being developed on Unity cross-platform engine.

The prototyping process is aimed at team learning process, gamification in the design of an isolated power system and modeling of its operation parameters, development and revision of a unified approach to the design of digital twins for various models. The ontological approach in such studies is relevant not only for the design of digital twins, structuring information in planning, functioning and forecasting the application of energy technologies, but also for the development team to structure information about a multidisciplinary subject area.

Acknowledgments. The reported study was funded by Russian Science Foundation, according to the research project No. 23-21-00382, https://rscf.ru/en/project/23-21-00382.

Author Contributions. Conceptualization, A.G.; Data curation, A.R., N.I.; Investigation, A.R., D.A.; Software, A.R., N.I.; Writing, A.R., D.A.

References

1. Emerging Technology Trends and 2018 Hype Cycle. https://www.gartner.com/en/newsroom/press-releases/2018-08-20-gartner-identifies-five-emerging-technology-trends-that-will-blur-the-lines-between-human-and-machine. Accessed 08 Feb 2024
2. Breakthrough Ideas in Energy for the Next 10 Years. https://globalenergyprize.org/en/2023/06/15/10-breakthrough-ideas-in-energy-for-the-next-10-years. Accessed 13 Feb 2024
3. Shmotin, Y.: Digital Twin in Manufacturing: Tasks, Issues, Prospects. http://www.up-pro.ru/library/information_systems/project/d7fb9dd59e1ffa29.html. Accessed 08 Feb 2024. [in Russian]
4. Prohorov, A., Lysachev, M.: Digital twin. Analysis, trends, world experience P: Al'yansPrint (2020). 401 p. [in Russian]
5. Abiodun, O.I., Jantan, A., Omolara, A.E., Dada, K.V., Mohamed, N.A., Arshad, H.: State-of-the-art in artificial neural network applications: a survey. Heliyon **4**(11) (2018). https://doi.org/10.1016/j.heliyon.2018.e00938
6. Massel, L.V., Vorozhtsova, T.N.: Ontological approach to the creation of digital twins of energy objects and systems. Ontol. Des. **10**(3), 327–337 (2020). https://doi.org/10.18287/2223-9537-2020-10-3-327-337. (in Russian)
7. Booshehri, M., Emele, L., Flügel, S., Förster, H., et al.: Introducing the Open Energy Ontology: enhancing data interpretation and interfacing in energy systems analysis. Energy AI **5** (2021). https://doi.org/10.1016/j.egyai.2021.100074
8. Liu, Y., Yu, S., Zhu, Y., Wang, D., Liu, J.: Modeling, planning, application and management of energy systems for isolated areas: a review. Renew. Sustain. Energy Rev. **82**(Part 1), 460–470 (2018)
9. Candas, S., Muschner, C., Buchholz, S., et al.: Code exposed: review of five open-source frameworks for modeling renewable energy systems. Renew. Sustain. Energy Rev. **161**, 112272 (2022). https://doi.org/10.1016/j.rser.2022.112272
10. Gavrilova, T., Laird, D.: Practical design of business enterprise ontologies. In: Proceedings of the IASW, pp. 65–81 (2005)
11. Monaco, R., Liu, X., Murino, T., Cheng, X., Nielsen, P.S.: A non-functional requirements-based ontology for supporting the development of industrial energy management systems. J. Clean. Prod. **414**, 137614 (2023). https://doi.org/10.1016/j.jclepro.2023.137614

12. Hippolyte, J.-L., Rezgui, Y., Li, H., Jayan, B., Howell, S.: Ontology-driven development of web services to support district energy applications. Autom. Constr. **86**, 210–225 (2018). https://doi.org/10.1016/j.autcon.2017.10.004
13. Massel, L.V.: Fractal approach to constructing ontological knowledge space. In: 2018 3rd Russian-Pacific Conference on Computer Technology and Applications (RPC), pp. 1–5. IEEE (2018). https://doi.org/10.1109/RPC.2018.8482138
14. Massel, L., Massel, A.: Smart digital twins as a trend of energy systems intellectualization in Russia. In: Proceedings of the Seventh International Scientific Conference "Intelligent Information Technologies for Industry" (IITI 2023), vol. 2, pp. 334–346 (2023). https://doi.org/10.1007/978-3-031-43792-2_32
15. Steinmetz, C., Rettberg, A., Ribeiro, F.G.C., Schroeder, G., Pereira, C.E.: Internet of things ontology for digital twin in cyber physical systems. In: 2018 VIII Brazilian Symposium on Computing Systems Engineering (SBESC), pp. 154–159 (2018). https://doi.org/10.1109/SBESC.2018.00030
16. Steindl, G., Stagl, M., Kasper, L., Kastner, W., Hofmann, R.: Generic digital twin architecture for industrial energy systems. Appl. Sci. **10**(24), 8903 (2020). https://doi.org/10.3390/app10248903
17. Akroyd, J., et al.: Universal digital twin: land use. Data-Centric Eng. **3** (2022). Article e3. https://doi.org/10.1017/dce.2021.21
18. Massel, L.V., Massel, A.G., Shchukin, N.I., Tsybikov, A.R.: Designing a digital twin of a wind farm. In: Proceedings of the 15th International Conference "Intelligent Systems", vol. 33, no. 1, p. 30 (2023). https://doi.org/10.3390/engproc2023033030
19. Massel, L., Shchukin, N., Cybikov, A.: Digital twin development of a solar power plant. E3S Web Conf. **289**, 03002 (2021). https://doi.org/10.1051/e3sconf/202128903002
20. Gorodetsky, V.I.: Multi-agent systems: basic properties and models of behavior coordination. Inf. Technol. Comput. Syst. **1**, 22–34 (1998)
21. Massel, A., Galperov, V., Kuzmin, V.: Agent-service approach for development of intelligent decision-making support systems. In: Proceedings of the VIth International Workshop "Critical Infrastructures: Contingency Management, Intelligent, Agent-Based, Cloud Computing and Cyber Security" (IWCI 2019), pp. 211–215 (2019). https://doi.org/10.2991/iwci-19.2019.37
22. Deissenroth, M., Klein, M., Nienhaus, K., Reeg, M.: Assessing the plurality of actors and policy interactions: agent-based modelling of renewable energy market integration. Energy Complex. **2017** (2017). https://doi.org/10.1155/2017/7494313
23. Marah, H., Challenger, M.: MADTwin: a framework for multi-agent digital twin development: smart warehouse case study. Ann. Math. Artif. Intell. **91** (2023). https://doi.org/10.1007/s10472-023-09872-z

Design of Augmented Diffusion Model for Text-to-Image Representation Using Hybrid GAN

Subuhi Kashif Ansari[✉] and Rakesh Kumar

School of Engineering and Technology, Shri Venkateshwara University, Gajraula, UP, India
subuhikashifansari@gmail.com

Abstract. One of the most active areas of study in processor idea and regular language handling as of late has been the problem of text-to-image generation. With descriptive language text as input, this job aims to produce an image that consistently contains text. A novel method that enhances the training of GANs, which can synthesis various pictures from text input, is presented. The objective is to facilitate the generation of novel, user-defined ideas using language. Encoding the related concepts into an existing text-to-image model typically allows for this. This research produces embedding vectors employing a language model that follows the generative adversarial networks (GAN) architecture for image synthesis. Making realistic visuals consistently in specified settings is the most difficult endeavor. The current state of text-to-image-generating algorithms produces images that misrepresent the text. We need to upgrade the proposed approach with a hybrid GAN architecture. The datasets used in this study are CUB-200 and Oxford-102. The F1 Score, the Frechet inception distance (FID), as well as the Inception Score (IS) have all been used to quantify the effectiveness of the framework. The trial findings show that our model can make flower photographs seem more realistic with the specified descriptions. Future plans include exercise the proposed model on a selection of datasets.

Keywords: Generative Adversarial Network · Generative model · Text-to-Image Synthesis · Datasets · Frechet inception distance

1 Introduction

One deep learning (DL) model that can generate images from text is text-to-image generation using GAN. For a long time, law enforcement officers had to rely on sketch artists to help them find criminals because of limited technology tools. The proposed method leverages documented inputs of human face features and outputs the associated image of the illegal to circumvent this laborious procedure. The conversion of data between text and image is difficult for artificial intelligence (AI) systems that integrate natural language text along with image processing. Consequently, we provide a novel GAN-based retrieval system that will enhance performance through straightforward procedures [1].

A generator neural network, which is included in GANs, generates what is ostensibly a truthful image from either noise or a valuable training mutable. The discriminator identifies the images as one or the other a false image or a real image created by the generator, which determines the success. GANs have shown the feasibility of producing convincingly realistic-looking fake images. By training the discriminator to differentiate among real as well as fake pairings, the easiest method to produce images from text employing GANs is to consider the text and image pairs as joint observations [2].

For most text-to-image synthesis tasks, a huge dataset with associated text and images is used for exercise a variational autoencoder (VAE) or a GAN. The model is able to translate text into a visual representation by recognizing and internalizing the correlations and patterns present in the training data. Visual content creation from text has come a long way, but it's still difficult to create extremely complete, truthful images that perfectly represent the sensitivities of text descriptions. However, there have been encouraging developments in DL approaches, such as larger models along with enhanced training procedures, that take displayed the ability to produce visually clear and contextually appropriate images in response to text prompts [3].

The rest of this work is planned as surveys. Section 2 provides an outline of some current and recent works. The proposed technique is defined in Sect. 3. After a summary of the findings as well as analysis in Sect. 4, the references are provided.

2 Recent Works for Research

While Goodfellow in 2014 [4] was the first to present GANs, Reed et al. in 2016 [5] was the earliest to usage them for text-to-image creation. This section reviews a few recent publications that have been published on the topic of Text-to-image generation. You may find all the information you need in Table 1, which includes a summary of the methods proposed for text-to-image creation as well as their merits and cons.

Table 1. Literature review

Paper and Author	Method	Advantages	Limitation
Xiuping Li et al. [6]	KT-GAN	Improved performance	The generator is unable to accurately generate images
Xin Li et al. [7]	SDM and DNM	T2I techniques better capture the real image when the image is less complicated	It is difficult for the text encoder
Deng, Zijun, Xiangteng He, Yuxin Peng [8]	LFR-GAN	Image is photo-realistic and looks attractive	The entered text has uncleared properties. These parameters are not well-defined and difficult

(*continued*)

Table 1. (*continued*)

Paper and Author	Method	Advantages	Limitation
Hongchen Tan et al. [9]	CSM-GAN	Make the synthesised image and text description more semantically consistent	Challenging large-scale MS-COCO dataset

Some new approaches are detailed in Table 1. KT GAN, DR GAN, LFR GAN, and CSM GAN are some of the many techniques proposed in current approaches. Improved performance, superior quality, and reduced complexity are just a few of the benefits that all of these technologies provide. However, other drawbacks, such as the absence of pre-processing methods, are also mentioned.

Natural surroundings and faces are more suited to the researchers' proposed model. This study is not just about improving GAN's performance but also about highlighting its robustness [10]. Yanhua Li et al. developed fitting GAN, a method for generating clothing images from input images. Using the input images as a basis, the model learns to create output that is suitable. The perfect used L1 regularization and the adversarial loss function [11].

A model was developed by Jezia et al. to assist in the synthesis of realistic images from narrative texts by using the spatial relations of the words. The next step is to use a KNN to link the image quality mark after converting the images from low-resolution to high-resolution using two-stage discriminator and generator models [12]. The field of computer vision has achieved significant strides in the area of image synthesis. The preservation of the images' semantic content was the primary focus of the researchers. Improving the clarity and sharpness of low-resolution images is the job of super-resolution GAN. Improving the quality of an image by scaling it up without sacrificing detail or creating unwanted artifacts is very helpful. A resolution generator is designed for generator network training to generate higher-resolution images from lower-resolution ones.

The rich, bidirectional context included in natural language writings may be used by computers with the help of BERT, an over-all language image model. The attention mechanism makes use of the sequence-transduction model transformer. To assess if individually chat may function as an ancestor, classification is performed in matching for each chat in the input word order. To make the text machine-readable, a language model is needed. Unidirectional training seems to be the foundation of most language models used in research. When compared to Elmo, BERT is bidirectional. Word embedding based on transformer encoders is employed [13].

From Table 1, the advantages observed with the existing works include improved performance, the T2I techniques better capture the real image when the image is less complicated, the image is photo-realistic and looks attractive, and the synthesised image and text description are more semantically consistent. Also, the limitations identified include that the generator is unable to accurately generate images, it is difficult for the text encoder, the entered text has uncleared properties, and these parameters are not well defined and difficult. Also, the existing works face challenges with the large-scale

MS-COCO dataset. Though several works are made for text-to-image, some issues still arise, as mentioned in Table 1. Hence, to tackle these limitations, this work makes the following contributions:

- Initially, this work uses two datasets such as the CUB 200 and Oxford 102 datasets.
- An innovation model termed hybrid GAN, or H-GAN, is proposed. This H-GAN comprises a two-stage GAN model.
- The input text is given as input to the BERT BASECASE model and an output is received. The BERT BASECASE model works with the token count with the input text. This BERT BASECASE model has nearly 12 layers to perform the process of converting the text to tokens. This BERT BASECASE model output is given as the input to the first-stage GAN, while the second-stage GAN takes the output of the first-stage GAN model as input.
- Finally, the performance of the proposed H-GAN is measured by using metrics such as the inception score, frechet distance measure, and F1-score.

3 Proposed Text to Image Model

Synthesizing images with their matching text descriptions is the intended use of the architecture. Merging the Birds 200 and Oxford-102 datasets, a new dataset was developed at Caltech UCSD. Figure 1 depicts the architecture of the image synthesis system. In order to create useful sentence embeddings, the model makes use of BERTBASE-CASE's capabilities. By using the word BERT Embedding, the model is combined with BERT BASECASE and BASE GAN. On two challenging datasets, the proposed resolution technique produces better images than realistic ones for text. We have gathered the CUB 200 text and the Oxford 102 flower dataset. There are a total of 102 courses in the Oxford-102, and each one has its own collection of images and information. A further experimental dataset, the CUB 200, was also created.

3.1 BERT BASECASE Model

Through adjustment the past level of the handling model, the proposed language model attempted to employ the BERT language model trained on a text corpus. In the proposed BERT BASE CASE model, hidden layers' process input text sentences. There are 768 unseen units in the 12 layers of the BERT BASECASE model.

Think of the rulings as t and the values of the text tokens $[t_1, t_2, ..t_n]$ as input tokens to the input layer. Adding the past level vectors of the unknown layers of the transformer H_0 together is called concatenation. It is used to make feature vectors $[f_1, f_2, ..f_n]$ from the results as they move through the hidden layers. The BERT BASE CASE model's goal function is shown as:

$$\varphi(t) = t_1, t_2, \ldots t_n \qquad (1)$$

where n is the tokens count in the text, t is the text's tokens, and the different text tokens are represented by Eq. (1).

```
┌─────────────┐     ┌──────────┐     ┌──────────────┐     ┌─────────────┐
│ Pink flower │     │ Language │     │Latent vectors│     │             │
│ with yellow │────▶│  Model   │────▶│ of sentence  │────▶│Image feature│
│   center    │     │          │     │              │     │             │
└─────────────┘     └──────────┘     └──────┬───────┘     └──────┬──────┘
                                            │                    │
                        ┌─────────┐         ▼                    │
                        │  Noise  │     ┌──────────┐             │
                        │function │────▶│Generator │◀────────────┘
                        └─────────┘     │ Network  │
                                        └─────┬────┘
                        ┌─────────┐           ▼
                        │  Noise  │     ┌──────────────┐
                        │function │────▶│Discriminator │
                        └─────────┘     │   Network    │
                                        └──────┬───────┘
                                               ▼
                                        ┌────────────┐    ┌─────────────┐
                                        │ Synthesised│───▶│Loss function│
                                        │   Image    │    │             │
                                        └────────────┘    └─────────────┘
```

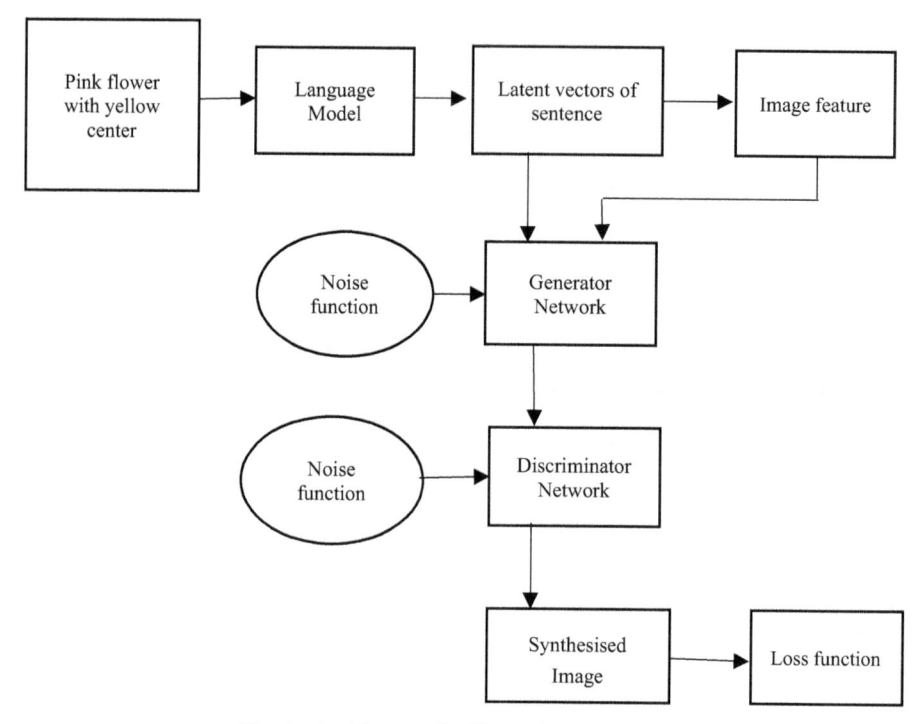

Fig. 1. Architecture for Text to Image Creation

3.2 BASEGAN Model for Image Generation

The proposed GAN is a text-to-image creation network organized basis model for image synthesis. Receiving latent vectors from the BERT BASE CASE model the prior language model is how the model under investigation operates. The noise function, generator network, along with preprocessed image feature vectors are given the latent output vectors. The discriminator receives the generator noise function and the generator network's output in a similar fashion.

3.3 Hybrid GAN (HGAN)

While the traditional GAN model is useful in many contexts, the hybrid GAN (H GAN) model is more akin to a two-stage GAN model. The synthesised images from stage I (S-I) are the building blocks of the two-stage model. Although single-stage GAN networks are useful for many applications, they cannot capture the fine details that are crucial to a synthesised image. The model uses slabs of residuals. The two GAN stages operate similarly to the base GAN stage examined in Model I, then the output is passed into Model II to improve resolution. A model with dividing, converting, and aggregating functions is like a residual block in a computer program. Latent vectors, which are the image vectors representation, allow the generator to access the necessary feature vectors in latent space and produce images.

To further enhance its resolution, the Stage II (S-II) GAN gets output images from S-I. The discriminator and generator both make use of the Wasserstein loss function (WLF). One major benefit of the WLF is that it reduces the detection threshold for generated fake and real images. Both the P_{Real} and $P_{Generated}$ components, which represent the natural distribution of values across the generated images, are involved. Mathematically, it's the shortest path that takes into account the transfer plan that turns data into real and generated images, so it can track the Earth's distance. One benefit of using the WLF is that it makes it easy to tell the difference between generated real as well as fake images, which should help with the difficulty of determining whether an image is real or not (Fig. 2).

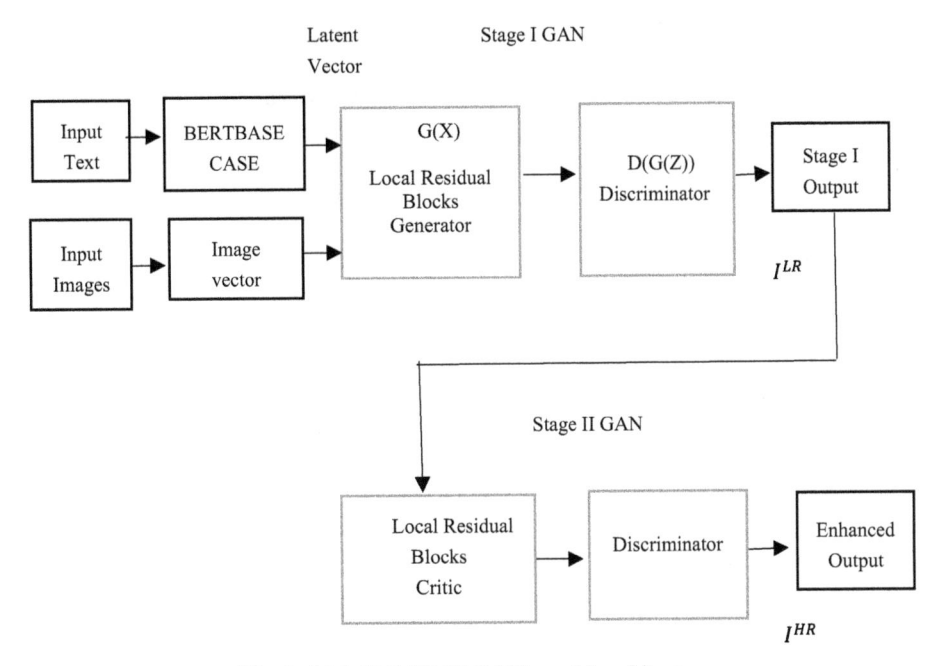

Fig. 2. Hybrid GAN (H GAN) model architecture

Additionally, it supports the model's stabilization throughout training. The WLF views the discriminator as a critic that aims to draw attention to significant gradient information throughout the training model. The following is how H GAN is represented: I^{LR} is a representation of the S-I stage network's low-resolution image, whereas I^{HR} stands for the image's high resolution. In Eq. (2), the objective function is depicted.

$$minmaxE_{I^{HR}}(G,D) = E_{x \sim pdata}\left[loglogD\left(I^{HR}\right)\right] + E_{I^{LR} \sim p I^{LR}}\left[loglog\left(1 - D\left(G\left(I^{LR}\right)\right)\right)\right] \quad (2)$$

The WLF, which is denoted as, is the loss function associated with S-II.

$$Loss_{WDG} = E(C(x_{real})) - E(C(G(z))) \quad (3)$$

It is evident from Eq. (3) that the WLF seeks to compare the generated fake images with the real image distribution in terms of critic value. The letter C stands for the loss function's critic value. The discriminator output is calculated as critic output, which is dependent on the Lipschitz constant and is represented by Eqs. (4 and 5). The critic value can be any number.

$$c = 1 - \text{Lipschitz Continuous} \tag{4}$$

$$Distance_{EMD} = \sum_{i=1}^{m} \sum_{j=1}^{n} [x_{Real} G(z)]ij \tag{5}$$

where I^{LR} denotes the low-resolution image representation produced by the S-I stage network. The term I^{HR} describes the high-resolution image that the stage-II network is producing. Total Real Data expected of the high-resolution image produced by the S-II network is indicated by the symbol E_{IHR}. Expected across all Real Data of the low-resolution image produced by the S-I network is indicated by the notation $E_{ILR} \sim P_{ILR}$. The probability that a fictitious occurrence of a low-resolution image is real is indicated by the symbol $D(G(I^{LR}))$. The output from the discriminator is identified as the critic output, and C is the critic value is any integer. The Earth mover distance among the real as well as false distributions is specified by $Distance_{EMD}$.

4 Results and Discussions

FID, IS, along with F1 score are utilized for the model evaluation. The IS calculates the Kullback-Leibler (KL) deviation, or Inception Score, among the conditional distribution $p(y|x)$ also the marginal distribution $p(y)$. The F1 score determines the synthesized images' Precision along with Recall values. The images have a tendency to have lesser quality resolution, but it may be improved employing a two-stage GAN, as the upcoming model explains. Though it still lacks high-resolution elements, the resulting picture is compelling. By adopting the H GAN model, it opens the door to improving the BASEGAN model output. Table 2 displays the training and testing set.

Table 2. CUB-200 as well as Oxford-102 Dataset

Datasets	Test	Train
CUB-200	2374	9414
Oxford-102	1155	7034

where μ_{HR} along with μ_{LR} are the means, σ_{HR} and σ_{LR} are the standard deviations, also the generated images x along with real image sequential input cross-covariance is σ_{HRLR}. The IS metric is equated as in Eq. (6)

$$IS = exp(E_x D_{KL}(P(y|x)||P(y))) \tag{6}$$

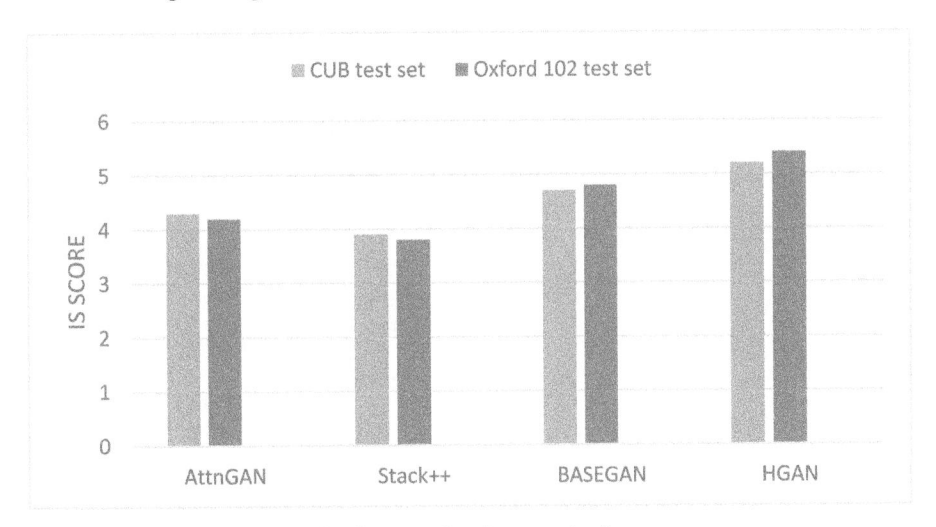

Fig. 3. Inception Score evaluation

The proposed H-GAN's IS score is 20.93% higher than the existing AttnGAN, 33.33% higher than the existing Stack++, and 10.63% higher than the existing BaseGAN with the CUB 200 dataset. Furthermore, the proposed H-GAN's IS score is 28.57% better than existing AttnGAN, 42.10% better than existing Stack++, and 12.5% better than existing BaseGAN with the Oxford 102 dataset.

X is an analysis of generated imagery, as well as y is a pre-trained Inception v3 network image label. A higher IS yields categorized images of superior quality. FID is an additional Frechet distance measure. By utilizing the trained Inception v3 network, FID is able to predict feature space pictures. We can see the FID score in Eq. (7).

$$FID = \|\mu_x - \mu_y\|^2 + Trace\left(\sum_x \sum_z -2* + \sqrt{\sum_x \sum_y}\right) \quad (7)$$

The proposed H-GAN's FID score is 20% higher than the existing AttnGAN, 13.33% higher than the existing Stack++, and 17.78% higher than the existing BaseGAN with the CUB 200 dataset. Furthermore, the proposed H-GAN's IS score is 41.37% better than existing AttnGAN, 13.88% better than existing Stack++, and 17.14% better than existing BaseGAN with the Oxford 102 dataset.

Here the synthesised and real images' mean and covariance FID on the minimum value, in contrast to IS, displays more realistic images and similar distributions. The F1 metric offers a unified representation of recall and precision that encompasses both characteristics. Equation (8) represents the F1 measure.

$$F1Measure = \frac{2 * Precision * Recall}{Precision + Recall} \quad (8)$$

The proposed H-GAN's F1 score is 23.07% higher than the existing AttnGAN, same as the existing Stack++, and 14.28% higher than the existing BaseGAN with the CUB 200 dataset. Furthermore, the proposed H-GAN's IS score is 22.73% better than

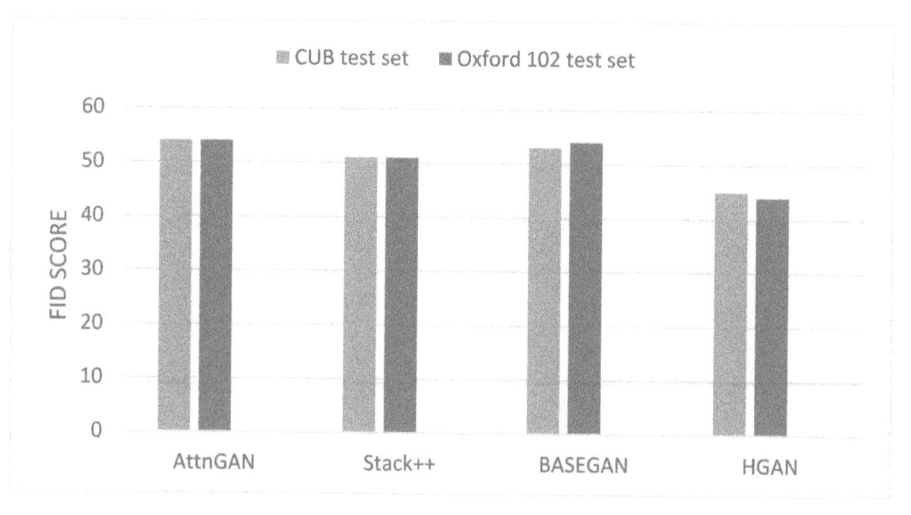

Fig. 4. FID score performance estimation.

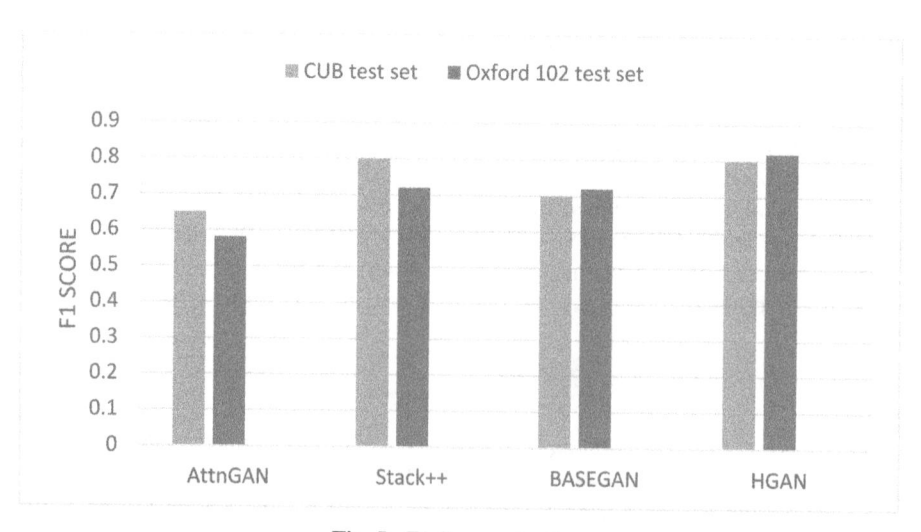

Fig. 5. F1-Score valuation

existing AttnGAN, 15.91% better than existing Stack++, and 22.73% better than existing BaseGAN with the Oxford 102 dataset.

GAN showed itself to be an excellent tool for image synthesis applications. The Base GAN model along with the H GAN model are the models currently in use for image synthesis at two performance levels. The proposed architecture can serve as a base for additional development that accommodates a range of applications. The model's initial goal is to produce vector demonstrations for text input. The GAN models create images in the backend that match the text vectors. The model's ability to produce images is what gives it its strength. AttnGAN and the GAN model match. GAN makes use of text and image encoders. Using the pre-trained GAN network, including AttnGAN and Stack+ + GAN, and the embedding vectors made using the BERTBASECASE language model, a comparison of their performance was made.

The demonstration of the proposed architecture is estimated in comparison to the current architecture. The value of the IS measure on the CUB-200 and Oxford-102 test sets is displayed in Fig. 3. The proposed GAN architecture, H GAN, performs better than the BASEGAN model as well as the trained GAN model. Comparatively speaking, BASEGAN and the other trained models perform better. The performance with respect to the FID score is shown in Fig. 4. The proposed H GAN achieves improved output than the trained architecture in this instance as well. The results are good and compelling. The presentation of the designs for the F1 score is seen in Fig. 5, which follows the run. The predicted work outperforms the other models in the evaluation. The proposed model's result matches StackGAN++, despite the text processing difficulty. Quantitative comparisons, however, show that performance in the creation of realistic, high-resolution images accustomed with text is achieved.

5 Conclusion

The creation of images for text is a fascinating area of computer vision investigation. Due to its complex morphology, image synthesis for text is essential. The popular GAN model is in the initial stages of merging with the BERTBASECASE language and BASEGAN models. Nevertheless, the fundamental architecture's performance is still convincing. It requires an upgrade that incorporates super-resolution. Architecture of GAN to further progress the resolution of the images, the BASE GAN model is improved employing a two-stage GAN model called Hybrid GAN (H GAN). This work's two-stage GAN produced better results when creating images from text. Performance parameters like the IS, FID, and F1-score serve as measurement tools. This research also conducted the analysis using two datasets, namely the CUB 200 and Oxford 102 datasets. The IR score for the proposed H-GAN is 5.2 with the CUB 200 dataset and 5.4 with the Oxford 102 dataset. The proposed H-GAN's FID score is 45 with the CUB 200 dataset and 44 with the Oxford 102 dataset. The proposed H-GAN's F1 score is 0.8 with the CUB 200 dataset and 0.82 with the Oxford 102 dataset. This research compares it with other existing algorithms like AttnGAN, Stack++, and base GAN. This comparison proved visually that the proposed H-GAN algorithm shows better results than the existing approaches. This is due to the implementation of a two-stage GAN. Since any misclassifications by the first stage GAN are rectified with the second stage GAN. Improved high-resolution patterns enhanced GAN models along with autoregressive models may be used to further advance the model.

References

1. Sawant, R., Shaikh, A., Sabat, S., Bhole, V.: Text to image generation using GAN. In: Proceedings of the International Conference on IoT Based Control Networks & Intelligent Systems - ICICNIS (2021)

2. Nichol, A., et al.: GLIDE: towards photorealistic image generation and editing with text-guided diffusion models. arXiv preprint arXiv:2112.10741 (2021)
3. Diviya, M., Karmel, A.: Deep neural architecture for natural language image synthesis for Tamil text using BASEGAN and hybrid super resolution GAN (HSRGAN). Sci. Rep. **13**(1), 14455 (2023)
4. Goodfellow, I.J., et al.: Generative adversarial networks. arXiv:1406.2661 (2014)
5. Reed, S., Akata, Z., Yan, X., Logeswaran, L., Schiele, B., Lee, H.: Generative adversarial text to image synthesis. arXiv:1605.05396 (2016)
6. Tan, H., Liu, X., Liu, M., Yin, B., Li, X.: KT-GAN: knowledge-transfer generative adversarial network for text-to-image synthesis. IEEE Trans. Image Process. **30**, 1275–1290 (2020)
7. Tan, H., Liu, X., Yin, B., Li, X.: DR-GAN: distribution regularization for text-to-image generation. IEEE Trans. Neural Netw. Learn. Syst. (2022)
8. Deng, Z., He, X., Peng, Y.: LFR-GAN: local feature refinement based generative adversarial network for text-to-image generation. ACM Trans. Multimed. Comput. Commun. Appl. (2023)
9. Zhang, H., Koh, J.Y., Baldridge, J., Lee, H., Yang, Y.: Cross-modal contrastive learning for text-to-image generation. In: Proceedings of the IEEE/CVF Conference on Computer Vision and Pattern Recognition, pp. 833–842 (2021)
10. Chrysos, G.G., Kossaif, J., Zafeiriou, S.: RoCGAN.: robust conditional GA. Int. J. Comput. Vis. **128**, 2665–2683 (2020)
11. Li, Y., Wang, J., Zhang, X., Cao, Y.: Fitting GAN: fitting image generation based on conditional generative adversarial networks. In: 2019 14th International Conference on Computer Science & Education (ICCSE), pp. 741–45. IEEE. (2019)
12. Zakraoui, J., Saleh, M., Al-Maadeed, S., Jaam, J.M.: Improving text-to-image generation with object layout guidance. Multimed. Tools Appl. **80**(18), 27423–27443 (2021)
13. Kim, Y., Ra, D., Lim, S.: Zero: anaphora resolution in Korean based on deep language representation model: BERT. ETRI J. **43**(2), 299–312 (2021)

A Hybrid Algorithm for Detection of Cloud-Based Email Phishing Attack

Saahira Banu Ahamed[1]([✉]) [iD], Anne Anoop[1] [iD], Rejna Azeez Nazeema[1] [iD], and Mujtaba Ali Khan[2] [iD]

[1] Department of Computer Science, College of Engineering and Computer Science, Jazan University, Jazan, Saudi Arabia
saahiraresearch@gmail.com, {aanup,razeez}@jazanu.edu.sa
[2] College of Computing and Informatics, University of North Carolina, Charlotte, NC, USA
malikha1@uncc.edu

Abstract. The term "cloud computing" describes the phenomenon wherein resources such as data storage and processing power are made available on demand by personal computer systems, often without the client's intervention. People and businesses alike often use email for the transfer of data. Credit reports and financial data are examples of the sensitive information that is often sent over the Internet. Con artists employ a technique called phishing to trick consumers into giving over vital information by making bogus emails seem official. A phished email may trick into divulging vital information via deceit. The email phishing attacks issue may happen at any point in the process, from sending to receiving. The attacker exploits your personal information when open as well as read an email to transmit spam. It has been a huge issue recently. This research uses different amounts of legitimate along with phishing data to detect fresh emails, categorise them using diverse features as well as algorithms, and draw conclusions. A fresh dataset is generated once the present methods are evaluated. This research used a hybrid strategy that combined deep learning (DL) and machine learning (ML) after creating a feature-extracted CSV file and a label file. Recognising a phished email is the focus of this experiment's classification challenge. Several preexisting ML and DL methods are compared and put into practice. The results of the proposed hybrid algorithm demonstrate an improved as well as more accurate performance in identifying email phishing attacks.

Keywords: Phishing · cloud computing · DL · ML · classification

1 Introduction

Phishing is a social engineering attack type that takes advantage of system users' vulnerabilities in system procedures. An attacker can send a phishing Uniform Resource Locator (URL) that directs users to a phishing website upon clicking on the link. Clicking on a link in another phishing attacks might install backdoors, download malware or spyware, or capture session data [1]. One of the most serious crimes in the world is phishing, which includes stealing private information from users. Phishing websites typically target websites belonging to people, businesses, cloud storage providers, and governments. During internet usage, the majority of individuals are not aware of phishing attacks. Many of the phishing methods have not been able to well talk the difficulties instigated by email attacks [2].

In this work, a phishing email classifier model that enhances the accuracy of phishing detection by using natural language processing and DL algorithms through the use of a graph convolutional network (GCN) across an email body text. The works has established GCN's effectiveness in text categorization, along with this work has verified its ability to increase email phishing detection accuracy [3]. Through the use of phishing emails, cybercriminals have effectively gained access to several crucial information systems in recent years, resulting in significant losses. Public attention has been focused on the identification of phishing emails from large email data sets. The two key phases of the novel approach are the sample expansion stage and the testing step when there are enough samples [4].

DL and ML approaches have drawn interest recently due to their promise to increase the accuracy of phishing detection. DL algorithms, including convolutional neural networks (CNNs) as well as long short-term memory (LSTMs), are better at spotting complex phishing attempts because they are built to learn from patterns and spot abnormalities in data [5]. Where data and processes are located matters a great deal in the field of computing. A person is in total control of the information and functions on their computer. Conversely, cloud computing (CC) involves a provider that maintains and provides services for data. In addition, the client or customer has no idea where the data is stored or where the operations are being run [6].

Phishing detection has drawn a lot of interest from the academic and business communities. A quick fix was required for the losses and data breaches brought on by email phishing attacks that affected both public and commercial organizations. The creation of an ideal solution was difficult due to the variety of attack methods and attack patterns connected to phishing attacks [7]. A Systematic Literature Review (SLR) of cloud security and ML approaches as well as methods in this work. ML is one method of cloud security. ML methods have been applied in diverse ways to stop or detect attacks along with security holes. Numerous businesses are making investments here, either for their own needs or to give services to others [8].

The rest of this work is planned as surveys. Section 2 delivers an outline of some current and recent works. The proposed technique is defined in Sect. 3. After a summary of the findings as well as analysis in Sect. 4, the references are provided.

2 Recent Works for Research

This part, take a look back at some of the more recent articles written on DL techniques.

Alzahrani et al. [9] defined to target a person or organization, suggesting a method for identifying a serious threat that aims to get private and sensitive data, comprising usernames, credit card numbers, along with passwords. A phishing attack is by definition when unscrupulous individuals assume the identity of reliable sources in order to steal user information. One category of social engineering attack is phishing. A victim has to be persuaded to open an email or direct message in order for a phishing attack to take place. The victim must click on the link that is included in the email or direct message. The victim of a phishing attack may suffer catastrophic consequences. Confidential and sensitive information may end up in the hands of bad actors. Identity theft is another terrible result of phishing attacks.

Bagui et al. [10] described Natural language processing (NLP) involves a lot of tasks, one of which is text representation. Recently, NLP tasks such as topic categorization, sentiment analysis, and language translation have made extensive use of DL and ML. Semantic analysis has received little attention in the phishing email field and phishing discovery until recently. This work is innovative in that it captures the intrinsic text body properties through the use of deep semantic analysis. Emails were classified as phishing or nonphishing using DL and ML algorithms combined with one-hot encoding.

Adebowale et al. [11] discussed the global economic expansion brought about by high technology has led to a change in phishing attacks. The surge in fraudulent losses across all categories in 2019 has been ascribed to the escalation of deception schemes and spoofing, in addition to advanced cyberattacks like phishing. Phishing attacks will become more widespread, thus in order to safeguard online user activity, a more effective phishing detection technique is needed. This study focused on the design as well as development of a DL-based phishing detection system that made use of website content as well as the universal resource locator in order to meet this demand.

Rashid et al. [12] implemented the information security concerns have increased in recent years due to cyberspace's fast expansion. Website phishing is one of the most hazardous attacks because it is intricate and hard to identify in real time. Because cloud ML uses cloud computing services to provide fast and precise results, it has become a viable method for identifying phishing websites. Therefore, utilizing three built-in SageMaker algorithms: Linear Learner, Extreme Gradient Boosting as well as k-Nearest Neighbor (KNN) this study proposes a Cloud ML approach for analyzing and measuring the time necessary to detect website phishing. A vast dataset is stored, trained, evaluated, and deployed online using Amazon Web Services.

Nayomi et al. [13] described the phishing attacks that target the infrastructure of smart cities. The safety as well as security of smart cities may be greatly impacted by these attacks. A cloud-assisted strategy for thwarting phishing attacks in smart cities is presented in this research. To identify and stop phishing attacks, the system combines blockchain technology with ML. Employing a phishing email dataset, the framework was assessed and shown to be very accurate in identifying phishing attacks. The framework also provides cost-effectiveness in terms of setup and upkeep.

Dutta et al. [14] have contributed to a notable rise in electronic trade in recent years, where customers conduct transactions and purchases online. This expansion harms an enterprise's resources by allowing unwanted access to sensitive user data. One well-known attack that deceives people into seeing dangerous content and obtaining their personal data is phishing. The majority of phishing webpages have the exact same URL and user experience as legitimate webpages. There are several methods that have been proposed for classifying phishing websites. However, the victims count is growing exponentially as a result of ineffective security systems.

Parra et al. [15] provided a distributed DL architecture for the cloud that is designed to identify and mitigate botnet and phishing attacks. The model consists of two main security mechanisms that work together: a Distributed CNN (DCNN) cloud-based temporal LSTM network model hosted on the back-end for noticing Botnet attacks, also ingest CNN embeddings to spot distributed phishing attacks across multiple Internet of Things (IoT) devices. The CNN model is embedded as an add-on for micro-security on IoT devices and can detect phishing as well as application layer distributed denial of service (DDoS) attacks.

Do et al. [16] discussed the phishing has drawn the attention of security professionals and end users. Phishing detection algorithms still have poor performance accuracy and an inability to detect unexpected attacks. Many cybersecurity experts have turned their focus to phishing detection that uses ML techniques in an effort to address these issues. In recent years, DL has become a popular area of ML that has great promise for phishing detection. The available material is then categorized into different groups using taxonomies for phishing detection and DL algorithms.

The primary objective of this research is to provide a new technique for identifying phishing attacks as well as figuring out how to guard against them. If the email worker is the target of a phishing attack, this method may identify it and stop it. What follows is the job contribution that has been proposed:

- The feature extraction process relies on a CNN with many layers, and the CNN features are then classified using the widely used K-nearest neighbour (KNN) classifier.
- A deep evaluation of CNN's DL characteristics is possible. Different layers make up the CNN architecture. This includes layers, such as convolutional, max-pooling, dropout, fully connected, and a classifier called Softmax.
- To determine the distance between any two locations in a system, the Euclidian technique in the KNN classifier takes the square root of the total number of features.
- CNN feature output is used as KNN input. The outcomes of the proposed approach are then assessed using several metrics, including f1score, recall, precision, and accuracy.

3 Proposed Methodology

The steps involved in the proposed architecture are as follows: data collection, feature extraction, algorithm selection, output classification, and performance assessment. Using variable amounts of actual and phishing data, this research discovers fresh emails and classifies them using various features and algorithms. A fresh dataset is generated and then the proposed methods are evaluated. Following the generation of a CSV file and label file that had features extracted from them, this research used a hybrid strategy that included DL and ML. Figure 1 shows the proposed architecture diagram.

3.1 Preprocessing

As part of the data mining as well as analysis processes, preprocessing transforms raw data into a form that ML and computers can comprehend and assess. Data preprocessing includes tasks like cleaning, normalisation, transformation, and more.

- Cleaning and purifying data-There is often noise, inconsistency, and inadequate data in the actual world. Filling in missing numbers, reducing noise while detecting outliers, and addressing data inconsistencies are the goals of data cleaning techniques.

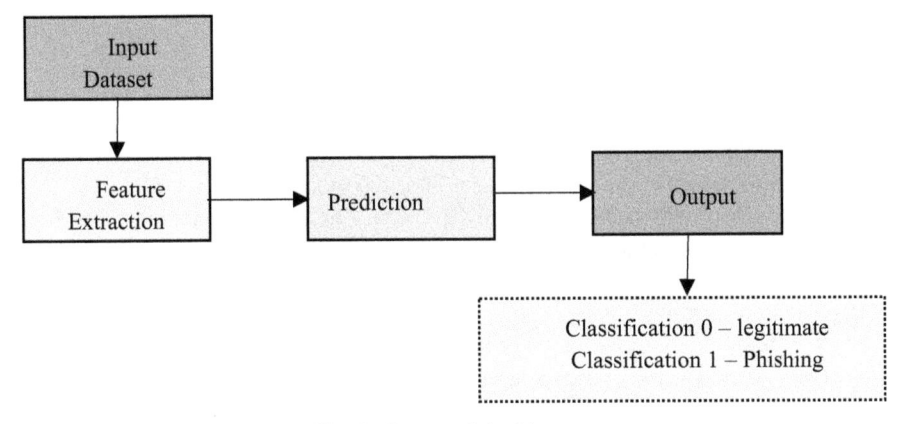

Fig. 1. Proposed Architecture

- Transformation of data-The data is transformed into situationally appropriate mining forms. Data transformation includes the following steps.
- Normalisation is the process of adjusting the attribute data such that it falls inside a specific range, like -1.0 to 1.0 or -1.0.
- Reduction of data-Complex data analysis and mining on massive datasets may take an inordinate amount of time. To get qualitative insight out of a smaller subset of dataset without sacrificing the original data's integrity, data reduction techniques are the way to go [19].

3.2 Feature Extraction and Classification

In feature space, the KNN method maintains all the relevant instances that may be employed to classify objects based on their surroundings. The approach in this study included finding the root of the pixels sum by performing a pixel-wide square of the difference. It may determine the distance between two locations in a coordinate system using this method, which is termed as the Euclidian distance method. As seen in Eq. (1), it may be expressed as follows:

$$D = \sqrt{\sum_{i=1}^{K} (x_i - y_i)^2} \quad (1)$$

Here, D stands for the distance between two points in three-dimensional space. The distance between two points (x_i, y_i) in xy plane space, where i = 1, 2 ..., K is the data space, is two if the dimension is two. In order to train and evaluate the KNN approach for pattern recognition, it used a Gaussian distribution. In order to classify using the majority rule, KNN is used and shown in Eq. (2), the majority rule is:

$$Majority\ voting = \sum_{c(p_i, q_i) D_r}^{argmax} W(c = q_i) \quad (2)$$

The class label (CL) is represented by c, the CL for the ith nearest neighbour is denoted by q_i, and W is an indicator function (IF) that equals 1 when the argument is true and 0 when it is false. Classification accuracy, however, is a limitation of this classifier.

Three different kinds of layers—convolutional, max-pooling, and classification make up the CNN architecture. Two kinds of layers, one at the bottom of the network and one in the middle, are the convolutional and max-pooling layers, respectively. The 2D plane is used to organise the convolutional and max-pooling outputs. Different from max pooling, which abstracts features by averaging or spreading them across input nodes, each convolutional layer extracts features via a convolutional operation on each input node. Feature extraction as well as classification are the two last components of the context, according to CNN. To begin, features, also referred to as neurons, are extracted by applying the convolution process to an input and passing it through a kernel, which is often called a convolutional kernel. Applying a downsampling technique to the input maps obtained from the convolutional layer's output, the pooling step aids to data simplicfication. By reducing the pixel values count to a single value within the neuron, this step effectively makes a feature dimension smaller and more controllable and as shown in (3),

$$x_j^l = \left(f\left(\beta_j^l down\left(x_j^{l-1}\right) + b_j^l\right)\right) \tag{3}$$

Here, down denotes a function that does subsampling. When considering the two dimensions of the feature maps, the output map dimension is thus decreased to 'n' times. Being a component of the hidden layer helps us limit the number of parameters and arrive at an image representation that is invariant. Compared to KNN, the performance rate was higher in this study [18].

4 Results

The dataset is used to evaluate the findings [17]. The accuracy formula is used to accomplish this task with the aid of Keras and TenserFlow-GPU. The proposed model uses these measurements to evaluate the model in Eq. (4):

$$Accuracy = \left(\frac{(TP + TN)}{(TP + TN + FP + FN)} * 100\right)\% \tag{4}$$

Precision is termed by the minimal beneficial recoverable elements counts. Here, the messages count that are successfully delegated are phished. The precision equation is shown in Eq. (5).

$$Precision = \left(\frac{TP}{(TP + FP)} * 100\right)\% \tag{5}$$

To calculate recall, it divides the relevant objects count retrieved by the total number of significant things. This ratio measures how many phishing messages were really phished from the dataset. Following the precision report, the results were double-checked using Recall Eq. (6).

$$Recall = \left(\frac{TP}{(TP + FN)} * 100\right)\% \tag{6}$$

The consonant mean of precision as well as recall is known as the F-measure. Equation 11 below finds an F-measure using the precision and recall formula in Eq. (7).

$$F1score = ((2 * precision * recall)/precision + recall) * 100 \qquad (7)$$

The term "true positive" (TP) refers to the situation in which a perception is correctly classified after expecting it to be part of a certain class. When one expects that a perception does not belong in a certain class and, sure enough, the perception does not belong in that class, it gets true negatives (TN). When a perception fits the criteria for a certain class but isn't really a part of that class, and get a false positive (FP). FN or false negatives, occur when a class isn't a good fit for the projected impression.

4.1 Comparative Analysis

Nowadays, people rely on email as a primary means of communication. With the rise of connected web users, email has become an essential tool for online communication. The authorities are facing a significant challenge in analysing and eliminating the phishing email. There is an increase in the amount of phishing emails that include trojans, contaminations, and malware. Claiming that approaching communications is spam or ham, this article employed many methods to detect phishing emails and discard them. The chart illustrates the distribution of mail in the dataset that was used. Figure 2 shows the categories distribution.

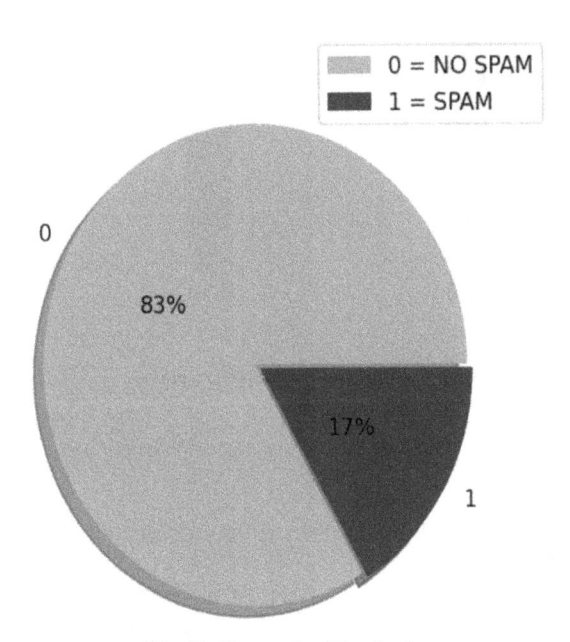

Fig. 2. Categories Distribution

Table 1 presents a comparison of the performance metrics of various techniques. The proposed model seems to outperform competing models across all parameters, including

Table 1. Comparison Table

Approach	Precision	Recall	F1-Score
Proposed	0.9845	0.9827	0.9835
KNN	0.9707	0.8724	0.9189
CNN	0.9728	0.9689	0.9708

CNN and KNN. The proposed model achieves a precision of around 98% on the input dataset. This model outperforms CNN and KNN by a small margin of 0.011%. Like the existing model, the proposed one has a recall of about 98%. As compared to CNN and KNN, this model outperforms them by a margin of just 0.013%. Another option is the proposed model, which has a f1score of over 98%. This model surpasses CNN and 0.0646% KNN in terms of performance, with a difference of 0.0127 percent. Figure 3 shows the graph representation of performance metrics.

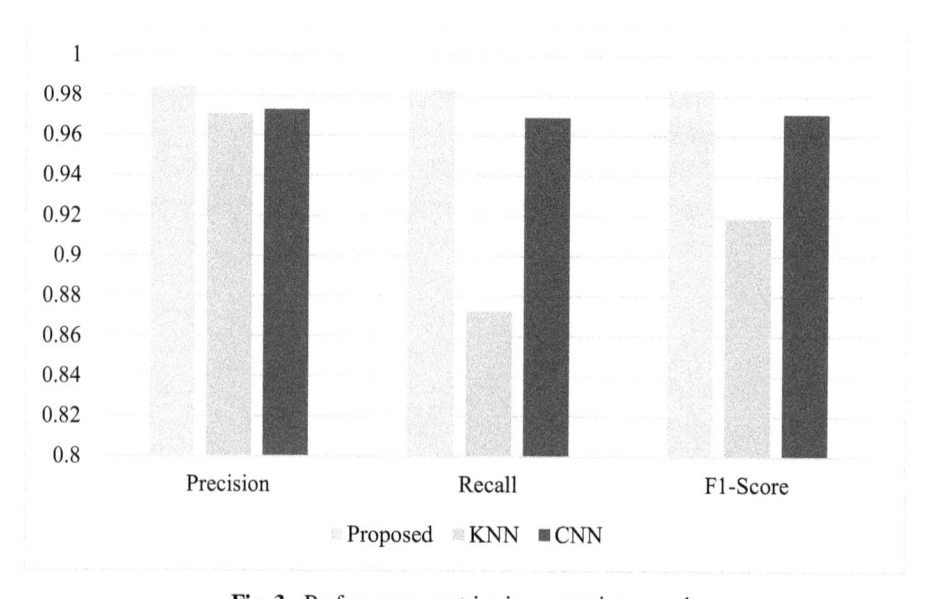

Fig. 3. Performance metrics in comparison graph

The confusion matrix graph representation for proposed and existing algorithms is illustrated in Fig. 4.

Table 2 presents an accuracy comparison of the performance metrics of various techniques. The proposed model achieves an accuracy of around 98% on the input dataset. This model outperforms CNN with 0.013 and KNN by a small margin of 0.110.

Figure 5 shows the accuracy comparison with various methods. To provide a more precise classification report and outcome, these algorithms do a comprehensive analysis of the phishing email attack classification presented in this article. The outcomes

```
[[242    5]        [[242   37]
 [  0   43]]        [  0   11]]
 (a) Proposed       (b) KNN

       [[241    8]
        [  1   40]]
 (C) CNN
```

Fig. 4. Confusion matrix graph

Table 2. Accuracy Comparison

Approach	Accuracy
Proposed	0.9827
KNN	0.8724
CNN	0.9689

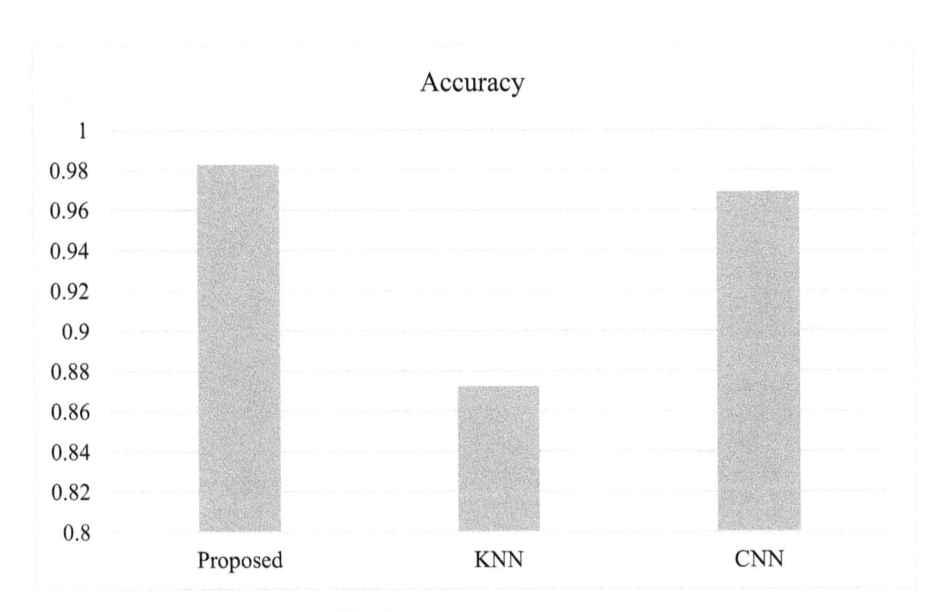

Fig. 5. Accuracy comparison

demonstrate the superior classification performance of the proposed hybrid CNN-KNN method.

5 Conclusion

With the use of hybrid DL algorithms, this study proposes a method for identifying emails as phishing or non-phishing and email spam assaults. To prepare the dataset for building classifiers from its features, it was preprocessed and transformed into an appropriate design. In Python, the selected features are obtained. In order to sort the test set, the DL algorithms that are used need an arrangement set. Both the CNN and KNN classifiers are evaluated independently to evaluate their performance alongside the suggested hybrid CNN and KNN classifier. The results are just as good as those of a hybrid algorithm when these algorithms are run independently. At 0.98%, 0.87%, and 0.96%, respectively, accuracy rates are achieved by the hybrid, KNN, and CNN classifiers. Working with the real-world situation, where fraudsters are always upgrading their strategies by changing up email forms (both phished and non-phished), may help enhance this framework in the future.

References

1. Alani, M.M., Tawfik, H.: PhishNot: a cloud-based machine-learning approach to phishing URL detection. Comput. Netw. **218**, 109407 (2022)
2. Mohamed, G., Visumathi, J., Mahdal, M., Anand, J., Elangovan, M.: An effective and secure mechanism for phishing attacks using a machine learning approach. Processes **10**(7), 1356 (2022)
3. Alhogail, A., Alsabih, A.: Applying machine learning and natural language processing to detect phishing email. Comput. Secur. **110**, 102414 (2021)
4. Li, Q., Cheng, M., Wang, J., Sun, B.: LSTM based phishing detection for big email data. IEEE Trans. Big Data **8**(1), 278–288 (2020)
5. Thakur, K., Ali, M.L., Obaidat, M.A., Kamruzzaman, A.: A systematic review on deep-learning-based phishing email detection. Electronics **12**(21), 4545 (2023)
6. Prasad, V.K., Dansana, D., Mishra, B.K., Bhavsar, M.: Intensify cloud security and privacy against phishing attacks. ECS Trans. **107**(1), 1387 (2022)
7. Alotaibi, R., Al-Turaiki, I., Alakeel, F.: Mitigating email phishing attacks using convolutional neural networks. In: 2020 3rd International Conference on Computer Applications & Information Security (ICCAIS), pp. 1–6. IEEE (2020)
8. Nassif, A.B., Talib, M.A., Nasir, Q., Albadani, H., Dakalbab, F.M.: Machine learning for cloud security: a systematic review. IEEE Access **9**, 20717–20735 (2021)
9. Alzahrani, S.M.: Phishing attack detection using deep learning. Int. J. Comput. Sci. Netw. Secur. **21**(12), 213–218 (2021)
10. Bagui, S., Nandi, D., Bagui, S., White, R.J.: Machine learning and deep learning for phishing email classification using one-hot encoding. J. Comput. Sci. **17**, 610–623 (2021)
11. Adebowale, M.A., Lwin, K.T., Hossain, M.A.: Intelligent phishing detection scheme using deep learning algorithms. J. Enterp. Inf. Manag. **36**(3), 747–766 (2023)
12. Rashid, S.H., Abdullah, W.D.: Cloud-based machine learning approach for accurate detection of website phishing. Int. J. Intell. Syst. Appl. Eng. **11**(6s), 451–460 (2023)
13. Nayomi, B.D.D., Mallika, S.S., Sowmya, T., Janardhan, G., Laxmikanth, P., Bhavsingh, M.: A cloud-assisted framework utilizing blockchain, machine learning, and artificial intelligence to countermeasure phishing attacks in smart cities. Int. J. Intell. Syst. Appl. Eng. **12**(1s), 313–327 (2024)

14. Dutta, A.K.: Detecting phishing websites using machine learning technique. PloS ONE **16**(10), e0258361 (2021)
15. Parra, G.T., Rad, P., Choo, K.-K.R., Beebe, N.: Detecting Internet of Things attacks using distributed deep learning. J. Netw. Comput. Appl. **163**, 102662 (2020)
16. Do, N.Q., Ali, S., Ondrej, K., Herrera-Viedma, E., Fujita, H.: Deep learning for phishing detection: Taxonomy, current challenges and future directions. IEEE Access **10**, 36429–36463 (2022)
17. https://www.kaggle.com/code/surekharamireddy/spam-detection-with-99-accuracy/input
18. Butt, U.A., Amin, R., Aldabbas, H., Mohan, S., Alouffi, B., Ahmadian, A.: Cloud-based email phishing attack using machine and deep learning algorithm. Complex Intell. Syst. **9**(3), 3043–3070 (2023)
19. Makkar, T., Kumar, Y., Dubey, A.K., Rocha, Á., Goyal, A.: Analogizing time complexity of KNN and CNN in recognizing handwritten digits. In: 2017 Fourth International Conference on Image Information Processing (ICIIP), pp. 1–6. IEEE (2017)

Using a Language Model to Analyze the Mental State of an Individual

Arsenij Taratukhin[✉] and Mais Farkhadov Pasha Ogly[iD]

Institute of Control Sciences, Russian Academy of Sciences, Profsoyuznaya 65, 117342 Moscow, Russian Federation
`avt@ipu.ru`

Abstract. The following paper discusses the use of machine learning in identifying the emotional state of the user using analysis of their written and verbal speech. Most importantly, the model in question will do so passively, without prompting the user to describe how they are feeling. Furthermore, the following work will discuss the potential techniques in constructing this prototype, pitfalls and ways how it can be integrated into a broader health monitoring system.

Keywords: Artificial Intelligence · Natural Language Processing · Large Language Models · Sociolinguistics · Corpus Linguistics

1 Introduction

The following paper will discuss a proposed system that will analyze a user's written and verbal speech and use it to read the user's mental state or well being. In rough terms, a kind of biometric monitor for the user's psychological state. The need to monitor the well being of the individual is highly important in fields such as space exploration, ocean fairing and polar research, where individuals may spend a prolonged period of time in isolation or in a small group of people in a confined space. Being in a confined space for an extended period of time may lead to various mental health disorders emerging or existing ones becoming more acute [10]. One thing all those groups of professionals have in common is that they submit standardized reports or logs on a regular basis in either a recorded or written form. Those speech samples, as well as fragments of chat messages, can be analyzed using machine learning systems in order to create an "early warning" mechanism. In a sense, we're creating a kind of therapist model that doesn't ask questions or probe the patient, but simply listens to their speech and takes notes. In case of spotting severe distress it may notify other groups that may reach out or offer help.

This may be vital, as being under a high degree of stress for a prolonged amount of time may end up putting the individual into an affective state, which in turn will jeopardize their decision making [4], especially when coordinating in a group.

Most importantly, such a language model may be integrated into a larger information system consisting out of various algorithms and trackers that monitor different markers of the user's behavior, such as their eye movement, appearance, body language, etc.

In future developments, the model will benefit greatly from being connected to other biometric monitors and similar models.

The first section will discuss the psychological theory connecting speech to user's mental state. The second section will cover the proposed architecture of the model and the third section will discuss licensing, potential uses and integration into multimodal systems. The conclusion will mention the potential future and development of such a model and how it can be scaled down to help the layman.

1.1 Methodology and Theory

First of all, it's would be helpful for logistics to give the project a distinctive name for ease of communication. One possible name is PSALM, which stands for Passive Speech Analysis Language Model. A psalm is a poem or hymn from Old Testament and Torah scripture, often sung in belief that it would offer protection. The passive part would indicate that the model wouldn't be asking for user's input, unlike other attempts at creating a digital therapist model (aka ELIZA, etc.) but rather simply analyses their text for intent and stylistic deviation over time, which would later be fit into a hypothetical larger information system that can display a more accurate picture of the user's health. This is contrasted to projects that utilize self-reported narratives for their structure [3].

Written and spoken speech has often been used as a primary indicator of mental health of an individual. In psychiatry analyzing speech is often used to indicate the potential for psychological disorders [1, 6], such as depression [3, 7, 8] or autism [13]. This goes in-line with a variety of conducted research on the subject as well as the widely adopted theory of cognitive-behavioral therapy. We can use some aspects of cognitive behavioral therapy as the basis and the techniques that we can use in the prototype.

The model relies on identifying a baseline for healthy speech and spotting deviations outside the norm that may signal distress. For doing this we need to define what the 'norm' is, for that we need to first differentiate between a mood, emotion the user is experiencing versus a long term trend [12]. Typically, this can be done by simply measuring the length of time that the user is affected by it. An emotion can last up to a few hours, a mood for a few days to several months (in case of traumatic events, such as grief) and a disorder has the effect last for over six months. This means that for the model to be effective, it needs to be utilized for years to have sufficient enough data to draw conclusions from. Second, the model is to utilize methodology from computational social science and corpus linguistics to determine "healthy stylistic averages" [11]. It's worth taking into account that stylistic averages vary from individual to individual. Most English speakers are non-native, which the system will be forced to take into account, due to certain kinds of phonetic, spelling and grammatical mistakes being the norm, even in the case of highly qualified professionals such as cosmonauts. That being said, if the model is well trained on stylistic differences, it will not only be able to take that into account, but actually try to guess certain demographic and cultural aspects of the user using conventional corpus linguistic methods [9, 14, 20].

There's two possible approaches at calculating a "linguistic norm" from which deviations will be calculated. One is to tailor the model to a niche profession with a strict selection for personnel. For example, cosmonauts and astronauts. There is a large database of communication data between space explorers in English, Russian and continental Chinese. Ergo, it's possible to deduce a 'typical' style and mannerism of communication for individuals working in the field. In addition to that, both cosmonauts and astronauts and well renowned for being mentally stable in extreme situations and maintain composure under stress. So, if the model detects that a 'by the numbers' station/ship log suddenly containing markers of distress [16, 18], it may send out a notification to ground control [20].

A second approach is to base this model on the average speech patterns of a median citizen of an English-speaking Western country, then try to specialize it for specific professions later on. This approach is far more economical due to there being extensive research beforehand in the fields of sociology, linguistics, corpus linguistics, big data analytics, and other similar fields that may help in collecting the necessary data for model training weights.

Essentially, the two approaches are to either start with an upscale model based around serving in a stressful and highly niche environment and then grow towards generalizing it for the greater public. That or we create a general baseline and then tailor it for cosmonauts and polar exploration. Both methods have a unique set of issues. Should the project take the approach of using an existing language model such as BERT, then it would have the benefit of having measurements of what the 'mean average' is for human speech in the alglophone internet. Then said model could be fine tuned in for more professional/formal language, only to later see if there are any possible deviations from that.

For the sake of simplicity let's take the popular cited paper on analyzing the *Schwartz, H. Andrew, et al. "Personality, gender, and age in the language of social media: The open-vocabulary approach."* [18]. The paper uses the big five OCEAN [5] model (Openness, Creativity, Extroversion, Agreeableness and Neuroticism) for their project. Our model can simply take the findings correlated to trait neuroticism of an individual. For example, the researchers notice that more stressed out individuals tend to swear more often as well as openly express their distress through expressions such as "I fear", "I worry". This can be used as a crude measure of general neuroticism in an individual. Should the subject express that emotion for a few hours to a few weeks, then it can be seen as normal, if the emotional state lasts for an extensive amount of time (several months to a year), then we can draw the conclusion that the subject is in a state of distress. Upon drawing the conclusion, the model may end up sending a signal to relevant parties to "check up" on the individual or offer more extensive psychological support.

2 Issues Regarding Model Architecture

2.1 Calculating Stylistic Averages

The first thing to be addressed is the kind of model that will be used and its associated weights. The stylistic averages will be integrated into the model weights, which will be based on the average speech of the median person residing in a Western English-Speaking country. Regardless, the model is to be trained on both the "neutral" manner of speaking in a casual conversation, as well as the more professional manner of speech that is expected from cosmonauts, astronauts and arctic explorers. The priorities for training and fine tuning may end up being somewhat altered due to the model being built not as a generative model, but a transformer that may identify the intent and the emotional bent of the text messages [19, 20].

Cultural differences are to be taken into account when calibrating the averages. For example, even individuals of a similar background and culture may have differences in terms of speech due to the region they were raised in. In the case of astronauts, an American crew member that was raised in the Southern parts of the United States may not only speak with a distinctive accent, but have unique lexical and grammatical properties characteristic of that dialect. This may cause issues as the project develops due to not every professional sphere having the equivalent of the NATO phonetic alphabet to rely on for pronunciation. One way to go about solving this is to attempt to generalize the dataset by moving to generalize it. For example, this can be done by using data from public broadcasting services, such as PBS in the United States or the BBC in the United Kingdom. Both of which try to highlight the different manners of speaking from across their cultures in both the presenters and the various guests. This may end up creating a more accurate model, but at the cost of increased time fine tuning the model and creating transcriptions for the audio and video training data. The transcription part of the process is likely to be automated using third party neural networks that are specialized in the task. Which leads us into another potential source for high quality training data, which are audiobooks, specifically those created by volunteer organizations for educational reasons. Not only are the speakers vetted for quality and pronunciation, but there is a transcription of everything that is being said presented in the source text, which makes it highly convenient for our project.

Should the project attempt to incorporate speaking styles from non-native English speaking cultures, the system may end up starting to flag certain mannerisms as signs of stress or exhaustion. For example, certain languages, such as German, have an accent that comes off as 'flat' and unemotional to native English speakers that are unfamiliar with the culture at hand. This in turn may end up in a scenario where should an individual for whom English is not a native language attempts to use the system, the model may end up construing an accent or certain mannerisms as signs of stress or mental distress. Ergo, we cannot disregard non-native English speakers from the data either, but attempt to figure out a method of making the system more forgiving of regional variance when operating with certain users. That being said, creating a truly broad set of training data for every single possible method of pronunciation of the English language may end up bloating the scope of the project beyond its available means. One possible means of avoiding that is to see which specific groups cause the bulk of the false-positives and hallucinations, then focus on them in the training data. Ergo, the final database would contain data from professional discourse, examples of journalistic speech, examples of accurate reading of certain literary and technical texts and, lastly, examples of pronunciation from certain groups with a distinct regional accent.

Regardless of the manner the training data used, the overall process will require a large degree of fine tuning in order to be functional to any degree. Specifically, most models struggle understanding and interpreting technical jargon, especially delivered with a heavy regional accent. The best way to correct those issues is to do it manually, nevertheless, it's likely certain artifacts and hallucinations will remain.

The largest engineering challenge will be balancing the model learning and building the profile of the end user with their distinct characteristics versus a stylistic average which can be highly broad even for a highly specific technical or professional group that said individual belongs to.

2.2 Approaches Towards Model Architecture

The main approach towards building the PSALM model will likely be based around taking an existing model, then fine turning it for the needs of the project. There are several contenders, such as BERT, RoBERTa and OpenAssistant/OpenChat that meet the criteria. The model needs to be open source and be able to run on local hardware. As the model is first and foremost built to be used on the ISS, Arctic research bases, ships in international waters and other locations that may not have the most reliable internet, it's important that the model be able to run on either a local area network or an isolated terminal. Lastly, it has to be fine tuned, due to it being difficult, if not impossible to update the model that cannot interface with the internet and that's located on a remote local server.

The issue of training weights and "stylistic medium" can be used via utilization of one of the forks of LLaMA (Large Language Model Meta AI) models, which are trained on a varying amount of parameters depending on how "compact" the model needs to be [21].

While the initial prototype will likely use a fork of an existing model, it's favorable to eventually develop a custom model trained on a custom dataset in order to properly fulfill all of the tasks the project is set out to do. Specifically, the goal of the project is to use some of the advancements in the field of natural language process to interpret and transform natural human speech into data that can be processed and fed into an information system. The vast majority of language models existing today are made to generate human-sounding language, in one form or another. This, inadvertently, may lead to certain artifacts and hallucinations that can only be avoided by creating a custom model or at very least using a unique dataset custom-fitted for the task at hand. It is highly likely that repurposing existing models for data processing may be the most taxing part of the overall project, especially as it involves making the models function well with legacy systems and information systems. In simpler terms, a text generator with a user interface bent as a data processing tool is being used and there's an effort to make sure there are as little points of failure as possible when it is incorporated into a larger system.

3 Examples of Similar Models in Works of Fiction

For a rough ballpark of what we're aiming for, it's great to refer to works of science fiction where similar devises are constructed and utilized. The Blade runner films are a good repository for reference. The film introduces two tests, the Void-Kampf empathy test in the first film and the Baseline test in the sequel. Void-Kampf is a science fiction version of the lie detector test that measures pupil dilation in order to test the individual for empathy. That is done for detecting human-appearing androids known as "replicants", which are said to be incapable of showing compassion. The second test is somewhat closer to what we're aiming for. For context, the character taking the test is a replicant androids and has to be tested for emotional stability after completing an assignment. They are placed in a blank room and asked to recite a poem while an interlocutor asks them questions that are meant to provoke a reaction. In front is a camera that observes the subject's posture, facial expression, position. In addition a microphone and other sensors record trembling in the voice, tempo and likely other factors such as the sweating of the skin. How close the subject is or is far from the 'baseline' is displayed on a monitor for both the supervisor and the interlocutor that makes the judgment if the individual passed a test or not. It's heavily implied that androids undergoing the following tests are compared across a long period of time and are assigned bonuses and privileges depending on their baseline stability. The test results are not as 'binary' as the Void-Kampf test and often lead to a wide variety of outcomes ranging from rewards, to limited leave, to disciplinary measures with the station authorities. Which is a good highlight for the fact that the agency over the individual isn't carried over to the system, but rather is used as a measuring tool for the organization the humanoid android is a part of.

Overall, this is a work of fiction and we should be heavily skeptical of such depictions of technology, as they are made to entertain first rather than show something that's technologically feasible. That being said, it is a useful approximation of what our laboratory is going for, with one major exception. First is that the subject may not have to be seated in one room for a 5–10 min session, but rather can go about their daily routine as the devise records them. Second, is that the 'test' will be operational on the span of months, rather than in short bursts. Everything else is is, roughly accurate as far as the monitoring side goes. One thing that the works of science fiction and reality will have in-common is that the faculties and discretion of the interlocutor will play a large role in the accuracy and usefulness of the tests than the technology involved in their use.

4 Multimodality and Integration with Information Systems

For best, most accurate results, the model would have to have a way to integrate into other biometric systems which would feed into an information system. PSALM, at the time of writing, is planned to work with text input, as well as verbal speech that's translated into text through voice-to-text software. Integrating something akin to voice cadence analysis [15, 16] would potentially greatly increase both the accuracy and the depth of the results. That being said, one of the major challenges would be making sure that the desperate biometric monitors (voice cadence analysis, eye tracking) works well not only with the data derived from the language model, but also with the part of the system that tracks the data over a period of months. The part of PSALM that governs long-term tracking can be labeled the "clock module" (Fig. 1).

In addition, should the system be implemented in space exploration, it has to be cross compatible both with legacy biometric monitors, as well as potential future ones, such as BMIs (brain-machine interfaces) [19]. The proposed solution for that is to make sure that PSALM is open source, which would essentially create a development kit for others to develop cross compatibility with. Should the system move into a more commercial sphere, it would be possible to create integration with other pieces of hardware, such as smart bracelets that monitor sleep patterns and heart rate of the individual. In that case,

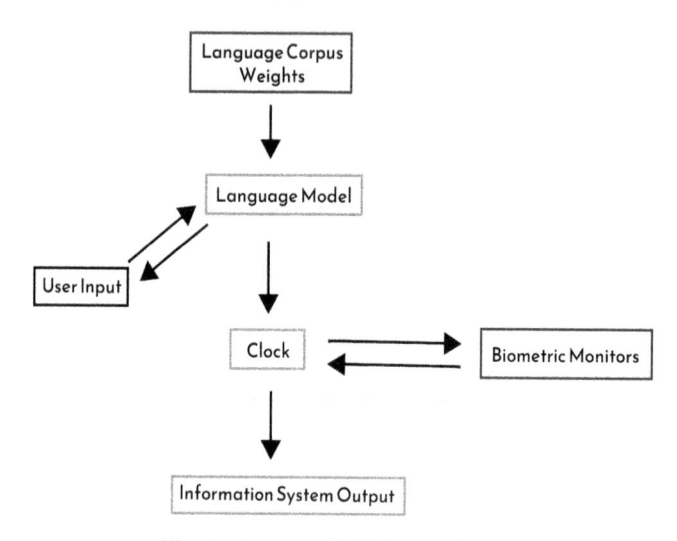

Fig. 1. Proposed PSALM architecture

PSALM will be available as a piece of computer software or a smartphone application. This, however, creates issues that are common to other pieces of open source software. Specifically the possibility of exploits and security vulnerabilities that are common to open projects run by small teams. Should one of those exploits include some form of data leakage, the system would be simply be too untrustworthy to be used by any individual for an extensive period of time once it's no longer run on a handful of terminals in low Earth orbit. As a result, while the ability to make the system more modular is paramount to its success, we should not do so while sacrificing privacy and security of the end user considering the nature of the system. Likely this would entail some form of data encryption with only other PSALM modules having a unique decryption key. That being said, this may end up creating the issue of increasing processing time for data, especially coupled with the inherent issues of locally run language models.

In addition, there should be space left for the system to not only build complex psychological profiles of individuals, but to work with an overarching system that may be used to compare several existing profiles to see how they may act in a group dynamic. For example, using the data gathered by PSALM, it may be possible to find out that a major source of stress for an individual may be the interaction with another member of their group, which would prompt a suggestion for a transfer or removal of said individual. In addition, the potential overarching model may not only analyze the dynamics of a specific group, but the psychological dynamics between groups and how that affects the mental well being of individuals.

For example, if the system identifies that a particular group is consistently causing stress to another group, it could suggest interventions to address the root cause of the conflict. This might involve facilitating communication between the groups, providing training on conflict resolution, or implementing policies to promote a more harmonious working environment.

By taking a holistic approach to mental health and well-being, the system could not only help individuals manage their stress and improve their psychological well-being but also foster healthier relationships and dynamics within and between groups. In short, it's important to make sure that the overall architecture of the system is as open ended to different kinds of integration as possible, which may end up pushing the project into adopting an open source approach to aid with that. The endgame of that is to create a system that may be able to interact and exchange data with copies of itself. Say, for example, we have two space stations both running a version of PSALM. The stations want to perform a Soyuz-Apollo docking procedure and the systems have to make sure that both teams are adjusted enough to be up to the task and will not erupt into conflict once the airlock opens.

5 Conclusion and Future Prospects

In conclusion, the aim of the following project is to aid decision making in complex missions by creating a model that's capable of monitoring the mental state of the individual. First through text and speech input recordings, then by taking into account other changes in biometric activity, such as voice cadence, posture, eye movement, duration of REM (Rapid Eye Movement) sleep, etc. Long term stress is known to impact decision making [4] and group coordination. An outside party being aware of it may help large projects to stay on track or even have some other entity take over decision making tasks.

In addition, the future of this project and its many challenges lie in miniaturizing the model and potentially marketing it to a wider market. Initially, it may be given to professionals working in commercial sailing, arctic research groups and individuals that are forced to spend extended amounts of time in prolonged isolation and/or stress. However, when that is perfected it's possible to turn it into an app that not only monitors the mental well-being of the individual, but also of entire teams or groups of people. This may be used, if not as an alternative to therapy, but as a kind of 'preventative' medicine, by having someone the user trusts check up on them if they have been under distress for an extended amount of time. This is especially important due to reports of loneliness and increased stress in the post-covid world.

As there are gradual improvements in machine learning and integration of various models, it may be possible to create a kind of descriptive mirror that not only monitors the behavior and mental state of the individual, but uses collected data to assess the probability of future behavior and possible deviations from said patterns. The final challenge of such a system is using said models in order to predict group behavioral dynamics. For example, an individual PSALM model may create a profile of an individual, then proceed to compare this profile to that of other members of their group in order to see how well they would coordinate and the probability of potential conflict between said individuals. This would start out in rather limited capacity, mostly focusing on small groups of two to five people, but can potentially later be expanded to medium or even large organizations consisting out of thousands of profiles. Say, a firm is building a new department consisting out of varying professionals. PSALM may be used to assess the risk of this new department lagging behind in terms of productivity due to potential conflict brought upon by stress and different psychological profiles.

Lastly, while this somewhat falls outside of the scope of the project, the data and profiles constructed by PSALM can be integrated with a model that guides human resources and management professionals in resolving interpersonal conflict brought upon by stress, in addition to aiding already affected individuals in recovery. This may be used as a guide on transferring individuals away from groups that do not cooperate well with their psychological profile or even changing the amount or nature of the work carried out by said individual. This, in turn, can be used as a method of practicing holistic psychology where there is not only the focus on the well-being of the individual, but also their place in the group and the relationship between groups. In the long term, different PSALM systems can be linked up to create a broad information system network. For the sake of argument, said network may be dubbed 'PSALMnet'. A decentralized network of systems that monitors the interaction between different groups in order to monitor and protect the mental well being of individuals in said groups. A potential application of said 'PSALMnet' is to aid in management and coordination process by offloading work to different groups in the production process should any one unit exceed certain stress parameters. Essentially, that would mean the transformation of PSALM from a pure monitoring tool to one that has the capability to assist in management of large organizations and firms.

References

1. Goldstein, H.: Multi-level Statistical Models. Halsted, Manchester (1995)
2. Corcoran, C.M., Cecchi, G.A.: Using language processing and speech analysis for the identification of psychosis and other disorders. Biol. Psychiatry: Cogn. Neurosci. Neuroimaging **5**(8), 770–779 (2020)
3. Kramer, A.: An unobtrusive behavioral model of gross national happiness. In: Proceedings of the 28th International Conference on Human Factors in Computing Systems, pp. 287–290. ACM (2010)
4. Rodriguez, A.J., Holleran, S.E., Mehl, M.R.: Reading between the lines: the lay assessment of subclinical depression from written self-descriptions. J. Pers. **78**(2), 575–598 (2010)
5. Peters, E., Västfjäll, D., Gärling, T., Slovic, P.: Affect and decision making: a 'hot' topic. J. Behav. Decis. Mak. **19**(2), 79–85 (2006)
6. Goldberg, L.R.: An alternative "'description of personality'": the big-five factor structure. J. Pers. Soc. Psychol. **59**, 1216–1229 (1990)
7. Golder, S., Macy, M.: Diurnal and seasonal mood vary with work, sleep, and daylength across diverse cultures. Science **333**, 1878–1881 (2011)
8. Hashim, N.W., Wilkes, M., Salomon, R., Meggs, J., France, D.J.: Evaluation of voice acoustics as predictors of clinical depression scores. J. Voice **31**(2), 256-e1 (2017)
9. Kehoe, J.P., Abbott, A.P.: Suicide and Attempted Suicide in the Yukon Territory. Can. Psychiatr. Assoc. J. **20**(1), 15–23 (1975). https://doi.org/10.1177/070674377502000104
10. Kosinski, M., Stillwell, D., Graepel, Y.: Private traits and attributes are predictable from digital records of human behavior. Proceedings of the National Academy of Sciences (PNAS) (2013)
11. Kupers, T.A.: What to do with the survivors? Coping with the long-term effects of isolated confinement. Crim. Justice Behav. **35**(8), 1005–1016 (2008). https://doi.org/10.1177/0093854808318591
12. Lazer, D., Pentland, A., Adamic, L., Aral, S., Barabasi, A.L., et al.: Computational social science. Science **323**, 721–723 (2009)

13. Houben, M., Van Den Noortgate, W., Kuppens, P.: The relation between short term emotion dynamics and psychological well-being: a meta-analysis. Psychol. Bull. **141**(4), 901–930 (2015)
14. Kumar, M., Gupta, R., Bone, D., Malandrakis, N., Bishop, S., Narayanan, S.: Objective language feature analysis in children with neurodevelopmental disorders during autism assessment. In: Proceedings INTERSPEECH 2016, 17th Annual Conference of the International Speech Communication Association, pp. 2721–2725 (2016)
15. Michel, J.B., Shen, Y.K., Aiden, A.P., Veres, A., Gray, M.K., et al.: Quantitative analysis of culture using millions of digitized books. Science **331**, 176–182 (2011)
16. Robinson, R.L., Navea, R., Ickes, W.: Predicting final course performance from students' written self-introductions: a LIWC analysis. J. Lang. Soc. Psychol. **32**(4), 469–479 (2013)
17. Rathner, E.M., Terhorst, Y., Cummins, N., Schuller, B., Baumeister, H.: State of mind: classification through self-reported affect and word use in speech (2018)
18. Pressman, S.D., Cohen, S.: Positive emotion word use and longevity in famous deceased psychologists. Heal. Psychol. **31**(3), 297–305 (2012)
19. Schwartz, H.A., et al.: Personality, gender, and age in the language of social media: the open-vocabulary approach. PloS ONE **8**(9), e73791 (2013)
20. Stone, P., Dunphy, D., Smith, M.: The General Inquirer: A Computer Approach to Content Analysis. MIT Press, Cambridge (1966)
21. Holtgraves, T.: Text messaging, personality, and the social context. J. Res. Pers. **45**, 92–99 (2011)
22. https://ai.facebook.com/blog/large-language-model-llama-meta-ai/

Digital Transformation as a Driver of the Fashion Industry

Melnikova Anastasiya[✉]

Plekhanov Russian University of Economics, Moscow, Russia
`Melnikova.av@rea.ru`

Abstract. Digital transformation is becoming increasingly important in all areas of the global market. Moreover, the scale of digitalization is growing exponentially. The fashion industry is not an exception. Digitalization has a significant impact on various processes of the fashion industry. This paper is devoted to the main innovations of digital technologies in the apparel market in recent years, such as blockchain technology, artificial intelligence, virtual and augmented reality, and even digital clothing. For instance, blockchain technology provides protection against counterfeiting for manufacturing companies. Luxury brands such as Louis Vuitton and Moët Hennessy, Hugo boss use this technology to simplify the authentication of their products. Another example is digital clothing which is growing in popularity among consumers owing to a number of advantages over ordinary clothes: it is cheaper, requires less time to create, exists in more limited quantities and does not pollute the environment. The study analyzes the benefits and drawbacks, and the perspectives of further development of digital transformation in the fashion industry. Furthermore, the author is conducting a research for a small local store in order to evaluate the effectiveness of the integration of blockchain technology.

Keywords: Digitalization · Fashion industry · Blockchain · Digital clothing · Artificial intelligence

1 Digitalization

This paragraph is devoted to the disclosure of the concept of "digitalization".

The most important direction of the development of the economies of various countries in modern conditions is the transition to the digital economy, due to changes in the forms and methods of providing consumers with various kinds of high-tech services. It should be noted that the scientific literature has not yet developed a clear definition of the concept of the digital economy. The root cause of the emergence of the digital economy in the middle of the twentieth century was the "Internetization" of society. Therefore, it is internetization as a process of expanding access to information and the possibility of conducting certain operations that can be used as the basis for the concept of the digital economy in the narrow sense of the word. By the digital economy in the broadest sense of the word, we mean a set of industries related to the emergence of new technologies and the development of robotics, in which digital platforms, new technologies, robotics, smart technologies, etc. are used. The digital economy in the narrow sense of the word accounts for about 5% of global GDP, and the digital economy in the broad sense of the word accounts for 22% of global GDP [1].

There are 5 stages of digitalization [2]:

- The first stage (1850–1950s). The formation of the digital economy is directly related to the emergence of the first telecommunications technologies and inventions;
- The digital economy begins to develop actively at the second stage. Since the 1960s, when in digital innovations aimed at the mass consumer are beginning to spread widely in the world;
- The third stage of digitalization started around the beginning of the 1990s. With the advent of the global spread of the Internet in all spheres of public life is taking place;
- At the fourth stage (2001–2009), active commercial operation of high-speed mobile communication systems begins, smartphones appear, an international information and communication infrastructure is being formed, electronic payment systems and Internet services are spreading;
- Since 2010, we can talk about the fifth stage of digitalization associated with rapid expansion the market for mobile and cloud applications, the beginning of mass use of new digital technologies, and the spread of cryptocurrencies in the global economy.

In 2011, the term Industry 4.0 was announced at the Davos Forum, after which the formation of government programs for the development and stimulation of digital transformation of industry began in many countries.

Thus, have considered the stages of the formation of the digital economy, we can conclude, that the main reasons for its development are:

- The emergence of the Internet and its rapid growth;
- The spread of a fundamentally new level of telephone communication and a sharp jump in the density of information flows;
- The growth of computing power.

Modern digital technologies play an important role in stimulating the economic growth of countries, while the digital economy is growing many times faster than the traditional one.

For example, the number of Internet users has almost doubled over the past 10 years, reaching 5.35 billion by the beginning of 2024. On average, there are 400 min per day per user, and this year the world will spend a total of 780 trillion minutes using the Internet, which corresponds to almost 1.5 billion years of humanity's collective existence [3].

However, the average figures vary significantly depending on geography.

There are three groups of countries that create the global potential of the digital economy:

- The first group of countries includes the leaders of the digitalization of the economy – the USA, Germany, France, Austria, Japan and some Asian countries. These countries form the core of this process and demonstrate significant growth potential in the field of digital technologies.

- The second group includes "small" European countries with very high rates of digitalization of the economy, such countries as Belgium, Estonia, Denmark, Finland, Ireland, the Netherlands, Norway and Sweden.
- The third group includes countries that usually rely more on their large domestic markets for economic growth – Brazil, Australia, Canada, and India. In these countries, digitalization rates are relatively high, but do not exceed those of digital technology leaders.

In order to implement an effective digitalization scenario, all stakeholders in the economy, in which there is a problem of introducing digital technologies, should actively participate in the digital transformation of the economy and economic relations.

2 The Fashion Industry

The fashion industry is a set of types of creative, economic and managerial activities combined into a process aimed at the design, production, marketing and sale of a fashion product, with the constant movement of conditional boundaries between the stages of this process [4].

There are four main segments of the fashion industry [5]:

1. Primary segment: manufacturers of raw materials, accessories, special production equipment;
2. Secondary segment: designers, manufacturers of ready-made fashion products. Sometimes this segment is also called the "designers and manufacturers" segment;
3. Shopping segment: uniting retailers of a fashionable product. This includes boutiques, specialty stores, retail chains, department stores, drains, factory stores;
4. Auxiliary segment: specialized media, specialized advertising and PR agencies, style consultants, fashion bloggers. This segment plays an important role in shaping the fashion industry. Because by means of an auxiliary segment, information is exchanged between all four levels. Thus, the main function of this segment is the formation and direction of information flows between consumers, manufacturers and sellers. Some of this information exchange takes place directly, but most of it takes place through an auxiliary segment. In the auxiliary segment, the product itself is not created, but here the main percentage of the value of the product for the consumer is created, which in turn directly affects the perception of a fashionable product.

And there are some statistics data of fashion industry. According to Expert Market Research the global apparel, accessories, and footwear market size was approximately USD 2098.55 billion in 2023. The market is assessed to grow at a CAGR of 6.1% between 2024 and 2032, reaching a value of USD 3565.53 billion by 2032 [6].

In this case it should be determined one more concept "Sustainable Fashion". This term describes efforts within the fashion industry to reduce its environmental impacts, protect workers producing garments and etc. Sustainability in fashion includes wide range of factors such as cutting CO_2 emissions, addressing overproduction, reducing pollution and waste and ensuring that garment workers are paid a fair wage and have safe working conditions [7].

Sustainable fashion is one of the main trends in the fashion market, which has been actively gaining momentum in recent years [4]. This phenomenon is especially typical for countries with advanced economies. Figure 1 shows the data of the global sustainable fashion market depending on the region [8].

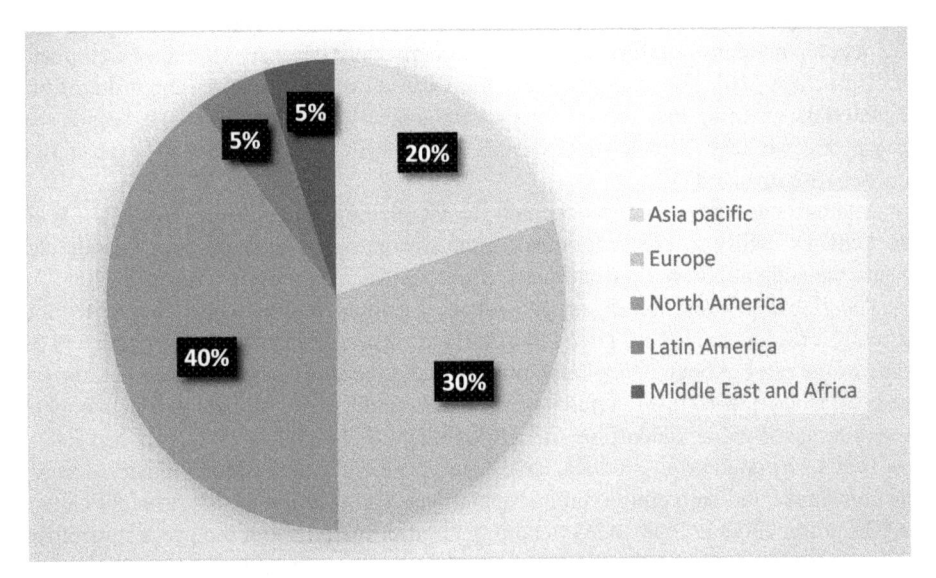

Fig. 1. Global Sustainable Fashion Market Share (%), By Region, 2023.

3 Digitalization in the Fashion Industry

As mentioned above, digitalization in the modern world penetrates into almost all processes and spheres. The fashion industry is no exception. However, this area has its own peculiarities of the digitalization process and ways of its application.

The main innovations in recent years of digital technologies in the fashion industry are represented in this chapter. There are blockchain technology, artificial intelligence, virtual and augmented reality, digital clothing. Each of these technologies are described in more detail below.

3.1 Blockchain Technology

Blockchain technology, widely known for its use in cryptocurrencies, is increasingly being adopted across various industries for its ability to provide transparency and security. The fashion industry is no exception, as blockchain can offer numerous benefits ranging from supply chain management to anti-counterfeiting measures.

Blockchain technology was introduced to the fashion world for the first time in the Shanghai Fashion Week 2016, the technology has today expanded its use cases in the direction of making the sector highly efficient and transparent [9].

There are several purposes for which we can use blockchain technology in the fashion industry.

First of all it is to provide transparent and secure supply chain ecosystem. Each step of the garment's lifecycle, from raw material sourcing to manufacturing, transportation, and retail, is recorded on the blockchain. This creates an unbroken chain of data that can be accessed by all stakeholders, ensuring accountability and authenticity. In this way a company convey information to consumers about ensuring ethical sourcing and labor practices [10]. For example, consumers can access information about the origin of materials, ensuring they are sustainably and ethically sourced. Likewise, brands can ensure that workers in their supply chain are treated fairly and that no exploitative practices are involved.

Another case of using blockchain is Combating Counterfeit products. With blockchain's ability to create unique digital identifiers for each product, brands can ensure the authenticity of their products. Some statistics data is provided below.

The global counterfeit industry as a whole is estimated to be worth over $3 trillion annually. Fashion and luxury goods like clothing, shoes, and leather items happen to be some of the most. About 20% of fashion products advertised on social media platforms are fake. Up to 3 in 10 fashion purchases are fake, and 8 out of 10 fake products bought were purchased online (according to Certilogo data) [11].

That's why counterfeit products have been a problem in the fashion industry, deceiving consumers and damaging brands' reputations. The solution of this problem can be an NFC chip with a unique code containing all information about the product installed in the item (during production). Each scan of this code updates the information on the chip itself and in the blockchain, thus, counterfeiting chips become meaningless [12].

ENDO Legacy Program works according to this principle. The product code can be scanned using the application of this program and determine the originality of the item as well as its status. For example, "on sale", "lost", "stolen", "belongs to", etc. [13].

3.2 Artificial Intelligence

The next paragraph of the chapter is devoted to artificial intelligence in fashion industry. As a blockchain this technology is widely used in various fields. But in fashion industry there some special products based on this technology. There are some cases of the various uses of artificial intelligence in the fashion industry.

Alejandro Giacometti from EDITED company has found an opportunity to predict demand with the help of artificial intelligence. By training artificial intelligence on the clothes of various designers, Alejandro's team was able to teach the computer to distinguish the models of one designer from others, to find characteristic elements of style. Moreover, it has become possible to predict the appearance of new collections, to anticipate consumer demand.

Another example is The American company Stitch Fix. Artificial intelligence analyzes fashion trends with the company's designers together and issues recommendations. As a result, the time to create new models is significantly reduced. In addition, this approach becomes a marketing tool, which helps the company stand out from competitors and attract the attention of consumers. Now several dozen models of clothing developed with the help of various types of artificial intelligence are successfully sold in stores.

And the last example is the neural network of American programmer Robbie Barratt.

The neural network has created a fashion collection in the style of Demna Gvasalia, designer of the fashion house Balenciaga. To do this, Barrat used photos from fashion shows and brand clothes from online stores, information from magazines and books. The result is a collection with Balenciaga-specific elements [14].

3.3 Virtual and Augmented Reality

The next technology is virtual and augmented reality. Three cases are considered in detail: virtual fitting rooms, virtual fashion shows and augmented reality for clothes.

VR can be used to create virtual fitting rooms, where customers can try on clothes and accessories without the need for physical fitting rooms. This can provide a more convenient and personalized shopping experience for customers [15].

Another interesting application of VR technology is virtual fashion shows. It allows fashion companies to showcase their collections to customers in a more immersive and interactive way [15].

One more example of a new experience of interacting with a product can be an animated virtual print on a T-shirt. To see it, a smartphone is enough: the print on the clothes is revealed when the camera is pointed at the application or mask for Instagram [16].

3.4 Digital Clothing

The last case is digital clothing. Digital clothing is a trend gaining popularity worldwide. The idea of digital clothing came to the fashion industry from video games, where you can change your character's wardrobe for real money. The trend was quickly picked up by brands [17].

There are several interesting facts of the history of digital clothing. In 2016 After bitmoji collaborated with Bergdorf Goodman, users were able to try on images of fashion brands on their avatars: Zac Posen, Alexander McQueen, Calvin Klein and other top designers [18].

In 2018, Milan Fashion Week saw a real breakthrough in the field of digital fashion – a virtual model Lil Miquela appeared with her first million Instagram followers, Cat Taylor (Sattytay) presented her digital versions of famous Balenciaga, Burberry and Vetements outfits [18].

Scandinavian retailer Carlings released its first digital clothing collection and a "digital fashion house" the Fabricant. One of the "digital fashion" outfits from the Fabricant was sold at auction in 2019 for $ 9.5 thousand [19].

Nowadays there are already quite a few virtual ateliers where everybody can order digital clothing. It is cheaper, requires less time to create, exists in more limited quantities and does not pollute the environment.

4 Research

This section is devoted to the research conducted by the author for a small local brand of beachwear "KupalnikiMoskva.ru".

KupalnikiMoskva.ru this is a small store, the main volume of sales is on the Internet platform, and there is also a showroom in Moscow. The main target audience is women between the ages of 16 and 45 with an average and above average income [20]. The objective of the study is to evaluate the effectiveness of the implementation of blockchain technology for this store. Since it is difficult to assess financial indicators before the introduction of technology, this analysis is aimed more at qualitative indicators than quantitative ones. Thus, the consumer's perception of the brand, which provides a product manufactured under environmentally friendly conditions at all stages of production and transportation, will be evaluated, as the buyer can verify by scanning the chip from the product label. In order to assess the effect of the introduction of blockchain technology for this store, a survey was prepared for the store's customers, as well as potential buyers who are part of the target audience. In the survey, respondents indicated their age, gender and income, which allowed us to segment our target audience. So, 111 people were interviewed. Their distribution by age and income is shown in Table 1.

Table 1. Segmentation of respondents by age and income.

Age	Number of responses	Income, thousands rubles	Number of responses
From 18 to 25	5	up to 50	5
From 26 to 35	34	up to 50	4
		from 50 to 80	15
		from 80 to 150	15
From 36 to 45	49	from 50 to 80	5
		from 80 to 150	34
		more than 150	10
Over 45	23	up to 50	2
		from 50 to 80	5
		from 80 to 150	13
		more than 150	3

Thus, the most significant segments were: women aged 36 to 45 with an income of 80 to 150 thousand rubles (30,6%), then women aged 26 to 35 with income of 50 to 150 thousand rubles (30%) and women over 45 with an income of 80 to 150 thousand rubles (12%).

In order to identify the importance of the principles of sustainable fashion for consumers of the brand, the following questions were asked with the possibility to choose an answer option or write your own (link to the survey: https://docs.google.com/forms/d/e/1FAIpQLSe4hxXN0t3uj0yDwCRLureLnfFufXY-frxyFqi8a1fNBGQ5w/viewform):

- Do you pay attention to the conditions under which the product you are purchasing was created?
- Does the availability of information about what, how and by whom the product is made affect your purchase decision?

- Would you like to be able to easily identify the origin of the product, its brand and other production details by scanning the chip on the label?
- How would you characterize a brand that provides open information about the environmental friendliness of its products at all stages?
- Are you willing to pay more for such a brand? And if yes, how much more?

The answers to these questions allowed us to assess the willingness of consumers to use blockchain technology to authenticate the brand and obtain information about the conditions of its production, as well as the willingness to pay extra money for this service. According to the results of the survey, the following data were obtained:

- 43% of respondents indicated that information about working conditions in production is extremely important to them, 53% replied that they would be interested if such information was available and less than 4% indicated that they were not interested in this information at all.
- Almost 37% of respondents confirmed that the availability of information about what, how and by whom the product is made is an extremely important factor in making a purchase decision. More than 40% of respondents also refer to the factors influencing the purchase decision, but not the main one. Less than 20% do not attach importance to this when making a purchase decision.
- More than 57% of respondents were interested in the idea of being able to receive all the information they are interested in regarding the manufacturer and brand authentication through scanning the product label. 40% would like to try this technology first to determine if it is convenient. Less than 3% replied that they were not interested in this information.
- The question of the characteristics of a brand that meets the values of sustainable fashion was open. The respondents had to figure out how to characterize such a brand. Everyone's answers turned out to be only positive: correct, caring, good, adequate, eco-friendly, sustainable, trending, high-quality, necessary, long-awaited, honest, as it should be, etc.
- The last question was about assessing the willingness to pay more for such a brand. Most of the respondents (almost 80%) agreed that such goods should cost more. 31.5%, however, could not determine how much more they are willing to pay. Almost 30% are willing to overpay no more than 5%. The price of 10% is more than 13% are willing to pay. And only about 5% of respondents are willing to pay up to 20% more for a sustainable brand.

These results are presented in the form of histograms in Fig. 2.

It is also interesting to highlight information on the most significant segment of the target audience separately. Above, we have indicated that the most significant for this brand are 3 segments:

1. women aged 36 to 45 with an income of 80 to 150 thousand rubles (1st segment)
2. women aged 26 to 35 with income of 50 to 150 thousand rubles (2nd segment)
3. women over 45 with an income of 80 to 150 thousand rubles (3rd segment)

The survey results for these three segments only are presented in Table 2.

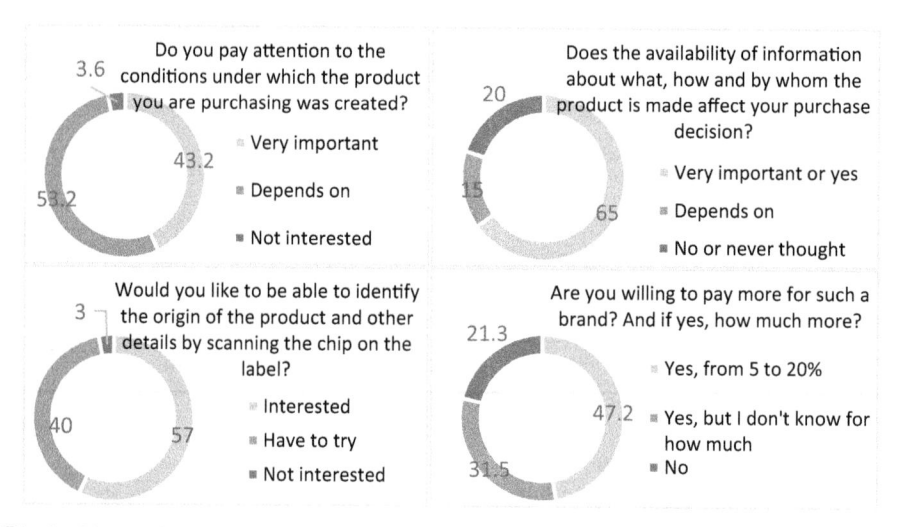

Fig. 2. The results of the survey of the target audience of the «Kupalniki Moskva» brand, 2024.

Table 2. The answers of main segments

Questions	Answers	1st segment PPL	%	2nd segment PPL	%	3rd segment PPL	%
Do you pay attention to the conditions under which the product you are purchasing was created?	It is extremely important to me that the conditions of the employees are at the proper level	14	41	13	43,3	8	61,5
	If this is indicated, then I will ask, if not, then it is not so important	17	50	15	50,0	4	30,8
	It doesn't matter to me	3	8	0	0,0	0	0,0
Does the availability of information about what, how and by whom the product is made affect your purchase decision?	Yes, it's very important to me	13	38	10	33,3	6	46,2
	Yes rather than no	8	23,5	8	26,7	3	23,1

(*continued*)

Table 2. (*continued*)

Questions	Answers	1st segment PPL	%	2nd segment PPL	%	3rd segment PPL	%
	This is one of the factors, but not the main one	3	8	2	6,7	2	15,4
	I've never thought about it	4	12	3	10,0	0	0,0
	Rather no than yes	6	17,6	5	16,7	1	7,7
Would you like to be able to easily identify the origin of the product, its brand and other production details by scanning the chip on the label?	I am always interested in the origin of the goods, and it will be more convenient this way	8	23,5	7	23,3	2	15,4
	That would be interesting	7	20,5	10	**33,3**	5	**38,5**
	I don't know, I have to try	17	**50**	11	**36,7**	4	**30,8**
	I'm not interested in such details	2	6	0	0,0	1	7,7
Are you willing to pay more for such a brand? And if yes, how much more?	Yes, by 10%	6	17,6	4	13,3	1	7,7
	Yes, by 5%	9	26,5	7	23,3	4	**30,8**
	Yes, no more than 20%	2	6	1	3,3		0,0
	Yes, but I don't know for how much	6	17,6	11	**36,7**	3	23,1
	No	8	23,5	5	16,7	4	**30,8**

After analyzing the table, we can conclude that the third segment is the most interested. However, among the respondents of the second segment, there are more other answers who are willing to pay for additional options.

5 Conclusion

The digitalization is one of global mega trend, which have significant impact of all spheres of society and it is a factor of growth of the modern economy.

In this paper we have analyzed the concept of digitalization and the fashion industry. Next, we considered the formats for the use of digital technologies in the fashion industry.

The most interesting for consideration by the author were 4 areas: blockchain technology, artificial intelligence, virtual and augmented reality and digital clothing. These technologies are widely used by both large well-known brands and small local ones. If analytics on large brands are available enough, then there is very little information on small brands.

Using the example of a local brand, an assessment of the effectiveness of introducing blockchain technology into operation was carried out. The analysis showed that brand consumers are extremely interested in the ability to receive open information about all stages of product creation and easily authenticate the brand using the blockchain system. In addition, consumers are willing to pay more for a brand with this option.

Thus, digitalization in terms of economic potential is effective for both well-known large brands and small ones.

References

1. Markova, O., Starodubceva, E.: Digital transformation of the global economy, Vestnik ASTU (2018). https://vestnik.astu.org/ru/nauka/article/33075/view. Accessed 21 Jan 2024
2. Umec, A.: Digitalization as a key factor of economic growth, 58th Scientific Conference of postgraduates, undergraduates and students of BSUIR (2022). https://libeldoc.bsuir.by/bitstream/123456789/48537/1/Umets_Didzhitalizatsiya.pdf. Accessed 21 Jan 2024
3. Kemp, S.: Digital 2024: global overview report, Datareportal (2024). https://datareportal.com/reports/digital-2024-global-overview-report. Accessed 21 Jan 2024
4. Melnikova, A.: The evolution of the theory of consumption of luxury goods. Econ. Entrepreneurship Law (2024). https://doi.org/10.18334/epp.14.3.120638
5. Melnikova, A.: Consumers' perception of fashion industry products. Econ. Entrepreneurship Law, 297–308 (2020). https://doi.org/10.18334/epp.10.2.100474
6. Global apparel, accessories, and footwear market outlook. https://www.expertmarketresearch.com/reports/apparel-and-footwear-market#:~:text=The%20global%20apparel%2C%20accessories%2C%20and,USD%203565.53%20billion%20by%202032. Accessed 21 Jan 2024
7. Farley, J., Colleen, H.: Sustainable Fashion: Past, Present, and Future. Bloomsbury Academic, New York (2015)
8. Global sustainable fashion market size and share analysis, Coherent market insights. https://www.coherentmarketinsights.com/industry-reports/global-sustainable-fashion-market. Accessed 21 Jan 2024
9. How Does Blockchain Technology Impact the Fashion Industry. https://dopewope.com/how-does-blockchain-technology-impact-the-fashion-industry/. Accessed 21 Jan 2024
10. Blockchain and transparency in fashion, Fashinnovation (2023). https://fashinnovation.nyc/blockchain-and-transparency-in-fashion/. Accessed 21 Jan 2024
11. How much money do brands lose to the counterfeit fashion industry. https://alpvision.com/counterfeit-fashion-industry/#:~:text=Counterfeit%20fashion%20products%20include%20both,counterfeited%20products%20across%20all%20industries. Accessed 21 Jan 2024
12. Bartlett, J.: A look at how new NFC chips prevent counterfeiting (2021). https://mindmatters.ai/2021/07/a-look-at-how-new-nfc-chips-prevent-counterfeiting/. Accessed 21 Jan 2024
13. ENDO Applications and User-Cases (2018). https://steemit.com/upvoteforupvote/@poshare/endo-applications-and-user-cases-or-no-more-tones-of-papers. Accessed 21 Jan 2024
14. Wilkins, A.: Will we all be wearing clothes designed by artificial intelligence (2020). https://metro.co.uk/2020/03/04/will-wearing-clothes-designed-artificial-intelligence-12342122/. Accessed 21 Jan 2024
15. Digital Transformation in Fashion. https://digitaltransformationskills.com/digital-transformation-in-fashion/. Accessed 21 Jan 2024

16. Maye-Delius, H.: 20 reasons why T-shirt printing is good for your business (2017). https://blog.printsome.com/20-reasons-t-shirt-printing-good-business/. Accessed 21 Jan 2024
17. What is digital clothing and how does it impact the fashion industry. https://audaces.com/en/blog/digital-clothing. Accessed 21 Jan 2024
18. Designers are now selling digital clothes that don't actually exist. https://www.designboom.com/technology/digital-clothes-virtual-fashion-carlings-the-fabricant-11-18-2019/#:~:text=It%E2%80%99s%20not%20an%20entirely%20new,neo%2Dex%2C%20a%2019%2Dpiece%20genderless%20collection. Accessed 21 Jan 2024
19. Sharkey, L.: Get to know digital fashion, the futuristic trend that wants to save the planet (2019). https://www.bustle.com/p/how-digital-fashion-could-let-you-own-clothes-that-dont-exist-19358438. Accessed 21 Jan 2024
20. Melnikova, A.: Import substitution in the fashion industry in Russsia. Econ. Entrepreneurship Law, 1211–1220 (2023). https://doi.org/10.18334/epp.13.4.117480

Sustainability and Environmental Impact of Innovations

Key Drivers and Barriers to Digital Transformation of the Electric Power Industry in CIS Countries

Tatsiana Zoryna[1,2], Olga Yurkevich[2,3](✉), and Pavel Kabanov[4,5]

[1] Institute of Power Engineering of the National Academy of Sciences of Belarus, 15/2, Akademicheskaya Street, 220072 Minsk, Republic of Belarus
[2] Belarus State Economic University, 26, Partizanski Av, 220070 Minsk, Republic of Belarus
oi.yurkevich@yandex.by
[3] RUE "Vitebskenergo", 30, Pravdy Street, 210029 Vitebsk, Republic of Belarus
[4] Belarusian National Technical University, 65, Nezavisimosti Av, 220013 Minsk, Republic of Belarus
[5] The Branch "Educational Center" of RUE "Vitebskenergo", 38A, Polyarnaya St., 220017 Vitebsk, Republic of Belarus

Abstract. Digitalization is one of the priority areas of strategic development and is crucial for the stable development of the economy. The article is devoted to the study of the process of digital transformation of the electric power industry of the Commonwealth of Independent States (CIS) countries, which opens up opportunities to improve energy efficiency, optimize equipment operation, improve energy demand forecasting and ensure more reliable operation of the energy system. The authors describe the principle scheme of digital transformation of the energy sector and note that successful digital transformation of the CIS power sector requires a comprehensive approach that takes into account both incentive factors and existing barriers, the most significant of which are discussed in the article. The article reflects the peculiarities of the CIS power industry, presents the stages of implementation of digital technologies in different countries and indicates the expected economic effect of their implementation, which consists in reducing the costs of energy companies, reducing the growth of the price burden on consumers and increasing the flexibility of the tariff policy for energy resources. It also describes the main ways and possible strategies for overcoming barriers to successful digital transformation of the energy sector, which require the development of a multidimensional long-term plan and coordinated efforts on the part of the government and energy companies.

Keywords: Digital Transformation · Power Engineering · Electric Power Industry

1 Introduction

The energy industry is the backbone of any country's economic progress, performing the critical function of energy supplier for industry, housing and utilities, and population.

The global energy industry is on the cusp of technological and structural reform driven by digitalization, a key trend for all countries [1]. In today's dynamic economic environment, marked by rapid technological advances and the need to adapt to changing climatic conditions, the digitalization of the energy industry represents a strategic imperative to maintain and strengthen its sustainable development.

Digital transformation in the electric power industry is a comprehensive transformation of the industry using modern information and communication technologies to improve the efficiency, reliability and availability of energy resources. It represents the process of introducing digital technologies into all aspects of energy companies' operations, from the automation of production processes to the introduction of smart metering systems for end-users.

1.1 Concept of Digital Transformation of the Energy Sector

The global smart energy market size was exhibited at USD 160.8 billion in 2023 and is projected to be worth around USD 395.0 billion by 2032, registering a compound annual growth rate (CAGR) of 10.50% during the forecast period from 2023 to 2032 (Fig. 1) [2].

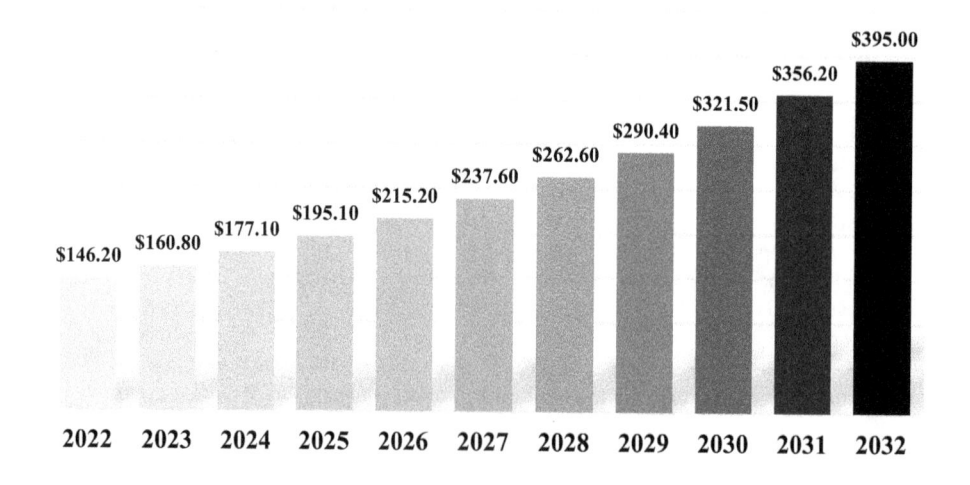

Fig. 1. Размер мирового рынка интеллектуальной энергии

In the context of the CIS countries, where energy systems are often in dire need of modernization and innovation, digitalization is particularly relevant and opens up new opportunities for development and integration at the international level.

Digitalization of the electric power industry for the member states is one of the key tools for improving the efficiency of monitoring, collection and analysis of large data sets, their comparison and analysis for study, modeling, forecasting, and as a result, improving the efficiency of the industry as a whole.

The current stage of digitalization in the energy industry of the CIS countries is characterized by a transition from the point implementation of digital technologies to an integrated approach to the administration of the industry, taking into account the peculiarities of integrity and interconnectedness, changes the existing architecture of interaction between industry participants and requires the intensification of cooperation in the field of digital transformation of the electric power industry of the CIS countries.

The principle scheme of digital transformation of the power industry can be presented as follows (Fig. 2).

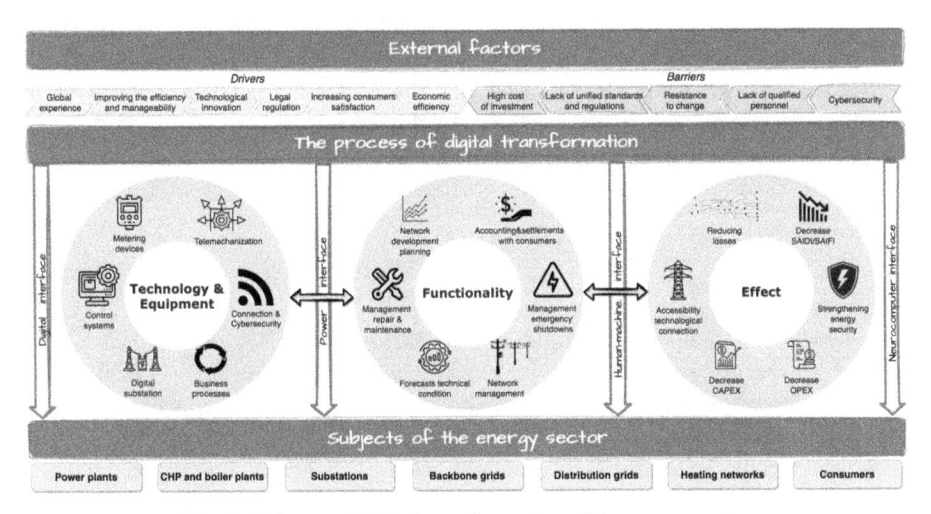

Fig. 2. Scheme of digital transformation of the energy sector

Using digitalization functionalities such as network development planning, management repair and maintenance, forecasts technical condition, network management, management emergency shutdowns, accounting and settlements with consumers in the areas of control systems, metering devices, telemechanization, connection and cybersecurity, business processes and digital substations it is possible to significantly improve the efficiency of the industry: reduce losses, improve power system reliability indices (SAIDI/SAIFI/CAIDI), decrease CAPEX and OPEX and strengthen energy security.

1.2 Characteristics of the Electricity Sector in the CIS Countries

Historically, the electricity sector of the CIS countries was formed as part of the unified energy system of the former Soviet Union. After the collapse of the USSR, each country began to develop its energy system independently, but close ties and integration processes are still in place. The structure of the electricity sector in the CIS countries remains quite diverse, combining public and private companies, as well as various forms of interstate cooperation.

The coordinated approaches of the CIS member states to the goals, main tasks, principles, main directions, as well as mechanisms of interstate cooperation in the field of digital transformation are reflected in the Concept of Cooperation of the Member States of the Commonwealth of Independent States in the field of digital development of society, adopted on October 25, 2019.

The electricity sector in the CIS countries in 2024 is characterized by active cooperation in long-term planning and coordination of power system development. In 2024, joint actions are planned in accordance with the creation of a common information space and unification of information exchange using a common digital data model (CIM). Thus, international expert interaction taking place on different platforms such as International Electrotechnical Comission (IEC), Conseil International des Grands Reseaux Electriques (CIGRE), GO15 and CIS Electric Power Council (EPC) is synchronized and increases mutual productivity.

But it should be noted, the path to digital transformation is full of both powerful incentives and significant obstacles, which should be carefully analyzed and taken into account when forming long-term development plans.

1.3 Key Drivers of Digital Transformation

1. World experience.

A powerful stimulus for the digital transformation of the CIS power industry is the successful experience of implementing digital technologies around the world, which testifies to the opportunities for optimizing production, increasing energy efficiency and improving the management of power systems.

A key example, in terms of global experience, is the introduction of smart grid systems (Smart Grids). This technology allows efficient management of power generation, distribution and consumption, ensuring more reliable and economical operation of the energy system.

Global experience shows that the implementation of smart grids can significantly increase the efficiency of resource utilization, reduce power losses in the grid, integrate renewable energy sources, and provide more flexible load management. In addition, smart grids contribute to the development of digital infrastructure and the creation of new services for consumers [3].

2. Improving the efficiency and manageability.

Digital innovations offer unique opportunities to improve the efficiency of management of all aspects of the electricity process, from generation and transmission to distribution of energy resources. The integration of digital automated control and monitoring systems and grid load optimization not only contributes to increased security of supply, but also to the overall quality of energy supply by improving load forecasting, optimizing energy consumption, enhancing system reliability, and enabling faster response to potential emergencies.

3. Technological innovation.

Advances in digital technologies such as artificial intelligence, predictive diagnostics, big data, virtual and augmented reality, Internet of Things and blockchain are creating new opportunities to improve efficiency and optimize the operation of energy systems.

Maintenance has always been a challenge for asset-intensive industries such as power generation plants. In a five-year study analyzing practices and identifying best practices for power plant maintenance, it was found that the best results were achieved when up to 71% of predictive diagnostics were used - significantly more than other types of maintenance (for example, emergency or planned corrective) [4].

Predictive diagnostics is a set of methods and technologies aimed at predicting and preventing equipment failures and breakdowns based on the analysis of data on its current condition and operating history [5]. The main goal of predictive diagnostics is the timely detection of signs of equipment degradation and determination of the optimal timing for maintenance or repair.

The use of predictive diagnostics of the state of electrical power equipment allows reducing maintenance costs by up to 40% [6], which makes it one of the most effective digital solutions.

The cost-effectiveness of predictive diagnostics is achieved due to several key factors:

- reduction of losses from production downtime due to timely detection and elimination of faults;
- reducing the cost of determining the root cause of a malfunction through data analysis and failure prediction;
- optimization of operating costs by maximizing the remaining service life of equipment (RUL).

According to an IoT Analytics report [7], the global predictive maintenance market grew to $5.5 billion in 2022 – up 11% from 2021 – with a projected CAGR of 17% through 2028.

It is clear that the average cost-effectiveness of using predictive diagnostics in electrical power plants will be high, especially when considering the long-term perspective and potential for reducing unexpected failures and increasing the intervals between scheduled maintenance shutdowns.

Thus, the implementation of advanced technologies, including predictive diagnostics, can significantly contribute to improving the efficiency of power systems and has significant potential for improving the operational performance of electric power plants between scheduled maintenance shutdowns.

4. Legal regulation.

In December 2020, the Strategy for Cooperation of the CIS Member States in the Electric Power Industry until 2030 and the action plan for its implementation were approved. The strategy defines goals and strategic objectives by areas of activity, among which the issues of digital transformation of the electric power industry are among the priorities of the energy agenda of the CIS countries.

The governments of the CIS countries are actively developing and implementing legislative acts aimed at supporting the digitalization of the electric power industry, which serves as an important incentive for the development of the industry.

All CIS states have adopted packages of strategic documents for the transformation of national economies, most states have adopted sectoral strategic documents for the digital transformation of the electric power industry and most energy companies have also adopted strategic documents and are implementing specific digital transformation projects (the multilevel nature of strategic documents on the example of the Republic of Belarus is presented in Table 1 [8]).

Strategic documents and regulatory legal acts adopted in the CIS countries reflect both similar and different decisions in support of the digital transformation of economies in general and electricity sectors in particular. The extensive regulatory legal framework developed in the CIS member states regulates the main stages of supporting digital transformation from the formulation of basic principles and objectives (laws and strategies) to the determination of mechanisms for using these principles in solving problems (programs and projects).

In order to unify terminology and eliminate different interpretations in the regulatory documents of the CIS countries, the CIS EPC for 2024 has determined the task of forming a consolidated list of terms for the digital transformation of the electric power industry of the CIS member states.

5. Increasing consumers satisfaction.

Electricity consumers are increasingly demanding better and more convenient services, expecting a high level of personalization, convenience and accessibility. This encourages energy companies to seek new digital solutions to meet these demands, expand the digitalization of energy sales activities and offer consumers new digital services.

6. Economic efficiency.

Digitalization of the energy sector can bring significant economic benefits by optimizing processes, increasing production efficiency and reducing maintenance costs. The use of modern technologies makes it possible to improve the management of power systems, increase forecasting of energy demand, optimize equipment maintenance costs and reduce energy losses [9].

In global practice, the effect of implementing digital solutions in the electric power industry includes the reduction of operating and investment costs and revenue growth [10] (Fig. 3):

For CIS countries, the resulting economic effect will not only reduce the costs of energy companies, but also reduce the growth of the price burden on consumers.

Thus, digital transformation opens up new opportunities for tariff regulation in the power sector:

1. Reduced tariffs (or reduced rate of tariff growth) due to cost optimization: more accurate forecasting of energy consumption, possible with the use of digital technologies, contributes to optimizing the load on the energy system and allows energy companies to manage assets and resources more efficiently.
7. Increased tariff flexibility: electronic metering systems allow the introduction of differentiated tariffs depending on the time of day or current energy demand, which contributes to a more efficient distribution of the load on the grid and encourages consumers to be more conscious of their energy consumption, thus reducing energy costs.
8. Personalization of tariff offers: taking into account all objective parameters such as power consumption, network voltage, distance to generation sources, technical

Table 1. Strategic documents in the field of digital transformation

Level	Strategic documents
State level	- Law of the Republic of Belarus №455-Z of 10.11.2008 "On Information, Informatization and Protection of Information"; - Decree of the Council of Ministers of the Republic of Belarus №673 of 26.05.2009 "On some measures to implement the Law of the Republic of Belarus 'On Information, Informatization and Information Protection and on invalidating some decrees of the Council of Ministers of the Republic of Belarus"; - Decree of the President of the Republic of Belarus №486 of 25.10.2011 "On Some Measures to Ensure the Security of Critically Important Informatization Objects"; - Decree of the President of the Republic of Belarus №531 of 02.12.2013 "On Some Issues of Informatization"; - Decree of the President of the Republic of Belarus №8 of 21.12.2017 "On the Development of Digital Economy"; - Decree of the President of the Republic of Belarus № 292 of 29.07.2021 "On Approving the Program of Socio-Economic Development of the Republic of Belarus for 2021–2025"; - Presidential Decree №46 of 23.01. 2014 "On the Use of Telecommunication Technologies by State Bodies and Other State Organizations"; - State Program "Digital Development of Belarus" for 2021–2025. Approved by Resolution of the Council of Ministers of the Republic of Belarus №66 of 02.02.2021; - Decree of the President of the Republic of Belarus №36 of 07.04.2022 "On the body of state administration in the sphere of digital development and informatization issues"
Industry level	- Industry development program for the electric power industry for 2016–2020. Approved by Resolution of the Ministry of Energy dated September 4, 2019 №31 - Concept for the development of electricity generating capacities and electrical networks for the period until 2030. Approved by Resolution of the Ministry of Energy dated February 25, 2020 №7 - Program for the comprehensive modernization of energy sector production for 2021–2025. Approved by Resolution of the Ministry of Energy dated April 5, 2021 №19
Corporate level	- The concept of creating an integrated automated control system for GPO Belenergo (IASU GPO Belenergo. Approved by order of GPO Belenergo dated September 1, 2016) - Comprehensive program for the development of automation of the Belarusian energy system for 2018–2022. Approved by order of the State Production Association "Belenergo" dated 05.08.2018 №112 - Strategy for informatization and digital transformation of SPA Belenergo for the period 2021–2025. Approved by order of the State Production Association "Belenergo" dated 04.09.2021 №7

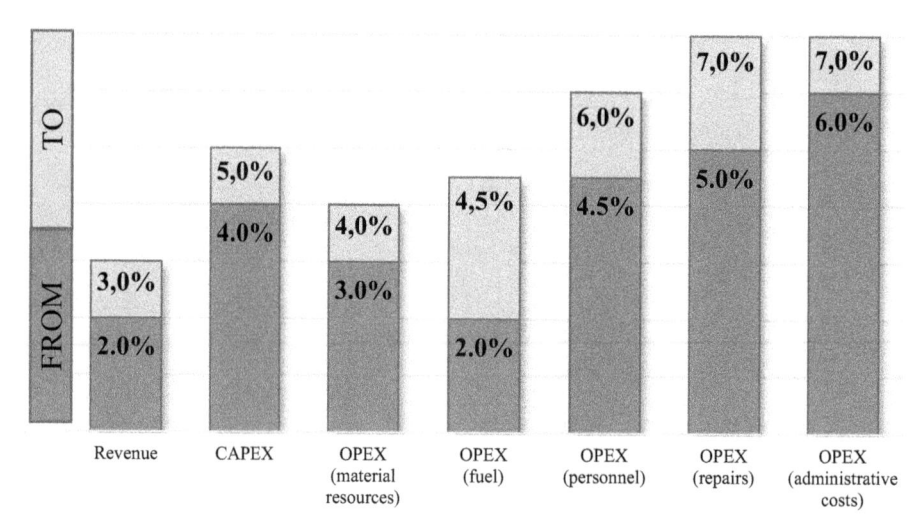

Fig. 3. Estimated economic effect from implementation of digital solutions [% of base]

condition of networks and equipment, consumption volumes, regional peculiarities of consumers' location, etc., energy companies can offer individual tariffs and services, which allows to achieve greater objectivity in tariff formation, enhances consumers loyalty and can stimulate more efficient use of energy.

9. Adaptability of tariff policy: digitalization makes it possible to quickly adapt tariffs to current economic conditions and demand, and to introduce new tariff groups, for example, to encourage the use of renewable energy sources or to promote rational electricity consumption.

An important area of this work is the introduction of an Automatic system for commercial accounting of power consumption (ASCAPC), which serves for automated collection, transmission, processing and documentation of electric power consumption. ASCAPC allow energy companies to automate settlements with consumers, to achieve increased reliability and efficiency of electricity metering, to provide automated control of the technical condition of electric power systems.

Automated energy control and metering systems are widely used in the CIS countries for effective monitoring and optimization of energy consumption and are the most widespread in the CIS countries among other digital technologies.

For example, in the Republic of Belarus, the share of metering devices integrated into the ASCUE system has more than tripled over the past 5 years: from 16.1% in 2019 to 49.4% in 2023.

Since the CIS countries in general are characterized by a high level of energy intensity of enterprises, which reduces the competitiveness of products in foreign markets [11], the possibility of reducing tariffs and increasing the flexibility of energy tariff policy make the digital transformation of the energy sector quite a significant factor in the development of industry and the economy of these countries as a whole. At the same time, digitalization

Key Drivers and Barriers to Digital Transformation 221

in the electric power industry of the CIS countries continues to develop, and its impact on tariff regulation will only increase, which will not only improve the quality of services for end consumers, but also increase the overall efficiency of the industry.

Thus, digitalization in the electricity sector opens new horizons for fairer and more efficient tariff regulation, which can stimulate economic growth and, at the same time, promote energy saving and energy efficiency.

It should be noted that all of the above drivers interact with each other, creating a synergistic effect that significantly accelerates the process of digital transformation of the industry.

1.4 Barriers to Digitalization of the Electricity Sector in the CIS

Nevertheless, the path to full-fledged digitalization of the industry is also characterized by the presence of serious barriers that should be carefully analyzed and taken into account in the formation of long-term development plans, and among which the following should be noted:

1. High cost of investment in the latest technologies.

The introduction of new technologies, large-scale infrastructure modernization, including the introduction of control and management systems, specialized software development, and staff retraining still require significant capital investments, which creates significant barriers to the large-scale integration of digital innovations.

2. Lack of unified standards and regulations in the field of digital technologies.

Most CIS countries have adopted sectoral strategic documents for digital transformation of the energy sector: concepts, strategic roadmaps, programs and projects for industry development and modernization, wholesale market rules, standards in the field of information and communication technologies and automation of control and management in the electric power industry. At the same time, the diversity of regulatory approaches in different CIS countries makes it difficult to implement universal digital solutions and requires additional development of common approaches in order to create a common information space for the introduction of a unified methodology for information exchange between power systems.

3. Resistance to change.

Traditional energy companies often have difficulty adopting new technologies. Resistance to change can arise for various reasons, such as lack of awareness of the benefits of digital technologies, fear of new changes, established processes, corporate culture, the need to retrain and adapt to new ways of working.

4. Lack of Qualified Personnel.

Lack of qualified personnel in the field of digital technologies is a serious problem faced by many companies and organizations, including the energy industry. There is a shortage of specialists with the necessary skills in the field of digital technologies in the CIS labor market, which complicates the process of digital transformation.

5. Cybersecurity.

As digital technologies are introduced, the risk of cyberattacks increases: insufficient data protection can lead to confidential information leaks, viruses and other negative consequences. To combat this problem, it is necessary to implement modern encryption methods, multi-layered security, train employees on cyber hygiene and regularly update software. With digitalization, it is becoming increasingly important to secure data and protect information from cyber threats, which also requires significant investment in security systems.

1.5 Electricity Digitalization Projects in CIS Countries

There are significant differences between CIS electricity organizations in the status of digital transformation: while some are starting digital transformation, others have already successfully implemented innovative digital solutions in their current operations and are piloting digital solutions in the area of new business models (Fig. 4).

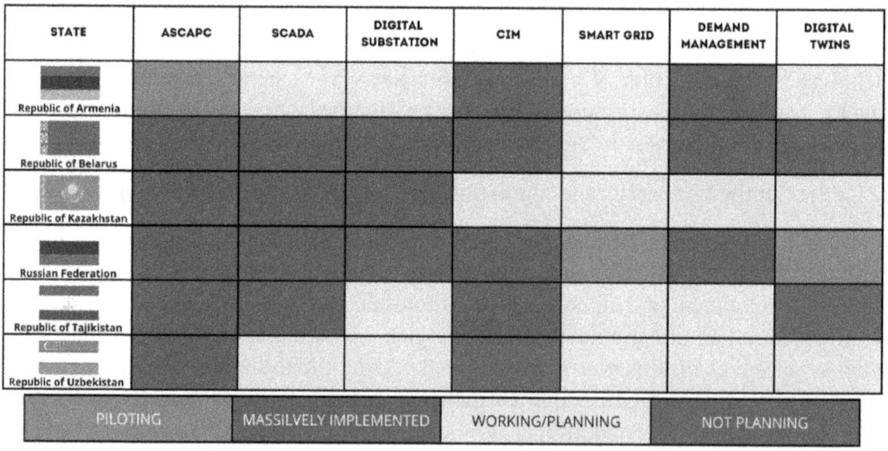

Fig. 4. Introduction of digital technologies in the electric power industry of CIS member states (based on data [12])

The highest level of implementation in the CIS countries has the "ASCAPC" and "SCADA" technologies, to a lesser extent the "Smart Grid" technology is implemented. The Common Information Model (CIM) is implemented and distributed to individual business processes in the Republic of Belarus and the Russian Federation.

It can also be noted that the opportunities and prospects for sharing experience and joint implementation of national projects of digitalization of the electric power industry are great, which puts the task of intensifying cooperation in the field of digitalization of the electric power industry of the CIS member states to the forefront.

1.6 A Set of Measures to Overcome Barriers

Overcoming barriers to the digital transformation of the CIS electricity sector is possible using the following key areas:

1. Formation of an effective investment model:

    Public-private partnerships: Stimulating investments through public-private partnerships, providing incentives and guarantees for private investors.
    Grant programs and subsidies: Establishment of grant programs to support innovative projects in the electricity sector.
    Investment funds: Organization of specialized investment funds aimed at financing digitalization projects.
    Attracting international financing: Using international financing and lending opportunities, including funds from international financial institutions.

2. Personnel training and development:

    Retraining programs: Development and implementation of retraining programs for existing employees to meet the new requirements of the digital economy.
    Partnerships with educational institutions: Cooperation with technical universities and colleges to train specialists capable of working in the digital transformation environment.
    Corporate training programs: Implementation of in-house training programs, including online courses and trainings on digital skills.

3. Creating a favorable regulatory and legislative space:

    Reforming legislation: Adaptation of legislation to simplify the process of implementing digital technologies, including regulations on cybersecurity;
    Standardization: Development and implementation of standards for digital technologies in the electric power sector, formation of a unified list of digital transformation terms;
    Market liberalization: Creating conditions for liberalization of the electricity market to increase competition and stimulate innovation;
    Support for innovative entrepreneurship: Introduction of measures to support startups and innovative companies in the electricity sector.

The implementation of these measures will require coordinated efforts on the part of government agencies and energy companies. The key success factor is an integrated approach focused on long-term partnership of all stakeholders.

1.7 Conclusion

Thus, despite the strong incentives for digital transformation, the CIS electricity sector faces serious obstacles that require careful consideration and an integrated approach in strategic planning. To realize the potential of digital transformation, CIS countries need to focus on creating a favorable investment climate, developing human capital and updating legislation.

Ultimately, successful digitalization of the power industry can not only fundamentally change the industry itself, but also become a catalyst for economic growth in the region, contributing to an improvement in the overall standard of living and sustainable development of the CIS countries.

The key to a successful future of the digital power industry will be the development and implementation of multidimensional strategies that take into account the unique characteristics of each state and are aimed at overcoming existing barriers and effectively using the drivers of innovation in the form of creating a favorable investment climate, developing human capital and updating legislation.

References

1. Zoryna, T., Prusov, S.: Digital transformation of the Belarus' electric power industry within the bounds of common approaches to the CIS fuel and energy sector digitalization. Sci. Innov. **2**, 59–65 (2022)
2. Precedence Research. https://www.precedenceresearch.com/smart-energy-market. Accessed 21 Feb 2024
3. Wang, R.M., Tian, Z., Ren, Fr.: Energy efficiency in China: optimization and comparison between hydropower and thermal power. Energy Sustain. Soc. **11**, 36 (2021)
4. Velayutham, P., Ismail, F.B.: A review on power plant maintenance and operational performance. Web Conf. **225**, 05003 (2018)
5. Kabanov, P.: Predictive capabilities condition diagnostics power equipment and prospects for its use in the Belarusian energy system. Energy Strateg. **6**(96), 20–22 (2023)
6. Uptimeai. https://www.uptimeai.com/resources/predictive-maintenance-in-power-plants. Accessed 21 Feb 2024
7. IoT Analytics. https://iot-analytics.com/predictive-maintenance-market. Accessed 21 Feb 2024
8. Zoryna, T., Salieva, R., Prusov, S., et al.: Economic and legal aspects of creating an integrated information system of the fuel and energy complex in the union state. International forum KAZAN DIGITAL WEEK. State Budgetary Institution "NCBZhD", Kazan. Part 1, pp. 158–162 (2023)
9. Gulnaz Galeeva. Digital transformation of the energy industry in the Russian economy. E3S Web Conf. **288**, 01065 (2021). SUSE-2021
10. Mikhaylenko, M., Koroleva, D.: International experience of digital transformation of the electric power industry. Report at the strategic session of the Association of Industry Digital Development Organizations "Digital Energy". Roland Berger, Moscow (2020)
11. Zoryna, T., Yurkevich, O.: Electricity intensity of GDP of the Republic of Belarus: an analysis in a sectoral and regional context, including comparative analysis with EAEU countries. Probl. Energy Resour. Saving **3**, 81–92 (2022)
12. Kupchikov, T., Bormatin, V., Gerikh, V., Ermolenko, G., Rakhimov, A., Frolova, O.: Digital transformation of the electric power industry: from the union of Soviet socialist republics to the commonwealth of independent states. Energeticheskii vestnik **28**, 20–39 (2023)

Sustainability as Collective Action: Co-design Model Leveraging University Stakeholders to Design Sustainable Seaweed-Based Menu

Hazel H. Kim[✉], Summer D. Jung, Katherine Yoon, Evelyn Hur, and Soh Kim

Stanford University, Stanford, CA 94305, USA
hjkim45@stanford.edu

Abstract. This research tackles the challenge of introducing and adopting sustainable marine-based food menus within university environments. As society transitions towards sustainable food sourcing and consumption, university students are positioned as future leaders, playing a vital role in this critical transformation. Facilitating adoption of novel and foreign ingredients among this demographic necessitates a collaborative approach with various stakeholders–including university dining chefs and student evaluators. This paper outlines a co-design model with university stakeholders to develop a novel and sustainable food menu, emphasizing the incorporation of seaweed into the Western diet. Four products are evaluated: seaweed pasta, salad, protein bar, and brownie. The success of this project is further evaluated through a survey-based sensory test among university students. The result shows that the students highly rated the sensory profile of the novel seaweed-based prototypes, with an average re-try willingness score of 4.5/5. In conclusion, the results of the project underscore the promise of seaweed as an environmentally friendly and nourishing food option, which can be effectively incorporated into university dining services by prioritizing sensory appeal and student involvement.

Keywords: Co-design · Sustainable ingredient · Food prototyping · Gen Z · Food innovation · Sustainability · Seaweed

1 Introduction

The awareness of sustainable food choices and the benefits of plant-based diets is constantly rising. Among other marine foods, seaweed is a highly nutritious and sustainable marine algae, notable for its abundant protein content, as well as antioxidant and antidiabetic properties [26]. Despite its numerous health benefits and culinary versatility, seaweed remains underutilized in the American diet. Recognizing the importance of adopting sustainable and nutritious food options on university campuses, we introduced a seaweed-based menu with a Western focus in campus dining halls. We took a co-design approach [25] and iterative design process (IDP), an early-stage product development method recognized as a valuable approach to reduce risks and elicit creative and effective solutions [18]. During the student tasting iterations, we conducted sensory evaluations of seaweed dishes to measure the perceived taste, odor, healthiness, and visual appeal on a scale. Based on the survey results and analysis, we suggest future directions for the promotion of seaweed-based menus in university settings.

2 Literature Review

2.1 Rise of Seaweed as a Sustainable Marine Ingredient

Sustainable marine ingredients in the food industry have garnered significant attention in recent years due to their nutritional benefits, environmental impacts, and potential to address future food security issues [6]. While the adoption of marine ingredients is widespread in Asia, a gap exists in the US market. Seaweed, among many marine ingredients, contains essential nutrients such as proteins, minerals, and vitamins, lowers blood glucose levels, and promotes antioxidant activity [26]. Moreover, the cultivation of marine ingredients requires fewer resources such as freshwater, chemical fertilizer, or land, lowering environmental impacts compared to traditional land-based agriculture [27]. However, seaweed aquaculture is still an emerging sector in the US [12].

Europe has been at the forefront of seaweed product development. Acknowledging the potential of seaweed, numerous studies took place in Northern Europe, testing its culinary applications [10,19]. A pilot consumer study conducted in Sweden reported high acceptability of seaweed-based food products among Swedish consumers [10]. Another consumer study from Sweden revealed consumers' positive perceptions and preferences among distinct consumer groups regarding seaweed food products, highlighting sustainability in their dietary choices [29]. Furthermore, one market research by Redway et al. [22] showed that seaweed food product availability has increased by 2.3-fold in the UK market compared to data in 2015. They developed seaweed-based products by recognizing consumer preferences and attitudes towards seaweed food products. The results of this study revealed that the majority of respondents were willing to purchase seaweed-related products in grocery stores and restaurants.

Despite the growing interest in seaweed, related research in the US is still limited. US consumers consider it as a highly foreign ingredient [20] and avoid seaweed due to its novelty [16]. Li et al.'s survey results indicated that only 36% to 43% of participants in the US were willing to purchase seaweed-based food products. To address this gap in seaweed-related research in the United States, the current research focuses on increasing consumer acceptance and preferences for seaweed-based food products by developing novel seaweed prototypes that specifically cater to American consumers.

2.2 Campus-Based Food Co-design Practices

Rather than targeting the US population at large, we decided to first introduce seaweed to a smaller segment of the population. Generation Z is known for its sustainable food choices, exemplified by higher adoption of a plant-based diet [1,13]. We hypothesized that prioritizing this expanding demographic, which is anticipated to become the primary consumer segment in the near future, would be a viable approach for promoting the adoption of seaweed-based diets.

Among various settings to introduce seaweed-based diets to the younger generation, we chose a university setting. Most importantly, university dining halls have served as a great space for food-related experiments and interventions. In dining halls, researchers have tested various methods to promote healthy eating, including introducing trayless dining [21], incorporating nutrition labels [5], increasing the availability of healthy food [14], decreasing the portion size of unhealthy foods, and more [24]. One common feature of such initiatives is their collaborative nature, never reliant solely on the efforts of a single individual or research team.

A co-design model with more active involvement of the university dining can further impact student education and the campus community. When done right, university stakeholders, especially student dining services, are a great resource for driving change in all stages of Human-Food Interaction [2]. Regarding the consumption of food, nutrition major students worked on a food science research project with campus food service staff [8]. Being able to work closely with the staff and offering tangible food to the campus community greatly enhanced the motivation and learning of the nutrition majors. In waste management, a comparable initiative was undertaken to involve design students in cross-disciplinary research focused on addressing food waste on campus. The initiative brought together design academics, campus facilities management, industry professionals, government experts, and design majors. This diverse array of stakeholders enabled students to create designs that are sensitive to social and cultural considerations. Beyond the application to food, co-design or co-creation in campus settings has led to numerous successful projects, such as in space design [4,17,28] and reduction of energy consumption [9].

Collectively, the examples mentioned offer a practical roadmap for effectively collaborating with university stakeholders in co-design projects. However, recognizing a significant void in existing research regarding empirical cases focused on promoting sustainable ingredients, we aim to fill this gap by detailing a unique co-design initiative. Specifically, we outline the partnership structure between student designers and university dining services. Moreover, we recognize the significance of engaging a broader spectrum of stakeholders within the food industry, including those involved in food sourcing [3]. Therefore, we delineate the complete menu development process with various stakeholders, including local food startups and suppliers. Food startups have demonstrated effective co-design practices, both within-industry and cross-industry [11]. The design process encompasses ideation, recipe creation, and ingredient procurement, providing a comprehensive overview of the initiative.

3 Research Progress

3.1 Approach

In this project, we collaborated with campus dining chefs, dietitians, food startups, and seaweed farmers. Furthermore, we solicited feedback from students through quantitative surveys to assess the acceptability of the dishes. The results were used to assess the possibility of incorporating seaweed-based menus into campus dining halls and develop future menu to better meet the needs and preferences of students.

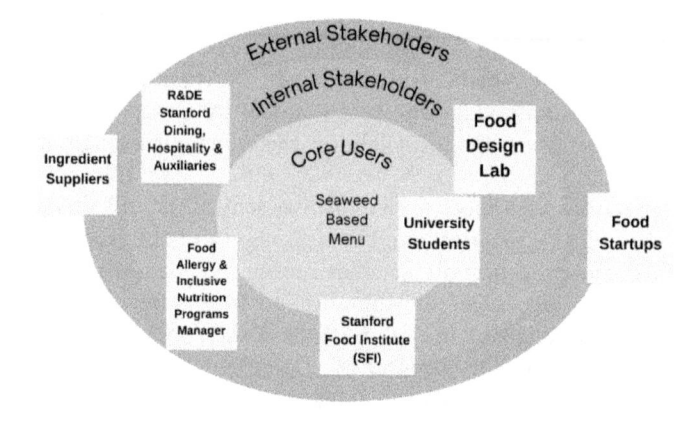

Fig. 1. Stakeholder map of campus-based seaweed co-design project

3.2 Related Stakeholders of the Campus-Based Seaweed Co-design Project

As exemplified by the UC Berkeley Foodscape Mapping Project [7], a crucial aspect of improving the campus food system involves identifying decision-makers and understanding the interplay among various elements of the foodscape. A co-design model can be described and analyzed in terms of stakeholder relationships. Figure 1 below shows the stakeholder map of this project showing how stakeholders are actively involved and communicating with each other to drive sustainability and innovation within university setting.

1) Stanford Residential & Dining Enterprises (R&DE) (internal) is leading sustainability efforts to incorporate more sustainable diets and food systems on campus and collaborating with various stakeholders to improve the sustainability, health, and safety of food supply chains. 2) Food Design Lab (internal) is where the project initiative initially came from, with researchers leading and facilitating communication among stakeholders. 3) Stanford Food Institute (SFI) (internal) is a platform to holistically enhance food quality, accessibility, and societal significance in the dining halls through collaborative research, education,

and innovative solutions involving diverse stakeholders, with a focus on sustainability and health for future generations. 4) Food Allergy & Inclusive Nutrition Programs Manager (internal) works closely with dining hall chefs and teams to provide nutritional information on the menus and manage food purchases, offering expertise and guidance on nutritional service within the dining hall. 5) University students (internal) who consume foods are central in this co-design model as they are the primary beneficiaries and core users of the dining experience. 6) Food Startups (Midwife & The Baker, Umaro) (external) introduce their innovative products by collaborating with researchers and dining professionals. They can leverage their creativity to complement existing efforts and drive positive changes in campus food system. 7) Ingredient suppliers (external) play a crucial role in food supply chain by providing essential components for the food products offered within the dining halls maintaining sourcing responsibility, and adapting to the evolving needs and preferences of campus community.

Through this co-design approach, internal stakeholders such as R&DE, Food Design Lab, SFI, and Food Allergy & Inclusive Nutrition Program Manager worked as a cohesive team to drive initiatives for sustainable food practices and menu development and implementation within campus dining halls. Additionally, food startups and ingredient suppliers brought innovative perspectives to the co-design model. Students were also central stakeholders in this project, providing feedback to improve the prototypes.

Overall, we present a dynamic network among stakeholders which drove positive changes in the campus dining halls. By teaming up with internal and external stakeholders, the co-design model seeks to promote the sustainability and health of campus community (Fig. 2).

Fig. 2. Various types of seaweed used for prototyping

Design Process. *Pilot Tasting and Prototyping:* In this initial stage, design researchers teamed up with R&DE chefs to craft the recipes, ensuring the dishes were not only innovative but also feasible for large-scale production. This partnership leveraged existing vendor agreements for ingredient supply, while also incorporating specially sourced seaweed to enhance the dishes' flavor profiles. This collaborative effort aimed to validate the concept of using seaweed in diverse culinary applications and assess the practicality of including such innovative dishes in the broader university dining context.

To refine the use of seaweed based on expert feedback, we conducted a pilot test, engaging a group of industry experts-including chefs, sustainable protein investors, blue food product developers, food scientists, design researchers, and expert tasters. They gathered to critically evaluate the first series of sustainable menu prototypes. The primary objective was to move beyond creating just a "minimum viable product" and instead unveil a "maximum innovative product" (MIP) that would showcase the sustainable and creative potential of seaweed in the culinary arts. A buffet-style tasting event was organized as a platform for open dialogue, where experts could share their insights on the selected range of dishes. These dishes were carefully chosen to demonstrate the versatility, unique flavors, and sustainability of seaweed, as showcased below (Fig. 3).

- **Sourdough Bread & Seaweed Butter**: A sourdough bread made from cultivated wheat starter, accompanied by butter infused with marine algae. [Vegetarian, Contains milk and wheat | Seaweed used: Kelp (S. japonica)]
- **Sunchoke Velouté and Pickled Hijiki Seaweed** Creamy sunchoke soup topped with tangy, pickled hijiki seaweed. [Vegetarian, Gluten-free, Contains milk, soy, fish | Seaweed used: Hijiki (S. fusiforme)]
- **Nori Omelet Roll** An omelet prepared with eggs and soy, rolled with nori. [Vegetarian, Gluten-free, Contains egg and soy | Seaweed used: Nori (N.tenera)]
- **Dulse Arancini with Romesco**
  Crispy rice balls with dulse seaweed, served with a nutty romesco sauce. [Vegetarian, Gluten-free, Contains egg, milk, and tree nut | Seaweed used: Dulse (P. palmata)]
- **Kale Wakame, & Quinoa Salad** A fresh mix of kale, wakame seaweed, and quinoa [Vegan, Gluten-free, Contains soy and wakame | Seaweed used: Wakame (U. pinnatifida)]
- **Clam and Mussel Risotto with Kelp Nage** A rice dish cooked with clams and mussels, in a broth flavored with large brown algae.[Gluten-free, Contains shellfish and milk | Seaweed used: Kelp (S. japonica)]
- **Seaweed Pesto & Mushroom Radiatore Pasta** Pasta shaped like ocean waves, served with a sauce made from blended seaweed, mushrooms, and nuts, offering unique earthy flavors. [Vegan, Contains tree nut and wheat | Seaweed used: Kelp (S. japonica)]
- **Chocolate Seaweed & Avocado Brownie** Moist brownies made with chocolate, seaweed, and avocado for a rich taste. [Gluten-free, Contains egg | Seaweed used: Nori (N.tenera)]

- **Umaro Bacon** Savory plant-based bacon made with red seaweed, chickpea, coconut oil, sunflower oil, plant flavors, natural colors and sea salt [Vegan | Seaweed used:Agar agar (Gelidium amansii)]
- **Seaweed Matcha Latte** Matcha latte with notes of sweetness and umami consists of seaweed powder and milk [Gluten-free, Contains milk | Seaweed used: Kelp (S. japonica)]

Fig. 3. Food prototypes tested during the pilot test

The experts engaged in the pilot tasting were tasked with identifying their top choices among the dishes, basing their selection on taste, nutritional value, visual appeal, and the sustainability of the dishes. The feedback highlighted a preference for Dulse Arancini with Romesco, Seaweed Pesto & Mushroom Radiatore Pasta, and Kale Wakame & Quinoa Salad. Despite the popularity of Dulse Arancini, practical considerations regarding scalability led to a focus on the latter two dishes. This iterative feedback loop was instrumental in refining the menu offerings, ensuring that the selected dishes not only resonated with the culinary team's vision but were also viable for large-scale production.

Subsequent stages involved multiple rounds of student tastings at tasting tables in the university dining area. The Stanford Flavor Lab serves as the research and development kitchen for R&DE, where chefs work on creating innovative menus to enhance students' dining experience, promote health, and advance food sustainability. The Tasting Table Program gathers student feedback on new dining hall menus, introducing them to unfamiliar foods and educating them about the food system. Through the Tasting Table Program, students sampled the chosen dishes and offered insights through surveys, allowing for menu refinement based on real user feedback.

Evaluation Process. *1st Iteration:* During the student tasting iterations, sensory evaluation of seaweed dishes was conducted to measure taste, odor, healthiness, and visual appeal on a scale. Two seaweed dishes were introduced to students during the first round–seaweed salad and seaweed pasta (Fig. 4). These dishes were evaluated by students who were asked to rate the sensory characteristics by giving a scale from 1 to 5 (with 5 representing excellence). Sensory

Fig. 4. Picture of the seaweed pasta and seaweed salad tested during the first iteration

evaluation is described as a scientific approach to quantifying, analyzing, and interpreting students' responses to products as experienced through visual, odor, taste, and hearing [15]. Additionally, we have incorporated healthiness into our evaluation criteria, as we aim to promote the sustainable and functional characteristics of seaweed. The 5-point numbered scale, which is most commonly used to perceive sensory intensities [23], has been used for student tasting iterations. The sensory evaluation was aimed to answer the following questions:

- *What considerations should be taken into account in menu planning and development?*
- *How acceptable are the seaweed-based menus flavor-wise to college students?*

Student feedback from a total of 44 respondents, consisting of 38 individuals aged 18–27 and 6 individuals aged 28–37, was obtained during the first test. The results in Table 1 indicate that students evaluated seaweed salad as better in taste, healthiness, and visual appeal compared to seaweed pasta.

Table 1. Student ratings of the four seaweed menu items, on a scale from 1 to 5

Menu	Taste	Flavor	Texture	Odor	Appearance	Healthiness	Accept
Pasta	4.0			4.5	4.3	4.0	
Salad	4.2			4.2	4.5	4.8	
Protein bar	3.7	3.6	3.8	3.4	3.6		3.8
Brownie	4.2	4.2	4.0	4.1	4.2		4.2

2nd Iteration: The sensory characteristics needed to be more specified to collect valuable information for further menu expansion. Therefore, in the second round of student tasting, students were asked to rate the taste, flavor, texture, odor, appearance, and overall acceptability on a scale from 1 to 5. As we aimed to explore students' preferences towards the seaweed-based menu items by testing a wide variety of seaweed products, seaweed protein bars and seaweed brownies were set up to be tested during this round (Fig. 5).

Fig. 5. Picture of seaweed protein bar and seaweed brownie tested during the second iteration

The results from 35 students, consisting of 28 individuals aged 18–27 and 7 individuals aged 28–34 are reported: students consistently evaluated seaweed brownies higher in all sensory characteristics than seaweed protein bars as Fig. 5 shown below. This suggests a preference among the university students population for the sensory profile of seaweed brownies over seaweed protein bars, which could inform future menu planning and implementation strategies within dining halls.

Willingness to Try Again: The question of willingness to try those menus again can guide and provide insights for shaping menu enhancements and application strategies at campus dining halls. By giving a scale from 1 to 5, students answered their inclination to try the seaweed-based menu again. Seaweed brownies received the highest average rating of 4.6, as they found them to taste like traditional brownies without an ocean-like taste or flavor. In contrast, seaweed protein bars ranked the lowest with a rating of 4.4, as they were too seaweedy in taste and had a noticeable seaweed texture within the bar. Similarly, students expressed a preference for seaweed pasta, which received a rating of 4.5, without an overly ocean-like flavor. For the seaweed salad, also rated at 4.5, students provided feedback suggesting the addition of another layer of texture such as crunch.

4 Conclusion

The survey results from two tasting iterations among university students provide insights into the acceptance and preference for seaweed-based menu items. In the first iteration, students preferred to eat seaweed salad over seaweed pasta, indicating that it has better taste, healthiness, and visual appeal. Subsequently, in the second iteration, seaweed brownies came out as the preferred option, outscoring seaweed protein bars across all sensory evaluation characteristics. These findings suggest that balancing the promotion of sustainability and sensory characteristics is crucial to incorporate seaweed-based dishes into campus dining halls.

In conclusion, the project's findings highlight the potential of seaweed as a sustainable and nutritious food source that can be successfully integrated into university dining services through careful consideration of sensory appeal, student engagement, and educational support. Iteratively refining the menu based on direct feedback ensures that the offerings not only contribute to environmental sustainability but also cater to the evolving tastes and preferences of the student population, paving the way for broader acceptance of sustainable food choices. Additionally, the iterative design process, as demonstrated through student tasting sessions, exemplifies a commitment to human-centered innovation by prioritizing user feedback and iterative refinement to meet the evolving needs and preferences of the audience.

5 Limitations and Future Directions

This study has potential limitations. First, the sample size and selection of students may not be representative of the entire student population nor be completely representative of Gen Z's food consumption preferences and behaviors. In the second tasting session, 43% of the respondents were born in Asian countries. Due to this selection bias, it's probable that the ratings of the Asian respondents were influenced by their familiarity with seaweed.

Furthermore, while students were provided with a simple sensory evaluation survey prompting rating of odor, taste, perceived healthiness, visual appeal, and willingness to try again on a scale of 1 to 5, the numerical ratings may not have been enough to capture nuances in students' opinions and preferences. Significance tests were also not performed on the average ratings. Characteristics such as odor and perceived healthiness may also be difficult to rate on a simple quantitative scale given that certain dishes may have little to no odor and students are not experts in nutrition respectively. Therefore, for future studies, we plan to adopt more qualitative approaches, including observation, follow-up interviews, and focus groups.

Lastly, the actual adoption of seaweed products in regular dining hall menus was not tested. While the tasting experiments invited students to rate the seaweed-based dishes, there needs to be further studies on the regular integration of seaweed items in dining halls in order to assess operational feasibility and continued student interest in blue foods. Especially due to the novelty effect, it's crucial to assess whether the co-design model can sustain interest in blue foods.

Based on the feedback gathered through the comprehensive tasting iterations, the integration of seaweed-based dishes into campus dining halls is core for the next step. Future efforts focus on seamlessly introducing innovative seaweed-based dishes in alignment with sustainability goals, enriching sensory profiles through collaboration with campus dining chefs, and fostering partnerships with environmentally responsible local suppliers and food startups. Through these collaborations and co-design, the aim is to enrich the dining experience and foster the importance of culinary innovation and consciousness on university campuses.

Acknowledgments. We would like to acknowledge the important contributions of Chefs Tami Lin and Junelle Fronda from Stanford R&DE, as well as Alice Pyo and Sophie Egan from Stanford Food Institute(SFI). Their expertise and dedication were invaluable in shaping and advancing our research on sustainable food practices and the integration of seaweed into the culinary landscape.

References

1. Aguirre Sánchez, L., et al.: What influences the sustainable food consumption behaviours of university students? A systematic review. Int. J. Public Health **66**, 1604149 (2021)
2. Altarriba Bertran, F., Jhaveri, S., Lutz, R., Isbister, K., Wilde, D.: Making sense of human-food interaction. In: Proceedings of the 2019 CHI Conference on Human Factors in Computing Systems, pp. 1–13 (2019)
3. Chesbrough, H., Kim, S., Agogino, A.: Chez panisse: building an open innovation ecosystem. Calif. Manage. Rev. **56**(4), 144–171 (2014)
4. Diep, M.Q.L.: Multi-sensory environments and student wellness on urban campuses: co-designing an inclusive space at butterfield park to help support student mental health (2019)
5. Driskell, J.A., Schake, M.C., Detter, H.A.: Using nutrition labeling as a potential tool for changing eating habits of university dining hall patrons. J. Am. Diet. Assoc. **108**(12), 2071–2076 (2008)
6. Duarte, C.M., Bruhn, A., Krause-Jensen, D.: A seaweed aquaculture imperative to meet global sustainability targets. Nat. Sustain. **5**(3), 185–193 (2022)
7. Fanshel, R.Z., Iles, A.: Transforming the campus foodscape through participatory mapping. Case Stud. Environ. **4**(1), 1120325 (2020)
8. Goto, K., Bianco-Simeral, S.: Campus community involvement in an experimental food research project increases students' motivation and improves perceived learning outcomes. J. Food Sci. Educ. **8**(2), 39–44 (2009)
9. Gwilt, I., Davis, A., et al.: Revealing the hidden: using a co-design approach to explore on campus energy use through the representation of consumption data. In: Proceedings of the Sixth International Conference on Design Creativity (ICDC 2020), pp. 133–143 (2020)
10. Jönsson, M., Maubert, E., Merkel, A., Fredriksson, C., Karlsson, E.N., Wendin, K.: A sense of seaweed: consumer liking of bread and spreads with the addition of four different species of northern european seaweeds. a pilot study among swedish consumers. Future Foods **9**, 100292 (2024)
11. Jung, S.D., Perttunen, E., Kirjavainen, S., Björklund, T., Kim, S.: Peer designers as strong influencers on the design process of food startups. Proc. Des. Soc. **1**, 2409–2418 (2021)
12. Kim, J., Stekoll, M., Yarish, C.: Opportunities, challenges and future directions of open-water seaweed aquaculture in the united states. Phycologia **58**(5), 446–461 (2019)

13. Kymäläinen, T., Seisto, A., Malila, R.: Generation z, food waste, diet and consumption habits: a finnish social design study with future consumers. Sustainability **13**(4), 2124 (2021)
14. Lachat, C.K., et al.: Availability of free fruits and vegetables at canteen lunch improves lunch and daily nutritional profiles: a randomised controlled trial. Br. J. Nutr. **102**(7), 1030–1037 (2009)
15. Lawless, H.T., Heymann, H.: Sensory Evaluation of Food: Principles and Practices. Springer, Heidelberg (2010)
16. Li, T., Ahsanuzzaman, Messer, K.D.: Is there a potential us market for seaweed-based products? A framed field experiment on consumer acceptance. Mar. Resour. Econ. **36**(3), 255–268 (2021)
17. Lundström, A., Savolainen, J., Kostiainen, E.: Case study: developing campus spaces through co-creation. Archit. Eng. Des. Manag. **12**(6), 409–426 (2016)
18. McClain, A.D., Hekler, E.B., Gardner, C.D.: Incorporating prototyping and iteration into intervention development: a case study of a dining hall-based intervention. J. Am. Coll. Health **61**(2), 122–131 (2013)
19. Mouritsen, O.G., Duelund, L., Petersen, M.A., Hartmann, A.L., Frøst, M.B.: Umami taste, free amino acid composition, and volatile compounds of brown seaweeds. J. Appl. Phycol. **31**, 1213–1232 (2019)
20. Prager, H.R.: What can be done to increase acceptance of seaweed into the western diet. Department of Product Design. Norwegian University of Science and Technology. TPD4505. Henry. Prager. pdf (ntnu. edu) (2017)
21. Rajbhandari-Thapa, J., Ingerson, K., Lewis, K.H.: Impact of trayless dining intervention on food choices of university students. Arch. Public Health **76**, 1–6 (2018)
22. Redway, M.L., Combet, E.: Seaweed as food: survey of the UK market and appraisal of opportunities and risks in the context of iodine nutrition. Br. Food J. **125**(10), 3601–3622 (2023)
23. Rousseau, B.: Sensory evaluation techniques. Food Science and Technology-New York-Marcel Dekker, vol. 138, no. 1, p. 21 (2004)
24. Roy, R., Kelly, B., Rangan, A., Allman-Farinelli, M.: Food environment interventions to improve the dietary behavior of young adults in tertiary education settings: a systematic literature review. J. Acad. Nutr. Diet. **115**(10), 1647–1681 (2015)
25. Sanders, E.B.N., Stappers, P.J.: Co-creation and the new landscapes of design. Co-design **4**(1), 5–18 (2008)
26. Thiviya, P., Gamage, A., Gama-Arachchige, N.S., Merah, O., Madhujith, T.: Seaweeds as a source of functional proteins. Phycology **2**(2), 216–243 (2022)
27. Tiwari, B.K., Troy, D.J.: Seaweed sustainability–food and nonfood applications. In: Seaweed Sustainability, pp. 1–6. Elsevier (2015)
28. Victorino, G., Bandeira, R., Painho, M., Henriques, R., Coelho, P.S.: Rethinking the campus experience in a post-covid world: a multi-stakeholder design thinking experiment. Sustainability **14**(13), 7655 (2022)
29. Wendin, K., Undeland, I.: Seaweed as food–attitudes and preferences among swedish consumers. a pilot study. Int. J. Gastronomy Food Sci. **22**, 100265 (2020)

Pioneering Renewable Energy Transition in US: A Comparative Case Study of Google, Apple, and Microsoft's Utilization of Power Purchase Agreements

TaeHyung Kwon and Soh Kim

Stanford University, Stanford, CA 94305, USA
sohkim@stanford.edu

Abstract. This paper presents a comprehensive analysis of the significant roles corporate Power Purchase Agreements (PPAs) play in the expansion of the U.S. renewable energy market through a detailed case study of three major technology companies - Google, Apple, and Microsoft - from 2018 to 2022. By employing a case-study methodology, the study examines the annual sustainability reports and numerical data of each company to assess their engagement with renewable energy procurement strategies through PPAs. The findings highlight how these corporations leverage PPAs not only to meet their energy needs and sustainability goals but also to establish the overall renewable-ecosystem of the United States, promoting the shift towards sustainability. The analysis further explores the impact of these strategies, quantitatively offering a progressive comparison between the PPA investments from companies and their contribution to the advancement of the renewable energy sector in the United States, underscoring their pivotal role in the power sector's transition towards decarbonization.

Keywords: Corporate Power Purchase Agreement · Renewable Energy · Sustainability

1 Introduction

In response to the desperate need of a climate agreement, in December 2015, 195 countries in UN Framework Convention on Climate Change adopted the Paris Agreement at the 21st Conference of the Parties (COP) to prevent further human-induced pollutions and stabilize the concentration of the GHG in the atmosphere to hold the global warming to a 1.5 °C limit [1]. The Paris Agreement had created an international framework for voluntarily making and evaluating commitments, aiming to boost global efforts by enabling the comparison and

---

Supported by organization x.

scrutiny of these pledges, with the intention that public exposure will motivate increased ambition. As the Paris Agreement was signed, the United States President Barack Obama [2] affirmed it as the "turning point for the world" and a new moment for the "United States into the global leader in fighting climate change".

Building on this momentum, a series of new legislations and climate policies were initiated by the United States to reduce carbon emissions, foster investment in renewable energy technologies, and support the development of clean energy infrastructure. Since the Paris Agreement, large US technology companies - including Apple, Google, and Microsoft - have each adopted proactive and strategic approaches towards sustainability and clean energy transition [3].

Hence, Apple has emphasized local renewable energy facility sourcing and construction through direct investments and contracts [14]. Similarly, Google has embedded environmental sustainability into its core values since its inception, as shown by its carbon neutrality since 2007 [13]. Microsoft has also outlined ambitious objectives, aiming to achieve carbon negativity by 2030. This involves utilizing its technologies to minimize environmental impact while making substantial investments in renewable energy sources [17]. Collectively, these three companies have demonstrated a shared approach to sustainability investment. In addition to government tax credits and benefits, these companies have increasingly invested directly in renewable energy development. This is evident through the emergence of Power Purchase Agreements (PPAs).

PPAs are contracts between energy buyers and sellers where the buyer agrees to purchase energy from the seller for a specified period at a predetermined price. In contrast to the government directly building new renewable energy facilities, PPAs offer a more flexible and market-driven approach [4]. Upon analyzing the annual sustainability reports produced by the three companies, PPAs have become a crucial tool in enabling businesses and utilities to invest in renewable energy sources.

In this paper, a primary analysis is conducted on the renewable energy investment of the aforementioned three prominent technology companies-Apple, Google, and Microsoft-by studying their published annual sustainability reports over the most recent five years (2018–2022). This analysis aims to comprehensively elaborate the collaborative dynamics among the companies in the context of stimulating the demand of the US renewable energy market.

2 Literature Review

In 2022, annual corporate PPAs volume across the US, Europe and Asia has reached its all-time high with 36 gigawatt (GW) of renewable energy [5]. PPAs are increasingly common due to the unique financial structure of renewable energy projects, which, despite high initial construction costs, benefit from significantly lower operation and maintenance expenses [6]. This efficiency not only allows energy producers to recover their investments with a reasonable profit margin but also enables companies to secure clean electricity at competitively low predetermined prices through PPAs [7,8]. Notably, long-term PPAs, spanning 10 to 20 years, are increasingly invested, reflecting a financial move by companies to lock in energy prices and ensure supply stability over extended periods [9]. This trend highlights the broader shift towards renewable energy, driven by both environmental necessities and the economic rationale of long-term cost savings and price stability. As a result, global trend further underscores the PPAs as a key mechanism for companies to meet their energy demands while voluntarily achieving sustainability goals and reducing carbon footprints. In fact, as global innovation continues to grow in tandem with the surging demand for electricity, by 2030, communication technology has been identified as accounting for nearly 50% of the total electricity demand, encompassing consumer devices, network infrastructure, and data centers [10]. This revelation has led to international initiatives like COP26 highlighting the critical role of corporate clean energy projects, thus illustrating the pivotal role of renewable energy procurement in meeting global sustainability ambitions [11]. Consequently, the strategic acquisition of renewable energy by companies is increasingly recognized as a fundamental driver in the power sector's transition towards decarbonization [12].

Under the hood of corporate strategies within their drive for environmental sustainability, the ultimate goal of this paper is to present a case study of three companies: Apple, Google, and Microsoft. It comprehensively elaborates on the role of PPAs in the expansion of the US renewable market, tangentially aligning the companies' stances with outcomes and various parameters affecting further investments.

3 Research Design

This study employs a case-study methodology to analyze Google, Apple, and Microsoft by examining their annual sustainability reports, drawing progressive insights from the report contents, and assessing numerical data from each company's data factsheet. Specifically, upon the meticulous content analysis of the each annual sustainability reports, the study aims to uncover the depth of corporate engagement with sustainability practices. This examination focuses on the companies' publicly stated commitments, goals, and progress, as well as any new approaches to sustainability and operational strategies. By dissecting these reports, we intend to extract both insights and quantifiable data to gain a holistic understanding of each company's annual stance on sustainability.

Transitioning from the analysis of the sustainable report content, the quantitative segment examines how the procurement of renewable electricity through PPAs by the three companies compares to the aggregate data of PPAs at the national level in the U.S. The initial dataset is exclusively extracted from the companies' factsheets, while the comparative national data is sourced from the National Renewable Energy Laboratory (NREL). NREL functions under the U.S. Department of Energy's Office of Energy Efficiency and Renewable Energy and offers an exhaustive overview of annual state-level PPAs volumes. The analysis conducts a year-on-year evaluation of the percentage growth or decline in these metrics, set against the comprehensive national data from NREL. The purpose of this comparison is to highlight the pivotal role and influence that the examined companies have in leading the renewable energy sector in the United States.

Upon the quantitative analysis, for Google and Apple, the study directly utilizes the reported figures, applying various assumptions over calculations to distinguish between domestic and international PPA values as needed. For Microsoft, the analysis became more intricate with the inclusion of RECs alongside PPA volumes as a single value in their reports post-2019. This complexity necessitated adopting a unique methodological stance, using the Ordinary Least Squares (OLS) regression to estimate the individual PPA figures. In statistically discerning the relative parameters for OLS equation, Stepwise Akaike Information Criterion (stepAIC) is adopted alongwith additional datasets spanning from 2015 to 2019 [18–20] to increase the accuracy of the model, as detailed in the available factsheets. This multifaceted approach allowed a quantitative assessment of each company's commitment to renewable energy through PPAs, facilitating a comparative analysis of their strategic engagements over the years.

4 Data Analysis

The examination aims to compare and contrast the reported sustainability information across different years, thereby quantitatively demonstrating the changes, advancements, and strategies each company employs in relation to renewable energy investment. The subsequent sections will delve deeply into interconnected discussions and conclusions about each company, particularly focusing on the quantitative impact of PPAs in their sustainability strategies, as detailed in the Discussion section.

4.1 Google's Advancements in Sustainability Initiatives

Starting in 2018 [13], Google made substantial progress in sustainability, launching a strategic five-year plan focusing on carbon-free energy, technology empowerment, and community benefits. The company acquired over 3.75 GW of renewable energy, translating into approximately $5 billion in new global investments, and for the twelfth year in a row, achieved carbon neutrality. Remarkably, Google matched its global operations' electricity consumption with renewable energy sources, a significant remark in corporate sustainability.

During the fiscal years of 2019 and 2020 [13], amidst the COVID-19 pandemic, Google advanced its sustainability agenda by incorporating consumer hardware products into its sustainability report and ensuring carbon-neutral shipping. The company undertook the world's largest solar-plus-storage project with Nevada utility NV Energy and led in clean energy transition initiatives. Globally, Google executed the largest corporate renewable energy purchase to date, securing a 1.6 GW package across 18 new energy deals, expanding their renewable energy portfolio by over 40%. This initiative led to over $7 billion in new renewable energy investments worldwide and matched 100% of their global operations' electricity usage with renewable energy, totaling over 12 million MWh.

In 2021, Google continued its leadership in sustainability, matching 66% of its data center electricity use with regional carbon-free sources on an hourly basis, while maintaining a 100% renewable energy match for its global electricity consumption since 2017. This effort showcased Google's dedication to green energy, with the company signing contracts for an additional 2.8 GW of clean energy capacity in 2022 [13]. These efforts underscore Google's role as a pioneer in the renewable energy sector, striving towards a more sustainable future with substantial investments and innovative policies in green energy.

Progressing further, the study pivots to evaluating the numerical volumes of documented PPAs [13], convering both domestic and international figures into a single metric. In order to calculate the PPA values pertinent to the US market, this analysis operates under the assumption of equitable distribution of PPAs in relation to domestic and international electricity consumption figures. This assumption is substantiated by the alignment of total renewable electricity acquisition with overall electricity demand, underscoring that all consumed electricity is sourced from renewables. Thus, the ratio of domestic to international electricity usage provides a basis for estimating the share of domestic PPAs.

Figure 1 encapsulates the trajectory of Google's commitment to renewable energy, where it reveals a steady rise in PPA procurement from 5.8 million MWh in 2018 to nearly 11.9 million MWh in 2022. It is worth highlighting the substantial spike in 2020, where the year-over-year percentage increase in PPA procurement reached an impressive 27.64%. The annual increments in PPA procurement values, which span from 960,987 MWh to as high as 1,927,577 MWh, reflect Google's escalating investments in renewable energy sources, signifying the corporate commitment to sustainability through increase of reliance on renewable energy to power its company operations.

4.2 Apple's Sustainable Commitments and Investments

From 2018 to 2022, Apple's journey in sustainability has been marked by significant achievements. In 2018 [14], Apple achieved a significant reduction in its carbon footprint, decreasing it by 35% compared to 2015 levels, and successfully powered all of its facilities worldwide with 100% renewable energy. This milestone was complemented by initiatives to enhance product energy efficiency, such as improvements in the iPad Pro, and a focus on reducing material usage while increasing the use of recycled resources. Apple's energy conservation measures led to substantial savings in electricity and thermal energy, effectively preventing a significant amount of CO_2 emissions. The company's active stance against fossil fuel subsidies and advocacy for renewable energy underscored its dedication to environmental responsibility.

The momentum continued in 2019 [14], with Apple expanding its renewable energy investments through strategic initiatives like a 75-megawatt wind project in Texas and the deployment of a utility-scale battery storage system to optimize solar electricity delivery to the grid. Apple's approach included venturing into subsidy-free renewable projects and investing in innovative technologies like biomethanation to convert organic materials into renewable natural gas. These initiatives contributed to a remarkable 71% reduction in Apple's scope 1 and scope 2 emissions since 2011, highlighting the company's ongoing commitment to reducing its environmental impact.

By 2020 [14], Apple further solidified its position as a leader in sustainability, focusing on expanding its renewable energy projects both domestically and internationally. Notable projects included a 180-acre solar initiative in Reno, Nevada, and a significant investment in a grid-scale energy storage project in California with a capacity of 240 MWh. Apple's Supplier Clean Energy Program aimed to transition its entire manufacturing supply chain to 100% renewable electricity by 2030, with over 4 GW of renewable energy added to the supply chain by the end of 2020. Apple's strategic investments, advocacy for clean energy policies, and focus on energy efficiency within its operations and data centers highlights its comprehensive approach to promoting environmental sustainability through establishing the collaborative ecosystem.

In their pursuit of its carbon neutrality, all annual reports highlight their dedication to renewable energy, particularly through engagement in various renewable energy projects [14]. These initiatives are categorized into Direct Ownership, Equity Investments, and Long-term Power Purchase Agreements (PPAs). In fact, among the categories, it becomes clear that long-term PPAs constitute a significant portion - nearly 90% - of Apple's projects. By applying the long-term PPAs proportion into total volume of purchased renewable energy, the analysis reveals a marked spike in PPA value by 535,200 MWh in 2019, translating to a 44.3% increase, which is substantially higher than in subsequent years. While there is a consistent annual increase in the absolute value of PPA purchases, the growth rate is not uniform. In particular, 2021 witnessed the smallest increase at 8.44% (depicted in Fig. 1).

4.3 Microsoft's Sustainability Efforts

Microsoft's approach to sustainability encompasses a diverse set of strategies, focusing on energy conservation and the development of renewable energy sources. Initiatives begun in 2018 include the collaboration on the 'Factory of the Future' solar panel installation and the implementation of intelligent building systems at a supplier's facility, aimed at reducing greenhouse gas emissions through increased efficiency. In the same year, Microsoft initiated a 315 MW solar project in Virginia and engaged in research into efficient fuel cell and energy storage technologies, indicating a move towards bridging the gap between the current reliance on fossil fuels and future sustainability objectives. The company sets goals for its data centers to achieve 60% renewable energy usage and construct 100% carbon-free 17 new buildings in Seattle [15,16].

Starting in 2020, Microsoft began releasing a detailed Annual Sustainability Report [17], separate from its previous Corporate Social Responsibility (CSR)

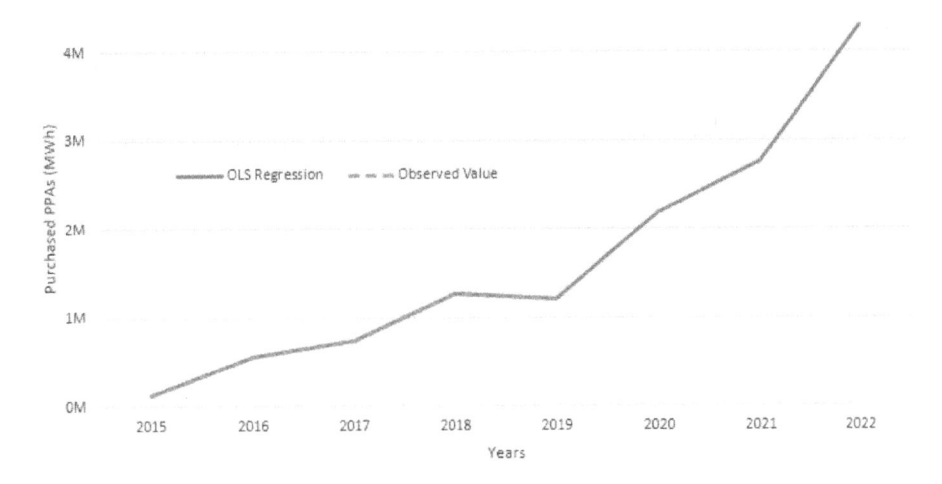

Fig. 1. Graph showing Microsoft's domestic PPA energy purchases from 2015 to 2022, with an OLS regression model fitted up to 2019 and predicted purchases significantly exceeding predictions in later years.

Reports, marking an increased focus on transparency in its sustainability efforts. This period saw the company moving closer to achieving net-zero emissions through strategic long-term PPAs and managing to supply 25% of its Silicon Valley campus's energy needs with on-site solar power. The company also made a partnership with Volt Energy, the only African American owned US solar facility, for a 250-MW project and the introduction of hydrogen fuel cells for backup power in data centers, reflecting a combination of technological innovation and social responsibility. Furthermore, Microsoft has focused on increasing energy efficiency, particularly in its data centers, by optimizing existing infrastructure. This includes leveraging surplus power and enhancing server density, which resulted in a significant increase in server density by up to 33% in 2022. This strategy not only reduces the demand for new data center construction but also minimizes the environmental impact associated with such expansions [17]. Through these various initiatives, Microsoft's sustainability strategy encompasses renewable energy, technology innovations, and social equity, representing a comprehensive environmental approach.

In the subsequent analysis of quantitative data, this study examined Microsoft's methodology for reporting environmental metrics, with a specific focus on PPAs and RECs. As mentioned in the Research Design section, contrary to the practices observed in other companies, Microsoft amalgamated the data for PPAs and RECs without individual breakdowns, necessitating the derivation of PPA figures through statistical means [17]. To address this, the research employed a linear regression model leveraging OLS. The choice of OLS was predicated on its diminished propensity for data overfitting, thereby enhancing the model's reliability.

For the construction of the OLS model, initial parameter selection was guided by an assessment of variables that potentially influence or correlate with PPAs, including metrics such as Renewable Energy Purchased and Total Electricity Consumption (Table 1). From an initial set of seven parameters, the study incorporated the stepAIC methodology. This iterative process refines the model by systematically adding or removing parameters to minimize the AIC value, thus achieving an optimal balance between model simplicity and the fidelity of data representation. Consequently, the research delineates a linear regression model that elucidates the data through a minimized subset of predictive variables as shown by Fig. 2.

Table 1. Selected parameters determined for the OLS regression model

Selected Parameters	Unit
Renewable Energy Purchased & Consumed - North America	MWh
Total Electricity Consumed	MWh
Offsets Purchased (Emission Compensation)	mtCO2e
On-Site Renewable Energy	MWh
Total Energy Used (portion of non-fuel Electricity)	MWh

The analysis revealed PPAs constituting nearly 20% of the combined total, highlighting a greater emphasis on RECs than PPAs. Figure 2 further illustrates that Microsoft significantly ramped up its investments in PPAs by 50% from the fiscal year 2019 to 2020. Moreover, with the transformation of the CSR Report into a Sustainability Report, Microsoft began to publicly underscore its commitment to increasing investments in sustainability. Indeed, from the fiscal year 2020 to 2022, the investment in solar electricity surged, annually increasing 100% and 300% [17]. Over the 5 year time-frame, there was a notable leap in PPA investments from 1,264,926 MWh in 2018 to 4,278,725 MWh in 2022, with the most pronounced annual growth occurring between 2021 and 2022. This trajectory showcases Microsoft's deepened dedication to sustainability, evidenced by a substantial surge in its renewable energy investments, particularly noticeable in the years following 2019.

4.4 Progressive Comparison Between 3 Companies and the United States

In the subsequent phase of the analysis, the calculated PPAs values from three companies combine to indicate a pivotal influence on the advancement of the US renewable energy sector. In order to illustrate the proportional amount of PPAs that the companies are responsible for, data from the NREL is employed [21]. The data shows a consistent annual increase in both corporate and national PPA acquisitions, as depicted in Fig. 1. Notably, national PPAs have generally grown more rapidly than corporate PPAs. An analysis of the period between 2018 and 2019 reveals that corporate PPAs saw an increase of approximately 18%, whereas national PPAs experienced a notable surge of nearly 48%. Nonetheless, a shift in growth dynamics was observed from 2021 to 2022, wherein corporate PPAs demonstrated a higher growth rate, outstripping national PPAs, which recorded a deceleration from 43% to 22%. Despite these fluctuations, the combined efforts of companies indicate their commitment to corporate responsibility and leadership, surpassing national initiatives. In fact, since the fiscal year 2019, the cumulative investment in PPAs by the companies has consistently represented about 20% of the total PPA contracts executed in the United States, stressing their significant role in the PPA landscape. This trend further highlights the pivotal role of corporate entities in advancing sustainable energy initiatives, thereby catalyzing a paradigm shift in the procurement of renewable energy through PPAs.

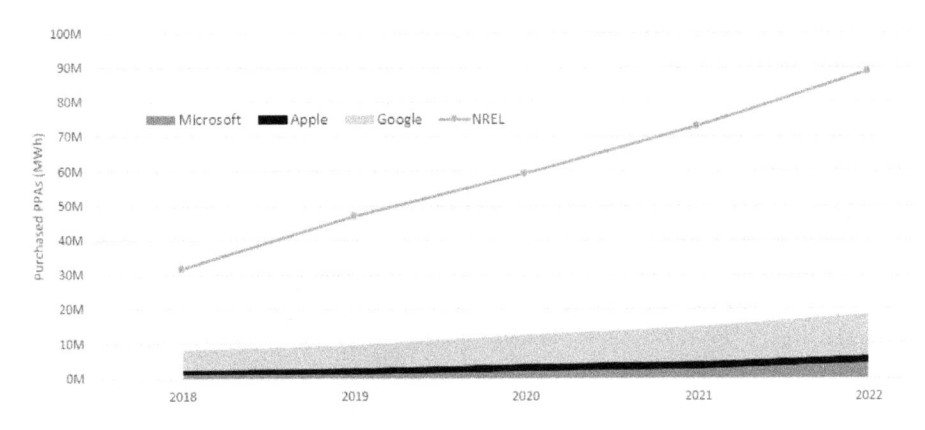

Fig. 2. Comparative bar and line chart illustrating the growth in Corporate PPAs for renewable energy by Microsoft, Apple, and Google from 2018 to 2022, alongside the NREL national PPA purchases, with NREL leading the increase

5 Discussion and Conclusion

Throughout the analysis, the study highlights the significant contribution of three companies to the nation's PPAs investment, accounting for one-fifth of the total. Expanding the scope to include other major corporations such as Meta Platforms, Inc., and Amazon.com, Inc., the study projects the large U.S. technology companies to account for over half of all national PPAs projects. This collective approach, as detailed in previous sections, emphasizes the critical role of not only individual company initiatives in achieving Net-Zero objectives but also the development of a renewable-ecosystems over the nationwide community. By leveraging market-oriented mechanisms like PPAs, these entities have the potential to markedly influence sustainable market trends through their significant brand influence and product demand. Yet, the study further anticipates that such corporate responsibilities cannot be the only parameter driving the PPAs market, highlighting the need for a multifaceted approach to energy sustainability.

Addressing the accelerants and barriers to increased investment in renewable energy is a multifaceted challenge, magnified by the significant political and economic shifts over the past five years. These shifts include pivotal presidential administration transitions, the unprecedented global upheaval caused by the COVID-19 pandemic, and subsequent economic recessions. As national leading companies, their investment and profit-generating activities are inextricably linked to the broader political and economic environment, requiring vigilant attention to evolving laws and regulations. In dissecting the data, our analysis hones in on two critical barriers: the fluctuating political landscape and the significant changes in market dynamics during the pandemic.

Political activities, in terms of laws and regulations, have deterred corporate investment in various ways. As the main catalyst of corporate investment is the profit gain, despite its role of corporate responsibility, political actions regarding the monetary policies must affect the money flows. As shown by the result, current study has reported that the rate increase of PPAs was only 17% between 2018 and 2019. In fact, starting in 2018, Tax Cuts and Jobs Act's [22] reduction of the corporate tax rate to 21% presents challenges for renewable energy financing through corporate PPAs. This change undermines the attractiveness of renewable energy investments to tax equity investors, as the lower tax rate diminishes the value of tax benefits, such as depreciation deductions, thereby reducing the incentive for companies to engage in renewable energy PPAs. Meanwhile, during the surge increase rate of 25% between 2021 and 2022, the Consolidated Appropriations Act of 2021 [23] significantly bolsters corporate investment in renewable energy through extensions and enhancements in the Investment Tax Credit and Production Tax Credit, which directly lower the cost and risk of renewable projects, making renewable energy projects like solar and wind more financially attractive for corporate PPAs. Consequently, while it's wrong to attribute corporate PPA trends solely to political actions, the significant influence of these political actions on the profitability and viability of corporate investments in renewable energy cannot be overlooked.

The transition to renewable energy sources has encountered both barriers and accelerants, with market dynamics playing a pivotal role alongside political factors. In 2019 towards the end of 2020, the current study has observed a significant rate of surge from 18% to 31% in corporate PPAs purchase. In fact, this period saw a temporary decline in global CO_2 emissions by 6% due to reduced fossil fuel demand. However, as the global economy began to recover in 2021, emissions rebounded, nearly reaching pre-pandemic levels, driven by increased energy demand, particularly in China and India [24]. Despite the initial boost in renewable energy deployment, the rebound in emissions and the rise in the carbon intensity of electricity in 2021 demonstrated that the swift resurgence in economic activity and energy demand outpaced the gains made by renewable energy during the pandemic, highlighting the ongoing challenge of decoupling economic growth from carbon emissions and the need for sustained policy efforts to support renewable energy adoption.

5.1 Limitations and Future Works

This study encounters several limitations that could affect the comprehensiveness of its findings. A primary constraint is the limited scope of data collection as it primarily examined three major companies to illustrate the dynamics of PPAs and their impact on the U.S. renewable energy market. Meanwhile, an ideal approach would entail a broader investigation across all major Silicon Valley tech companies-Google, Amazon, Facebook, Apple, and Microsoft (GAFAM)-for a more holistic understanding. Moreover, there is a lack of explicit data regarding their investments, particularly, in the case of incomplete data from Microsoft and Google, injects a degree of uncertainty into the results. The improvements could not only enhance the accuracy of future research but also contribute to the global effort towards achieving net-zero emissions. Looking ahead, opportunities lie in expanding the study's scope to include more companies beyond GAFAM and mathematically integrating current qualitative variables like market dynamics and political factors into parametric analyses for a deeper insight into the substantial role these large companies play in steering both the U.S. and global markets towards renewable energy adoption.

5.2 Conclusion

This analysis underscores the remarkable strides made by leading companies like Google, Apple, and Microsoft in the realm of renewable energy and sustainability, showcasing a collective commitment to environmental leadership through substantial investments and innovative policies. By examining the qualitative and quantitative shifts in corporate strategies over recent years, the findings illuminate the evolving landscape of renewable energy adoption and the critical role of PPAs in advancing the national renewable market under the corporate sustainability agendas. Moreover, the broader context of political and economic changes highlights the complexities and challenges faced by companies in navigating the renewable energy investment terrain, underscoring the necessity for adaptive strategies in the face of external pressures and opportunities for sustainable growth.

References

1. Blau, J.: The Paris Agreement. Springer, Heidelberg (2017). https://doi.org/10.1007/978-3-319-53541-8
2. President Cabinet Room: Statement by the President on the Paris Climate Agreement, The White House - President Barack Obama (2015). https://obamawhitehouse.archives.gov/the-press-office/2015/12/12/statement-president-paris-climate-agreement. Accessed 01 Feb 2024

3. Wirth, D.A.: Cracking the American climate negotiators' hidden code: united states law and the Paris agreement. Clim. Law **6**, 152–170 (2016)
4. Thumann, A., Woodroof, E.A.: Energy Project Financing: Resources and Strategies for Success, 1st edn, p. 93. River Publishers (2021)
5. Luis Cordova, J.G., Jiménez Zulueta, L., Byttebier, K.: Power purchase agreements and sustainable energy development: an approximation to the Cuban legal system. J. World Energy Law Bus. **16**, 506–515 (2023)
6. Vimpari, J.: Financing energy transition with real estate wealth. Energies **13**, 4289 (2020)
7. Bloomberg Nef.: companies Brush Aside Energy Crisis, Buy Record Clean Power. In: BloombergNEF (2023). https://about.bnef.com/blog/companies-brush-aside-energy-crisis-buy-record-clean-power/
8. Setya Budi, R.F., Sarjiya, Hadi, S.P.: Indonesia's deregulated generation expansion planning model based on mixed strategy game theory model for determining the optimal power purchase agreement. Energy **260**, 125014 (2022)
9. Wallace, P.: Long-term power purchase agreements: the factors that influence contract design. Research Handbook on International and Comparative Sale of Goods Law (2019)
10. Andrae, A., Edler, T.: On global electricity usage of communication technology: trends to 2030. Challenges **6**, 117–157 (2015)
11. Sthepani, Y.F., Sunitiyoso, Y.: Corporate Renewable Energy Procurement Prioritization Using Analytic Hierarchy Process (AHP) by Energy Service Company Perspective in Response to COP26. ijcsrr 05 (2022)
12. Johnson, D.: Corporate Procurement of Renewable Energy as a Key Driver in the Decarbonization of the Power Industry. Duke University (2018)
13. Alphabet Inc.: Google Sustainability Reports (2023). https://sustainability.google/reports/
14. Apple Inc.: Environment (2023). https://www.apple.com/environment/
15. Microsoft: Microsoft 2018 Corporate Social Responsibility Report (2018). https://query.prod.cms.rt.microsoft.com/cms/api/am/binary/RE2IDuR
16. Microsoft: Corporate Social Responsibility Report. Microsoft Corporation, Inc. (2019). https://query.prod.cms.rt.microsoft.com/cms/api/am/binary/RE4R1l8
17. Microsoft Corporation, Inc.: Microsoft Environmental Sustainability Report (2023). https://www.microsoft.com/en-us/corporate-responsibility/sustainability/report
18. Microsoft: 2016 Data Factsheet Environmental Indicators. Microsoft Corporation, Inc. (2016). http://download.microsoft.com/download/0/1/4/014D812D-B2E3-43A0-A89A-16E3C7CD46EE/2016_Data_Factsheet_Environmental_Indicators.pdf
19. Microsoft: 2017 Data Factsheet Environmental Indicators. Microsoft Corporation, Inc. (2017). https://download.microsoft.com/download/0/0/6/00604579-134B-4D0E-97C3-D525DFB7890A/Microsoft_2017_Environmental_Data_Factsheet.pdf
20. Microsoft: 2019 Data Factsheet Environmental Indicators. Microsoft Corporation, Inc. (2019). https://query.prod.cms.rt.microsoft.com/cms/api/am/binary/RE3455q
21. Jena, S.: Voluntary Green Power Procurement. https://www.nrel.gov/analysis/green-power.html

22. Brady, K.: H.R. 1 (IH) - Tax Cuts and Jobs Act. U.S. Government Publishing Office (2017)
23. Cuellar, H.: Consolidated Appropriations Act, 2021. Authenticated U.S, Government Information (2020)
24. Davis, S.J., Liu, Z., Deng, Z., et al.: Emissions rebound from the COVID-19 pandemic. Nat. Clim. Chang. **12**, 412–414 (2022)

Towards a Renewable City: A Case Study of CleanPowerSF's Impact on Reducing GHG from Residential Buildings in San Francisco

Jeung Lee[ID] and Soh Kim[✉][ID]

Stanford University, Stanford, CA 94305, USA
sohkim@stanford.edu

Abstract. This case study critically examines the impact of CleanPowerSF's impact on reducing greenhouse gas emissions in San Francisco's residential sector, with a special emphasis on the effectiveness of green retrofitting and electrification measures. Through a detailed analysis of the "San Francisco Communitywide Greenhouse Gas Inventory" and data from the DOE's "2023 Better Buildings Progress Report," the research evaluates the role of these initiatives in the city's overall sustainability efforts. The findings demonstrate a disconnect between increased electricity consumption and greenhouse gas emissions, signaling the positive effects of CleanPowerSF's integration of greener energy sources. The paper also addresses the socio-economic challenges related to retrofitting costs, highlighting the need for more effective incentives to encourage wider participation among homeowners, particularly for the retrofitting of older buildings. By offering a comprehensive overview of CleanPowerSF's strategies and their tangible impacts, this study contributes to the understanding of urban energy policy and sustainable development, providing valuable insights for policymakers and stakeholders aiming to replicate similar success in urban settings.

Keywords: CleanPowerSF · Green Retrofitting · Electrification · Renewable Energy · Urban Sustainability · Greenhouse Gas Emissions

1 Introduction

The transition to sustainable urban environments is imperative in the face of escalating climate change challenges, with residential buildings playing a critical role due to their substantial energy consumption and associated greenhouse gas (GHG) emissions. The International Energy Agency (IEA) has reported a global increase in energy-related CO2 emissions by 0.9% in 2022, reaching an all-time high of over 36.8 gigatons (Gt), amidst a complex backdrop of energy price shocks, inflation, and geopolitical tensions [12]. Despite these pressures, the growth rate of emissions was tempered, thanks in part to the accelerated deployment of clean energy technologies, underscoring the potential of electrification and renewable energy in curbing emissions growth.

The Department of Energy (DOE) emphasizes the necessity of transitioning towards electrification in the "Industrial Decarbonization Roadmap", alongside energy efficiency improvements, as central to the decarbonization of industrial and residential sectors. This transition involves replacing fossil fuel-based energy systems with electric systems that can be powered by renewable energy, thereby reducing direct emissions from buildings. Such strategies are vital in addressing the dual challenges of energy security and climate change, offering a pathway to a more sustainable and resilient energy future [20].

In San Francisco, the CleanPowerSF program, as detailed in its "2022 Integrated Resource Plan," serves as a leading example of how local initiatives can significantly impact the transition towards renewable energy. This plan outlines the program's approach to achieving 100% renewable energy by 2025, emphasizing the prioritization of local resources and the integration of community goals such as transportation electrification and building decarbonization. Through strategic investments and comprehensive modeling, CleanPowerSF aims to not only meet but exceed the city's ambitious environmental targets, marking a substantial contribution to the broader objectives of reducing carbon emissions and enhancing energy sustainability [4].

This paper explores the impact of the CleanPowerSF initiative within the context of San Francisco's renewable energy adoption, assessing its achievements and challenges in the pursuit of a cleaner, more sustainable energy future.

2 Literature Review

The transition towards sustainable urban environments necessitates both technological innovations and robust policy frameworks. Pistochini et al. demonstrate the environmental efficacy of transitioning from gas furnaces to heat pumps for space heating in residential homes. This shift, pivotal for reducing greenhouse gas emissions, takes into account factors such as regional climate variations, building energy efficiency, and the evolving carbon intensity of electricity generation. These technological strides align with CleanPowerSF's endeavors to mitigate GHG emissions through renewable energy adoption [18].

Parallelly, Hess & Gentry delve into the policy landscape, examining the intricacies of implementing 100% renewable energy policies in U.S. cities. Their analysis underscores the imperative of local policy initiatives in the broader context of climate change mitigation, particularly highlighting the significance of coalition building among civil society and government officials. The study sheds light on the practical challenges and strategic considerations necessary to foster urban transitions to renewable energy, providing a comprehensive backdrop the importance of local initiatives like CleanPowerSF [11].

McGee and Swaroop discuss how Community Choice Aggregation (CCA) programs in California serve as a mechanism for both advancing environmental justice and reducing greenhouse gas emissions. Their research emphasizes the role of CCAs in engaging communities, particularly low-income and marginalized groups, in renewable energy development and decision-making processes. This aligns with CleanPowerSF's efforts in San Francisco by highlighting the importance of local involvement and the potential of CCAs to democratize energy access and contribute to sustainable urban development [16].

The study by Dall'O' et al. introduces a comprehensive methodology for evaluating the potential energy savings of retrofitting residential building stocks, particularly within the context of the European Union where residential sectors significantly contribute to energy consumption. This research underscores the critical importance of retrofitting existing buildings to achieve energy efficiency and CO_2 reduction targets. By applying their methodology to municipalities committed to exceeding the EU's CO_2 reduction objectives, the authors provide valuable insights into the technical, legal, and economic feasibility of various energy retrofit interventions. This approach not only supports sustainable urban development but also complements CleanPowerSF's initiatives by illustrating the broader implications of retrofitting on energy savings and GHG emission reductions in residential buildings [5].

In summation, the literature presents a compelling narrative of the transformative potential that policy initiatives and technological advancements hold for sustainable urban development. Pistochini et al. and Hess & Gentry provide a foundational understanding of the technological shifts and policy frameworks essential for reducing greenhouse gas emissions, while McGee and Swaroop extend this discourse to the democratization of energy through Community Choice Aggregation, emphasizing environmental justice. Complementing these perspectives, Dall'O' et al. offer a practical methodology for evaluating the energy savings of retrofitting buildings—a critical step towards operationalizing these theoretical frameworks. However, these studies also reveal the complexity of fully integrating such strategies, highlighting the challenges associated with retrofitting costs, the participation of older buildings, and the overall adoption of electricity-based solutions in residential sectors [5, 11, 16, 18].

The current body of literature offers crucial insights into the transition towards sustainable urban energy systems, yet it often lacks detailed empirical evaluations of specific regional programs and their wider socio-economic impacts. This paper aims to bridge this gap by conducting a thorough examination of CleanPowerSF, evaluating the program's success in boosting renewable energy usage and reducing CO_2 emissions within the distinct urban setting of San Francisco. Moreover, this study will investigate the socio-economic implications of CleanPowerSF's incentive programs, particularly focusing on their effect on encouraging retrofitting activities among owners of older buildings. This detailed local analysis seeks to enhance our overall understanding of urban sustainability initiatives, providing targeted recommendations for policy refinement and guiding the strategic direction of similar projects.

Moving into the data analysis phase, this research will draw on public data to rigorously evaluate CleanPowerSF's achievements, including the increase in renewable energy adoption and the impact of its educational outreach on homeowner practices toward electrification and adopting a greener energy grid. This exploration aims to uncover how these educational efforts successfully raise awareness and modify homeowner behaviors, especially regarding retrofitting older buildings for better energy efficiency. Furthermore, the study will attempt to uncover the challenges faced, such as the relatively small proportion of electricity use compared to natural gas in residential areas, the significant costs associated with retrofitting, and the limited engagement of older building owners in these sustainability initiatives.

3 Data Collection and Methods

3.1 San Francisco Communitywide Greenhouse Gas Inventory

This study leverages the "San Francisco Communitywide Greenhouse Gas Inventory," a comprehensive dataset adhering to the Global Protocol for Community-Scale Greenhouse Gas Emissions Inventories (GPC). This protocol ensures global consistency and comparability, with San Francisco's emission tracking efforts dating back to 1990. Notably, methodologies and sectoral data have been subject to third-party verification, enhancing data integrity, with key years such as 2010 and 2012 offering publicly accessible verification memos. This rigorous adherence to the GPC framework, alongside the city's alignment with the Global Covenant of Mayors (GCOM) standards, provides a robust foundation for analyzing CleanPowerSF's impact on communitywide CO_2 emission reductions [7].

The data analysis employs statistical techniques and the use of graphical representations created with Microsoft Excel to illustrate temporal trends. Excel, known for its user-friendly interface and versatile data visualization tools, was the software of choice for producing the graph depicting CO_2 emissions and electricity usage of San Francisco's residential buildings.

3.2 DOE's 2023 Better Buildings Progress Report

This research incorporates an in-depth analysis of the "Low Carbon Technology Strategies" by the Department of Energy (DOE). This component of the study examines nine key technologies identified within the Better Buildings Initiative, assessing their role in reducing carbon emissions and their compatibility with electrification and green grid initiatives. By reviewing relevant research for each technology, the study categorizes their potential impact on electrification and grid compatibility as high, middle, or low. This methodical approach underscores the nuanced role each technology plays in advancing national energy efficiency and decarbonization goals, providing a comprehensive understanding of their applicability and effectiveness at both the municipal and national levels [21].

3.3 K-means Clustering Analysis

This study enhances its analytical depth by incorporating machine learning techniques through Python, particularly utilizing Pandas for data preprocessing, including the cleansing of missing columns from San Francisco's public dataset, and Scikit-learn for K-means clustering to analyze GHG emissions profiles across the city's varied building stock. Employing Python offers unmatched computational power and flexibility, allowing for the integration of both traditional statistical measures and machine learning insights. The approach includes calculating median and standard deviation (STD) for each cluster using Pandas, and clustering with Scikit-learn, providing a dual metric method that leverages Python's comprehensive capabilities for deeper insights [7].

The use of K-means clustering in Python provides an objective, data-driven examination of the city's building emissions, uncovering patterns and groupings not immediately apparent through traditional analysis. This approach is key in evaluating the impact of initiatives like the All-Electric New Construction Ordinance and the engagement levels among owners of older buildings towards electrification. Integrating statistical measures with machine learning insights highlights the diversity in energy efficiency and GHG emissions across different clusters, identifying strategic opportunities for intervention [3].

By employing this advanced clustering technique, supported by comprehensive statistical analysis, this study not only catalogues the extensive range of San Francisco's emissions data but also elevates this data into the realm of digital analytics through machine learning analysis. This transition signifies a shift from merely measuring emission data to transforming it into actionable insights within a digital analytics framework. Such an approach underscores the potential to not just quantify but also qualitatively enhance CleanPowerSF's strategies for a more inclusive and effective urban energy transition, showcasing the transformative power of digital technologies in interpreting and leveraging environmental data for sustainable development.

4 Data Analysis

The data presented in Fig. 1 and Fig. 2 illustrate the trends in CO_2 emissions and energy usage in San Francisco's residential buildings over a span of three decades.

In Fig. 1, a decreasing trend of CO_2 emissions is evident from 1990 to 2019, with a brief uptick in 2020. While electricity usage increased sharply in 2020, reaching 2,905 GWh, the CO_2 emissions did not reflect a parallel increase, which might suggest improvements in the carbon efficiency of electricity consumption.

Figure 2 provides a comparison between electricity and natural gas usage from 1990 to 2020. Despite the increase in electricity usage, particularly in 2020, natural gas usage remains consistently higher throughout the years. In 2020, while electricity usage shows a significant rise, the natural gas usage continues to dominate the energy mix in residential buildings, suggesting that while there is a notable shift towards greater electricity consumption, natural gas remains a significant energy source for San Francisco's residential sector.

The data, therefore, indicate that the transition towards increased electricity usage does not yet surpass the reliance on natural gas in San Francisco's residential buildings. This context of energy usage is important for understanding the city's overall energy profile and its implications for CO_2 emissions.

The assessment of electrification and green grid compatibility presented in Table 1 is grounded in an extensive literature review focused on each highlighted technology. This rigorous examination aimed to gauge the effectiveness and alignment of various low carbon strategies with electrification efforts and their potential to integrate seamlessly with a greener grid. By analyzing peer-reviewed studies and seminal works in the field, the evaluation sheds light on the critical role of technological advancements and innovative solutions in driving down greenhouse gas emissions and promoting sustainable energy consumption.

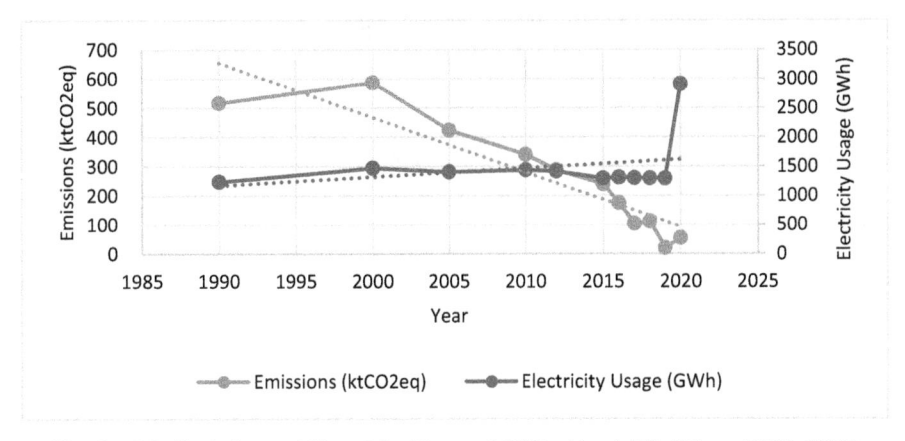

Fig. 1. CO_2 Emission and Electricity Usage of SF Residential Buildings (1990–2020)

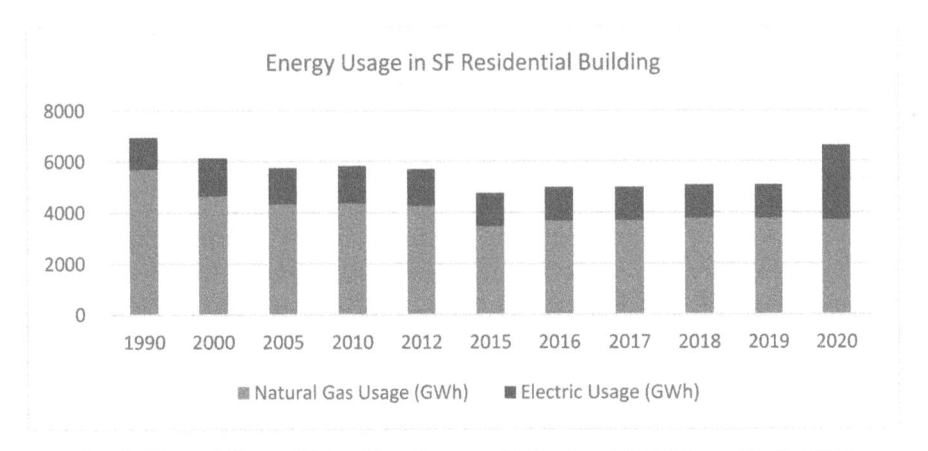

Fig. 2. Natural Gas and Electricity Usage in SF Residential Buildings (1990–2020)

The exploration into lighting smart controls reveals that the architectural variables of a room can significantly impact the performance of these controls. This finding underscores the importance of considering physical space in the deployment of energy-saving technologies, which are rated highly compatible with electrification efforts [1].

Similarly, the emphasis on electric heat pumps for space conditioning and water heating showcases their potential in contributing to carbon neutrality goals. The high compatibility of these technologies with green grid initiatives points towards their pivotal role in transitioning to sustainable energy sources [9].

Smart controls and analytics play a crucial role in optimizing building electrification efforts. While these controls have a medium rating in terms of electrification compatibility, their contribution to enhancing energy efficiency is undeniable, suggesting a balanced approach to their integration into energy management systems [15].

The significance of building envelope enhancements, particularly through advanced insulation within facade retrofit initiatives, is underscored in contemporary research.

Despite being rated low in electrification compatibility, such measures significantly reduce the energy demand for heating and cooling, demonstrating the energy efficiency potential in existing buildings [19].

A comparison of electric versus gas-powered appliances presents electrification as a beneficial strategy for climate impact mitigation with a high rating for electrification compatibility. This comparison supports the shift towards electric appliances for their environmental benefits [8].

Furthermore, the role of renewables and battery storage in enhancing smart home energy efficiency and cost savings though rated middle in compatibility, indicates the evolving nature of distributed demand side management and its contribution to a sustainable energy ecosystem [14].

The evaluation of refrigerants in refrigeration systems and the promotion of electric cooking through induction stoves both highlight the high compatibility of these technologies with electrification efforts. These studies advocate for a shift towards greener solutions and underscore the importance of choosing sustainable options in everyday appliances [13].

The promotion of induction stoves nationwide in Ecuador illustrates the environmental and health benefits of electric cooking. Highlighted for its high compatibility with electrification efforts, electrification of kitchen equipment underscores the significant reduction in greenhouse gas emissions and hospitalization rates, positioning electric kitchen equipment as a crucial component of sustainable living practices [10].

Collectively, these strategies and technologies present a comprehensive view of the potential pathways for achieving reduced carbon emissions and higher energy efficiency through electrification and grid compatibility enhancements. The varied compatibility ratings across technologies suggest a nuanced approach to implementing low carbon strategies, where the integration of various systems and considerations for specific building characteristics are essential for optimizing energy savings and reducing environmental impact.

The analysis of cluster data showcases variance in Site Energy Use Intensity (EUI) and electricity usage across different building ages within San Francisco. Cluster 1, with a median construction year of 1927, exhibits a median Site EUI of 18.8 $kBtu/ft^2$ and an electricity usage percentage of 20.0%. Conversely, Cluster 2 buildings, predominantly from 1997, show a median Site EUI of 26.5 $kBtu/ft^2$ with a higher electricity usage percentage at 57.6%. Clusters 3 and 4, median years 1936 and 1991, respectively, display their own unique EUI and electricity usage profiles, emphasizing the diverse energy profiles across the city's building stock (see Table 2) [12].

5 Discussion

5.1 Enhancing CleanPowerSF Utilization for CO_2 Emission Reduction and Boosting Residential Electricity Use

The progression of CleanPowerSF's utilization marks a promising direction in reducing CO_2 emissions, as demonstrated by the considerable decline from 516,752 $mtCO_2eq$ in 1990 to 19,396 $mtCO_2eq$ by 2019 (see Fig. 1). This positive trend underscores the

Table 1. Evaluation of Carbon Reduction Technologies for Electrification Compatibility

Technologies	Carbon Emission Reduction Strategy	Electrification and Green Grid Compatibility
Lighting	The exploration of lighting smart controls on energy consumption has shown that architectural variables of a room significantly impact the performance of these controls [1]	High
Space Conditioning and Water Heating	Electric heat pumps are emphasized for their carbon reduction potential, especially towards achieving carbon neutrality goals [9]	High
Controls and Analytics	Smart controls play a pivotal role in optimizing building electrification efforts, enhancing energy efficiency [15]	Middle
Building Envelop	Enhancing building insulation as part of facade retrofit measures significantly reduces energy demand for heating and cooling, highlighting the energy efficiency potential in existing buildings [19]	Low
Plug and Process Loads	A comparison of electric versus gas-powered appliances reveals the climate impact benefits of electrification [8]	High
Renewables and Battery Storage	Distributed demand side management with battery storage enhances smart home energy efficiency and cost savings [14]	Low
Refrigeration	An evaluation of R134a versus R744 refrigerants in refrigeration systems highlights a shift towards greener solutions [13]	High
Kitchen Equipment	The nationwide induction stove promotion in Ecuador suggests electric cooking reduces greenhouse gas emissions and hospitalization rates [10]	High

program's vital role in facilitating the shift towards more sustainable energy sources. Despite this success, Fig. 2 reveals a relatively low engagement in terms of the overall percentage of electricity use within residential settings, emphasizing an area for strategic improvement.

This research emphasizes that while CleanPowerSF's achievements in diminishing CO2 emissions are commendable, broader adoption and deeper penetration into residential energy use remain crucial objectives. The substantial increase in electric usage

Table 2. Clustering of San Francisco Buildings

Cluster	Year Built		Site EUI ($kBtu/ft^2$)		Electricity Usage (%)		GHG Emission Intensity ($kgCO_2eq/ft^2$)	
	Median	STD	Median	STD	Median	STD	Median	STD
1	1927.0	18.8	36.8	13.1	20.0	11.4	2.1	0.7
2	1997.0	26.5	26.2	10.7	57.6	11.5	1.6	0.7
3	1936.0	27.5	68.6	20.3	19.6	11.3	3.9	1.1
4	1991.0	17.5	35.8	12.1	32.9	9.7	2.1	0.7

in 2020 to 2,905 *GWh*, juxtaposed with a slight uptick in CO_2 emissions as shown in Fig. 1, indicates the complexities of managing energy sources and demands effectively. It highlights a pivotal opportunity for CleanPowerSF to expand its reach and impact, making sustainable energy solutions more accessible and appealing to a broader segment of San Francisco's population.

To bridge the gap between the program's potential and its current state of residential electricity utilization, a multifaceted approach is necessary. This should include targeted initiatives to enhance community awareness and understanding of the benefits associated with CleanPowerSF. Additionally, policy adjustments and incentives could be designed to encourage a shift towards increased residential electricity usage from clean energy sources. Figure 2 illustrates the energy usage in SF residential buildings, showing a steady level of natural gas usage compared to a variable pattern of electricity usage over the years. By addressing the existing challenges and leveraging the program's successes, CleanPowerSF can significantly contribute to creating a more sustainable and environmentally friendly energy landscape in San Francisco.

Through strategic efforts to increase engagement and adoption of CleanPowerSF among residents, there is substantial potential to further reduce CO_2 emissions while enhancing the quality of life and environmental health in the community. The low overall percentage of electricity usage in residential homes, as depicted in Fig. 2, signals a critical area for intervention, where increased participation in CleanPowerSF could lead to more pronounced environmental benefits and move San Francisco closer to its sustainability goals.

5.2 Educational Outreach and Incentivization: Overcoming the Cost Barrier in Home Energy Retrofits

The adoption of low-carbon technologies in residential settings is critical for achieving broader environmental sustainability targets. Table 2 showcases a diverse range of technologies, from innovative lighting systems and space conditioning to renewable energy solutions and modern kitchen appliances, all underlining the critical emphasis on electrification and its compatibility with a more sustainable grid. This comprehensive overview demonstrates the significant potential these technologies hold for reducing carbon emissions, with electrification serving as a key player across various strategies to mitigate green-house gas emissions and align with ambitious climate action initiatives [20, 21].

To address the barriers hindering the adoption of these transformative technologies, educating homeowners emerges as a primary strategy. This initiative aims to enhance awareness around the environmental and economic benefits of low-carbon technologies, equipping homeowners with the knowledge necessary to make informed choices. The focus on electrification, as highlighted in Table 2, is crucial for illustrating its impact on reducing emissions and fostering a transition to cleaner energy sources.

However, education alone may not suffice to catalyze widespread adoption. Financial incentives, such as those provided by the U.S. Department of Energy's Home Energy Rebates program, play a pivotal role in making energy-efficient improvements more financially viable for a wider audience. By offering rebates and financial assistance for specific home improvement projects, this program significantly contributes to reducing overall household energy consumption, delivering both economic and environmental dividends [16].

Despite the presence of such incentives, the substantial costs associated with comprehensive home retrofits, including the adoption of efficient heat pumps, present a notable challenge. The American Council for an Energy-Efficient Economy outlines that these retrofits can lead to considerable reductions in energy use and emissions. Still, these retrofits also come with high initial costs, estimated between $42,600 and $56,750, which remain out of reach for many homeowners without further support [1].

By intertwining educational efforts with the robust incentive schemes offered by programs like the DOE Home Energy Rebates and addressing the upfront costs of comprehensive retrofits, a holistic strategy can be developed. This approach not only promotes the adoption of critical electrification technologies but also moves us closer to realizing a more sustainable and energy efficient future for residential living [16].

5.3 The All-Electric New Construction Ordinance: Integrating Older Buildings for Comprehensive Urban Sustainability

The All-Electric New Construction Ordinance is a significant step towards enhancing urban sustainability by favoring electricity over other energy sources in new buildings. Yet, the integration of older buildings into this green paradigm reveals considerable challenges. Analysis of the energy profiles across different building ages in San Francisco, as presented in Table 2, accentuates these challenges.

Older buildings, specifically those categorized under Clusters 1 and 3, which correspond to median construction years of 1927 and 1936, respectively, are marked by significantly lower percentages of electricity usage compared to their newer counterparts. For example, buildings in Cluster 1 have a median electricity usage percentage of only 20.0%, coupled with a median Site EUI of 18.8 $kBtu/ft^2$. This contrasts with buildings from Cluster 2, constructed around 1997, which not only have a higher median Site EUI of 26.5 $kBtu/ft^2$ but also a substantially higher median electricity usage percentage of 57.6%.

This disparity in electricity usage and energy efficiency between old and new buildings underscores a broader issue: older buildings are not keeping pace with the sustainability standards set forth by initiatives like the All-Electric New Construction Ordinance. The data implies that newer buildings are more likely to adopt electric energy sources and incorporate energy-efficient technologies, aligning with the goals of reducing greenhouse gas emissions.

Addressing the energy inefficiency and low electricity usage of older buildings requires targeted interventions. These may include incentivizing retrofitting efforts, offering technical support for energy efficiency upgrades, and enhancing owner awareness about the benefits and available resources for transitioning to electric-based systems. By focusing on these areas, the potential environmental impact of the All-Electric New Construction Ordinance can be fully realized, ensuring a comprehensive approach to urban sustainability that includes both new and existing buildings.

6 Conclusion

The assessment of CleanPowerSF's role in reducing San Francisco's residential CO_2 emissions indicates notable advancements. Nonetheless, opportunities for enhancement remain, particularly in aging homes characterized by minimal electricity consumption. Electrification stands out as a crucial approach towards sustainability; however, the substantial expenses associated with retrofitting present a significant obstacle to its broad implementation.

The disparity in energy efficiency between new and old buildings is pronounced. New constructions are increasingly embracing sustainability, yet older buildings remain behind, underscoring a misalignment with current environmental standards. A comprehensive approach is crucial, going beyond policy to tackle the economic and infrastructure hurdles associated with modernizing older buildings. Implementing such measures is critical to guarantee that sustainability initiatives equitably benefit the entire urban residential landscape.

Acknowledgements. The research is funded by Ninewatt.

References

1. Acosta, I., Campano, M.A., Bustamante, P., Molina, J.F.: Smart controls for lighting design: towards a study of the boundary conditions. Int. J. Eng. Technol **10**(6), 481–486 (2018)
2. Amann, J., Srivastava, R., Henner, N.: Pathways for Deep Energy Use Reductions and Decarbonization in Homes. American Council for an Energy-Efficient Economy, Washington, DC (2021). aceee.org/research-report/b2103
3. City and County of San Francisco. All-electric new construction ordinance (2020). https://www.sf.gov/all-electric-new-construction-ordinance. Accessed 6 Mar 2024
4. CleanPowerSF. CleanPowerSF 2022 integrated resource plan (2022). https://www.cleanpowersf.org/resourceplan. Accessed 16 Feb 2024
5. Dall'o', G., Galante, A., Pasetti, G.: A methodology for evaluating the potential energy savings of retrofitting residential building stocks Elsevier BV (2012). https://doi.org/10.1016/j.scs.2012.01.004

6. DataSF. Existing buildings energy performance ordinance report (2024). https://data.sfgov.org/Energy-and-Environment/Existing-Buildings-Energy-Performance-Ordinance-Re/96ck-qcfe/about_data. Accessed 6 Mar 2024
7. DataSF. San francisco communitywide greenhouse gas inventory (2024). https://data.sfgov.org/Energy-and-Environment/San-Francisco-Communitywide-Greenhouse-Gas-Invento/btm4-e4ak/about_data. Accessed 29 Mar 2024
8. Dietrich, F., Chen, J., Shekhar, A., Lober, S., Krämer, K., Leggett, G., et al.: Climate impact comparison of electric and Gas-Powered End-User appliances American Geophysical Union (AGU) (2023). https://doi.org/10.1029/2022ef002877
9. Dong, S., Zhao, H., Zheng, Y., Ni, L.: Carbon reduction analysis of electric heat pumps in carbon neutrality in china Elsevier BV (2023). https://doi.org/10.1016/j.scs.2023.104758
10. Gould, C.F., et al.: Climate and health benefits of a transition from gas to electric cooking. Proc. Natl. Acad. Sci. **120**(34), e2301061120 (2023)
11. Hess, D.J., Gentry, H.: 100% renewable energy policies in US cities: strategies, recommendations, and implementation challenges. Sustain.: Sci. Pract. Policy **15**(1), 45–61 (2019)
12. International Energy Agency. CO2 emissions in 2022 (2022). https://www.iea.org/reports/co2-emissions-in-2022. Accessed 29 Mar 2024
13. Korotkiy, I., Korotkaya, E., Neverov, E., Korotkikh, P.: Evaluating the energy efficiency and environmental impact of R134a versus R744 refrigerants in refrigeration systems. Int. J. Heat Technol. **41**(6), 1461–1467 (2023)
14. Longe, O.M., Ouahada, K., Rimer, S., Harutyunyan, A.N., Ferreira, H.C.: Distributed demand side management with battery storage for smart home energy scheduling. Sustainability **9**(1), 120 (2017)
15. Marinina, O., Nechitailo, A., Stroykov, G., Tsvetkova, A., Reshneva, E., Turovskaya, L.: Technical and economic assessment of energy efficiency of electrification of hydrocarbon production facilities in underdeveloped areas. Sustainability **15**(12), 9614 (2023)
16. McGee, A., Swaroop, S.: The power of power. Ecol. Law Quart. **46**(4), 985–1016 (2019)
17. Office of State and Community Energy Programs. Home Energy Rebates Programs (2024). https://www.energy.gov/scep/home-energy-rebates-programs. Accessed 3 Apr 2024
18. Pistochini, T., Dichter, M., Chakraborty, S., Dichter, N., Aboud, A.: Greenhouse gas emission forecasts for electrification of space heating in residential homes in the US. Energy Policy **163**, 112813 (2022)
19. Sarihi, S., Faizi, M., Saradj, F.M.: Prioritization of façade retrofit measures to achieve energy efficiency in existing office buildings in Tehran. Energy **63** (2013)
20. U.S. Department of Energy (DOE). Industrial decarbonization roadmap (2022). https://www.energy.gov/industrial-technologies/doe-industrial-decarbonization-roadmap. Accessed 3 Apr 2024
21. U.S. Department of Energy (DOE). Better buildings progress report 2023 (2023). https://betterbuildingssolutioncenter.energy.gov/resources/2023-better-buildings-progress-report. Accessed 3 Apr 2024

Evaluation Model for the Quality of Electronic Services to Clients of a Non-profit Institution

Svetlana Begicheva[1](✉) and Antonina Begicheva[2]

[1] Ural State University of Economics, 8 Marta 62/45, 620144 Yekaterinburg, Russia
`begichevas@mail.ru`
[2] National Research University Higher School of Economics, Pokrovsky Boulevard 11, 109028 Moscow, Russia

Abstract. One of the main values of modern public services aimed at meeting the needs of citizens is their focus on increasing customer satisfaction. The re-search is aimed at developing a model for assessing the quality of electronic services provided by the Social Fund of Russia, which performs functions for pension provision, compulsory pension insurance, social insurance, etc. Due to advanced technologies and a large amount of accumulated information, the Fund makes many payments completely remotely through electronic services, without the need to provide additional certificates and supporting documents. The purpose of the study is to create an effective tool that can assess the level of customer satisfaction while receiving electronic services and offer recommendations for their improvement. The study identified key factors affecting the quality of electronic services, such as citizens' awareness of Social Fund services, reliability and accuracy of information provided by the client, functional and organizational accessibility of the system, and the speed of processing user applications. To account for the uncertainty and fuzziness in the assessment of these factors, the mathematical apparatus of fuzzy logic was used. The analysis of modeling results contributes to improving the efficiency and competitiveness of a non-profit organization, improving customer satisfaction, strengthening their trust and more accurate service quality management. In addition, the simulation results allow to identify weaknesses, determine priorities for making improvements and make informed decisions based on data analysis and customer feedback.

Keywords: quality of electronic services · fuzzy model · Social Fund of Russia · electronic service · evaluation of the quality of electronic services

1 Introduction

One of the main goals of a modern state is to orient all public services towards meeting the needs of its citizens, increasing transparency and accessibility, ensuring convenience and efficiency, as well as regularly informing during the service process and receiving feedback from both citizens and businesses.

Modern non-profit institutions such as charities, public foundations or government agencies focus on providing electronic services to their customers, which al-lows them to simplify and speed up service processes, increase the availability of services and improve customer satisfaction [1]. However, it is necessary to have effective tools for assessing the quality of electronic services and determining their compliance with customer expectations. Despite the urgent need to solve the problem of improving the quality of public services, there is still no single comprehensive methodology for assessing them. There are various methods based on different indicators and criteria for evaluating the quality of government services. The works of researchers such as A. Parasuraman, V.A. Zeithaml, L.L. Berry [2–4], C. N. Madu and A. Madu [5], S. Cai [6], L. Gaster [7] and G. Van Ryzin [8] are devoted to methods of evaluating service quality, including government-provided services. However, despite the availability of methods for quality assessment, the monitoring and evaluation system for public service quality is not fully developed and needs improvement. The relevance of the research topic is due to the need to develop tools for assessing the quality of electronic services, taking into account the vagueness of evaluation criteria and the subjective perception of the service by customers.

The aim of this research is to develop an effective tool to assess customer satisfaction with electronic services provided by the Social Fund of Russia and to provide recommendations for improvement.

2 Methods

The Social Fund is one of the extra-budgetary state funds of the Russian Federation that performs a variety of functions. It provides pensions, mandatory pension insurance, and certain social benefits, such as maternity and temporary disability benefits. The fund also provides compulsory social insurance against accidents at work and occupational diseases. Additionally, it ensures social security for certain groups of citizens and provides social protection measures.

The Social Fund operates one of the largest information systems in Russia, which contains data on pensions, social and labor rights for citizens and foreign citizens who work in Russian organizations. All services provided by the Social Fund in electronic form are combined into a single portal of the Social Fund of Russia at: https://sfr.gov.ru. Thanks to advanced technologies and a large amount of accumulated information, the fund can make many payments completely remotely through electronic services, without the need for additional certificates and supporting documents.

The information system of the Social Fund of Russia is a complex structure that combines various components for effective information management and provision of social services. The information system provides the following functions: accounting and client registration; processing of applications and documents; calculation and payment of social benefits; monitoring and control of compliance with service terms; and statistical reporting.

The system ensures the availability and security of data, as well as the consistency and integrity of information. It allows participants in the Social Fund of Russia, including employees of organizations, clients, and other interested parties, to interact effectively, exchange information and receive necessary support.

To make it easier for users, the portal is organized according to the types of services received (pensions, benefits, payments, maternity capital, disability certificates, and others). As of today, the Social Fund offers one hundred and three electronic services.

In order to achieve a high level of citizen satisfaction with the quality of state and municipal services provided, the Social Fund of the Russian Federation collects feedback from customers, evaluates the quality of electronic services, and makes appropriate changes to service delivery processes. The Social Fund uses the "Information and Analytical System for Monitoring the Quality of Public Services in the Russian Federation" to monitor and analyze the quality of public services. This system automatically collects data on the quality of services from various sources:

- SMS surveys and telephone surveys of citizens;
- surveys from terminal devices located in customer service;
- reviews provided by customers on the "Your Control" website;
- a questionnaire form available in the "Citizen's Personal Account".

In addition, to identify problems that arise during the provision of social fund services in an electronic format, monitoring of citizens' feedback on social networks, forums, and other public sources is carried out. Data analysis of customer service requests in the Sverdlovsk region is also conducted. To assess the effectiveness of the electronic services provided by the Customer Service software and hardware complex, statistical data such as the time spent processing electronic applications and errors made by citizens when filling out applications is used.

Based on a survey of clients, we have identified the main reasons why citizens find it difficult to use electronic services, which forces them to contact the Social Fund's customer services "in person":

- Lack of technical knowledge and skills in the field of computer technology can make it difficult for some people to work with electronic devices.
- The absence of internet connectivity makes it impossible to use electronic services. This may be due to a lack of internet access at home, insufficient coverage of mobile networks, or financial constraints that prevent individuals from paying for internet services;
- The need to provide original documents for some services makes it impossible to send them electronically. In this case, customers must contact customer service to provide the documents.
- The complexity and inconvenience associated with using electronic services presents a challenge for citizens. Citizens may experience difficulties in completing forms, lack understanding regarding the required documents, or discomfort using technology.
- Lack of trust in electronic services is due to concerns about privacy and security. Customers may fear that their personal information will be stolen or used without permission.

In addition, citizens who have used electronic services may leave negative feedback for the following reasons:

- Technical problems with the system (logging in, filling out forms, uploading documents, etc.)
- Insufficient information from citizens on the use of electronic services leads to misuse of the services.
- Quality of service is negatively assessed by users if they do not receive sufficient help or support while using the electronic service.

- Long processing times for electronic services cause dissatisfaction among citizens, especially when they expect results within the shortest time possible.
- Non-compliance with expectations – citizens may evaluate an electronic service negatively if it fails to meet their expectations as described in the information provided.
- Inconvenience of use – users may find using an electronic system inconvenient, especially if it requires a lot of time or complex functions.

The database, which is formed through the analysis of customer experience, serves as the basis for improving the process of providing public services in order to increase citizens' satisfaction with the quality of services provided in electronic form.

In general, public service quality can be represented as follows: the quality of the preparation (before applying) stage, the quality of service receipt, and the quality of its final outcome. At the preparation stage, the need for a service is formulated, along with measures to start the service provision process, including organizing the collection of required information. Service receipt is a direct communication and interaction act between the customer and service provider regarding provision. Its final outcome content is the results which comply with regulations regarding completeness and timeliness of service delivery [9].

We will define the quality of an electronic service as a measure of its compliance with the expectations, requirements, and needs of users, as well as the level of user satisfaction and the success of achieving user goals. We will consider the assessment of electronic service quality as a process of measuring and analyzing different aspects and features of the provision of these services in order to establish their conformance with established standards and requirements. Therefore, the aim of evaluating the quality of a digital service is to guarantee a high level of customer satisfaction, identify strengths and weaknesses in the digital services offered, as well as optimize the processes involved in providing services and enhance the efficiency of the organization [9].

The quality of electronic services is characterized by:

- Usability – the level of accessibility for all categories of users, including people with disabilities.
- Reliability – the level of system performance, the reliability of data transmission, the speed of operations, and protection against information loss. The service works reliably without failures and errors.
- Functionality – the adequacy of the provided services, the ability to perform various operations, and support for various types of requests and transactions. The service provides all the necessary functions and features,
- Performance – the time of operations, the quality of solutions provided, and the degree of compliance with user expectations. The service provides a quick and timely response to user requests and requests,
- Security – the quality of the authentication, encryption, and access control measures is being evaluated. The service ensures the protection and safety of user data.
- User satisfaction – the level of satisfaction with the result of the service provided.

Let's consider the main methods of assessing the quality of electronic services, which can be applied depending on the specific goals, type of service and the context in which it is provided. The main assessment methods are as follows:

- The user survey method is based on a survey of users by providing them with a questionnaire or a sociological questionnaire.
- The method of using metrics and indicators is based on the defining and measurement of specific indicators and metrics.
- The method of analyzing complaints and feedback is based on the analysis of complaints, reviews and user comments.
- The "Mystery Shopper" method is based on obtaining an independent assessment in the course of simulating the service receiving process by an expert.
- The "Critical Cases" method is based on the analysis of cases that are critical, or negative events that occurred in the process of providing services.

The existing methods for quality assessment have several disadvantages, including bias in the results due to the subjective perceptions and opinions of a limited number of users surveyed. To overcome this drawback, we have chosen the apparatus of fuzzy set theory and fuzzy logic to develop the model, which provides powerful tools for modeling and analyzing complex systems where uncertainty, fuzziness, and subjective estimates exist.

Fuzzy Logic is a mathematical model that allows you to work with fuzzy (blurred) data and uncertainty. Using the method of linguistic variables, it does not require traditional binary logic where the values of variables must be either true (1) or false (0). In fuzzy logic, values are determined using specific membership functions [10].

The sequence of stages in the development of a fuzzy model is as follows:

- defining the purpose of modeling and the problem that needs to be solved using fuzzy logic;
- data collection and definition of linguistic variables;
- construction of fuzzy sets and membership functions;
- defining fuzzy inference rules that relate linguistic variables and evaluation criteria;
- development of a fuzzy inference algorithm based on fuzzy rules and membership functions;
- testing and validation of the model on real or simulated data;
- interpretation of the results obtained using fuzzy logic [11].

The choice of variables was based on the analysis of expert interviews. Employees of the client service of the Social Fund in the Sverdlovsk region noted that, in their opinion, the result is influenced by the quality of service provided by four blocks:

1. The first block determines organizational and information accessibility and evaluates customer efforts to receive an electronic service. The input parameters for the first intermediate variable Y1, which determine the client's efforts to receive the service, are three linguistic variables: X_1 – the level of computer literacy of the client, X_2 – the level at which citizens are informed, and X_3 – an indicator of feedback from representatives of the organization.
2. The second block evaluates the quality of the input data provided by the client for processing. To assess the quality of data provided in real time, the following parameters are used: X4 is an indicator of the client's choice of a necessary service, and X5 is an indicator of accuracy and reliability of data provided for processing by the client.

3. The third block determines functional availability and estimates time spent on providing a service. The variables in this block are: X6 – preparation time for receiving service (filling out the application form by client, sending application), X7 – time spent processing client's application by organization employees.
4. The fourth block evaluates the final result of the provided electronic service and is evaluated by two linguistic variables: X8 – an indicator of the accuracy, completeness, and comprehensibility of the information provided to the client, and X9 – an indicator of whether the result of providing the service meets the client's expectations.

The step-by-step creation and configuration of a fuzzy model to evaluate the quality of electronic services was carried out using fuzzyTECH as a tool to model and manage systems using fuzzy logic, and an obtained fuzzy conclusion for evaluating the quality of the electronic services based on the values of the variables. The final fuzzy model for evaluating service quality is shown in Fig. 1, where Q represents the final evaluation of electronic service quality.

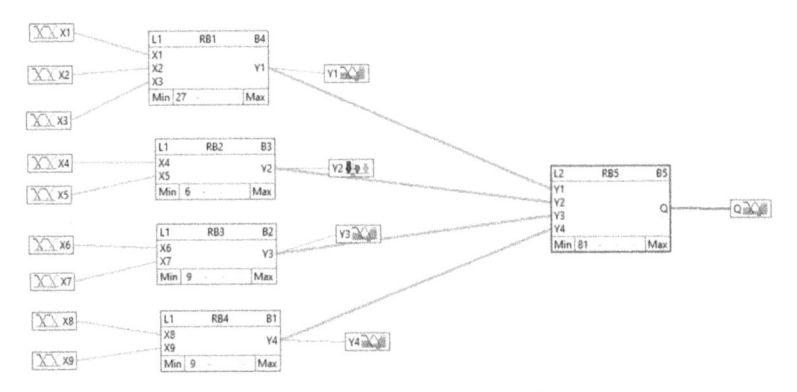

Fig. 1. Fuzzy model for evaluating the quality of services

The values of the terms sets of variables and the rules of fuzzy inference were formed based on the analysis of data from monitoring citizen feedback on social networks, forums, and other open data sources for customer service requests in the Sverdlovsk region. In addition to publicly available data, the data downloaded from software and hardware complex "Client Service" of Social Fund of Russia's information system were also analyzed.

Table 1 shows the term sets of input linguistic variables.
The terms of the intermediate and output variables take on values:

- Y_1 – from 0 to 10, where: values from 0 to 4 – customer efforts are low; from 4 to 8 – customer efforts are average; from 8 to 10 – customer efforts are high;
- Y_2 – from 0 to 1, where: 0 – incorrect data provided by the client; 0.5 – required to clarify the data; 1 – the data provided correctly;
- Y_3 – from 0 to 10, where: values from 0 to 4 – low time costs; from 4 to 8 – average time costs; from 8 to 10 – high time costs;
- Y_4 – from 0 to 10, where: values from 0 to 3 – a low result indicator; from 3 to 8 – an average result indicator; from 8 to 10 – a high result indicator;

Table 1. Description of input linguistic variables

Indicator name	Variable name	Indicator value range	The term set value
Level of computer literacy of the client	X1	0–2	low – 0 medium – 1 high – 2
Level of the citizen informing about the service	X2	0–10	low – from 0 to 5 medium – from 5 to 8 high – from 8 to 10
Feedback from representatives of the organization	X3	0–5	low – from 0 to 2 medium – from 2 to 3 high – from 3 to 5
Client's choice of the necessary service	X4	0–1	0 – wrong choice 1 – right choice
Accuracy and reliability of the data provided by the client for processing	X5	0–2	0 – incorrectly filed data 1 – requires data clarification 2 – correctly filled data
Preparation time for receiving the service	X6	0–10	low – from 0 to 5 medium – from 5 to 8 high – from 8 to 10
The time spent on processing the client's application by the organization's employees	X7	0–10	low – from 0 to 4 medium – from 4 to 8 high – from 8 to 10
Accuracy, completeness and comprehensibility of the information provided to the client as a result of the service provided	X8	0–5	low – from 0 to 2 medium – from 2 to 3 high – from 3 to 5
Compliance with customer expectations	X9	0–10	low – from 0 to 5 medium – from 5 to 7 high – from 7 to 10

- Q – from 0 to 10, where: values from 0 to 4 – a low assessment of the quality of an electronic service; from 4 to 7 – an average assessment of the quality of an electronic service; from 7 to 10 – a high assessment of the quality of an electronic service.

Next, a block of heuristic rules was compiled for the intermediate variables Y1, Y2, Y3 and Y4. Using these rules the final output variable Q is calculated. A fragment of the heuristic rules block for the variable Y1 is shown in Fig. 2.

For the resulting model testing, we will enter input data for which the outcome is known. With the help of the model, we evaluate the quality of electronic service provision, after which we compare the results with empirical data. Let's consider a situation where, as a result of conducted research, indicators assume average values (Fig. 3).

Name	If	And	And	Operators	Then
B4 RB1	1	2	3	Min / Max	1
.G1	X1	X2	X3		Y1
.R1	X1.low	X2.low	X3.low	→	Y1.low
.R2	X1.low	X2.low	X3.medium	→	Y1.low
.R3	X1.low	X2.low	X3.high	→	Y1.low
.R4	X1.low	X2.medium	X3.low	→	Y1.low
.R5	X1.low	X2.medium	X3.medium	→	Y1.medium
.R6	X1.low	X2.medium	X3.high	→	Y1.medium

Fig. 2. A fragment of heuristic rules block for the variable Y_1

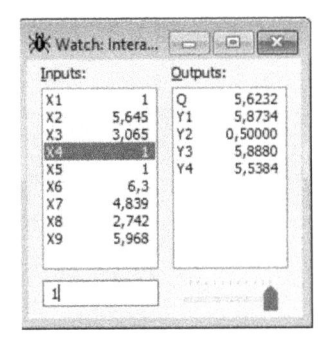

Fig. 3. Inputs and Outputs values for the model testing

For the average values of the variables, the term sets of intermediate indicators were used: Y_1 - 5,8734, Y_2 - 0,5, Y_3 - 5,888 and Y_4 - 5,5384. The quality assessment of electronic services was 5.6232, which was the average result. The conducted testing of the model using averaged values showed its ability to reliably assess customer satisfaction level and produce relevant results.

For an analysis of the simulation results, plots were created showing the dependence of the initial variables on the final output variable, Q. In order to determine the impact of the intermediate variables, Y1–Y4, on the output variable, we set minimum values for each of these parameters and maximum values for the remaining variables.

Figure 4 and Fig. 5 show, as examples, the resulting graphs of the impact of the client's effort indicator and of the indicator of the result of the provided electronic service on the assessment of service quality, respectively.

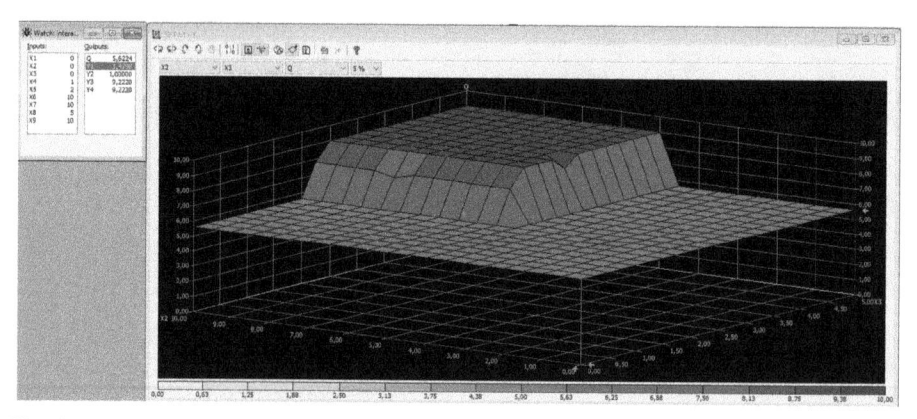

Fig. 4. The output surface illustrates the effect of the customer effort indicator on the assessment of service quality

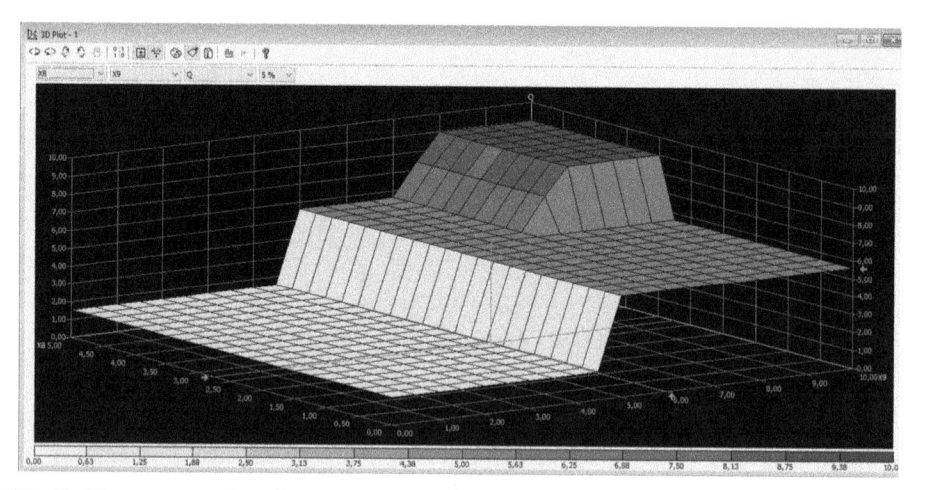

Fig. 5. The output surface illustrates the effect of the indicator of the result of the provided electronic service on the assessment of service quality

3 Results

The analysis of the simulation results shows that:

- The impact of the customer effort indicator on the assessment of service quality is insignificant when ratings are low and average, but it becomes crucial for achieving high indicators.
- The impact of the input data indicator provided by the client on the assessment of service quality is critical, as at its zero value the service cannot be delivered to the client.
- The value of time spent on providing services has a negligible impact on the assessment of service quality at a low level, but it becomes significant when aiming for a high assessment.

- The indicator of the result of rendered electronic service has the greatest influence on the quality of service assessment (except for the indicator of input data provided by the client for processing). Even with high values of other indicators, a low estimate of this indicator would provoke a poor assessment of service quality.

Thus, the application of the fuzzy inference model to the assessment of the quality of the provision of electronic social fund services allows us to account for the uncertainty and fuzziness of the data that may arise when evaluating service quality. Using rules and a knowledge base, the model produces a fuzzy conclusion to assess the quality of a service based on collected data. This approach allows us to take into consideration the influence of various factors and identify causes of negative quality assessments of electronic services, in order to make more informed decisions based on analysis results.

An analysis of the causes of negative assessments of the quality of electronic services led us to identify the following measures to improve the assessment of quality for electronic services provided by the Social Fund. A description of the measures that should be taken in each situation, as shown in Table 2.

Table 2. Measures to Improve Service

Reasons for Negative User Ratings	Measures to Improve Service
Technical problems with using the system (difficulties logging in, filling out forms, uploading documents, etc.)	• improving the convenience of the interface and navigation in the service delivery system; • customer training and support in using electronic services (providing documentation, video tutorials, FAQs and other resources)
Low awareness of citizens about electronic services leads to misuse	• conducting information work and explanatory activities by posting relevant information on official websites, social networks, publications, etc. • informing through social marketing
Poor quality of feedback from representatives of the organization (insufficient help or support)	• providing information support to clients through communication channels (email, online chat, phone); • training personnel serving citizens about how to work correctly and effectively with electronic services
Long processing times for electronic services lead to dissatisfaction of citizens, especially when they expect results in the shortest possible time	• simplifying the service provision process by minimizing the number of steps needed to receive the service; • updating and upgrading systems to improve its performance and functionality

(continued)

Table 2. (*continued*)

Reasons for Negative User Ratings	Measures to Improve Service
Non-compliance with citizens' expectations of the result of the provided service described in the "information form"	• collecting feedback from clients about their experience with the electronic service • monitoring and analyzing data on the quality of service provision in order to identify areas for improvement

The developed model has practical significance for the Social Fund as it allows identification of weaknesses in the provision of electronic services and suggests measures to improve these. It can be used to monitor and analyze the quality of services as well as make informed decisions in order to optimize customer service processes.

References

1. Order of the Government of the Russian Federation of April 11, 2022 No. 837-r "The concept of transition to the provision of the absolute majority of state and municipal services 24 hours a day, 7 days a week without the need for the personal presence of citizens"
2. Parasuraman, A., Zeithaml, V., Berry, L.: A conceptual model of service quality and its implications for future research. J. Mark. **49**(4), 45–50 (1985)
3. Parasuraman, A., Zeithaml, V., Berry, L.: SERVQUAL: a multiple-item scale for measuring consumer perception of service quality. J. Retail. **64**(1), 12–40 (1988)
4. Parasuraman, A., Zeithaml, V., Berry, L.: E-S-QUAL a multiple-item scale for assessing electronic service quality. J. Serv. Res. **7**, 213–233 (2005)
5. Madu, C.N., Madu, A.: Dimensions of e-quality. Int. J. Qual. Reliab. Manag. **19**(3), 246–258 (2002)
6. Cai, S., Jun, M.: Internet users' perceptions of online service quality - a comparison of online buyers and information searchers. Manag. Serv. Qual.: Int. J. **13**(6), 504–519 (2003)
7. Gaster, L., Squire, A.: Providing Quality in the Public Sector: A Practical Approach to Improving Public Services. Open University Press, Maidenhead (2003)
8. Van Ryzin, G.G.: The measurement of overall citizen satisfaction. Public Perform. Manag. Rev. **27**(3), 9–28 (2024)
9. Kuznetsova, P.: Improvement of methodology of assessment of quality and availability of providing public and municipal services. State Munic. Manag. Sch. Notes **3**, 53–58 (2019)
10. Zadeh, L.A.: Fuzzy logic. IEEE Trans. Comput. **21**(4), 83–93 (1988)
11. Konysheva, L.K., Nazarov, D.M.: Osnovy teorii nechetkikh mnozhestv (Elements of Theory of Fuzzy Sets). Piter, Saint-Petersburg (2011)

ESG 2.0: Revolutionizing Sustainability Through the Power of Digitalization

A. Zimin[1](✉), N. Sedova[1,2], and N. Pulyavina[2]

[1] Russian Foreign Trade Academy Ministry of Economic Development of the Russian Federation (RFTA), Moscow, Russia
`ajax_z@mail.ru`
[2] Plekhanov Russian University of Economics (PRUE), Moscow, Russia

Abstract. On the way to the sustainable development, the Environmental, Social, and Governance (ESG) agenda stands as a pillar or basis, guiding corporate responsibility and societal progress. This article explores the intricate interplay between digitalization and ESG objectives, emphasizing the transformative impact of contemporary technologies on the path to sustainability. With ESG considerations now integral to corporate decision-making, this research illuminates how digital tools play a pivotal role in optimizing sustainable practices. By delving into the strategic implementation of digital solutions, ranging from advanced data analytics and artificial intelligence to blockchain and the Internet of Things (IoT), we demonstrate their capacity to streamline ESG reporting, ensure compliance, and foster innovation. Real-world case studies underscore the efficacy of these technologies in resource optimization, transparency enhancement, and stakeholder empowerment. This comprehensive survey contributes valuable insights to the ongoing discourse, illustrating the potential of responsibly integrating technology into ESG frameworks for a resilient and sustainable future. This research serves as a direction for organizations, governments and communities seeking to leverage digitalization to advance their ESG goals and contribute meaningfully to global sustainable development.

Keywords: digitalization · ESG · sustainability · technological advancements · AI

1 Introduction

In an era marked by unprecedented technological advancements, the fusion of Environmental, Social and Governance (ESG) principles with digitalization has given rise to a transformative paradigm – ESG 2.0. This revolutionary approach not only underscores the commitment to sustainable business practices but also leverages the immense potential of digital tools to propel organizations towards a greener, more socially responsible and ethically governed future.

The global landscape is witnessing a seismic shift in the way corporations perceive and engage with ESG considerations. Beyond traditional sustainability practices, ESG

2.0 represents a holistic and dynamic strategy that harnesses the power of digital technologies to drive positive impact across diverse facets of business operations. From optimizing resource utilization to fostering inclusive social practices and enhancing corporate governance, ESG 2.0 is redefining the benchmarks for responsible and resilient business conduct.

This article aims to unravel the layers of ESG 2.0, shedding light on how the fusion of ESG principles and digitalization represents not merely an incremental progression but a revolutionary leap toward a more sustainable and equitable future. As our world becomes increasingly interconnected, comprehending the nuances and consequences of ESG 2.0 is crucial for businesses, investors and policymakers.

2 The Transition from ESG 1.0 to ESG 2.0

The inception of the term ESG, denoting Environmental, Social and Governance, traces back to a pivotal moment in 2004 with the release of the landmark report titled "Who Cares Wins" [1]. Spearheaded by UN Secretary-General Kofi Annan, this transformative document addressed a distinguished gathering of over 50 CEOs from leading financial organizations.

In a call to action, Secretary-General Annan urged these influential leaders to actively engage in a collaborative initiative under the UN Global Compact. Supported by the International Finance Corporation (IFC) and the Swiss government, this initiative aimed to delve into and implement practices centered around Environmental, Social and Governance (ESG) in capital markets [1, p. vii].

The primary objective of this pioneering effort was to navigate and integrate ESG considerations into the structure of capital markets. By fostering collaboration between major financial entities and international organizations, the initiative sought to explore the multifaceted dimensions of ESG, acknowledging its significance in shaping responsible and sustainable business practices. This early groundwork laid the foundation for the subsequent evolution of ESG principles, ultimately giving rise to what we now refer to as ESG 2.0.

In the transition from ESG 1.0 to ESG 2.0, there is a notable shift in the scope and integration of environmental, social, and governance considerations. ESG 1.0 often saw these factors addressed as separate entities, with a primary focus on compliance and risk management. However, ESG 2.0 represents a more holistic and integrated approach, recognizing the interconnectedness of these elements within the fabric of business operations. Companies embracing ESG 2.0 weave sustainability considerations into their strategic planning and daily activities, acknowledging that a comprehensive approach is essential for lasting impact.

Another key distinction lies in the evolution of metrics and reporting. ESG 1.0 witnessed the early stages of sustainability reporting, often with basic metrics and a lack of standardized frameworks, making comparisons between organizations challenging. Contrastingly, ESG 2.0 emphasizes the importance of standardized reporting frameworks such as the Global Reporting Initiative (GRI) or Sustainability Accounting Standards Board (SASB). This shift towards standardized metrics enhances transparency and facilitates a more comprehensive evaluation of a company's sustainability efforts, fostering greater accountability and comparability.

The evolution from ESG 1.0 to ESG 2.0 is marked by significant changes in stakeholder engagement and the incorporation of technology. ESG 1.0 often involved reactive engagement with a limited set of stakeholders. In contrast, ESG 2.0 adopts a proactive and collaborative approach, recognizing the importance of involving diverse stakeholders in decision-making processes. Moreover, ESG 2.0 embraces the potential of technology, leveraging digital tools to enhance the effectiveness of sustainability initiatives. From advanced data analytics for environmental impact assessments to blockchain for transparent supply chains, technology plays a pivotal role in driving innovation and efficiency in ESG practices.

3 Tracing the Evolution of ESG and Digitalization Over the Time

Before delving into the realm of digital tools that play a pivotal role in advancing ESG goals, it is essential to trace the evolution of the intricate relationship between ESG principles and digitalization. Understanding how these two domains have become increasingly intertwined over time will provide valuable context for the transformative impact that digital tools have on reshaping and enhancing sustainability practices.

In tracing the historical trajectories of digitalization and sustainable development, it becomes evident that both have independently navigated extensive timelines, leaving indelible imprints on the landscape of modern business and societal evolution. The development of digitalization began in 1945 [2]. It has been characterized by successive technological shifts, moving from mainframes and minicomputers to the era of the integrated circuit revolution and, more recently, to personal computers. This technological evolution has had a significant impact on business in a variety of ways. Simultaneously, ESG principles, emerging in response to environmental awareness, social justice concerns, and the need for robust governance structures, have deep historical roots, evolving over time as a response to the changing dynamics of corporate responsibility.

However, it is in the past decade that a noteworthy shift has occurred, ushering in a transformative phase in the relationship between digitalization and ESG. While both trends have coexisted on the historical stage, it is only in recent years that digitalization has actively assumed the role of a catalyst, fostering and amplifying the impact of sustainability approaches such as ESG principles within the business landscape.

The convergence of digitalization and ESG in the last decade has been pivotal, marking a departure from a passive coexistence to an era where digital tools actively contribute to advancing sustainability, social responsibility and ethical governance.

This newfound interconnection, often referred to as ESG 2.0, signifies a paradigm shift where digitalization is not merely a facilitator but a proactive force in shaping responsible business practices. The integration of technology is now instrumental in measuring, managing, and enhancing ESG performance, transforming it from a static set of principles into a dynamic and impactful strategy for organizations worldwide.

4 Unleashing the Power of Digital Tools to Foster ESG

Sustainability has evolved over the years, traversing a transformative journey that has seen the integration of environmental, social, and governance (ESG) principles into the core of business operations. But it is important to evaluate at what stage we are right now to identify the appropriate next steps. In a recent Capital Group ESG Global Study, a comprehensive analysis was conducted by surveying 1130 global investors across 19 countries. The findings revealed a notable uptick in the adoption of Environmental, Social and Governance (ESG) practices. In 2022, an impressive 89% of surveyed investors reported incorporating ESG considerations into their decision-making processes, marking a substantial increase from the 84% reported just one year prior [3, p. 9]. These statistics underscore the growing significance of ESG factors in the realms of both investment and business strategy. The evident surge in ESG adoption implies a heightened awareness among investors and businesses regarding the impact of sustainable practices on financial performance and overall success. Recognizing the pivotal role of ESG, it becomes imperative for stakeholders to identify and implement practices that will further bolster ESG integration, thereby accelerating its positive effects on businesses globally.

As the global business landscape increasingly acknowledges the importance of ESG considerations, the need for effective tools to navigate and implement sustainable practices becomes paramount. Recognizing ESG as a critical component for investors and businesses alike, there arises a demand for streamlined approaches to incorporate these principles into decision-making processes. In response to this growing trend, various digital tools have emerged to facilitate the integration of ESG factors. These tools not only aid in the assessment of environmental, social, and governance risks but also contribute to the identification of opportunities for sustainable growth. Next, we will illustrate how some digital tools actively contribute to and foster sustainability initiatives (see Fig. 1).

Fig. 1. Diagram of the main digital tools influencing the development of the concept of sustainable development.

4.1 Artificial Intelligence (AI)

Artificial Intelligence (AI) refers to the development of computer systems that can perform tasks that typically require human intelligence. These tasks include learning from experience (machine learning), understanding natural language, recognizing patterns, and making decisions. AI encompasses various technologies, such as machine learning, natural language processing, computer vision, and robotics [4].

AI affects sustainability across multiple domains, contributing to environmental, social, and economic aspects:

a) Supply Chain Optimization: AI improves supply chain efficiency by predicting demand, optimizing logistics, and reducing waste. This contributes to sustainable practices by minimizing resource use and enhancing overall supply chain transparency.
b) Climate Modeling: AI aids in climate research by analyzing vast datasets. It improves climate modeling, helping scientists understand and predict climate patterns, contributing to informed decision-making for climate change mitigation and adaptation.
c) Smart Cities: AI technologies contribute to the development of smart cities.
d) Healthcare Optimization: AI enhances healthcare sustainability by improving diagnostic accuracy, optimizing treatment plans, and streamlining healthcare delivery.
e) Economic Innovation: AI fosters economic innovation by driving advancements in various industries. This can lead to the development of sustainable technologies, job creation, and economic growth with a focus on environmental and social responsibility.

AI in overall has significant importance for ESG. To prove that we could look at one example. In 1960, the total world population was 3.0 billion, grew to 6.1 billion by 2000 [5], and exceeded 8 billion in 2023. Experts estimate that by 2050, the world population will exceed 9.7 billion [6], creating an unprecedented demand for food, water and other critical resources. In this context, the deployment of AI algorithms combined with IoT-enabled sensors in agriculture becomes not just a solution but a necessity.

The integration of sensors into agricultural practices holds the promise of revolutionizing crop management and fostering sustainable agriculture. These sensors, equipped with cutting-edge technology, provide real-time data on various environmental factors crucial to plant growth – from soil moisture levels and nutrient content to weather conditions and pest infestations.

Moreover, the predictive capabilities of IoT sensors with AI algorithms contribute to more efficient resource allocation. By anticipating changes in weather patterns or identifying potential disease outbreaks, farmers can proactively implement strategies to mitigate risks and optimize yields. This not only enhances productivity but also reduces the environmental impact of agricultural practices by minimizing resource wastage.

4.2 Social Computing

Social computing is the intersection of social interaction and computing where people interact, collaborate and share information through digital platforms and networks. They include various online activities such as social networking interactions, online communities, collaborative content creation, and problem solving with the help of a group of people.

Social computing has been researched and worked on by many notable scholars and entrepreneurs, such as Mark Zuckerberg, co-founder and CEO of Facebook, who in his article "Building Global Community" discussed the role of social computing in building a global community [7], or Thomas Erickson, a social computing researcher at IBM

Research, who studies the social and collaborative aspects of information systems and develops new methods and technologies to improve social interaction.

In the context of sustainable development, social computing plays a transformative role by:

a) Information Dissemination and Awareness: Social computing platforms enable the rapid dissemination of information and awareness about sustainable practices, environmental issues, and social causes. This widespread sharing of knowledge helps raise public consciousness and encourages collective action towards sustainability.
b) Crowdsourced Solutions: Online communities and platforms facilitate crowdsourced solutions to sustainability challenges. People from diverse backgrounds can collaborate to find innovative solutions, design eco-friendly technologies, and address local environmental concerns more effectively.
c) Behavioral Change: Social computing can influence individual and collective behavior towards sustainable choices. Through social networks and peer interactions, people can share their eco-friendly practices, inspiring others to adopt similar behaviors and reduce their environmental footprint.
d) Transparency and Accountability: Social media platforms create opportunities for citizens to hold governments, corporations, and organizations accountable for their sustainability commitments. Transparency in reporting and communication is enhanced, driving entities to adopt more responsible practices.
e) Collaborative Advocacy: Online activism and digital campaigns amplify the voices of those advocating for sustainable policies and practices. Social computing provides a platform for organizing and mobilizing efforts to push for positive environmental and social change.
f) Data Analysis and Decision-Making: Social computing generates vast amounts of data about public sentiment, trends, and opinions related to sustainability. Analyzing this data can provide valuable insights for policymakers, businesses, and organizations to make informed decisions aligned with sustainable goals.
g) Global Collaboration: Social computing breaks down geographical barriers, enabling global collaboration on sustainability initiatives. Individuals and groups can work together on international projects, sharing knowledge and resources for a more interconnected approach to sustainable development.

4.3 Big Data

The term "big data" began to be actively used in the 1990s, and the term was popularized by John R. Mashey [8], who was the chief scientist at Silicon Graphics.

In the context of sustainable development, Big Data plays a transformative role by:

a) Supply Chain Optimization: Ensures transparency and sustainability in sourcing and manufacturing.
b) Renewable Energy Integration: Predicts demand, manages resources for efficient renewable energy use.
c) Climate Monitoring: Analyzes data for climate research, supporting resilience and adaptation.
d) Precision Agriculture: Optimizes farming practices for increased yield and reduced environmental impact.

e) Waste Management: Tracks waste patterns, facilitates recycling, and reduces environmental impact.
f) Consumer Behavior Influence: Utilizes data to drive awareness and promote sustainable choices.
g) Corporate Sustainability Reporting: Supports accurate measurement and reporting of sustainability initiatives.
h) Resource Efficiency: Big data optimizes energy, water, and material usage, reducing waste.

4.4 Business Analysis and Analytics

The use of Big Data has facilitated the emergence of technologies that offer intelligent business intelligence solutions to help make sense of and optimize data as part of sustainable business development. This advancement paves the way for the creation of connected and truly intelligent businesses, which offers significant opportunities for sustainable development. Notable examples of the adoption of intelligent technology solutions can be seen in industries such as banking, insurance, retail and transportation, where they are helping to detect and prevent fraudulent activities and improve the overall customer experience, which plays a key role in driving sustainable economic growth and societal well-being.

4.5 Cloud Computing

The term Cloud Computing was originally introduced by Prof. Ramnath K. Chellappa [9]. Cloud Computing refers to the provision of various computing services over the Internet. Instead of owning and maintaining physical servers or computing infrastructure, individuals and organizations can access and use computing resources such as servers, storage, databases, networks, software, etc. through remote data centers of a cloud service provider. Utilization of these services can reduce storage and computing resource costs and provide the convenience of accessing large amounts of data from various devices anywhere. This promotes global collaboration and accelerates business processes.

Cloud computing offers several benefits that contribute to sustainability across various dimensions:

a) Renewable Energy Adoption: Many cloud service providers commit to using renewable energy sources to power their data centers, contributing to a cleaner and more sustainable energy mix in the IT sector.
b) Reduced Hardware Footprint: By consolidating computing resources in centralized data centers, cloud computing reduces the need for individual organizations to maintain extensive hardware infrastructure, leading to lower e-waste and a smaller overall carbon footprint.
c) Remote Collaboration: Cloud-based collaboration tools enable remote work and virtual meetings, reducing the need for extensive business travel and associated carbon emissions.
d) Green Building Standards: Cloud providers often adhere to green building standards for their data centers, incorporating energy-efficient design principles and sustainable construction materials.

e) Energy Efficiency: Cloud service providers invest in energy-efficient data centers with advanced cooling and power management systems, resulting in lower overall energy consumption compared to traditional on-premises data centers.

5 Conclusions

In conclusion, it can be emphasized that sustainable development in the era of digital transformation entails a delicate balance between actively pursuing innovation and caring for the needs of both current and future generations. This equilibrium, in turn, facilitates the harmonization of economic growth, social justice, and environmental preservation amidst the integration of digital technologies. By applying digital innovations to address global challenges such as poverty, inequality and climate change, digital transformation serves as a pivotal tool for enhancing resource efficiency, improving education and healthcare, and fostering citizen engagement in decision-making processes. However, achieving genuine sustainability in the digital age requires astute management of the ethical aspects of data use, ensuring privacy protection, combating digital inequality, and making efforts to minimize the negative impact on the environment, including prudent energy consumption and electronic waste management. Thus, sustainable development in the era of digital transformation stands as a strategic path toward creating an innovative and sustainable future for all.

References

1. United Nations, The Global Compact. Who Cares Wins: Connecting the Financial Markets to a Changing World? United Nations (2004)
2. Key Events in the Development of the First General Purpose Electronic Digital Computer, the ENIAC. https://www.historyofinformation.com/detail.php?id=636. Accessed 27 Aug 2023
3. Capital Group ESG Global Study 2022
4. History of artificial intelligence: Key dates and names. https://www.ibm.com/topics/artificial-intelligence. Accessed 15 Jan 2024
5. World Population. Worldometer (2023 and historical). https://www.worldometers.info/world-population/#table-historical. Accessed 11 Oct 2023
6. World Population Projections. Worldometer (2023). https://www.worldometers.info/world-population/world-population-projections. Accessed 11 Oct 2023
7. Zuckerberg, M.: Building a global community that works for everyone (2017). https://www.weforum.org/agenda/2017/02/mark-zuckerberg-building-a-global-community-that-works-for-everyone. Accessed 03 Oct 2023
8. Lohr, S.: The Origins of 'Big Data': An Etymological Detective Story (2013). https://archive.nytimes.com/bits.blogs.nytimes.com/2013/02/01/the-origins-of-big-data-an-etymological-detective-story. Accessed 03 Oct 2023
9. Mishra, D.: Cloud Computing: the era of virtual world. Int. J. Comput. Sci. Eng. (IJCSE) **3**(04), 204 (2014)
10. Cortada, J.W.: The Digital Flood: The Diffusion of Information Technology Across the U.S., Europe, and Asia. OUP, USA (2012)
11. Santarius, T., et al.: Digitalization and sustainability: a call for a digital green deal. Environ Sci Policy **147**, 11–14 (2023)

12. Edje, A.E., Abd Latiff, M.S., Howe Chan, W.: IoT data analytic algorithms on edge-cloud infrastructure: a review. Digit. Commun. Netw. **9**(6), 1486–1515 (2023). https://doi.org/10.1016/j.dcan.2023.10.002
13. Kutyauripo, I., Rushambwa, M., Chiwazi, L.: Artificial intelligence applications in the agrifood sectors. J. Agric. Food Res. **11**(2023). https://doi.org/10.1016/j.jafr.2023.100502
14. Sipola, J., Saunila, M., Ukko, J.: Adopting artificial intelligence in sustainable business. J. Clean. Prod. **426** (2023). https://doi.org/10.1016/j.jclepro.2023.139197
15. Guida, M., Caniato, F., Moretto, A., Ronchi, S.: The role of artificial intelligence in the procurement process: State of the art and research agenda. J. Purch. Supply Manag. **29**(2) (2023). https://doi.org/10.1016/j.pursup.2023.100823
16. Mandas, M., Lahmar, O., Piras, L., De Lisa, R.: ESG in the financial industry: what matters for rating analysts? Res. Int. Bus. Financ. **66** (2023). https://doi.org/10.1016/j.ribaf.2023.102045
17. Santarius, T., et al.: Digitalization and sustainability: a call for a digital green deal. Environ. Sci. Policy **147**, 11–14 (2023). https://doi.org/10.1016/j.envsci.2023.04.020
18. Irajifar, L., Chen, H., Lak, A., Sharifi, A., Cheshmehzangi, A.: The nexus between digitalization and sustainability: a scientometrics analysis. Heliyon **9** (2023). https://doi.org/10.1016/j.heliyon.2023.e15172
19. Pérez-Moure, H., Lampón, J.F., Velando-Rodriguez, M., Rodríguez-Comesaña, L.: Revolutionizing the road: how sustainable, autonomous, and connected vehicles are changing digital mobility business models. Eur. Res. Manag. Bus. Econ. **29**(3) (2023). https://doi.org/10.1016/j.iedeen.2023.100230
20. Verdecchia, R., Lago, P., de Vries, C.: The future of sustainable digital infrastructures: a landscape of solutions, adoption factors, impediments, open problems, and scenarios. Sustain. Comput.: Inform. Syst. **35** (2022). https://doi.org/10.1016/j.suscom.2022.100767
21. Guandalini, I.: Sustainability through digital transformation: a systematic literature review for research guidance. J. Bus. Res. **148**, 456–471 (2022). https://doi.org/10.1016/j.jbusres.2022.05.003.3
22. Andersen, A.D., et al.: On digitalization and sustainability transitions. Environ. Innov. Soc. Trans. **41**, 96–98 (2021). https://doi.org/10.1016/j.eist.2021.09.013
23. Yang, G., Deng, F.: Can digitalization improve enterprise sustainability?–Evidence from the resilience perspective of Chinese firms. Heliyon **9**(3) (2023). https://doi.org/10.1016/j.heliyon.2023.e14607
24. Harrison, K.B., Meneer, E., Zhu, B.: ESG 2.0-The Next Generation of Leadership (2021). https://corpgov.law.harvard.edu/2021/09/02/esg-2-0-the-next-generation-of-leadership. Accessed 15 Jan 2024
25. Bubenzer-Paim, A.: How The Tech Industry Can Shape ESG 2.0 (2022). https://www.forbes.com/sites/forbestechcouncil/2022/08/04/how-the-tech-industry-can-shape-esg-20/?sh=7c8e2b585af9. Accessed 15 Dec 2023
26. Green, A.: The Future Of ESG Investing (2022). https://www.forbes.com/sites/forbestechcouncil/2022/02/16/the-future-of-esg-investing/?sh=4dd00482573e. Accessed 15 Dec 2023
27. George, G., Schillebeeckx, S.J.D.: Digital transformation, sustainability, and purpose in the multinational enterprise. J. World Bus. **57**(3) (2022). https://doi.org/10.1016/j.jwb.2022.101326
28. Prabawani, B., Hadi, S.P., Wahyudi, F.E., Ainuddin, I.: Drivers and initial pattern for corporate social innovation: from responsibility to sustainability. Heliyon **9**(6) (2023). https://doi.org/10.1016/j.heliyon.2023.e16175
29. Mbaidin, H.O., Alsmairat, M.A.K., Al-Adaileh, R.: Blockchain adoption for sustainable development in developing countries: challenges and opportunities in the banking sector. Int. J. Inf. Manag. Data Insights **3**(2) (2023). https://doi.org/10.1016/j.jjimei.2023.100199

30. Yontar, E.: The role of blockchain technology in the sustainability of supply chain management: grey based DEMATEL implementation. Clean. Logist. Supply Chain **8** (2023). https://doi.org/10.1016/j.clscn.2023.100113
31. Alzoubi, Y.I., Mishra, A.: Green blockchain - a move towards sustainability. J. Clean. Prod. **430** (2023). https://doi.org/10.1016/j.jclepro.2023.139541
32. Wu, J.: Sustainable development of green reverse logistics based on blockchain. Energy Rep. **8**, 11547–11553 (2022). https://doi.org/10.1016/j.egyr.2022.08.219

Author Index

A
Ahamed, Saahira Banu   177
Anastasiya, Melnikova   198
Anoop, Anne   177
Ansari, Subuhi Kashif   166

B
Becker, Jörg   63
Begicheva, Antonina   262
Begicheva, Svetlana   262

C
Calvo, Jorge   135

D
Djalalov, Muzaffar   43
Dudkovskaia, Kristina   63

G
Gaskova, Daria   155

H
Hur, Evelyn   225

J
Jung, Summer D.   225

K
Kabanov, Pavel   213
Khan, Mujtaba Ali   177
Kim, Hazel H.   225
Kim, Soh   225, 237, 250
Kumar, Rakesh   166
Kwon, TaeHyung   237

L
Lee, Jeung   250
Levchenko, Artem   29

M
Massel, Aleksei G.   107
Massel, Aleksei   155
Massel, Liudmila V.   107
Mirzokhidova, Dilshoda   43

N
Nazeema, Rejna Azeez   177

O
Ogly, Mais Farkhadov Pasha   188

P
Parkhi, Shilpa   87
Pesterev, Dmitrii V.   107
Pulyavina, N.   273
Pulyavina, Natalia   3, 51, 120
Purohit, Yagnesh   87

S
Sedova, N.   273
Shchukin, Nikita   155
Singh, Mahendra   15
Starostin, Aleksei   120

T
Taratukhin, Arsenij   188
Taratukhin, Victor   3, 51, 63
Tsybikov, Aleksey   155

Y
Yoon, Katherine   225
Yurkevich, Olga   213

Z
Zimin, A.   273
Zoryna, Tatsiana   213